THE A TO Z OF THE DOCTRINE AND COVENANTS AND CHURCH HISTORY

RICHARD O. COWAN ❋ CRAIG K. MANSCILL

All artwork and photographs courtesy of the Visual Resource Library, Audio Video Department, The Church of Jesus Christ of Latter-day Saints

Leatherwood Press
8160 South Highland Drive
Sandy, Utah 84093
www.leatherwoodpress.com

ISBN: 978-1-59992-119-8

Printed in the United States

Contents

Preface

Both of us have taught the Doctrine and Covenants at Brigham Young University for many years, and we love this special book of modern scripture. We are grateful that God gives direction to His children on earth, as much in our day as in times past.

Our objective in this book is to provide a concise resource to the average Latter-day Saint to use in conjunction with a study of the Doctrine and Covenants. Other excellent commentaries are available to those who want greater depth. Our desire here is to provide just enough information to answer most questions that arise while studying the Doctrine and Covenants and to provide the kind of information that will enhance our appreciation of this scripture's message; this approach allows the scriptures to speak for themselves. This book has two major parts: the first part presents a treatment of each Doctrine and Covenants section in the order it appears in this standard work. The second half of the book, "A to Z of Church History," examines topics arranged alphabetically for easy reference.

The discussion of each section first describes the "Setting" in which that revelation was received. Knowing this background enables a reader to more fully appreciate the Lord's message. (Reading a revelation without knowing its setting is similar to sitting in a room listening to someone talking on the telephone and hearing only one side of the conversation.) Then, under the heading "Teachings," major themes of the section are considered. These brief explanations are designed to provide the reader with an understanding of the doctrines taught in the revelation. In some sections, there is a third heading, "Scripture Helps." Here, various other points are briefly covered with the intent of answering a reader's questions about a particular verse or section of scripture.

In the A to Z portion of the book, each entry explains a principle or provides information about a person, place, or event important to the Doctrine and Covenants. The A to Z portion is not intended to be exhaustive. For example, we do not include a biographical sketch on every person whose name is mentioned in this standard work. Instead, our goal was to give insight on topics or items that are central to an understanding of the Doctrine and Covenants.

One feature of this work is the inclusion of frequent quotations from Church leaders, especially those who are serving today. It is our testimony that these Brethren are inspired and that they truly are "prophets, seers, and revelators."

Another feature of this book is its cross-referencing system. Included in our discussion of individual Doctrine and Covenants sections are references to entries in the A to Z portion. Entries in the alphabetical portion of the book may also contain cross-references to other related items and also to discussions of individual Doctrine and Covenants sections. These cross-references are indicated by words written in small capitals. Normally, this reference word will be identical to the title of the entry. Sometimes, however, the capitalized word is a different form of the entry title, such as BAPTIZE, which refers to the entry on **Baptism,** and FORGIVEN, which refers to the entry on **Forgiveness**. Also, entries about individual persons in the A to Z portion will be alphabetized according to the person's last name. For example, a reference to JOSEPH SMITH will actually be found under **Smith, Joseph Jr**.

Speaking of His latter-day revelations, the Lord testified that "these words are not of men nor of man, but of me." He then promised: "You can testify that you have heard my voice and know my words" (D&C 18:34–36). We hope that *The A to Z of the Doctrine and Covenants and Church History* will enable you, the reader, to realize the fulfillment of this promise and share the love that we have for this wonderful book of latter-day scripture.

Richard O. Cowan and Craig K. Manscill
Provo, Utah

Acknowledgements

We express our deep appreciation to those who have helped us with this project. Four very capable BYU students have worked with us: Cameronne C. Newman has played a major role in preparing the manuscript for submission. Adrianne Carson Lee, Tyler Nebeker, and Sarah K. Terry have worked with us closely, helping research items, providing editorial help, and assisting in many other ways. In addition, Cami, Adri, and Sarah have each authored several of the sections in the A to Z portion of the book. Bruce Pearson at the Visual Resource Library at Church Headquarters provided essential assistance in identifying and preparing copies of photographs used in this book. We couldn't have accomplished this task without their help.

We have found it a pleasure to work with the people at Leatherwood Press. Their editor, Linda Prince, has provided important direction in a professional and pleasant manner. Amy Orton has provided important help with graphics and design. The typesetter, Kent Minson, has expertly designed and formatted the book's interior. Garry Mitchell, Leatherwood's owner, has given appreciated encouragement to this project.

Last, but certainly not least, we express our appreciation to our eternal companions for their support and encouragement. Dawn Cowan and Jana Manscill have been understandingly patient when we have needed to spend long hours on this project, especially during the final weeks of completing it. Here again, we could not have accomplished this work without their participation.

Abbreviations

AGQ	Joseph Fielding Smith, *Answers to Gospel Questions,* 5 vols. (Salt Lake City: Deseret Book Co., 1957–1966)
BD	Bible Dictionary, King James Bible, LDS Edition
CDC	Stephen E. Robinson and H. Dean Garrett, *A Commentary on the Doctrine and Covenants,* 4 vols. (Salt Lake City: Deseret Book Co., 2000–2005)
CHMR	Joseph Fielding Smith, *Church History and Modern Revelation,* 4 vols. (Salt Lake City: Deseret Book Co., 1946–1949)
CR	Conference Report
DCC	Hyrum M. Smith and Janne M. Sjodahl, *Doctrine and Covenants Commentary* (Salt Lake City: Deseret Book Co., 1923)
DS	Joseph Fielding Smith, *Doctrines of Salvation,* ed. Bruce R. McConkie, 3 vols. (Salt Lake City: Bookcraft, 1954–1956)
DE	Richard D. Draper, "Light, Truth, and Grace: Three Interrelated Salvation Themes in Doctrine and Covenants 93," in *Doctrines for Exaltation: The 1989 Sperry Symposium on the Doctrine and Covenants* (Salt Lake City: Deseret Book Co., 1989)
EM	Daniel H. Ludlow, ed., *Encyclopedia of Mormonism,* 5 vols. (New York: Macmillan, 1992)
GD	Joseph F. Smith, *Gospel Doctrine,* 5th ed. (Salt Lake City: Deseret Book Co., 1939)
GK	G. Homer Durham, ed., *The Gospel Kingdom: Selections from the Writings and Discourses of John Taylor, Third President of The Church of Jesus Christ of Latter-day Saints* (Salt Lake City: Bookcraft, 1987)
HC	Joseph Smith, B.H. Roberts, *History of The Church of Jesus Christ of Latter-day Saints,* 7 vols. (Salt Lake City: Deseret Book Co., 1902–1932)

HL	James E. Talmage, *House of the Lord* (Salt Lake City: Bookcraft, 1963)
HT	Boyd K. Packer, *The Holy Temple* (Salt Lake City: Bookcraft, 1980)
JD	George D. Watt, ed., *Journal of Discourses,* 26 vols. (London: LDS Book Depot, 1854–1886)
JSP	Joseph Smith Papers
JST	Joseph Smith Translation
LHCK	Orson F. Whitney, *Life of Heber C. Kimball* (Salt Lake City: Deseret Book Co., 1888)
MD	Bruce R. McConkie, *Mormon Doctrine* (Salt Lake City: Deseret Book Co., 1966)
MEL	Boyd K. Packer, *Mine Errand from the Lord,* comp. Clyde J. Williams (Salt Lake City: Deseret Book Co., 2008)
MF	Spencer W. Kimball, *Miracle of Forgiveness* (Salt Lake City: Bookcraft, 1969)
MFP	James R. Clark, ed., *Messages of the First Presidency,* 6 vols. (Salt Lake City: Bookcraft, 1965–1975)
MM	Bruce R. McConkie, *The Millennial Messiah: The Second Coming of the Son of Man* (Salt Lake City: Deseret Book Co., 1982)
PPP	Parley P. Pratt, *Autobiography of Parley Parker Pratt,* ed. Parley P. Pratt Jr. (Salt Lake City: Deseret Book Co., 1966)
RR	Joseph Fielding McConkie and Craig J. Ostler, *Revelations of the Restoration* (Salt Lake City: Deseret Book Co., 2000)
TDE	Richard O. Cowan, *Temples to Dot the Earth* (Springville, UT: Cedar Fort, 1997)
TPJS	*Teachings of the Prophet Joseph Smith* (Salt Lake City: Deseret Book Co., 1976)
v.	verse or verses
WW	Matthias F. Cowley, comp., *Wilford Woodruff, Fourth President of The Church of Jesus Christ of Latter-day Saints: History of His Life and Labors as Recorded in His Daily Journals* (Salt Lake City: Bookcraft, 1964)
WWDC	Susan Easton Black, *Who's Who in the Doctrine and Covenants* (Salt Lake City: Bookcraft, 1997)
WWJ	*Wilford Woodruff's Journal,* 9 vols. (Salt Lake City: Signature Books, 1982–1985)

The Doctrine and Covenants by Section

Explanatory Introduction

SETTING

In the earliest editions of the Doctrine and Covenants, the introductory material was titled the "Preface." Because D&C 1 is also titled the Preface, this seeming duplication led to confusion. To resolve this, in the 1921 edition the "Preface" was renamed the "Explanatory Introduction." On December 17, 1921, the FIRST PRESIDENCY, while making an official announcement about the new edition, stated that the Explanatory Introduction composed "in concise form the essential facts relating to the history of this sacred volume of latter-day REVELATION" (*MFP,* 5:207).

In the 1981 edition of the Doctrine and Covenants, the Explanatory Introduction was enlarged. The Explanatory Introduction has four parts. The first part explains the purpose and value of the Doctrine and Covenants; the second part gives the testimony of the 1835 Quorum of the Twelve Apostles about the revelations; the third part recounts the history of the various editions of the Doctrine and Covenants; and the fourth part is the Chronological Order of Contents.

PURPOSE AND VALUE OF THE DOCTRINE AND COVENANTS

Unlike previous versions, the Explanatory Introduction in the current edition of the Doctrine and Covenants gives several guiding themes on which a reader may base a study of the book. It speaks of "messages, warnings, and exhortations" that "are for the benefit of all mankind." In these revelations, we can hear "the tender but firm voice of the Lord Jesus Christ" speaking to us "for [our] temporal well-being and [our] everlasting salvation." The introduction points out that "these sacred revelations were received in answer to prayer, in times of need, and came out of real-life situations involving real people" and therefore afford us an insight into how the early Saints labored to establish God's kingdom on EARTH. The Doctrine and Covenants provides deeper understanding of many significant doctrines, traces the unfolding of Church organization, and shares powerful testimonies of our Savior Jesus Christ. All these things "make this book of great value to the human family and of more worth than the riches of the whole earth."

COMING FORTH OF THE DOCTRINE AND COVENANTS

1820 First Vision
1823 Section 2, earliest revelation in present D&C received (Sept. 21)
1830 Church organized (April 6)
Section 20 accepted as "Articles and Covenants" at first conference (June 9)
Joseph Smith began copying and arranging the revelations for publication (summer)
1831 Authorized publication of Book of Commandments with 65 "chapters" (Nov. 1)
More D&C revelations received than in any other year
1833 Press at Independence destroyed, halting publication (July 20)
1835 Doctrine and Covenants included Lectures on Faith and 102 "sections"
1844 The Prophet Joseph Smith martyred
New edition included 111 sections
1876 Edition included 136 sections
1921 New edition included Official Declaration 1 and omitted Lectures on Faith
1981 Edition included 138 sections, added Official Declaration 2 and incorporated improved headings and cross-references

The First Vision—the appearance of the Father and the Son to JOSEPH SMITH during the early spring of 1820—was the first communication from God through a living PROPHET in our time, thus opening the present DISPENSATION. Even though this revelation is not included in the Doctrine and Covenants, it should still be studied for the important truths that became the foundation for subsequent revelations. Read Joseph Smith's account of this experience in the Pearl of Great Price (JS–H 1:5–20). Other revelations followed, restoring basic gospel principles necessary for reestablishing God's kingdom on earth. The first of these, Moroni's visit on September 21, 1823, is now recorded as section 2 of the Doctrine and Covenants.

The Church of Jesus Christ was formally organized on April 6, 1830. At its first regular CONFERENCE, held in Fayette, NEW YORK, on June 9, 1830, the "Articles and Covenants [were] read by Joseph Smith, Jr., and received by unanimous voice of the whole congregation" (*Far West Record,* 1). The "Articles and Covenants" consisted of the revelations now known as sections 20 and 22. This document was reviewed at most of the Church's early conferences and can be regarded as the forerunner of our modern book of scripture, the Doctrine and Covenants. During this same year, 1830, Joseph Smith began the work of collecting, copying, and arranging the revelations in preparation for possible publication (*HC,* 1:104).

At the time the Church was organized, many revelations were received that set forth basic gospel doctrines and directions for Church operations. Of the revelations currently in the Doctrine and Covenants, more were received during 1831 than in any other year. During the years 1830 through 1832, more than half of the total were received.

At a special conference held November 1, 1831, Church leaders decided to publish 10,000 copies of the Book of Commandments, but the number was reduced to 3,000 before the book actually went to press the following year. This edition contained 65 chapters and was similar in content and arrangement to the first 64 sections in the present Doctrine and

The Book of Commandments

The Rollins sisters saving the Book of Commandments

Covenants. In 1833, a mob destroyed the press on which the Book of Commandments was being printed, not so much because of displeasure with the publication of the compiled revelations but because of opposition to a Latter-day Saint newspaper, the *Evening and Morning Star,* which was being issued from the same press. Nevertheless, the result was that only about one hundred full copies of the partially completed book remained.

During the fall of 1834, a committee composed of the First Presidency was constituted to bring the compilation of revelations up to date and publish it in book form. The 1835 edition appeared under the title of Doctrine and Covenants. The first part was entitled "Theology" and included the "Lectures on Faith" that had been given in the SCHOOL OF THE PROPHETS; these set forth the doctrine of the Church. The second part, entitled "Covenants and Commandments of the Lord," contained the revelations. Thus the book's new title reflected these two divisions. This compilation included 102 sections that covered about the same material as the first 107 sections, plus it included sections 133 and 134 in the present Doctrine and Covenants. The former chronological order was abandoned in favor of an arrangement that grouped the more significant revelations near the beginning of the book. At the conference where this book was officially accepted as scripture, the recently formed Quorum of the Twelve APOSTLES signed a testimony almost similar to that which the witnesses to the Book of Commandments had offered four years earlier.

Because of the large quantity printed in 1835, the next major edition of the Doctrine and Covenants was not issued until 1844, shortly after the Prophet's martyrdom. It included 111 sections and was similar in arrangement to the 1835 edition.

The 1876 edition, prepared under the supervision of Apostle ORSON PRATT, returned to the basic chronological arrangement and included 136 sections in the same order as in the current edition. Twenty-four revelations given through Joseph Smith, as well as the 1847 revelation to BRIGHAM YOUNG, were included for the first time. Also for the first time, the sections were divided into verses, and historical notes and footnote references were included.

The 1921 edition was prepared under the direction of the First Presidency and Apostle George F. Richards, with the capable assistance of Elder James E. Talmage. In this edition, the historical notes and cross-references were improved and the text was printed in double columns. The "Lectures on Faith," which had been included in several previous editions, were omitted.

President Spencer W. Kimball appointed a committee consisting of Elders Thomas S. Monson (acting as chair), Boyd K. Packer, and Bruce R. McConkie, to prepare new editions of the standard works. Robert J. Matthews, Ellis T. Rasmussen, and Robert C. Patch, professors of religious education at Brigham Young University, also played key roles in this endeavor. The current (1981) edition of the Doctrine and Covenants includes two more sections—137 and 138—as well as Official Declaration 2. It also contains improved section headings and cross-references. In addition, the 1981 edition features a map showing key locations related to the Doctrine and Covenants.

CHRONOLOGICAL ORDER OF CONTENTS

The list of the revelations summarized in the chart below reflects the geographical progression of early Church history. The fact that many revelations were necessary to restore fundamental truths when the Church was first being organized explains why more recorded revelations were received during 1830, 1831, and 1832 than during any other three-year period.

Geographical and Chronological Distribution of Sections of Doctrine and Covenants

Place	*1823–1828*	*1829*	*1830*	*1831*	*1832*	*1833*	*1834–1837*	*1838*	*1839–1844*	*1847*	*since 1844*	*Total*
Manchester, New York	1		3									4
Harmony, Pennsylvania	2	9	4									15
Fayette, New York		5	12	3								20
Kirtland, OHIO				19	5	12	11					47
Hiram, OHIO				7	8							15
Misc.—OHIO				2	1							3
Jackson County, Missouri				4	2							6
Far West, Missouri								7				7
Misc.—Missouri				2			1	1	3			7
Nauvoo, ILLINOIS									10			10
Utah											3	3
Others						1	1			1		3
Totals	3	14	19	37	16	13	13	8	13	1	3	140

*Vicinity

Section 1

"THE LORD'S PREFACE"

SETTING

At a conference held on November 1, 1831, in HIRAM, OHIO, a committee was appointed to draft a preface for a collection of revelations to be published as the Book of Commandments (see COMING FORTH OF THE DOCTRINE AND COVENANTS). The brethren united in prayer, with JOSEPH SMITH as voice. The PROPHET then dictated the words of this revelation by the Spirit, with SIDNEY RIGDON acting as scribe. Because section 1 is the Lord's "preface unto the book of [His] commandments" (v. 1), it has been placed at the beginning; it actually fits chronologically between sections 66 and 67.

TEACHINGS

Apostasy: The "anger of the Lord" (v. 13) is manifest because those living on the earth have "strayed from mine ordinances, and have broken the everlasting covenant"(v. 15). Today, many pursue their personal worldly interests (v. 16) rather than putting "first the Kingdom of God" (Matt. 6:33). This is a form of apostasy. The modern, wicked world, linked with the ancient kingdoms of BABYLON (v. 16) and IDUMEA or Edom (v. 36), will be destroyed, and peace will be taken from the earth (v. 35). However, because of God's love for His children, He sent His servant Joseph Smith (v. 17) and other prophets who have followed him (v. 18), that "faith might increase in the earth" (v. 21) and the NEW AND EVERLASTING COVENANT might be reestablished on earth (v. 22).

Latter-day Restoration: The Lord's REVELATIONS are a "voice of warning . . . unto all people" (v. 4). We must "prepare . . . for that which is to come, for the Lord is nigh" (v. 12). To help us prepare for His SECOND COMING, the Lord has given direction through His prophets (v. 17) in a manner we can understand (v. 24). Verses 19 through 30 list various benefits of these revelations, including an increase of faith, proclamation of the gospel, the publication of the BOOK OF MORMON (v. 29), and the organization of the one true church (v. 30). Even though the RESTORED CHURCH is the only one possessing the PRIESTHOOD and teaching the fulness of the gospel, there are honorable people in other churches who accomplish a great deal of good. At the same time, the Lord had to acknowledge the presence of members of His Church with whom He was not "well pleased."

Repentance: Because the Lord cannot tolerate SIN "with the least degree of allowance" (v. 31), He is pleased with members of His Church only "collectively" but not necessarily "individually" (v. 30). On a later occasion, the Lord condemned His Church, but once again only collectively but not individually (see D&C 105:2). A serious consequence of the sinner that chooses not to repent is a loss of the "light" or knowledge of the gospel, even one's testimony (v. 33). This can lead to individual apostasy. Nevertheless, those who REPENT will be FORGIVEN (v. 32).

Written and Living Scriptures: God affirms that these revelations are of Him and that the record is true (v. 39). We should not read the Lord's words casually, but we must "search these commandments" (v. 37). (During the early days of the restored Church, "commandments" often specifically referred to the revelations published in the "Book of Commandments.") This suggests studying them by the power of the Lord's SPIRIT (D&C 18:34–36) and applying their teachings in our lives (1 Ne. 19:23; Mosiah 4:10; Matt. 7:24–27). The Lord's promises will be fulfilled, whether given by His own voice or through His servants (v. 37–38; compare D&C 21:4–5). Finally, we are assured that the Spirit will confirm their truthfulness (v. 39).

Section 2

MORONI'S PARAPHRASE OF MALACHI

SETTING

This is the earliest section in the Doctrine and Covenants, given three years after the FIRST VISION. Confident of obtaining a divine manifestation, young JOSEPH SMITH prayed for forgiveness of his sins and a knowledge of his standing before God (see D&C 20:5). In answer, an angel, MORONI, appeared to Joseph on five occasions in three different locations, within the space of a few hours. He gave instructions about the coming forth of the Book of Mormon and cited biblical scripture about important

Smith family log cabin in Palmyra, New York

future events. The words of this section are Moroni's paraphrase of the Old Testament prophet Malachi (compare Mal. 4:5–6). See Joseph's more complete account in JS–H 1:27–53.

TEACHINGS

Of all the instructions imparted and scriptures quoted by Moroni, Joseph Smith included this excerpt from Malachi. While Joseph is silent as to the reason for selecting Malachi, the teachings within these verses certainly typify gospel priorities—PRIESTHOOD, the SECOND COMING of JESUS CHRIST, promises made to the fathers, the purpose of the EARTH, and family exaltation.

Priesthood Revealed by the Hand of Elijah: In his paraphrase of Malachi's prophecy, Moroni clarified that ELIJAH would restore the priesthood (v. 1). In 1836 at the KIRTLAND TEMPLE, Elijah restored the sealing keys, which allow families to be sealed forever in exaltation (see D&C 110).

Family Exaltation: The sealing keys authorize temple work for the living and the dead. These "promises to the fathers" may include the covenant God made with Abraham (see Abr. 2:8–11), as well as the assurance to those who receive the GOSPEL in the SPIRIT WORLD that one of their posterity on earth will perform needed priesthood ORDINANCES in their behalf. Without the sealing of families, the "whole earth would be utterly wasted" at Christ's Second Coming. This would be a "dreadful day" for the entire human family.

Section 3

Joseph Smith's Chastisement from the Lord

SETTING

Over four years had passed since Moroni told Joseph Smith about the plates buried in a hill near Joseph's home. Important events transpiring during this time include Joseph's marriage to Emma Hale in January 1827, the reception of the plates in September 1827, and a move from Manchester, New York, to Harmony, Pennsylvania, in December 1827, in order to begin the translation. Martin Harris, serving as a scribe in the translation of the Book of Mormon, repeatedly petitioned the prophet for the opportunity to show the manuscript to his family as proof of his involvement in the translation. Reluctantly, Joseph gave into Martin's request and loaned him the first 116 pages of manuscript. When Martin lost the manuscript, Joseph fell under the condemnation of the Lord. This revelation delivers a chastisement to Joseph for not following the Lord's prior instructions.

TEACHINGS

The Nature of God: Having lost the manuscript, Joseph wondered how he stood before the Lord. The first three verses of this revelation must have renewed the young Prophet's hope and given him new prospective. Because the Lord "knoweth all things" past, present, and future (see D&C 38:2), He can affirm that His purposes will not fail (v. 1). His paths are straight, or direct, yet they are also one eternal round (v. 2; see also 35:1). The end is the same as the beginning—we started in the presence of God

The Prophet Joseph Smith Jr.

and hope to return there. Furthermore, God's works are without beginning or end, like a circle.

Joseph's Accountability: When Joseph Smith returned from his parents' home in Manchester, New York, he knew he had incurred the vengeance of God (v. 4). In this revelation, the Lord publicly reminded Joseph of his failure to follow strict counsel regarding the care of the plates and manuscript (v. 4–6, 13, 15). The Lord also explained that a man (including Joseph himself) can have many revelations and power to do great works, but if that man is boastful, follows after the dictates of his own will and carnal desires, and shows disregard for God's counsel, that man will incur the wrath of God (v. 4). Joseph was also chastised for frequently transgressing the commandments and the laws of God, going on "in the persuasions of men," and fearing God more than man (v. 6–7). The Lord explained that as a consequence for Joseph's transgressions, the Prophet had "lost thy privileges [to translate] for a season, (v. 14)." In D&C 10:2, the Lord states that at the time Joseph lost the privilege of translating, his mind had become darkened.

The Lord Renews His Trust in Joseph: The Lord offered Joseph the path to repent of his transgressions (v. 10). Even though Joseph was chosen by the Lord for this special work, the Prophet was reminded that unrepented-for transgressions could result in the loss of his calling. However, because of the Lord's mercy, Joseph received a second chance. "Thou art still chosen," said the Lord, "and art again called to the work" (v. 10). About two months after this revelation, on September 22, 1828, the plates and Urim and Thummim were returned to Joseph.

A Wicked Man: Referring to the loss of the 116-page manuscript, the Lord described Martin Harris as a "wicked man, Who has set at naught the counsels of God" (v. 12–13). In a General Conference address, Elder Dallin H. Oaks stated, "Having a special interest in Martin Harris, I have been saddened at how he is remembered by most Church members. He deserves better than to be remembered solely as the man who unrighteously obtained and then lost the initial manuscript of the Book of Mormon" (*Ensign*, May 1999, 35). Elder Oaks reviewed the highlights of Martin's life and listed his positive contributions to the Church: Martin served as one of the Three Witnesses to the Book of Mormon, financed the initial publication of the Book of Mormon, was the first man the Lord called by name to consecrate his property in Zion, served on the Kirtland High

Council, and was called to select the first QUORUM of the Twelve Apostles (ibid).

Section 4

SERVICE TO GOD

SETTING

This revelation was received as JOSEPH SMITH JR. was waiting to resume his translation of the plates. Interested in the welfare of Joseph and his family, the PROPHET's father, JOSEPH SMITH SR., and others arrived in HARMONY, PENNSYLVANIA, from MANCHESTER, NEW YORK, in February 1829. During this visit, the Prophet received this revelation in behalf of his father.

TEACHINGS

Marvelous Work: The Lord announced that a "marvelous work" is soon to be established (v. 1). This has reference to future events of the RESTORATION. At this time, neither the PRIESTHOOD (D&C 13) nor the Church had been organized (D&C 20–21). In preparation for these and other future events, the "field," or the world, had been prepared and was ready for harvest (v. 4). People such as OLIVER COWDERY, MARTIN HARRIS, DAVID WHITMER, JOSEPH KNIGHT, and PARLEY P. PRATT were some of those whom the Lord was preparing to make important contributions. The same principle applies today. That is, Lord is preparing people from all nations to serve in many different capacities in the Church.

Called to Serve: The call to serve is an invitation to labor with God for the salvation of our own soul (v. 4) and the souls of others (see Moses 3:9). While a desire to serve is initially necessary (v. 3) it is *how* we are to serve that is essential. The Lord asks that we serve with all our "heart, might, mind, and strength" (v. 2), suggesting that we are to bring all of our talents, gifts, skills, and abilities. If that is not enough, we are add our faith, hope, charity, and love with an "eye single to the glory of God" (not our glory), then we will "stand blameless before God" in our service (v. 2 and 4).

Section 5

MARTIN'S DESIRE TO SEE THE PLATES

SETTING

Nearly a year after the manuscript was lost (see SECTION 3), a repentant MARTIN HARRIS asked JOSEPH SMITH to inquire of the Lord whether he would ever be privileged to see the plates. The subsequent revelation was received at Harmony, Pennsylvania, in March 1829.

TEACHINGS

Acquiring Spiritual Knowledge: The Lord's response to Martin provides insights into how we too can receive a spiritual witness: it will come from the Lord on His terms (v. 3, 12). Seeing SIGNS, like viewing the plates, will not necessarily convince one of the truth (v. 7); first we need the ability to discern spiritual things (see Mark 16:17). The Lord gives us understanding through His PROPHET (v. 10), and we can gain strength from the testimony of others (v. 11). Baptism and confirmation open the way to learning by the Spirit (v. 16). We must also humble ourselves, repent, pray sincerely with faith, and covenant with the Lord to keep His commandments (v. 24, 28). When we receive the desired witness we, like Martin, must bear testimony of what we know to be true, in order to keep our covenants and avoid condemnation (v. 25, 27).

Exaltation is the reward promised to those who are faithful (v. 35).

Manifestation of My Spirit: It is important to understand the difference between the manifestation of the Spirit and the gift of the HOLY GHOST. Manifestations of the Spirit are given to all of God's children who humbly seek Him. However, this does not mean that they have the right to the Holy Ghost as a constant companion—the gift of the Holy Ghost. This gift, bestowed during the ordinance of confirmation, is given only to those who have been baptized into the Lord's true Church, who accept and seek the gift, and who strive to be worthy of the Spirit's companionship (v. 24, 28).

SCRIPTURE HELPS

Ordained: Joseph had not received the priesthood so was unable to perform the ordinances of baptism and confirmation of the Holy Ghost, referred to in verse 16. However, Joseph was promised in verse 6 that he would soon be ordained to the priesthood. Approximately two months later, on May 15, 1829, Joseph and Oliver Cowdery received the AARONIC PRIESTHOOD from JOHN THE BAPTIST, on the banks of the Susquehannah River (see D&C 13).

Section 6

OLIVER'S DESIRE FOR A WITNESS

SETTING

While teaching school in MANCHESTER, NEW YORK, young OLIVER COWDERY boarded with the Joseph Smith Sr. family. From them, he learned about the work of their son Joseph. Oliver prayed to know the truth and was blessed with a vision in which the Lord showed him the plates and gave him a witness that the work was true (*JSP*, 9–10). When school ended, Oliver went to HARMONY, PENNSYLVANIA, to meet the Prophet and learn more. He arrived on April 5, and two days later he began working as JOSEPH SMITH'S scribe. When Oliver desired an additional divine witness that the work of translation was true, the Prophet inquired of the Lord for him through the URIM AND THUMMIM. This was the first of four revelations given at Harmony in April 1829.

Joseph Smith and Oliver Cowdery translating the plates

TEACHINGS

Ideas similar to those revealed earlier provide context for the specific ideas the Lord would reveal to Oliver (compare v. 1–6 with SECTION 4). SECTIONS 11, 12, and 14 also begin with these identical verses.

Acquiring Spiritual Knowledge: Proper priorities are essential in learning the MYSTERIES OF GOD (v. 7). Worldly wealth is not evil in itself, and it can be a tool for doing good (see Jacob 2:17–19). In order to learn the things of the Lord, we must have a sincere desire (v. 8, 20, 22, 25, 27). Oliver's gift, by which he would learn the truth, is the right to have revelation through the HOLY GHOST (v. 11–12).

What to Teach: The Lord's injunction to "say nothing but REPENTANCE" (v. 9) suggests that any GOSPEL topic should be presented in such a way that our listeners would want to change their lives for the better.

Oliver's Witness: To provide Oliver with the desired witness, the Lord revealed things that no one else could have known (v. 14–16, 22, 24). With this witness came a responsibility (v. 18).

Motivation: We sometimes fear to do good because of peer pressure or selfishness (v. 33).

Section 7

John's Desire

SETTING

While translating the PLATES (perhaps 3 Ne. 28), a difference of opinion arose between OLIVER COWDERY and JOSEPH SMITH concerning what had happened to JOHN THE BELOVED. They inquired of the Lord through the URIM AND THUMMIM. Whether Joseph actually had John's parchment in his hands or simply saw it by VISION is not known.

TEACHINGS

This revelation expands on the account found in John 21:20–22. JOHN was promised that he might continue his work on earth until the SECOND COMING (v. 1–6), so he became a TRANSLATED BEING. In 1831, JOSEPH

SMITH declared that John was then laboring among the TEN TRIBES (see *HC* 1:176).

Church Leaders: The Lord declared that PETER, JAMES, AND JOHN would hold the KEYS of presidency until He came again (v. 7; D&C 27:12–13).

Section 8

OLIVER'S DESIRE TO TRANSLATE

SETTING

OLIVER COWDERY had been promised an opportunity to translate (see D&C 6:25). He now desired to have this "gift" bestowed upon him.

TEACHINGS

Answers to Prayer: We must PRAY with FAITH and real intent (v. 1). The HOLY GHOST will speak to our mind and heart (v. 2). "For me, response to the mind is very specific, like dictated words, while response to the heart is generalized, like a feeling to pray more" (*Ensign,* May 2007, 10). The Holy Ghost is the power by which REVELATION comes (v. 3). We should only pray for that which is appropriate (v. 10; see also D&C 88:65). Knowing what to pray for is one of the GIFTS of the Holy Ghost (D&C 46:30).

Gift of Aaron: Like AARON, Oliver Cowdery was called to be a spokesman. Oliver may have had a tangible object that he could hold in his hand (v. 8) to symbolize the gift, but if so, the exact nature of this object is not known.

Section 9

OLIVER'S TRANSLATING EXPERIENCE

SETTING

OLIVER COWDERY began to TRANSLATE, but soon lost confidence and could not continue. This is similar to PETER's experience walking on the water (see Matt. 14:25–31). The PROPHET inquired of the Lord so that Oliver could understand his role in the translation.

TEACHINGS

Because Oliver could no longer translate, he returned to his role as scribe, a role he maintained until the translation was finished (v. 1–6, 10–11). Even though Oliver fell short of his own expectation to translate, he did learn that the process required a great deal of effort. In this way, Oliver became a second to the translation process (v. 9–10). This is what the Lord might have referred to when He said, "for it is wisdom in me" (v. 3, 6).

Answers to Prayer: In addition to PRAYING with FAITH, we need to weigh the merits of each possible answer to a question, or to weigh the merits of each course we might take (v. 7–8). The promised "burning" or "stupor" (v. 8–9) is often referred to as spiritual confirmation.

SCRIPTURE HELPS

Other Records: We do not know exactly what the "other records" are that the Prophet was told he might translate in the future (v. 2).

Section 10

SATAN'S PLAN TO DESTROY THE WORK OF GOD

SETTING

For a brief period after the first 116 pages of manuscript were lost, JOSEPH SMITH had lost the privilege of translating the plates. Once the plates and the Urim and Thummim were returned by Moroni, Joseph inquired of the Lord as to how he should proceed with the work of translation. Chronologically, this revelation follows section 3. (It is out of order because one early manuscript was dated May 1829.)

TEACHINGS

Satan's Objectives: Nowhere in scripture do we learn more about the evil designs and purposes of Satan than in section 10. We learn that Satan is cunning and enlists those who love darkness rather than light (v. 21), and that he stirreth up their hearts to commit iniquity against that which is good, that they may get glory of the world (v. 19, 20). Satan uses deception and flattery and encourages his people to lie and deceive (v. 25, 26). A major tactic of Satan is to stir up contention regarding Christ's doctrine (v. 63–69). Ultimately, the adversary wants to destroy the souls of men and drag them down to hell (v. 22, 26), and to destroy the work of God (v. 15, 23; see 2 Ne. 28:20–22).

Satan's Plan to Destroy the Work of Translation: Satan's plan was to destroy Joseph Smith and the work of the translation (v. 19). Had Joseph retranslated the lost material, Satan would have prompted the Prophet's enemies to alter the wording in this missing original so as to discredit the translator. Attempting to translate 116 pages exactly the same way a second time would have been "tempting" the Lord (v. 15).

The Lord's Counterplan: The Lord would not allow Satan to "accomplish his evil design" (v. 14). In order to appreciate the Lord's counterplan, we must understand the nature of the two sets of Book of Mormon plates. Nephi made two sets of plates "for a wise purpose in the Lord" (1 Ne. 9:5). On the small plates of Nephi, the prophets gave a religious history covering the period from 600 to 150 b.c., until the plates were full. The first six books of the present Book of Mormon were translated from the small plates. The kings kept a political and military history on the large plates of Nephi. The book of Lehi covers roughly the same period as the small plates. The book of Mosiah, which followed the book of Lehi on the large plates, provided a combined religious and secular history that continued until Mormon's day. Mormon then abridged the large plates. Joseph Smith began his work by translating from Mormon's abridgement of the book of Lehi, and it was this manuscript that Martin Harris lost. The Lord instructed Joseph not to retranslate the political history from the book of Lehi, but rather to translate the spiritual history from the small

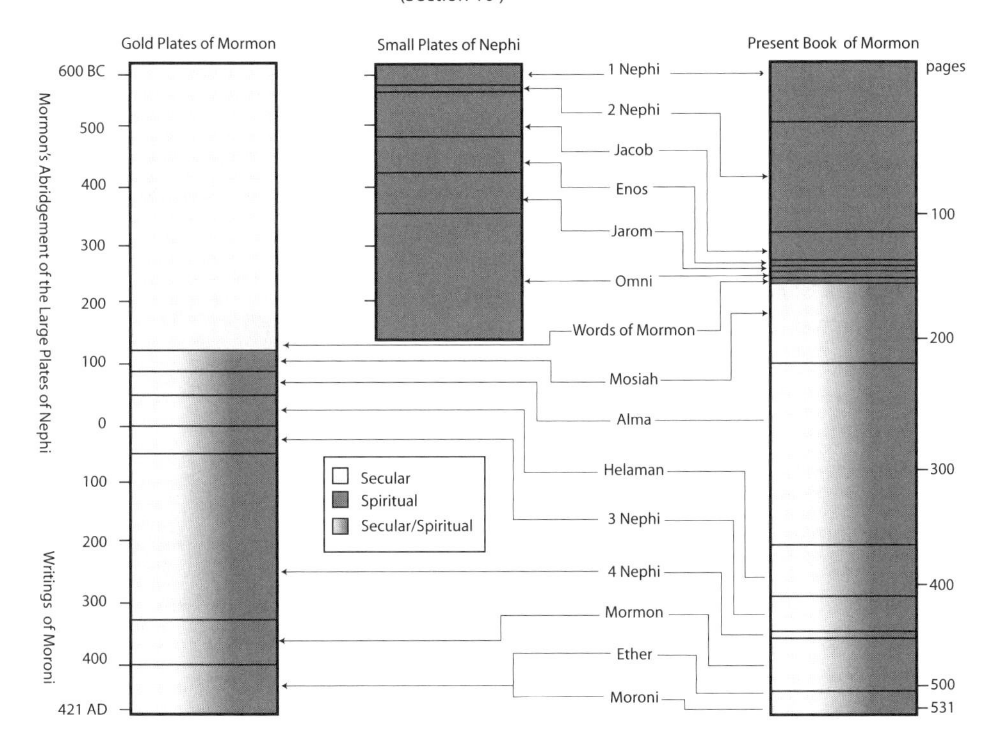

plates that covered the same period of time and threw a greater light on the gospel of Jesus Christ (v. 39–40). Then the Prophet was to continue translating from the abridged large plates, beginning with Mosiah, which also contained things of the Spirit (v. 41, 46).

Section 11

HYRUM SMITH'S MISSION PREPARATION

SETTING

Shortly after JOSEPH SMITH and OLIVER COWDERY resumed translation of the plates, HYRUM SMITH, Joseph's elder brother, paid a visit to Harmony. During the visit, the PROPHET received this REVELATION in his behalf.

TEACHINGS

The first nine verses of this revelation are similar to sections 4, 6, 12, 14, 15, and 16. This repetition provided perspective and emphasized the qualifications Hyrum would need to enter the Lord's service.

A Mission Call: Hyrum wanted to preach, but the Lord reminded him that he needed to be called first (v. 15). We are mistaken if we think we can serve by self-appointment.

Hyrum's Preparation: Hyrum's desire to preach was commendable, but the Lord asked him to wait a little longer until he was better prepared. Specifically, Hyrum is asked to keep the commandments (v. 9, 20), trust in the Spirit (v. 12–14), study the Bible and the BOOK OF MORMON (v. 21–22), and seek the kingdom of God (v. 23). President Gordon B. Hinckley declared, "The time has come when we must raise the standards of those who are called . . . as ambassadors of the Lord Jesus Christ. . . . To practice self discipline, to live above the low standards of the world, to avoid transgression and take the high road in all their activities" ("Missionary Service," Worldwide Leadership Training Meeting, Jan. 11, 2003, 17). Elder Russell M. Ballard has advised prospective missionaries to learn the doctrine better through focused scripture study, to learn how to PRAY sincerely, to be more disciplined and work harder, and to learn what is expected as a missionary (see *Ensign,* May 2005, 69).

Hyrum Smith

Section 12

JOSEPH KNIGHT'S CONTRIBUTIONS

SETTING

Joseph Knight Sr., a close friend of JOSEPH SMITH since 1826, traveled over twenty miles from COLESVILLE, NEW YORK, to HARMONY,

PENNSYLVANIA, to visit his friend. He was anxious to know of his duty and part in the work of the RESTORATION. Joseph received this revelation in his behalf.

TEACHINGS

In this revelation, the Lord stated that Father Knight, as Joseph often referred to him, would be remembered for his compassionate service to the Smith family. The Lord said, "No one can assist in this work except he shall be humble and full of love, having faith, hope, and charity, being temperate in all things (v. 8)." This is the standard for service in the GOSPEL. During the translation of the plates, Joseph Smith remembered how "[Joseph Knight] very kindly and considerately brought us a quantity of provisions, in order that we might not be interrupted in the work of translation."

Section 13

RESTORATION OF THE AARONIC PRIESTHOOD

SETTING

While translating the BOOK OF MORMON (perhaps 3 Ne. 11:22–41), Joseph Smith and Oliver Cowdery desired to know more about baptism for the remission of sins. They walked to the nearby bank of the Susquehanna River and prayed. (See the PROPHET's more complete account in JS–H 1:68–75, and Oliver Cowdery's account in the footnote of JS–H 1:71.)

Restoration of the Aaronic Priesthood

TEACHINGS

Authorized by PETER, JAMES, AND JOHN, and in the name of the

Messiah or Jesus Christ, John the Baptist bestowed divine authority. He announced: "I confer the Priesthood of Aaron." This priesthood deals with repentance and baptism and prepares one to receive the Priesthood of Melchizedek, which Joseph and Oliver received a short time later. Though the Aaronic Priesthood is referred to as the lesser priesthood, it is nevertheless significant. It holds the keys of the ministering of angels and is the power by which the sons of Levi will make their offering in the last days. The statement that this priesthood will remain "until" the offering is made does not mean that the lesser priesthood will then be withdrawn (see D&C 84:18).

Section 14

David Whitmer's Call to Serve

SETTING

Persecution was mounting in Harmony, Pennsylvania. In order to complete the translation of the Book of Mormon, Oliver Cowdery and Joseph Smith moved to the home of David Whitmer, a friend of Oliver's, in Fayette, New York. David was anxious to know his duty concerning the work of the Lord. The prophet inquired of the Lord through the Urim and Thummim on David's behalf.

TEACHINGS

To Stand as a Witness (v. 7–11): After receiving the same counsel the Lord gave at the beginning of sections 6, 11, and 12 (v. 1–6), David was called to assist in the work of the Restoration (v. 11). He was told to "stand as a witness of the things of which you shall both hear and see" (v. 8). He would be privileged to be one of the Three Witnesses to bear testimony of the Book of Mormon (D&C 17:1). In addition, David was promised the reward of eternal life if he would endure to the end and keep God's commandments (v. 7).

Sections 15

JOHN WHITMER TO CRY REPENTANCE

SETTING

Revealed to Joseph Smith in June 1829, Doctrine and Covenants 15 and 16 share the same historical setting. JOHN and PETER WHITMER JR., two sons of PETER WHITMER SR., were anxious to know their roles in the work of the Lord. The Prophet inquired through the URIM AND THUMMIM on their behalf.

TEACHINGS

The Lord reminded John that He, JESUS CHRIST, is the Savior (v. 1), and that He has power over the whole earth. The symbol of the arm (v. 2) represents strength and power.

Declare Repentance: A central theme from the revelations in the Doctrine and Covenants is the necessity to call people to repentance (v. 4; compare D&C 6:9). Repentance saves souls.

Section 16

PETER WHITMER ALSO TO CRY REPENTANCE

SETTING AND TEACHINGS

The setting and teachings of section 16 are the same as for SECTION 15, except this REVELATION was directed to JOHN WHITMER's brother PETER WHITMER JR.

Section 17

The Three Witnesses

SETTING

The privilege of seeing the plates or being a witness had previously been promised to Martin Harris (D&C 5:24), Oliver Cowdery (D&C 6:25), and David Whitmer (D&C 14:8). They now wanted to know if they might be the Three Witnesses spoken of in the Book of Mormon and in an earlier revelation (D&C 5:11–13).

TEACHINGS

Nature of Their Witness: Because of their faith and by the power of God, the three saw the plates and other sacred objects and heard God declare the translation to be true (v. 1–5; see also D&C 5:12–13). Even though all Three Witnesses left the Church later in life, they never denied their witness of the sacred work. Contrast their supernatural witness with the more natural experience of the Eight Witnesses, who were permitted to "heft" and "handle" the plates. The testimonies of the Three and Eight Witnesses can be found at the beginning of the Book of Mormon.

Section 18

The Foundation of the Gospel of Jesus Christ

SETTING

As the translation of the plates neared completion, Joseph Smith, Oliver Cowdery, and David Whitmer turned some attention to the matter of "building up my Church" (v. 5). Oliver desired to know what was necessary to organize or build up the Church of Christ (v. 1). This was the last revelation received through the Urim and Thummim.

TEACHINGS

The* Book of Mormon *'s vital role in the formation of the Church: Joseph, Oliver, and David were instructed to "rely upon the things which are written" (v. 3), the Book of Mormon, for the building up of the Church. Therefore, it is not surprising that the collection of inspired bylaws and teachings, as found in SECTION 20, were derived from the Book of Mormon. Such teachings include baptism for the remission of sins, priesthood authority, duties of the Aaronic Priesthood, and administration of the sacrament.

The Foundation of My Gospel: This section contains many important truths that are foundational to the GOSPEL, first and foremost that "Jesus Christ is the name . . . given whereby man can be saved" (v. 22–24). All people must take upon themselves the name of Christ (v. 24) through the ordinance of BAPTISM, which is preceded by REPENTANCE (v. 42–43) and followed by the reception of the HOLY GHOST (v. 18); otherwise they cannot have a place in the kingdom of God (v. 25).

The Worth of a Soul: So great was the worth of a soul to our Father in Heaven that He willingly offered His Son, who suffered the pains of all mankind, died on the cross, and rose from the dead, that all men might repent and come into Him (v. 10–13).

Section 19

Repentance and the Atonement

SETTING

In March 1830, a number of PALMYRA citizens held a meeting in opposition to the printing of the BOOK OF MORMON and agreed to boycott it when it was published. Mr. Egbert B. Grandin, who was printing the Book of Mormon in Palmyra, stopped work on the project, fearing that the Smiths might not make good on their debt if the boycott proved successful. MARTIN HARRIS had put up his 240-acre farm as collateral to guarantee payment of the three thousand dollars for the printing of the Book of Mormon. It was in this setting that Martin went to Joseph and demanded a revelation from the Lord. Joseph initially hesitated but Martin insisted, and section 19 is the result. In the revelation, Martin was commanded to impart of his land freely for the printing. After the revelation, Joseph and Martin when to Grandin and convinced him that he would be paid one way or another. Eleven months later, the debt for the printing was due. Obedient to the Lord's command, Martin sold 151 acres of his farm. Section 19, however, goes far beyond these circumstances. In order to impress upon Martin Harris the importance of keeping this commandment, the Lord clarified the relationship between the ATONEMENT, repentance, and the forgiveness of sins.

Grandin Print Shop in Palmyra, New York

TEACHINGS

This revelation is one of the most important in the Doctrine and Covenants because it teaches about the PLAN OF SALVATION. Namely, section 19 speaks of REPENTence, HELL, and the Atonement of JESUS CHRIST. Since the Lord had referred to Martin Harris as a "wicked man" (D&C 3:12–13), it was important for Martin to understand the judgments of God if he did not repent.

Eternal Punishment (v. 4–12). According to God's justice, punishment is the inevitable consequence of our misusing our AGENCY and breaking His laws (see Alma 42:22). Still, it is impossible to reconcile with the erroneous idea that some of His children are saved in heaven but the majority are condemned to suffer with the devil forever. What the scriptures call "eternal punishment" may be considered "eternal" in three senses:

1. Because "Endless" and "Eternal" are among God's names, the punishment inflicted under His law may be called *endless* or *eternal* punishment, or in other words, *Eternal's* punishment (v. 10–11).
2. God's law is eternal, and according to the principle of justice, punishment must always follow when the law is broken. Thus, punishment is an eternal principle. This may be compared to a prison, which is relatively permanent even though individuals come and go, serving sentences only in proportion to the seriousness of their offenses.
3. A few persons, who become SONS OF PERDITION, will actually suffer "eternal punishment" eternally because their offenses are unpardonable; thus, they have placed themselves permanently beyond the possibility of ever again enjoying God's presence or glory (see D&C 76:44). The majority of sinners, however, will suffer "eternal punishment" only temporarily, until the demands of justice are satisfied according to the number and seriousness of their sins.

Section 20

ARTICLES AND COVENANTS—A CONSTITUTION FOR THE CHURCH

SETTING

Known as the "Articles and COVENANTS" of the Church, this section is a combination of several inspired writings prepared by JOSEPH SMITH and OLIVER COWDERY from 1829 through April 1830 (see section 18). It provides a summary of basic DOCTRINES and organizational procedures in the restored Church, similar to documents being produced by other religious groups at the time. The italicized words in verses 37, 38, and 68 might be regarded as subheadings.

TEACHINGS

This REVELATION is associated with a number of firsts in Church history. In the first conference of the Church (June 9, 1830) this revelation, along with what is now known as section 22, was read to the Church membership and unanimously accepted by those present. It thus became the first revelation given through Joseph Smith to be formally sustained by Church membership.

Church of Christ was the original NAME OF THE CHURCH.

Date of Christ's Birth: The Church was organized on Tuesday, April 6, 1830, exactly 1,830 years from the time Jesus Christ had come into the world (v. 1). His springtime birth is confirmed by the New Testament, which reports that shepherds were out with their flocks at night when He was born. We learn in the New Testament that Jesus was crucified at Passover—in the springtime (see Matt. 26:17–18). This fact is confirmed by the Book of Mormon, which indicates that the Lord's Crucifixion took place at the same time of year as His birth (see 3 Ne. 8:5).

Impact of the Book of Mormon: A review of events leading up to the Church's organization (v. 2–16) emphasized the coming forth of the BOOK OF MORMON. Its "record of a fallen people" (v. 9) includes lessons relevant to the latter days. It also contains "the fulness of the gospel" (v. 9); its presentation of basic GOSPEL principles is powerful and beautiful. Studying the Book of Mormon strengthens one's faith in the Bible, and a testimony of the Book of Mormon's truthfulness has often become the foundation of a testimony of the restored Church itself (v. 11).

Gospel Doctrines Summarized: Verses 17 through 36 present a summary of key teachings of the newly organized Church. Namely, we learn that the Father, the Son, and the HOLY GHOST are united in purpose, that they form one Godhead (v. 28), and that the principles of JUSTIFICATION, SANCTIFICATION, and GRACE are true (v. 30–32).

Justification is a "judicial act" by which the Lord grants remission of sins, releasing the individual from the punishments required by justice—upon condition of FAITH, REPENTANCE, and BAPTISM (*DCC,* 104). This "preparatory gospel" is administered by the lesser PRIESTHOOD (see D&C 84:26–27), preparing us for the greater change of sanctification.

Sanctification: "To be sanctified," explained Elder Bruce R. McConkie, "is to become clean, pure, and spotless; to be free from the blood and sins of the world; to become a new creature of the Holy Ghost, one whose body has been renewed by the rebirth of the Spirit. Sanctification is a state of saintliness, a state attained only by conformity to the laws and ORDINANCES of the gospel. The plan of salvation is the system and means provided whereby men may sanctify their souls and thereby become worthy of a celestial inheritance" (*MD*, 675).

Priesthood Ordinance—Baptism: Those who are baptized should desire to join the Church and should have truly repented. The LIGHT OF CHRIST should have led them to the point that they are prepared to receive a REMISSION of their sins. Notice how baptism involves not only a covenant with God but also with the Church (v. 37). Compare these teachings with Alma the Elder's instructions to his converts (see Mosiah 18:8–10). Verses 72 through 74 set forth the procedure to be followed; today we use the wording revealed in verse 73 rather than the similar prayer translated from the Nephite record (see 3 Ne. 11:25). Verse 68 may give the impression that people should be baptized before they are instructed, but remember that the italicized words are a caption. Therefore, the intent is that people should be taught before they receive such ordinances as baptism, confirmation, or the sacrament. The age of accountability (v. 71) is specified in D&C 68:25.

Traveling Bishops: EDWARD PARTRIDGE became the Church's first BISHOP in February 1831 (see D&C 41:9). NEWEL K. WHITNEY was called in December of that year to be the second bishop. Bishop Whitney was given responsibility for the SAINTS in OHIO (see D&C 72), and Bishop Partridge was responsible for the Saints in ZION, or MISSOURI. Because the Saints were scattered geographically, both bishops had to travel among several small congregations to perform their duties. Not until 1839, when the Saints settled in Nauvoo, were bishops associated with specific local congregations known as wards.

The sacrament is explained in verses 75 through 79. SACRAMENT MEETINGS are to be held regularly (v. 75). The instruction in verse 76 means that the person offering the prayer kneels in the presence of the congregation. Notice how the sacrament prayers specifically renew covenants made at baptism (compare v. 77 with v. 37). Four months after the Church was organized, water replaced wine as the usual emblem for Christ's blood (D&C 27:2–4); its clearness and purity remind us of the cleansing power of His ATONEMENT.

Priesthood Offices and Duties are explained in verses 38 through 59. At the time the Church was restored, brethren were ordained to the offices of deacon, teacher, priest, and ELDER—the same four offices a faithful brother successively holds today as he grows in the Church. The Lord revealed that all these offices share the essential responsibility to teach and expound the gospel. Responsibilities are cumulative, with each successive office adding to the responsibilities of those that have gone before. "Priest" is an appropriate title for those authorized for the first time to perform such priesthood ordinances as BAPTISM, blessing the sacrament, and ordaining others. "Elder" is an appropriate title for those who receive this office at about the time they are regarded as adults and who receive responsibility in spiritual matters. The specific duties to "visit the house of each member, and exhort them to pray vocally and in secret and attend to family duties" (v. 47, 51) and to "watch over the church always" (v. 53) are now the particular assignments of home teachers. Ordinations are performed by the power of the priesthood; those performing ordinances or giving blessings should always seek the guidance of the Holy Ghost (v. 60).

Conferences should transact Church business (v. 61–62). CONFERENCES are held at general as well as local levels. For many years, STAKE conferences were held quarterly. President Harold B. Lee explained why conferences are so important to the Latter-day Saints: "Now, you Latter-day Saints, I think you have never attended a conference where in these three days you have heard more inspired declarations on most every subject and problem about which you have been worrying. If you want to know what the Lord would have the Saints know and to have his guidance and direction for the next six months, get a copy of the proceedings of this conference, and you will have the latest word of the Lord as far as the Saints are concerned" (*Ensign*, Jan. 1974, 128).

Certificates and Licenses: Licenses (v. 63–64) were documents authorizing a person to perform a specific service; hence, TEMPLE recommends today follow this pattern. A certificate (v. 64) is a document attesting that an ordinance such as baptism, ordination to the priesthood, or MARRIAGE has been received.

Voting to Sustain: Verses 65–67 set forth the principle of COMMON CONSENT; these verses reflect later revelation calling additional priesthood officers and were added to this section in the 1835 edition of the Doctrine and Covenants.

Standards: Members are to live worthy of being called Saints (v. 69).

When members fail to do so, regularly organized DISCIPLINARY COUNCILS deal with their transgressions (v. 80).

Membership records are to be maintained so that individuals may be remembered and "nourished by the good word of God" (Moro. 6:4). The procedures for handling membership records outlined in verses 83 and 84 were superseded as the Church grew larger and as new technology, such as computers, became available.

Blessing of Infants: President John Taylor stated, "Outside of the all important fact that this is a direct command of Jehovah [see D&C 20:70], and as such should be studiously complied with without hesitancy or objection, we think quite a number of excellent reasons can be adduced to prove that this command is attended with beneficial results to babe and to parents, who by bringing their child before the Church manifest their faith in the sight of their brethren and sisters, in God's word and in his promises, as well as their thankfulness to him for increasing their posterity and for the safe delivery of his handmaiden. The child is also benefited by the united faith and responsive prayers of the assembled Saints" (*Millennial Star,* Apr. 15, 1878, 235).

Section 21

THE CHURCH ORGANIZED

SETTING

During the meeting where the Church was officially organized, the Prophet JOSEPH SMITH dictated this revelation by the Spirit, with Oliver Cowdery acting as scribe.

Organization of the Church in Fayette, New York

TEACHINGS

Role of the Prophet: The first commandment given to the Church was to keep a record. The head of the Church was to be SEER, translator, PROPHET, APOSTLE, and ELDER (v. 1). Joseph Smith acted as a translator not only in conjunction with the BOOK OF MORMON but also with the Bible and book of ABRAHAM. Church members should look to the President of the Church, who speaks for the Lord (v. 4–5).

Section 22

A New and Everlasting Covenant

SETTING

People who had been BAPTIZED by immersion in other churches wanted to know whether they needed to be rebaptized in order to join the newly restored Church.

TEACHINGS

In New Testament times, the GOSPEL OF JESUS CHRIST superseded the law of MOSES. Similarly in the latter days, ORDINANCES within the NEW AND EVERLASTING COVENANT, the restored gospel, supersede those performed elsewhere without PRIESTHOOD authority.

Enter Ye in at the Gate: The Lord has used this phrase on a number of occasions (Matt. 7:13; 2 Ne. 31:17; Jacob 6:11; 3 Ne. 14:13; 3 Ne. 27:33). President Joseph Fielding Smith explained, "The scriptures are very definite in their instruction that there is but one plan of salvation, and one way by which we may be saved. Yet the notion prevails abundantly among all men, that the Lord is so liberal, so kind, so loving, that he will permit every man to seek his own salvation in any organization which he desires to join and that there are no set rules, except that a person live a clean life in order to return into the presence of the Lord" (*CHMR,* 1:102–103).

Section 23

INSTRUCTIONS TO FIVE EARLY BRETHREN

SETTING

OLIVER COWDERY, HYRUM SMITH, SAMUEL H. SMITH, JOSEPH SMITH SR., and JOSEPH KNIGHT were anxious to know their duties in the Lord's newly organized Church. This material was originally published as five separate sections, but was combined in the 1835 edition of the Doctrine and Covenants.

TEACHINGS

All five of these brethren were members of the Church except Joseph Knight. Those who had been BAPTIZED were told that their SINS were FORGIVEN and that they were "under no condemnation," while Brother Knight was directed to join the Church. Hyrum was told that because of his family, his duty was to the Church. Upon the death of his father, JOSEPH SMITH SR, he became the PATRIARCH to the Church (see D&C 124:91–93), and this office was subsequently held by his descendants.

Beware of Pride: The Lord warned Oliver to beware of pride (v. 1). As Joseph Fielding Smith stated, "This was one of Oliver Cowdery's besetting sins. If he could have humbled himself in the troubled days of KIRTLAND he would not have lost his place and membership in the Church. That which had been bestowed upon him was exceedingly great and had he been willing to humble himself, it was his privilege to stand with the Prophet Joseph Smith through all time and eternity holding the keys of the DISPENSATION of the Fulness of Times" (*CHMR,* 1:112–13).

Section 24

INSTRUCTIONS TO JOSEPH AND OLIVER

SETTING

After ministering to the branches of the Church in NEW YORK during a time of intense persecution, the PROPHET and OLIVER COWDERY arrived home in Harmony, Pennsylvania, in need of encouragement and instruction from the Lord.

TEACHINGS

Magnifying Callings: Joseph Smith was to magnify his calling by devoting his full attention to his role in the Church. The Lord promised to bless and strengthen him as he served (v. 3–9). Specifically, the Lord directed Joseph to begin writing what was revealed to him (v. 5). It was about this time that the Prophet began compiling the revelations or publication in book form. Also, Joseph began to make corrections and additions to the Bible, and the result was later known as the Joseph Smith Translation or JST.

Missionary Procedures: Miracles (v. 13–14) do not always bring conversion, but the Lord promised that signs would "follow them that believe" (Mark 16:17). Joseph and Oliver, like the Apostles of old, were to cast dust off their feet as a witness when their message was rejected (v. 15; compare Matt. 10:14). They were also to "take no purse nor scrip" but rather depend on the Church for support (v. 18; compare Matt. 10:9–10). These latter two instructions do not apply to missionaries.

Be Patient in Afflictions: Joseph Smith's life was one of almost constant affliction (v. 8), from nearly losing his leg at age seven to his martyrdom at age thirty-eight. Yet despite these great afflictions, just two years before his death, he said that like Paul, he "gloried in tribulation" (D&C 127:2), and that he was accustomed to swimming in "deep water" (ibid.). No wonder Brigham Young would later say that Joseph Smith became more perfect in his short lifetime with persecution than he could have in a thousand years without it (see *JD,* 2:7).

Section 25

Instructions to Emma Smith

SETTING

Emma Hale Smith, the wife of Joseph Smith Jr., had suffered much persecution, humiliation, and harassment from others over the past several months. The PROPHET received this REVELATION on her behalf to encourage, instruct, and strengthen her.

TEACHINGS

Speaking collectively to the women of the Church, President Gordon B. Hinckley said, "I remind you of a great and remarkable revelation given through the Prophet Joseph Smith to his wife Emma and applicable to every woman in the Church, for the Lord said in concluding this revelation 'that this is my voice unto all' [v. 16]. In the first verse of this revelation the Lord states that 'all those who receive my gospel are SONS AND DAUGHTERS in my kingdom.' Great and true are these words of divine promise. The revelation which follows these opening words is rich in counsel, in praise, in instruction, and in promise to Emma Smith, and to every other woman who heeds the word of the Lord as set forth therein" (*Ensign,* Nov. 1991, 97).

Emma Hale Smith

Promises to Emma: In verse 1, the Savior addressed Emma as "my daughter." This title of endearment is befitting a spiritually begotten daughter who had been born again through her BAPTISM and His ATONEMENT. (Emma was baptized on June 28, 1830, and this revelation was given in July 1830.) The Lord promised Emma that her life would be preserved and that she would have an inheritance in ZION (v. 2), if she would walk in the paths of FAITH and virtue. This must have been consoling, since she had been subjected to the violence associated with Joseph's recent arrests. Even more so, it must have been a comfort in the future as Emma and her family often found themselves in harm's way when the mobs attacked Joseph. In addition, Emma was promised an inheritance in Zion (v. 2), that her husband would support her (v. 9), and that her SINS were FORGIVEN (v. 3). Collectively, these many promises must have been a great strength to Emma in the difficult years ahead.

Callings: The Lord proclaimed, "Thou art an elect lady" (v. 3). This is not to say that she was above others but rather that she was chosen or elected. Later on in NAUVOO, Emma was elected by Joseph Smith to the presidency of the Relief Society. At that time, the Prophet said Emma's call to that position was in partial fulfillment of D&C 25:3. Emma was also called to act as scribe for the Prophet (v. 6), to expound the scriptures (v. 7), and to write and learn as much as she could (v. 8). It is obvious the Lord had a great deal of confidence in Emma's abilities.

Counsel and Warnings: Emma was told that her calling was to be a comfort and a delight to Joseph (v. 5, 14). She was admonished to cleave to her COVENANTS, keep the commandments, beware of pride, and murmur not about the things she had not seen (v. 4, 13–15). Perhaps as the Prophet's wife, Emma thought she should be entitled to certain privileges. For instance, she did not understand why she could not view the plates when others were allowed to do so. President Gordon B. Hinckley, speaking of the counsel the Lord gave to Emma, said, "He then went on to say to Emma, 'Murmur not because of the things which thou hast not seen' [v. 4]. He was speaking of the plates which her husband was translating, she serving at the time as his scribe. Evidently she complained because Joseph would not show them to her. The Lord is saying to her, 'Murmur not. Complain not. Accept what must be in my eternal wisdom, and do not find fault.' There are a few women in the Church who complain because they do not hold the priesthood. I think the Lord would say to you, 'murmur not because of the things which are not given thee.' This is his work. Joseph did not set the rule about not showing the plates to others. He was instructed concerning it. Nor have we set the rule concerning those who should receive the priesthood. That was established by him whose work this is, and he alone could change it" (*Ensign,* Nov. 1984, 89).

Finally Emma is warned to "go with him at the time of his going" (v. 6). In some regards, Emma could be likened to Ruth in the Old Testament (see Ruth 1:16). It was no secret that Emma' parents, Isaac and Elizabeth Hale, were hoping she would come to her senses and remain in Harmony when Joseph departed.

A Selection of Hymns: It was said of Emma that she possessed a beautiful singing voice. Emma and songwriter WILLIAM WINES PHELPS made a selection of hymns that was published in KIRTLAND, OHIO, in 1836. The hymnbook included ninety hymns, of which thirty-six were written by members of the Church.

SCRIPTURE HELPS

"Ordained under His Hand" (v. 7): These words do not have reference to ordination to priesthood offices but refer to being "set apart" for a calling.

Section 26

Done by Common Consent

SETTING

This REVELATION was one of three received after JOSEPH SMITH returned to HARMONY following the organization of the Church in FAYETTE, New York. OLIVER COWDERY, JOHN WHITMER, and the PROPHET disagreed about the wording of an earlier revelation, and these instructions helped resolve the matter.

TEACHINGS

Voting to Sustain: At the meeting where the Church was organized, Joseph Smith asked those present if they were willing to accept him and Oliver Cowdery as the first and second ELDERSS in the Church. Thus from the beginning, the pattern of sustaining those called to Church office was established. "And all things shall be done by common consent in the church, by much PRAYER and FAITH, for all things you shall receive by faith" (D&C 26:2; see *Ensign,* Nov. 2004, 23).

Section 27

Emblems of the Sacrament

SETTING

This REVELATION was probably received on two separate occasions. The first four verses were given in the context of a confirmation meeting. Earlier, EMMA SMITH and Sally Knight had been BAPTIZED but had not been confirmed members of the Church. Joseph Smith desired all to partake of the sacrament prior to these confirmations. Shortly after Joseph left home to buy wine for the service, a heavenly messenger appeared and gave him instructions. The latter verses were given a month later in Fayette, New York, in connection with a Church conference.

TEACHINGS

Emblems of the Sacrament (v. 2–4): The Lord declared that when His followers partake of the sacrament, it doesn't matter what we eat or drink, as long as it is with an eye single to the glory of God (v. 2). However, there is one exception to this rule: the Church was commanded not to use wine or any strong drink as a sacramental emblem (v. 3–4).

The Hour Cometh . . . Drink of the Fruit of the Vine: Jesus is referring to the remarks He made to His Apostles at the Last Supper (Matt. 26:29). This revelation has reference to a future sacrament meeting or meetings associated with the Second Coming, perhaps to be held at Adam-ondi-Ahman. Elder Bruce R. McConkie asserted, "Before the Lord Jesus descends openly and publicly in the clouds of glory, attended by all the hosts of heaven; before the great and dreadful day of the Lord sends terror and destruction from one end of the earth to the other; before he stands on Mount Zion, or sets his feet on Olivet, or utters his voice from an American Zion or a Jewish Jerusalem; before all flesh shall see him together; before any of his appearances, which taken together comprise the Second Coming of the Son of God—before all these, there is to be a secret appearance to selected members of his Church. He will come in private to his prophet and to the Apostles then living. Those who have held keys and powers and authorities in all ages from Adam to the present will also be present. And further, all the faithful members of the Church then living and all the faithful saints of all the ages past will be present. It will be the greatest congregation of faithful saints ever assembled on planet earth. It will be a sacrament meeting. It will be a day of judgment for the faithful of all the ages. And it will take place in Daviess County, Missouri, at a place called Adam-ondi-ahman" (*MM,* 578). Verses 6 through 13 speak of the great dispensational leaders and Patriarchs who will participate in this sacred meeting.

Restoration of Melchizedek Priesthood Keys (v. 12–13): This is the first mention in the Doctrine and Covenants of the restoration of the Melchizedek Priesthood. The description of the restoration of this priesthood by Peter, James, and John (v. 12) conforms precisely to the biblical pattern of priesthood restoration in an earlier dispensation (see Matt. 17:1–3; *TPJS,* 158).

The Armor of God: Verses 15 and 16 teach the necessity of putting on the armor of God as a protection from the evils in the last days. Elder Dallin H. Oaks stated, "I am . . . grateful for the warnings of the scriptures and Church leaders on things to avoid. By following that counsel I have been able to avoid pitfalls that might otherwise have trapped and enslaved me. Alcohol, tobacco, drugs, pornography, and gambling are but a few examples of dangerous substances and addictive practices we have been warned to avoid. I appeal to all—especially to young people—to hear and heed the words of the men and women God has called as your leaders and teachers. You will be blessed if you refrain from setting your own wisdom or desires ahead of the commandments of your Creator and the warnings of His servants. The scriptures tell us to take upon us the 'whole armor' of God that we 'may be able to withstand the evil day.' They promise that the 'breastplate of righteousness' and 'the shield of faith' will 'quench all the fiery darts of the wicked' (D&C 27:15–17). I urge you to obey those teachings and lay claim on those blessings. They include the personal spiritual conversion—the 'mighty change . . . in our hearts' (Mosiah 5:2)—that helps us become what our Heavenly Father desires us to become" (*Ensign,* May 2002, 33).

Section 28

Hiram Page's Seer Stone

SETTING

The prophet was distressed that Hiram Page claimed to receive divine revelations through a seer stone. Oliver Cowdery and some of the Whitmers had been deceived into believing Hiram's claims. Joseph was uneasy about commencing the second conference of the Church until he had settled this matter, so he inquired of the Lord for instruction.

TEACHINGS

Who May Receive Revelation: Hiram Page was reminded that although anyone may receive revelation for his or her own affairs, only the President of the Church can receive revelation for the entire Church (v. 2–7). To strengthen Oliver Cowdery, who had believed in the false revelations, the Lord instructed him to correct Hiram Page privately (v. 11–12).

President James E. Faust declared, "Some have said, 'My integrity will not permit me to yield my conscience to anyone.' A clear conscience is a very precious spiritual endowment when it is guided by the HOLY GHOST. Ultimately, everyone has the responsibility of making their own moral decisions" (*Ensign,* May 1996, 4). Nevertheless, the Lord commanded, "Thou shalt not command him who is at thy head, and at the head of the church" (v. 6). Joseph Smith stated that "it is contrary to the economy of God for any member of the Church . . . to receive instruction for those in authority, higher than themselves" (*TPJS,* 21).

Preach to the Lamanites: Oliver was to serve as a missionary among the LAMANTIES (v. 8). This verse may be though of as the charter for the Church's ongoing programs for this chosen people. The LAMANITE MISSION of 1830–1831 played a key role in eventually identifying the location of Zion as promised in verse 9.

Section 29

A Doctrinal Perspective

SETTING

This REVELATION was probably received before the second CONFERENCE of the Church on September 26, 1830. Given for the benefit of six ELDERS about to depart on their missions, this revelation came at a time when many were interested in prophecies about the LATTER DAYS.

TEACHINGS

The Elect to Gather (v. 1-8): This is one of the earliest mentions of the latter-day GATHERING. In this revelation, the Lord first commanded all Saints to gather to one place (v. 7–8), then declared that other gathering places would be designated later (D&C 101:20–23; 115:17–18). This gathering was to be in preparation for events of the latter days (v. 8).

Judgments Are at Hand (v. 9–30): Calamities will sweep the earth before Christ comes (v. 14–21). His coming, which is nigh, will be a time of JUDGMENT when the wicked will be destroyed and the righteous will reign with Christ during the MILLENNIUM (v. 9–11). The original Twelve (except Judas, who lost his standing and was replaced by Matthias; see Acts 1:26) will judge the tribes of ISRAEL (v. 12–13). After the thousand years have ended, there will be another time of judgment when Michael or ADAM (D&C 27:11) shall usher in the last RESURRECTION. Then the EARTH itself will be transformed into its CELESTIAL state (v. 22–30)

A Spiritual Perspective (v. 31–35): To the Lord, all things are spiritual and eternal (v. 34). Our MORTAL existence, on the other hand, is temporal, meaning that it can be measured by time. As we look back toward the beginning, we were in a spiritual state before we entered our present temporal condition; as we look to the future, we see that following our temporal existence we will once again exist in a spiritual condition (v. 32). None of the effects of God's commandments are limited to this temporal existence (v. 34). Even the Word of Wisdom (SECTION 89), with obvious temporal consequences, is essentially a spiritual commandment in terms of the lessons it teaches and blessings it promises.

Agency (v. 36–50): Even during our PREMORTAL EXISTENCE, there was AGENCY. This enabled SATAN to lead astray "a third part" of the spirits (v. 36; notice how this verse is much clearer than the symbolic description in Rev. 12:4, 7–9). Satan's temptations are an essential part of God's plan (v. 39). Still, the only power the devil has over us is what we choose to give him (v. 40), because he cannot tempt us beyond our power to resist (see 1 Cor. 10:13). Because of his transgression, Adam was cast out of God's presence, thus suffering SPIRITUAL DEATH; this is the same as the SECOND DEATH (v. 41). Even after the FALL, we are assured the opportunity to qualify for ETERNAL LIFE or DAMNATION (v. 42–45). Satan is not permitted to tempt little children, who cannot sin "until they begin to become accountable" (v. 46–48; see also D&C 68:25). Similarly, those who are "without understanding" remain in a like condition (v. 49–50).

Section 30

Revelations to the Whitmer Brothers

SETTING

The PROPHET received three separate revelations for DAVID, PETER, and JOHN WHITMER in the wake of their actions during the HIRAM PAGE incident (see SECTION 28).

TEACHINGS

Fearing God Rather Than Men (v. 1): President Ezra Taft Benson warned, "The proud stand more in fear of men's JUDGMENT than of God's judgment (D&C 3:6–7; 60:2.). 'What will men think of me?' weighs heavier than 'What will God think of me?' King Noah was about to free the prophet Abinadi, but an appeal to his pride by his wicked priests sent Abinadi to the flames. Herod sorrowed at the request of his wife to behead JOHN THE BAPTIST. But his prideful desire to look good to 'them which sat with him at meat' caused him to kill John (Mark 6:26). Fear of men's judgment manifests itself in competition for men's approval. The proud love 'the praise of men more than the praise of God' (John 12:42–43). Our motives for the things we do are where the SIN is manifest. Jesus said He did 'always those things' that pleased God. Would we not do well to have the pleasing of God as our motive rather than to try to elevate ourselves above our brother and outdo another?" (Ensign, May 1989, 4).

Follow Those in Authority: DAVID WHITMER was chastised for paying more attention to those the Lord had not authorized, such as Hiram Page (v. 2). Similarly, in calling Peter Whitmer Jr. to join the missionaries preaching to the LAMANTIES, the Lord reminded him that he should follow the direction of OLIVER COWDERY, who was in charge of this mission (v. 5–7). John Whitmer was also called to preach (v. 9–10). Both David and John were cautioned not to fear man more than God (v. 1, 11).

Section 31

CAUTIONS TO THOMAS B. MARSH

SETTING

This revelation, as well as sections 32, 33, and 34, was addressed to converts taught by the missionaries to the LAMANTIES. The men counseled in these revelations later became GENERAL AUTHORITIES of the Church. In fact, five years after the revelation now known as section 31 was received, THOMAS B. MARSH became the senior member of the QUORUM of the Twelve APOSTLES. Thomas had asked the PROPHET Joseph Smith to inquire as to the Lord's will concerning him, and section 31 was the result.

TEACHINGS

Family: Thomas had suffered much because of his family (v. 2), and the Lord counseled him to be patient and to "govern [his] house in meekness, and be steadfast" (v. 9). He was also directed to "PRAY always" so that he might not "lose [his] reward" (v. 12). Unfortunately, a disagreement involving his wife and a neighbor woman would eventually contribute to Marsh's APOSTASY and his loss of the office of Apostle.

Missionary Service: Addressing the concerns of couples who are considering missionary service, Elder Robert D. Hales taught, "In 1830 the Lord called Thomas B. Marsh to leave his family and go into the mission field. Brother Marsh was greatly concerned about leaving his family at that time. In a tender revelation, the Lord told him, 'I will bless you and your family, yea, your little ones. . . . Lift up your heart and rejoice, for the hour of your mission is come. . . . Wherefore, your family shall live. . . . Go from them only for a little time, and declare my word, and I will prepare a place for them' (D&C 31:2–3, 5–6). It is just possible that these are the blessings that are needed most for your children, grandchildren, great-grandchildren, and future posterity" (*Ensign,* May 2001, 25).

Urgency in Missionary Work: As Thomas B. Marsh was called to proclaim the GOSPEL, he was reminded that the "field . . . is white already to be burned" (v. 4). This suggests a much more advanced condition than the field being "white already to harvest" (D&C 4:4). Notice how many of the next few revelations end with the warning "I come quickly" and contain other evidence that the SECOND COMING is near.

Section 32

MORE CALLED TO THE LAMANITE MISSION

SETTING

OLIVER COWDERY and PETER WHITMER JR. wondered if the number of missionaries assigned to teach the gospel to the LAMANTIES could be increased. PARLEY P. PRATT had been baptized the previous month, and he would become a member of the original QUORUM of the Twelve APOSTLES. Ziba Peterson had been BAPTIZED less than two weeks after the Church was organized.

TEACHINGS

Parley P. Pratt and Ziba Peterson were to join the LAMANITE MISSION and were to study the scriptures prayerfully in preparation for this assignment (v. 1–5).

Elder Henry B. Erying taught, "The Lord will not only magnify the power of your efforts. He will work with you Himself. His voice to four missionaries, called through the Prophet Joseph Smith to a difficult task, gives courage to everyone He calls in His kingdom: 'And I myself will go with them and be in their midst; and I am their advocate with the Father, and nothing shall prevail against them' (D&C 32:3)" (*Ensign,* Nov. 2002, 75).

Missionaries to the Lamanites

Section 33

Missionary Labors in Difficult Times

SETTING

Ezra Thayre and Northrop Sweet were BAPTIZED the same month this REVELATION was received. As newly ordained elders, they desired to know the will of the Lord concerning them. Unfortunately, both eventually APOSTATIZED.

TEACHINGS

Urgency in preaching the gospel is once again stressed by the Lord. In biblical times, the day was divided into twelve hours; hence the "eleventh hour" and "last time" (v. 3) suggest that the end is near. In verses 10 through 12, the Lord defines His gospel briefly and links it with preparing for His SECOND COMING. "Articles and covenants" (v. 14) refers to SECTION 20. Verse 15 explains that we should "confirm" individuals as members of the Church in preparation for their receiving the Gift of the HOLY GHOST. "Holy scriptures" (v. 16) refers to the BIBLE.

Holy Ghost (v. 15): Speaking of the importance of the Holy Ghost, President Boyd K. Packer taught, "Members have had the Holy Ghost conferred upon them after their baptism. The Holy Ghost will teach and comfort them. They are then prepared to receive guidance, direction, and correction, whatever their position or needs require" (*Ensign,* Nov. 2007, 6–7).

Section 34

Orson Pratt

SETTING

ORSON PRATT had traveled two hundred miles from OHIO to see JOSEPH SMITH. He now wanted to learn the Lord's will concerning him.

Orson later became a member of the original QUORUM of the Twelve APOSTLES in this dispensation.

TEACHINGS

Atonement: Verse 3 clarifies that like His Father, Jesus loved the world, so He was willing to give His own life (compare John 3:16)

Missionary Work (v. 4–5): once again, the Lord referred to Latter-day prophecies to emphasize the urgency of preaching His gospel. Orson certainly did fulfill the call to "lift up [his] voice as with the sound of a trump, both long and loud, and cry repentance" (v. 6); he served multiple missions, and his writings and sermons in defense of the gospel are voluminous.

Second Coming (v. 6): While a member of the Quorum of the Twelve Apostles, Ezra Taft Benson taught: "The Lord made it plain to these humble ambassadors [missionaries] that they were 'preparing the way of the Lord for his Second Coming.' They were promised that their words would be prompted by the power of the HOLY GHOST and would be the will of the Lord and scripture unto the people, inasmuch as they were faithful. They were told in no uncertain terms that they were being sent 'out to prove the world,' that they should 'not be weary in mind, neither darkened,' and a hair of their head should 'not fall to the ground unnoticed'" (*Ensign,* May 1974, 104).

Section 35

SIDNEY RIGDON

SETTING

SIDNEY RIGDON, a Campbellite minister who had been baptized by the missionaries to the LAMANTIES, asked the PROPHET to reveal the Lord's will concerning him.

TEACHINGS

Relative Roles of Joseph and Sidney: Apparently Sidney Rigdon's labors as a Protestant minister were regarded as worthwhile, because the Lord now called him to "a greater work" (v. 3). He had served as a forerunner (v. 4), and he had taught his congregation the need for a restoration of the New Testament Church. He had specifically prepared the way for ELIJAH, since his followers would play a key role in building the KIRTLAND TEMPLE, in which Elijah would restore the sealing keys (D&C 110:13–16). Without authority, Sidney had baptized many people, and they had not received the HOLY GHOST. With the PRIESTHOOD he now held, he could lay his hands on a convert's head and bestow the gift of the holy ghost (v. 5–6). The Lord reminded Sidney that by the "unlearned" He will "thrash the nations" (v. 13). While Joseph's stewardship was to prophesy, Sidney was commanded to use his background as a former minister to "preach my gospel and to call on the words of the holy prophets to prove [Joseph's] words" (v. 23; compare D&C 100:9–11). Specifically, Sidney was to write for Joseph, who was working on what became known as the JOSEPH SMITH TRANSLATION of the Bible, and the Lord promised that the prophet would receive the scriptures "as they are in mine own bosom" (v. 20). As in previous revelations, the Lord communicated a sense of urgency by referring to the parable of the fig tree and declaring that His coming was "nigh at hand" (v. 15–16).

Sidney Rigdon

The Weak Things of the World (v. 13): Elder Neal A. Maxwell explained, "The Lord knows our circumstances and the intents of our hearts, and surely the talents and gifts He has given us. What we could and have done within our allotted acreage, therefore, is known perfectly by the Master of the vineyard. Their meekness and larger capacity for spiritual contentment may be one reason why God uses the weak of the world to accomplish His work. The worldly are usually not very interested in doing what they regard as the Lord's lowly work anyway" (*Ensign,* May 2000, 72).

Section 36

EDWARD PARTRIDGE

SETTING

EDWARD PARTRIDGE, who was first taught the message of the Restoration by missionaries serving in the LAMANITE MISSION, was not entirely convinced of the truth. To further investigate the Church, he journeyed from OHIO to NEW YORK to meet the PROPHET. After observing the good order of the Smith farm in MANCHESTER and checking with neighbors about the Smiths' character, he found JOSEPH SMITH and requested baptism. He then asked Joseph to inquire of the Lord on his behalf.

Edward Partridge

TEACHINGS

Role of the Priesthood: The Lord's words in verse 2 teach that when a priesthood bearer acts in the name of the Lord, it is as though the Lord were performing the action Himself. Once again, the Master stressed the urgency of proclaiming REPENTANCE to the nations (v. 4–8).

Peaceable Things of the Kingdom (v. 2): Elder M. Russell Ballard observed, "At one time or another I believe everyone yearns for the peace of God. That peace for our troubled hearts only comes to us as we follow the Light of Christ, which is 'given to every man, that he may know good from evil' (Moro. 7:16), as it leads us to repent of sins and seek forgiveness. For all there is a hunger to know 'the peaceable things of the kingdom' and to taste 'the fruit[s] of righteousness,' which are 'sown in peace of them that make peace (James 3:18).' In every home, neighborhood, and community, we ought to strive for peace and never be party to stirring up contention or division" (*Ensign,* May 2002, 87).

SCRIPTURE HELPS

"Hosanna" (v. 3) is a worshipful shout of praise that means "Help, I pray," or "Save, I pray."

"Gird Up Your Loins" (v. 8): This is a common biblical expression for putting yourself in readiness for any service you might be called upon to render. In biblical times, one would literally tie up the loose garments around his or her loins in preparation to go to work. In the context of this verse, the work alluded to is the preparation for the SECOND COMING.

Section 37

THE MOVE TO OHIO

SETTING

The Church in NEW YORK had been under constant persecution, and the lives of its leaders were in danger. As the PROPHET and SIDNEY RIGDON worked on the JOSEPH SMITH TRANSLATION of the Bible, the Lord gave the commandment to move to OHIO.

TEACHINGS

The Gathering: The Saints in western New York and PENNSYLVANIA were directed to GATHER "at the OHIO [country]," where many converts had been made by the LAMANITE MISSION in the KIRTLAND area. By this time, OLIVER COWDERY and the other missionaries had gone on to western MISSOURI, where they would also make converts.

The Importance of Missionary Work and Perfecting the Saints is seen in the Lord's instruction to Joseph and Sidney to preach the GOSPEL and strengthen the BRANCHES of the Church before making the move to OHIO (v. 2).

The Departure of the New York Saints to OHIO

Branch	*Leader*	*Members*
Colesville	Newel Knight	70
Fayette	Lucy Mack Smith	80
Manchester	Martin Harris	50

Section 38

PREPARING TO MOVE TO OHIO

SETTING

Many of the Saints were poverty stricken and expressed a desire to know more about how and why they should move to OHIO. This was the first Doctrine and Covenants section given in 1831, when more of these revelations were received than during any other single year.

TEACHINGS

The Roles of Jesus Christ (v. 1-4): ALPHA AND OMEGA are the first and last letters in the Greek alphabet, so this title (v. 1) suggests all-inclusiveness. The Lord knows all things (v. 2); if this were not so, something He didn't know could prevent Him from accomplishing His purposes. God's knowledge that something will happen does not cause it to happen; we possess moral AGENCY and are therefore free to choose. Jesus Christ created all things (v. 3; see Jn. 1:1–3, 10) under the direction of God the Father. Jesus Christ was the God of the Old Testament (v. 4), and is known by various names, including JEHOVAH or I AM (v. 1; see Ex. 3:14). "CHRIST" means "the anointed one"; in the PRE-EARTHLY EXISTENCE, He was anointed or chosen to be the Savior. He is the one who pleads for us before the Father (v. 4; see D&C 45:3–5).

Further Instructions Concerning Gathering: Although the specific goal of establishing ZION had not yet been revealed, the Lord was already encouraging qualities that would be required to accomplish this goal. He informed the Saints, "Ye are clean, but not all" (v. 10); and later admonished, "Be ye clean that bear the vessels of the Lord" (v. 42). He explained that the earth is "rich" and promised the faithful a "land of promise, a land flowing with milk and honey" (v. 17–20). Nevertheless, He exhorted the Saints to seek the kind of riches the Father desired to give them—the riches of eternity—and that by so doing they would be the "richest of all people" (v. 39; see D&C 6:7). Next, the Lord admonished the Saints to be united (v. 24–27), stating that in that way, they would be like the people of the City of Enoch who were "of one heart and one mind" (Moses 7:18). The Saints were warned of "enemies" in "secret chambers" who were plotting their destruction (v. 13, 28–29). Nevertheless, they received the assurance "If ye are prepared ye shall not fear" (v. 30). The Lord promised that in Ohio, He would reveal His law and endow His Saints "with power from on high" (v. 32). The first promise would be fulfilled the following month with the revelation of SECTION 42, while the second promise would be realized five years later with the dedication of the Kirtland Temple. The Saints were to organize themselves so that they could care for the poor and provide other needed assistance for the upcoming journey (v. 34–38). Once again, the Lord instructed the Saints to raise "the warning voice" before their departure (v. 40–41)

Vessels of the Lord (v. 42): In ancient Israel, certain vessels (bowls, urns, vases, and other containers) and utensils were used in religious feasts and ceremonies. The vessels used in the temple had special significance and were handled only by those who were worthy and authorized and who had properly prepared themselves. In a similar manner, the Lord has indicated that His Saints should come "out from among the wicked" and leave the worldliness of Babylon so they will be worthy to "bear the vessels of the Lord."

President James E. Faust remarked, "As members of the Church and particularly as holders of the PRIESTHOOD, we believe in being chaste. There is no different or double standard for moral cleanliness for men and women in the Church. In fact, I believe holders of the priesthood have a greater responsibility to maintain standards of chastity before MARRIAGE and fidelity after marriage. The Lord has said, 'Be ye clean that bear the vessels of the Lord'" (*Ensign,* May 1998, 43).

Section 39

James Covill

SETTING

James Covill, who had served as a Baptist minister for about forty years, promised to obey any command the Lord gave him through Joseph Smith. The Prophet inquired of the Lord on his behalf.

TEACHINGS

Christ and His Gospel: The author of this revelation identified Himself as the God of the Old Testament and as Jesus Christ, who was rejected by many in the days of the New Testament. As people accept Christ, live His gospel, and are spiritually born again (see Mosiah 5:7), they become His SONS AND DAUGHTERS (v. 4–5). The Savior defines His gospel as REPENTANCE, BAPTISM by water, and baptism by fire (v. 6). These principles and ORDINANCES, along with FAITH (v. 12, 16), compose the first four principles and ordinances of the gospel as listed in Article of Faith 4. The "baptism of fire" refers to the cleansing and purifying power of the HOLY GHOST, which brings SANCTIFICATION.

James Covill to Preach: The command for James Covill to be baptized (v. 10) may have been difficult for him to follow because, as a Baptist minister, he was probably convinced that he had already fulfilled this commandment. Similarly, he may have been reluctant to go to OHIO rather than to the East (v. 14), as the population was more scattered in OHIO and a missionary might not have as much influence there. The Lord then directed the Prophet to call missionaries to preach the gospel in preparation for His coming, which He declared was "at hand" (v. 17–24).

Section 40

JAMES COVILL'S FAILURE

SETTING

When JAMES COVILL rejected the commandment of the Lord to preach the gospel in OHIO, the PROPHET and SIDNEY RIGDON wondered why.

TEACHINGS

Honoring Commitments: The Lord's explanation of Covill's failure was relevant to Sidney Rigdon, who also had been a Protestant minister. All of us should consider whether the same factors (temptation, fear of persecution, and the cares of the world) sometimes cause us to reject the Lord's word and to fail to keep our promises to Him. Contrast the Lord's description of Covill's action in verse 2 with His affirmation that those who "receiveth my law and doeth it, the same is my disciple" (D&C 41:5).

Section 41

THE FIRST BISHOP

SETTING

This REVELATION was the first of many given in the state of OHIO. The PROPHET found some strange notions and false spirits among the Saints in OHIO. He inquired of the Lord to know how best to govern the Church. EDWARD PARTRIDGE had been baptized only a few weeks earlier (see SECTION 36), but was now being called as BISHOP.

TEACHINGS

Calling a Bishop: The Lord's promise to reveal His law to govern the Church was fulfilled just five days later with the revelation in SECTION 42. Among other things, the Lord would reveal the law of CONSECRATION in which the bishop would play a key role. This was the first new office added to the Church since its organization the previous year. Note the three steps in Bishop Partridge's call (v. 9) that are still essential in calls to serve today: (1) called by the Lord through those in authority, (2) sustained "by the voice of the church" under the principle of COMMON CONSENT, and (3) ordained or set apart by PRIESTHOOD authority. Providing a house for Joseph Smith (v. 7) was consistent with the principle of REMUNERATION for full-time Church officers.

Without Guile (v. 11): To be without guile is to be pure in heart—an essential virtue of those who would be counted among true followers of Jesus Christ. He taught in the Sermon on the Mount, "Blessed are the pure in heart: for they shall see God" (Matt. 5:8; see also 3 Ne. 12:8). The Lord also revealed to the Prophet Joseph Smith that Zion is the pure in heart (see D&C 97:21) and that a house is to be built in Zion in which the pure in heart shall see God (see D&C 97:10–16). If we are without guile, we are honest, true, and righteous. All of these are attributes of Deity and are required of the Saints (*Ensign,* May 1988, 90).

Section 42

"THE LAW OF THE CHURCH"

SETTING

Groups of ELDERS united in prayer on two separate occasions with the desire to receive the law of the Lord, as promised in D&C 38:32 and 41:2–3. They also wanted to know how to organize MISSIONARY WORK and how to proceed in cases where Church members had committed adultery or other serious transgressions.

TEACHINGS

Teaching the Gospel (v. 4–17): The elders were to go forth two by two, preaching and building up the Church in "the regions westward" (v. 4–9). Only those with known authority are to be recognized (v. 11); this principle has since been invoked when men have falsely claimed to have a commission to lead the Church. In this REVELATION, the Lord also commanded the elders to teach from the scriptures (v. 12). At this time, revelations in the Doctrine and Covenants had not yet been canonized or officially accepted as scripture, with the exception of SECTIONS 20 and 22, known as the "Articles and Covenants" of the Church (v. 13). The Lord admonished the elders of the Church to teach by the power of the HOLY GHOST (v. 14), which testifies of the Father and the Son (v. 17), reveals "the truth of all things" (Moro. 10:5), and will carry the truth "unto the hearts" of those who listen (2 Ne. 33:1).

The Ten Commandments Reemphasized (v. 18–29): The Lord gave these commandments to His people, the Israelites, when they were about to establish new homes in Canaan, their promised land (see Ex. 20). In the revelation now known as section 43, He restated the commandments for His people who were about to relocate to OHIO. Murderers do not commit the UNPARDONABLE SIN, but "it is not easy" for them to obtain FORGIVENESS (v. 18; see Alma 39:6). CAPITAL PUNISHMENT is an appropriate penalty for this crime (v. 19). Unrepentant thieves and liars are subject to CHURCH DISCIPLINE (v. 20–21). While verse 23 (and D&C 63:16) list some of the negative fruits of immorality, verse 22 suggests a positive reason for chastity—that one may save his full love for that person whom he chooses as his eternal companion.

Love Thy Wife . . . and None Else (v. 22): President Boyd K. Packer taught, "You should be attracted to one another and to marry. Then, and only then, may you worthily respond to the strong and good and constant desire to express that love through which children will bless your lives. By commandment of God our Father, that must happen only between husband and wife—man and woman—committed to one another in the covenant of marriage (see 1 Cor. 7:2). To do otherwise is forbidden and will bring sorrow" (*Ensign,* Nov. 2000, 72–74).

The Law of Consecration (v. 30-42) was to replace the system of collective ownership of property that people in KIRTLAND had established before receiving the restored gospel. Under CONSECRATION, individuals held deeds to their stewardships for which they were also accountable. This law was linked to the BISHOP'S responsibility to care for the poor and to manage properties needed for building up the Church and for establishing ZION.

Healing the Sick (v. 43-52): Faith and the PRIESTHOOD play a key role in healing the sick, which is a gift of the Spirit. People without faith should be cared for (v. 43), but even people with faith should do all possible to preserve or restore their health through obtaining proper care. This parallels the Lord's instruction that we seek answers through our own efforts (see D&C 9:7–9) as well as through asking Him. Administering to the sick is an important priesthood ORDINANCE (v. 44; compare James 5:14). The righteous are not promised that they will never die, but rather that they will not "taste of death," meaning that death will hold no fear for them (v. 46–47). God Himself has appointed the time when we enter and leave this mortal sphere (v. 48). We may hasten the time of our death, but we probably cannot delay it much (see Spencer W. Kimball, "Tragedy or Destiny," in *Faith Precedes the Miracle,* 95–106).

Appointed unto Death (v. 48): Elder Dallin H. Oaks explained, "Although the Savior could heal all whom He would heal, this is not true of those who hold His priesthood authority. Mortal exercises of that authority are limited by the will of Him whose priesthood it is. Consequently, we are told that some whom the elders bless are not healed because they are 'appointed unto death'" (*Ensign,* Nov. 2006, 6–9).

Use of the Joseph Smith Translation (v. 56-58): In his translation of the Bible, the prophet did not begin with Genesis and work his way through

Revelation; instead, he worked on particular books of the Bible, or certain topics as he was directed by the Spirit. On February 2, 1833, he finished the revision of the New Testament, and on July 2 of that same year, he finished the translation of the Bible, as far as the Lord permitted him to go at that time. The Prophet hoped to resume this project, but persecution prevented him from doing so (see *CHMR,* 1:242). Consistent with instructions given to the Church in verse 57, the JOSEPH SMITH TRANSLATION has not been published, but key parts of it are included in the LDS edition of the King James Version of the Bible.

More Revelation Promised (v. 61–68): The promise in verse 61 applies to the Saints today as much as to those in 1831. The faithful may know the MYSTERIES, while the world cannot (v. 65), but the faithful must ask (v. 68).

The Location of Zion was yet to be revealed (v. 62). Covenants would also be unfolded for Zion, or the NEW JERSUSALEM (v. 67).

Keys of the Kingdom (v. 69): These KEYS are the authority to direct the functioning of the priesthood and the Church.

Remuneration for Church Service (v. 70–73): At this time, the bishop and his counselors served full time in their callings, so they were entitled to receive REMUNERATION, or support, from the Church. Their full-time callings were, in effect, their stewardships, which should be a source of livelihood just as with individuals that have temporal stewardships (v. 71–73). Saints not required to work full time in their callings were to have temporal stewardships and did not need to receive support from the Church (v. 70).

Fornication vs. Adultery (v. 74–77): The First Presidency has declared: "The Lord has drawn no essential distinctions between fornication, adultery, and harlotry or prostitution" (CR, Oct. 1942, 11). Therefore, the distinction made in verses 74 and 75 is not between fornication and adultery but rather between those who are personally guilty or innocent of the offense. Verses 76 and 77 suggest that sexual immorality is a more serious transgression for married than for single individuals; a married person is not only committing the immoral act, but is also breaking the covenant of MARRIAGE.

Dealing with Transgressions (v. 78–92): The Church may deal with adultery (v. 80–83) and "any manner of iniquity," while the law of the land handles offenses such as murder (v. 79), robbery, and lying (v. 84–86). If a person has offended publicly, he may be dealt with openly, but if the offense was "in secret," it should be dealt with confidentially (v. 88–92).

Section 43

False Claims to Revelation

SETTING

A self-proclaimed prophetess named Hubble deceived some Saints with her supposed REVELATIONS and commandments. The PROPHET knew she was an imposter and inquired of the Lord concerning the matter.

TEACHINGS

Beware of False Prophets (v. 1–7): As He had done when Hiram Page professed to be receiving revelation for the Church, the Lord emphasized that only the prophet has this authority. Knowing that JOSEPH SMITH would not fall, the Lord declared that if a prophet falls he will have only the right to name his successor (v. 4). This statement had the effect of requiring that pretenders to Church leadership prove they had been appointed by the President of the Church. In a sense, PRESIDENTS OF THE CHURCH do name their successors through the process of the senior Apostle becoming the new leader. President Harold B. Lee explained, "The call of one to be President of the Church actually begins when he is called, ordained, and set apart to become a member of the Quorum of the Twelve Apostles" (CR, Apr. 1970, 123).

Come in at the Gate (v. 1–7): Elder Dallin H. Oaks said, "Another revelation reaffirmed to the ELDERS of the Church that 'commandments and revelations' [v. 3] for the Church would be received only by the prophet the Lord had appointed, and that 'none else shall be appointed unto this gift except it be through him' [v. 4]. Those selected by the Lord to exercise this gift would 'come in at the gate and be ordained as I have told you before' [v. 7]—thus excluding the possibility of secret callings or appointments to receive revelation" (*The Lord's Way,* 68–69). The gate is ordination into the QUORUM of the Twelve APOSTLES.

Church Meetings (v. 8–9): We should instruct and edify one another that we may understand God's laws and become sanctified. We then need to commit ourselves to act upon that which we have learned. Speaking of this commitment to act, Elder Paul V. Johnson of the SEVENTY taught, "In order for the messages of general conference to change our lives, we need to be willing to follow the counsel we hear. The Lord explained in a revelation to the Prophet Joseph Smith 'that when ye are assembled together ye shall instruct and edify each other, that ye may know . . . how to act upon the points of my law and commandment' [v. 8]. But knowing 'how to act' isn't enough. The Lord in the next verse said, 'Ye shall bind yourselves to act in all holiness before me' [v. 9]. This willingness to take action on what we have learned opens the doors for marvelous blessings" (*Ensign,* Nov. 2005, 50).

Support for Church Officers: The Lord had directed Joseph Smith to devote all his time to his calling as Prophet, and He instructed the Church to provide REMUNERATION for Joseph's support (see D&C 24:3, 7). Now the Lord reminded the Saints that they must fulfill this responsibility if they wanted to enjoy spiritual blessings (v. 13).

Calls to Teach: Although missions can be broadening experiences, this is not their purpose. Missionaries will be endowed with the Lord's SPIRIT and be "taught from on high" what they need to know (v. 15–16). They are to "call upon the nations to repent," after which the Lord will cry repentance by means of lightnings, pestilences, and other calamities (v. 20–25).

Latter-day Events: The Lord will call on the "sleeping nations" or people in the SPIRIT WORLD to awaken (v. 18); this will be part of the RESURRECTION of the just; the wicked will need to wait a thousand years until He calls again. The "great MILLENNIUM" is the thousand years when Christ will reign upon the earth and SATAN will be bound (v. 30–31). Afterwards, Satan will be loosed for a little season, the FINAL JUDGMENT will take place, and the earth will be consumed by fire and receive its ultimate CELESTIAL condition (v. 31–33).

Section 44

MEET IN CONFERENCE

SETTING

The Prophet JOSEPH SMITH inquired of the Lord for instructions concerning the next general meeting of the Church.

TEACHINGS

A Purpose of Church Conferences is to conduct Church business. The promised spiritual experiences (v. 2) were certainly realized at the conference held early in June (see SECTION 52, Setting).

Missionary work was to continue successfully so that new BRANCHES could be organized according to the law of the land (v. 3–5).

Caring for the Poor (v. 6) was a continuing priority.

Section 45

SIGNS OF THE LAST DAYS

SETTING

When the Church was almost one year old, missionary work was significantly hindered by many false stories that aroused prejudice against the Latter-day Saints. For example, many newspapers in the area carried the story of a Mormon girl predicting an earthquake in China that caused great destruction just six weeks later. These papers labeled the loss of thousands of lives in that disaster as being "'Mormonism' in China" (*HC*, 1:158). At a special CONFERENCE for elders leaving on missions, the PROPHET sought clarification of the meaning of prophecies concerning the SECOND COMING of Christ.

TEACHINGS

Jesus Christ, Our Advocate (v. 3-5): Because He is God's Son and lived a sinless life, Jesus Christ possesses power over both physical and SPIRITUAL DEATH. Nevertheless, on behalf of mankind, He willingly suffered both physical and spiritual death. Therefore, He could ask the Father to spare us on condition that we believe in Him and live His gospel.

Signs of the Times (v. 39-40) may be regarded as the keynote of this revelation. Those who respect the Lord will look for the signs of His SECOND COMING. Even though we cannot fix the exact date of His Coming (see D&C 49:7), we can recognize these signs (see D&C 68:11). Prophesied events can be grouped into five broad categories: (1) events of the LATTER DAYS in general; (2) developments to immediately precede the Second Coming; (3) events to accompany the Lord's Advent in glory; (4) conditions and events during the MILLENNIUM; and (5) events to follow the thousand years.

After commanding us to hearken to His words (v. 6–14), the Lord recounted what He taught His disciples on the Mount of Olives (v. 15–16; compare Matt. 24 and the Prophet's inspired revision in Joseph Smith—Matthew). The Lord first cited a promise made to those in the SPIRIT WORLD (v. 17; compare D&C 138:50), and then spoke of what would soon happen to Jerusalem and its temple (v. 18–24). He then turned to the latter days (v. 24–38). The "times of the GENTILES" will begin with the Restoration and refer to the time when the Gentile nations will receive the gospel (v. 28–30). After the times of the Gentiles are fulfilled, the gathering of Israel will be completed (v. 25). This will be a time of calamities (v. 26–27, 30–33), but the Lord's disciples will "stand in HOLY PLACES" (v. 32) and rejoice because they know the time of His Coming is near (v. 35). The Master then turned to events that will immediately precede and accompany His Advent (v. 41–55). "This place" (v. 43) and "this mount" (v. 48) refer to Jerusalem and the Mount of Olives, where Jesus originally spoke these words to His New Testament disciples. He then emphasized that the wise virgins, those who will be prepared for His Coming, are those who "have received the truth and have taken the Holy Spirit for their guide" (v. 57). Finally, He described the conditions that will prevail during the Millennium (v. 58–59).

Elder James E. Faust reminded us: "The parable of the ten virgins, five wise and five foolish, has both a spiritual and a temporal application. Each of us has a lamp to light the way, but it requires that every one of us put the oil in our own lamps to produce that light. It is not enough to sit idly by and say, 'The Lord will provide.' He has promised that they who are wise and 'have taken the Holy Spirit for their guide' will have the earth given unto them [v. 57–58]. It is further promised that 'the Lord shall be in their midst, and his glory shall be upon them, and he will be their king and their lawgiver' [v. 59]" (*Ensign,* May 1986, 20).

The Lord then reminded the elders in Kirtland that more concerning His discourse (recorded in Matt. 24) would not be known until the JOSEPH SMITH TRANSLATION of the Bible, the New Testament in particular, was completed (v. 60–61). He then spoke of wars that would sweep the earth, and reminded the elders that they had been commanded to gather in order to establish ZION or the NEW JERSUSALEM, which would be a refuge of peace and glory (v. 62–75). The Latter-day Saints were to accomplish this "with one heart and with one mind" (v. 65), just as the people of Enoch had done (see Moses 7:18).

Section 46

Gifts of the Spirit

SETTING

Despite instructions in the BOOK OF MORMON that all should be welcome in Church meetings (3 Ne. 18:22–34), members often excluded unbelievers from sacrament and confirmation meetings. Following a discussion of this matter, the PROPHET inquired of the Lord.

TEACHINGS

The Lord settled this matter in the first seven verses by reemphasizing the fact that no one is to be excluded from sacrament or other public meetings (v. 3–6). Those who conduct meetings are to proceed as "directed and guided by the Holy Spirit" (v. 2). The Lord further commanded his Saints "in all things to ask of God" so they might not be deceived by false ideas either from men or from devils (v. 7).

Spiritual Gifts: The Saints were then commanded, "Seek ye earnestly the best gifts." These are given for the benefit of those who love the Lord and keep all His commandments as well as for those who are striving to do so (v. 8–9). If we are to seek these gifts, we must know what they are (v. 10). Not all receive the same gifts, but "to some is given one, and to some is given another, that all may be profited thereby" (v. 12). In

1 Corinthians 12, Paul listed the various gifts of the Spirit and compared them, as well as the various officers in the Church, to a perfect human body, all of whose members are essential for the well-being of the whole. Paul's list of the gifts is similar to that found in section 46, as well as in Moroni 10.

In certain cases, these lists clarify one another. Paul stated that "no man can *say* that Jesus is the Christ but by the HOLY GHOST" (1 Cor. 12:3; italics added), while modern revelation suggests that "say" might better be translated "know" (D&C 46:13). The Doctrine and Covenants speaks of the "word of wisdom" and the "word of knowledge" (D&C 46:17–18); Moroni explained that the ability to *teach* these is a gift of the Spirit (Moro. 10:9–10).

Relying on the Testimony of Others (v. 14): President Harold B. Lee encouraged, "You young Latter-day Saints here tonight, some of you may not have that testimony as firmly rooted as you would like to. May I ask you then, if you don't have one, to cling to my testimony tonight, until you can develop one for yourselves. Say that you believe in one who holds the holy apostleship, that you believe what I said and then you start now to so search in the way that the scriptures have told us, as I have explained to you here tonight, until you too can say, as I say tonight, yes I know, by a witness that is more powerful than sight, I know that Jesus is the Savior of the world [v. 13]" (LDSSA Fireside, Utah State University, Oct. 1971).

"Differences of Administration" and "Diversities of Operations" (v. 15–16): The Greek work translated into "administration" refers to the various courses or duties of the priesthood. The Lord directs His authorized servants by revelation through the Holy Ghost. In light of the Greek oration, to know the "diversities of operations" means being able to discern whether or not a given form of spiritual manifestation is of the Lord.

The Gift of Tongues (v. 24–25): While some individuals publicly demonstrate the ability to speak in unknown tongues as an attempt to prove they have the Holy Spirit, JOSEPH SMITH pointed out that the weightier gifts, such as faith and wisdom, are not necessarily accompanied by visible outward manifestations. He also described the gift of tongues as the smallest of the gifts, its "ultimate destiny" being its power to enable one to speak with foreigners (*HC,* 5:27–31). In chapter 14 of 1 Corinthians, Paul discussed some of the abuses of the gift of tongues. Even though the Apostle was proud of the fact that he could speak in tongues as much as anyone in the Church, he said he would rather speak five words that could be understood than to speak ten thousand words in an unknown tongue (see 1 Cor. 14:18–19).

Discernment (v. 27) is a gift given to presiding priesthood officers so they can understand the source and purpose of various spiritual manifestations. President Boyd K. Packer observed, "There is a power of discernment granted 'unto such as God shall appoint . . . to watch over [his] church. To discern means to see. President Harold B. Lee told me once of a conversation he had with Elder Charles A. Callis of the Quorum of the Twelve. Brother Callis had remarked that the gift of discernment was an awesome burden to carry. To see clearly what is ahead and yet find members slow to respond or resistant to counsel or even rejecting the witness of the Apostles and prophets brings deep sorrow" (*Ensign,* Nov. 1996, 6).

Knowing what to pray for (v. 30) is also a gift of the Spirit. Elder Neal A. Maxwell taught, "God cannot . . . respond affirmatively to all of our petitions with an unbroken chain of 'yeses.' This would assume that all of our petitions are for that 'which is right' and are spiritually 'expedient' (3 Ne. 18:20; D&C 18:18; D&C 88:64–65)" (*Ensign,* May 1991, 88).

Section 47

Church Historian John Whitmer

SETTING

Oliver Cowdery, the first Church historian, had been called to the Lamanite Mission, leaving a need for someone else to record the history of the Church. John Whitmer was reluctant to accept the responsibility for keeping a history of the Church. He said he would do it, however, if it was the Lord's will. The prophet inquired of the Lord on John's behalf.

TEACHINGS

Historical Sources: Historians emphasize the importance of using good sources. John Whitmer was given a key for finding and evaluating information and for producing the written narrative: "It shall be given him, inasmuch as he is faithful, by the COMFORTER, to write these things" (v. 4).

Section 48

LAND FOR THE INCOMING SAINTS

SETTING

Church leaders were concerned about purchasing land in OHIO on which the NEW YORK Saints could settle. They also wondered if they should establish ZION in KIRTLAND or elsewhere. The PROPHET inquired of the Lord.

TEACHINGS

Be Prepared: The location of Zion was not to be revealed yet (v. 4–6), so the members in Kirtland should remain there for the time being (v. 1). They should share their lands and save money to buy more for the benefit of the New York Saints, whose arrival they anticipated (v. 2–4).

Section 49

MISSION TO THE SHAKERS

SETTING

Leman Copley was eager to share his newfound faith with his friends in the United Society of Believers in Christ's Second Appearing, a group popularly known as the Shakers. He asked the PROPHET JOSEPH SMITH to inquire of the Lord concerning some of the teachings of his former religion.

TEACHINGS

Source of Knowledge (v. 1-4): The Lord declared that the Shakers' desire to know the truth was limited, and that they were not "right" before the Lord and therefore needed to repent (v. 2). Leman Copley was to learn the truth from the Lord's authorized servants rather than from others (v. 4).

Has Christ Already Come? The Shakers believed that Jesus Christ had made His "second appearing" in the form of their founder—Ann Lee. Verse 7, which speaks of His Second Coming as a future occurrence, dismisses the notion that the event had already happened.

Ordinances: The Shakers taught that outward ordinances such as baptism by water and the laying on of hands for the gift of the Holy Ghost are unnecessary. Verses 11 through 14 specifically state that these ordinances are essential.

Marriage (v. 15–17): Although they did not condemn marriage, the Shakers regarded celibacy as a higher state. This revelation testifies that "marriage is ordained of God" as the means to provide earthly tabernacles for God's spirit children (see The Family: A Proclamation to the World, 1995). Notice that monogamy was the pattern for marriage (v. 16); the doctrine of plural marriage had not yet been revealed.

Eating Meat (v. 18–21): Shakers were vegetarians, not eating meat except in time of cold or famine. The Lord revealed that animals are "ordained for the use of man for food and for raiment," but cautioned that they should not be wasted.

God's Gender: The Shakers held that God had two natures, male and female. They believed that in His first appearing, God came in the form of the man Jesus, but that in His "second appearing" He was in the form of a woman, Ann Lee. Verse 22 specifically refutes the idea that the Son of Man would come to earth as a female or as an ordinary mortal ("a man traveling on the earth"); instead, He will come "in the clouds of glory" (Matt. 26:64).

Destiny of the Lamanites: Once again, the Lord ended a revelation with the affirmation, "I come quickly" (v. 27). He stressed, however, that various things needed to be accomplished before His Second Coming (v. 23–25). One of these is that the Lamanites must achieve their prophesied glorious destiny and "blossom as the rose" (v. 24).

Section 50

Discerning the Spirits

SETTING

Several elders asked the PROPHET to inquire of the Lord concerning the many curious spiritual manifestations seen even among the Saints. PARLEY P. PRATT described some of them as "very strange . . . Some persons would seem to swoon away, and make unseemly gestures, and be drawn or disfigured in their countenances." After joining with the elders in prayer, Joseph dictated the Lord's answer.

Parley then recorded one of the few eyewitness accounts of the Prophet receiving a revelation: "After we had joined in prayer in his translating room, he dictated in our presence the following revelation [section 50]. Each sentence was uttered slowly and very distinctly, and with a pause between each, sufficiently long for it to be recorded, by an ordinary writer, in long hand. This was the manner in which all his written revelations were dictated and written. There was never any hesitation, reviewing, or reading back, in order to keep the run of the subject; neither did any of these communications undergo revisions, interlinings, or corrections. As he dictated them so they stood, so far as I have witnessed; and I was present to witness the dictation of several communications of several pages each" (*PPP*, 61–62).

TEACHINGS

Teach by the Spirit of Truth: The Lord acknowledged that there were many "false spirits" in the land and "abominations in the church" (v. 2, 4). He then "reasoned" with the ELDERS by asking, "Unto what were ye ordained?" He then answered His own question, "To preach my gospel by the Spirit," and emphasized that "if it be by some other way it is not of God" (v. 10–18). Those who preach and those who listen "by the spirit of truth . . . understand one another, and both are edified and rejoice together." That which edifies is light and is from God; as we follow the Spirit, we receive "more light" which will grow "brighter and brighter until the perfect day"(v. 21–22, 24). On the other hand, that which does not edify is not of God and is darkness; the elders were admonished to "chase darkness from among you" (v. 23, 25). PRIESTHOOD leaders were promised the power to discern and rebuke false spirits (v. 26–33).

Depend on Christ: The Master likened the elders to children who needed to grow in the gospel. He then assured them, "Fear not, little children, for you are mine, and I have overcome the world, and you are of them that my Father hath given me" (v. 40–41).

Grow in Grace (v. 40): President James E. Faust observed, "We are told in the Doctrine and Covenants that we are to 'grow in grace.' Grace is a God-given virtue. It is a disposition to be kind and to do good. It is a charming trait or accomplishment . . . Charm is attractiveness which comes from a feeling of personal dignity, an inner beauty that comes from a feeling of self-worth" (*Ensign,* May 2003, 108). With the Lord's help we should seek to develop these qualities.

Section 51

Further Instructions to the Bishop

SETTING

As the Saints began to arrive from the East, BISHOP EDWARD PARTRIDGE sought further direction on implementing the law of CONSECRATION among them. The PROPHET's countenance shone as he dictated the revelation.

TEACHINGS

Further Instructions Concerning Consecration: The assignment of stewardships was not to be done routinely, but each individual's "circumstances . . . wants and needs" were to be considered (v. 3). (Of course, the "wants" had to be just; see D&C 82:17.) A person leaving the Church could retain his stewardship because it had been received by legal deed; however, he would have no claim on his original consecration that had been given to the bishop by deed (v. 4–5). The instruction to appoint an AGENT to assist the bishop (v. 8) was carried out the following month (see SECTION 53). The transfer of funds from one "church" (meaning BRANCH) to another was to be handled by the bishop or his agent (v. 10–12). The bishop was to establish a storehouse. Due to the full-time nature of the bishop's assignment, he was to be supported according to the principle of REMUNERATION for Church service (v. 13).

The Long View: Even though the Saints might be in KIRTLAND only "for a little season," the Lord counseled them to work as though they were going to be there "for years" (v. 16–17). He promised that a person who is faithful and wise in his stewardships or responsibilities "shall enter into the joy of his Lord, and shall inherit eternal life" (v. 19).

Section 52

ELDERS SENT TO MISSOURI

SETTING

According to instructions given the previous February (see D&C 44:1–2), the ELDERS met in CONFERENCE at KIRTLAND on June 3, 1831. During this conference, JOSEPH SMITH spoke with "great power as he was moved upon by the HOLY GHOST" and "the spirit of power and of testimony rested down upon the elders in a marvelous manner" (*PPP,* 68). Joseph prophesied that JOHN THE BELOVED was then laboring among the Lost TEN TRIBES. At this conference, the first HIGH PRIESTS were ordained during this DISPENSATION. The "man of sin" was revealed but rebuked. During the four-day gathering, "great harmony prevailed" (*HC,* 1:175–76). At its conclusion, the PROPHET inquired of the Lord what the elders should do until the convening of the next conference in INDEPENDENCE, MISSOURI.

TEACHINGS

Instructions to the Missionaries: Joseph Smith and SIDNEY RIGDON were to go to Missouri, where the land of their inheritance would be made known (v. 3–5). Twenty-six other elders were to travel by various routes to the same destination, "preaching the word by the way" (v. 6–34). Specifically, they should teach "none other thing than that which the prophets and APOSTLES have written, and that which is taught them by the COMFORTER" (v. 9). They were to "go two by two" (v. 10), thus providing protection for one another and fulfilling the principle that "in the mouth of two or three witnesses shall every word be established" (2 Cor. 13:1). The elders were given a "pattern" to judge spiritual manifestations; individuals who are "contrite" and exhibit spiritual GIFTS are acceptable only if "they obey mine ORDINANCES" and "bring forth fruits of praise and wisdom" (v. 14–19). Other elders were to "watch over the churches and declare the word in the regions round about." They were to "labor with their own hands" so there would be no time for "idolatry or wickedness." They were charged to "remember in all things the poor and the needy, the sick and the afflicted" (v. 39–40).

Section 53

THE CALLING OF AN AGENT

SETTING

In May 1831, the Lord had directed that an "AGENT" be called to assist the bishop with his weighty temporal responsibilities in the law of CONSECRATION (D&C 51:8). Having just been ordained an elder, SIDNEY GILBERT, a successful partner of NEWEL K. WHITNEY with business experience, asked the PROPHET to inquire of the Lord concerning the part he should play in sustaining the Church.

TEACHINGS

Counsel to Brother Gilbert: His "calling and election in the church" was to hold the offices of ELDER and agent (v. 1–4). Even though the latter calling involved temporal responsibilities, Sidney was counseled in verse 2 to "forsake the world"—in other words, to put spiritual goals above material concerns. He was instructed to accompany JOSEPH SMITH and SIDNEY RIGDON to MISSOURI (v. 5; see also D&C 52:3); he departed two weeks later for INDEPENDENCE, MISSOURI, where he would assist Bishop EDWARD PARTRIDGE (D&C 57:6–8)

Forsake the World (v. 2): President BRIGHAM YOUNG explained, "Some are fearful that the Lord will forsake them . . . Who does he forsake? None save those who first forsake him and begin to walk in by-and-forbidden paths, where neither he nor his angels walk; and then such persons say the Lord has forsaken them. They have forsaken the path of rectitude and are upon the grounds of the Devil, being led captive by his will, and do not enjoy the benign influence that flows from the Fountain of all intelligence as they did when they were in the path of truth. Never be fearful that the Lord will first forsake you; for you have first to leave him, since he never forsaketh those who are striving to do right" (Address given in Salt Lake Tabernacle, Aug. 4, 1859).

Section 54

Counsel to the Colesville Branch

SETTING

Saints from Colesville, New York, settled on land at Thompson, Ohio, that Leman Copley, a former Shaker, had consecrated. When the mission to the Shakers failed (see section 49), Copley ordered the Saints off the land. When this caused confusion among the Colesville Saints, their branch president, Newel Knight, and others asked the prophet what they should do.

TEACHINGS

Accountability: The Colesville Saints' covenant to enter the law of consecration in Ohio was now broken. The Savior emphasized that those responsible for it being broken would be held accountable, while the faithful Saints who had attempted to honor it would be blessed (v. 4–6). They were directed to move on to Missouri (v. 7–8), where they would play a key role in settling Jackson County.

Priorities: Those who have put Christ first in their lives are promised rest to their souls (v. 10). His rest has been defined as the fulness of celestial glory (see D&C 84:24).

Seek the Lord Early (v. 10): In regard to our priorities, Elder James E. Faust advised, "First, and perhaps most important, our faith and testimony can be strengthened. The faithful member of the Church learns that in times of economic stress the Lord helps those who have sought him early. But those members who haven't begun early in their religious life may resolve to seek the Lord more diligently. We learn to recognize the Lord's hand in helping us. In hard times we have a chance to reevaluate and reorder our priorities in life. We learn what is most important to us. The way is open to strengthen faith and testimony" (*Ensign*, Nov. 1982, 87).

Section 55

WILLIAM W. PHELPS

SETTING

WILLIAM W. PHELPS, a former newspaper editor, was a recent convert but had not yet been BAPTIZED. When he arrived in OHIO, he asked the PROPHET to inquire of the Lord on his behalf.

William W. Phelps

TEACHINGS

Outward Actions and Inward Preparation (v. 1–3): Phelps was promised a REMISSION of his sins and the GIFT OF THE HOLY GHOST if he was baptized with an eye single to God's glory. After being ordained an elder, he would have authority to bestow the Holy Ghost if those on whom he laid his hands were contrite.

Education (v. 4–5): Phelps' assignment to help prepare school books for children is evidence of the importance of EDUCATION in the restored Church since its early days. For the purpose of selecting and writing these books, Phelps was commanded to join JOSEPH SMITH and SIDNEY RIGDON on their journey to Missouri (see D&C 52:3).

W.W. Phelps is the author of fourteen hymns that appear in the modern LDS hymnal, including such favorites as "The Spirit of God," "Now Let Us Rejoice," "Redeemer of Israel," and "Praise to the Man."

Section 56

Changes in Assignments

SETTING

Of the twenty-two missionaries called to Missouri, two did not serve. Due to the problem over the land at Thompson, Ohio, Ezra Thayer was no longer willing to go on the mission to which he was called (D&C 52:22). Because of the land issue, Newel Knight was assigned to go with his branch to Missouri (D&C 54:7–8), and so was unable to fulfill his missionary assignment (D&C 52:32). Therefore, their two companions were reassigned to go on the mission together.

TEACHINGS

Commandments Revoked (v. 3–13): The Lord and His purposes are unchanging (see Heb. 13:8); however, we are not. Therefore, the Lord sometimes needs to modify His instructions that His unchanging purposes may be realized (v. 4). An illustration was the reassignment of missionary companions made in this revelation.

Speaking of the principle of revelation evidenced when the Lord revokes a previous commandment, Elder Boyd K. Packer testified, "Those who hold the keys have obtained knowledge on what to do. When changes have come, they have come through that process. The Lord does as He said He would do: 'I, the Lord, command and revoke, as it seemeth me good' (D&C 56:4). 'I command and men obey not; I revoke and they receive not the blessing' (D&C 58:32). He told the Saints that when enemies prevented them from keeping a commandment, he would no longer require them to do so" (*Ensign,* Nov. 1989, 14).

Attitudes about Wealth (v. 16–18): Money as such is neither good nor evil; it is simply a means of exchange that can be used for good or ill. Our attitude is all-important. Paul labeled "the love of money" rather than money itself as "the root of all evil" (1 Tim. 6:10). Jacob approved seeking for riches if we have first sought the kingdom of God, because we will then seek money in the right way and for the right reasons (Jacob 2:17–19). In the present revelation, the Lord specifically condemned wealthy people who refuse to share their means with the poor (v. 16). In like spirit, the Lord rebuked the poor whose hearts are not humbled and who are greedy and lazy (v. 17–18).

Section 57

ZION LOCATED

SETTING

Upon his arrival in western Missouri, the PROPHET greeted the Saints and viewed the countryside and its people. He diligently sought the Lord for answers to questions concerning the establishment of ZION in the LATTER DAYS. Prior to this revelation, the Lord had promised to reveal the location of ZION, or the NEW JERUSALEM (D&C 42:62). Members of the Church had read in the BOOK OF MORMON about a New Jerusalem that would be located in America (see 3 Ne. 20:22; 21:23–24; Ether 13:1–12). In addition, in September 1830 the Lord had explained that Zion would be erected "on the borders by the Lamanites" (D&C 28:9).

TEACHINGS

Location of Zion: The first three verses answer the Prophet's questions about where the center of Zion and its TEMPLE would be located. The Saints were to purchase lands out to "the line running directly between Jew and GENTILE" (v. 4), referring to the western boundary of Missouri; the land west of this line was designated as Indian Territory. The LAMANTIES had been referred to as a remnant of the Jews (see D&C 19:27), perhaps because Lehi's group had come from Jerusalem and because the Mulekites had brought Jewish blood to the Western Hemisphere. *Gentiles* was the term the Book of Mormon used to refer to those who came from Europe to people the Americas (see 1 Ne. 13:10–15). SIDNEY GILBERT was to function as AGENT (see SECTION 53) in assisting the BISHOP, EDWARD PARTRIDGE (v. 6–10), specifically in connection with the GATHERING (v. 15).

Elder Joseph Fielding Smith explained, "In accord with the revelations given to the Prophet Joseph Smith, we teach that the Garden of Eden was on the American continent located where the City Zion, or the New Jerusalem, will be built" (*DS,* 3:74).

A Latter-day Saint Press (v. 11–14): William W. Phelps was to set up a press, and Oliver Cowdery was to help him in selecting materials to be printed.

Section 58

Instructions to the Saints in Zion

SETTING

Many Saints in Jackson County, Missouri, were anxious to know the will of the Lord concerning where they would live, how they should be organized, and what they should do.

TEACHINGS

These Saints were honored to be "laying the foundations" for Zion (v. 6–7). They were reminded, however, that often the blessings come only following "much tribulation" (v. 3–4). Their situation was compared to a wedding feast to which many were invited, but only a few responded (v. 8–11; see Matt. 22:1–10).

After Much Tribulation (v. 4): President Marion G. Romney observed, "The Lord was reminding the Saints there that there was some tribulation ahead before they could enjoy the promised blessings of Zion. He was warning them that in Jackson County, Missouri—which was Zion then and will yet be Zion—where they were going, the law—that is, his law—had to be kept. Men had to be true disciples. This was clear notice to the Saints in Missouri, and it should and must be clear notice to us, that keeping the law of God is the principal thing that all who truly become his disciples must learn" (*Ensign,* Nov. 1978, 39).

Instructions to Bishop Partridge (v. 17–18): Edward Partridge was called to repentance. He was then reminded that the bishop was to be "a judge in Israel" such as in apportioning lands; his judgments were to be based on the testimony of competent witnesses and made with the help of his counselors (v. 17–18).

Obeying Laws (v. 19–22): God's law was to be kept in Zion. Still, obeying

God's law was no excuse for breaking the law of the land; we must "be subject to the powers that be" until Christ comes to reign. The Lord pointed out the inconsistency of the disobedient complaining that they receive no blessings after breaking the laws on which those blessings are predicated (v. 30–33; see D&C 82:10; 130:20–21).

Initiative (v. 26-29): We should not need to be commanded in all things, but should be "anxiously engaged," doing much good on our own.

Pride (v. 40-41): William W. Phelps was criticized for seeking to excel. Certainly, we should strive to do our best, but we should not be motivated only by a desire for worldly recognition.

Repentance (v. 42-43): These verses contain one of the clearest statements in the scriptures on the remarkable promise for those who repent, and what is involved in the process of true repentance. We may remember our former sins, but this memory will not pain us; rather, it can motivate us and others (see Alma's example in Alma 36:19–20).

Instructions Concerning Travel to Zion: The elders in Missouri were to return home, preaching along the way (v. 46–48). Sidney Rigdon was to write a description promoting the purchase of lands in Zion, and an agent was to be appointed in Ohio to collect funds for this purpose (v. 49–54). Newel K. Whitney was subsequently called to this position (D&C 63:42–45). The gathering was to proceed in an orderly manner, "not in haste" (v. 55–56). Sidney was to dedicate the land (v. 57); this was done the following day, August 2. The elders who were still en route should continue until they reached Zion so that they too could give positive reports of this land (v. 61–63).

Take the Gospel to the World: Verse 64 effectively states the Church's mission today: "The sound must go forth from this place into all the world, and unto the uttermost parts of the earth—the gospel must be preached unto every creature." In recent decades, modern technology such as satellites and the internet have made this goal more attainable.

Section 59

Keeping the Sabbath, and Other Commandments

SETTING

Soon after the arrival of the Colesville Saints, Polly Knight (wife of Joseph Knight, Sr.) passed away, the first Latter-day Saint to die in the land of Zion. Her funeral was held on Sunday, August 7, 1831. Later that day, the Prophet sought assurance from the Lord concerning the future prosperity of the Saints in Missouri.

TEACHINGS

The Lord assured the faithful that they would be blessed, whether they live or, like Sister Knight, die (v. 2).

Ten Commandments Stressed Once Again (v. 4–8): The Lord promised to give "commandments not a few," and "revelations in their time" (v. 4). The Ten Commandments had been given when the children of Israel were going to establish new homes in the promised land. The Lord reviewed some of the commandments for the Saints as they were about to settle in Ohio (D&C 42:18–29), and now again as settlement was commencing in Missouri. The first four commandments were summed up in the injunction in verse 5; notice the addition to the familiar version in Matthew 22:37. The remainder can be summed up by the injunction at the beginning of verse 6. Not only should we not steal, kill, or commit adultery, but we must avoid "anything like unto it" (v. 6); feeling greed or anger, having lustful thoughts, and viewing pornography are only a few of the unworthy behaviors prohibited by the final words in this verse. Recognizing the hand of the Lord in all things (v. 21) certainly should prompt us to thank Him for His blessings and guidance (v. 7). This, in turn, should lead us to be humble (v. 8).

Adultery or "Anything Like Unto It" (v. 6): The Savior taught, "Behold, it is written by them of old time, that thou shalt not commit adultery; But I say unto you, that whosoever looketh on a woman, to lust after her, hath committed adultery already in his heart. Behold I give unto you a commandment, that ye suffer none of these things to enter into your heart"

(3 Ne. 12:27–29). This is one reason why the addiction of pornography is to be avoided. Elder Richard G. Scott clarified, "Many youth have been led to believe that sexual intimacy is 'not that bad' as long as it does not involve the act that could cause pregnancy. That is false. Sexual intimacy in any of its forms, outside the covenant of MARRIAGE, is serious sin. Serious sin is addictive. It forges binding habits that are difficult to sever. If you have broken such laws, seek help from your bishop or stake president since such transgression requires a confession both to the Lord and to such a judge as a necessary step toward forgiveness" (*Ensign,* Nov. 2000, 25–27).

Murder or "Anything Like Unto It" (v. 6): Elder Dallin H. Oaks warned, "The ultimate act of destruction is to take a life. That is why abortion is such a serious sin. Our attitude toward abortion is not based on revealed knowledge of when mortal life begins for legal purposes. It is fixed by our knowledge that according to an eternal plan all of the spirit children of God must come to this earth for a glorious purpose, and that individual identity began long before conception and will continue for all the eternities to come" (*Ensign,* Nov. 1993, 72).

President Gordon B. Hinckley advised, "While we denounce [abortion], we make allowance in such circumstances as when pregnancy is the result of incest or rape, when the life or health of the mother is judged by competent medical authority to be in serious jeopardy, or when the fetus is known by competent medical authority to have serious defects that will not allow the baby to survive beyond birth. But such instances are rare, and there is only a negligible probability of their occurring. In these circumstances those who face the question are asked to consult with their local ecclesiastical leaders and to pray in great earnestness, receiving a confirmation through prayer before proceeding" (*Ensign,* Nov. 1998, 70).

Keeping the Sabbath day holy (v. 9–15) receives more attention than any other doctrine in this revelation. The faithful observance of the Sabbath can help us remain "unspotted from the world" (v. 9), as observing it focuses our attention on spiritual priorities. In judging which activities are appropriate for the SABBATH, we might well consider whether they contribute to the two purposes of this day: worshiping the Lord and resting from our daily work (v. 9–10). Even though we emphasize religious services on Sunday (v. 12), we should worship God every day (v. 11). Religious practices such as FASTING should not be regarded negatively, but our attitude should be one of rejoicing (v. 13–14). The joy of the gospel should result in our having "cheerful countenances." Nevertheless, we should avoid inappropriate laughter (v. 15); in a later revelation, the Lord commanded, "cast away your idle thoughts and your excess of laughter" (D&C 88:69).

Sabbath Observance: President Gordon B. Hinckley taught, "I mention the Sabbath day. The Sabbath of the Lord is becoming the play day of the people. It is a day of golf and football on television, of buying and selling in our stores and markets. Are we moving to mainstream America as some observers believe? In this I fear we are. What a telling thing it is to see the parking lots of the markets filled on Sunday in communities that are predominately LDS. Our strength for the future, our resolution to grow the Church across the world, will be weakened if we violate the will of the Lord in this important matter. He has so very clearly spoken anciently and again in modern revelation. We cannot disregard with impunity that which He has said" (*Ensign,* Nov. 1997, 67).

Rich Blessings (v. 16–23): The Creator tells us that He has given us the earth with all its marvelous resources to be used for righteous purposes (v. 16–20). This revelation closes with the affirmation that righteous living brings the richest of rewards, "even peace in this world, and eternal life in the world to come" (v. 23).

SCRIPTURE HELPS

Oblations: A dictionary published in Joseph Smith's day defined "oblation" as "any thing offered or presented in worship or sacred service."

Section 60

INSTRUCTIONS FOR THE RETURN TRIP

SETTING

As missionaries prepared to return home to OHIO, they inquired of the PROPHET about the return trip to KIRTLAND.

TEACHINGS

Sharing the Gospel (v. 2–4): The Lord is not pleased with those who do not "open their mouths . . . because of the fear of man." He likened our testimony to a talent that He has given us, and that can be lost if we do not use it. We do not need to be afraid, because His power is over all the earth.

Elder Dallin H. Oaks said, "There has never been a greater need for us to profess our faith, privately and publicly [see v. 2]. Though some profess atheism, there are many who are open to additional truths about God. To these sincere seekers, we need to affirm the existence of God the Eternal Father, the divine mission of our Lord and Savior, Jesus Christ, and the reality of the Restoration. We must be valiant in our testimony of Jesus. Each of us has many opportunities to proclaim our spiritual convictions to friends and neighbors, to fellow workers, and to casual acquaintances. We should use these opportunities to express our love for our Savior, our witness of His divine mission, and our determination to serve Him" (*Ensign,* May 2008, 26–29).

Travel Instructions (v. 5–15): Church leaders, including JOSEPH SMITH, SIDNEY RIGDON, and OLIVER COWDERY, were given specific directions. Concerning some details, the Lord explained, "It mattereth not unto me" (v. 5). From this divine statement, we can infer that as long as a righteous goal is achieved, we usually have some leeway in carrying out the related work. The Lord's declaration also demonstrates that we have been given the opportunity to grow through using our own judgment and initiative. Most of the ELDERS were to travel "two by two, and preach the word, not in haste, in the congregations of the wicked," meaning the "inhabitants of the earth" who had not yet accepted the gospel (see D&C 62:5). Those who were still on their way to Missouri received similar instructions (v. 12–14). If rejected, the elders could shake the DUST off their feet as a witness in the day of judgment; this was to be done privately rather than as a matter of public display (v. 15).

Section 61

DANGERS ON THE WATERS

SETTING

A serious canoe accident on the Missouri River caused the PROPHET and ten ELDERS to stop and make camp. WILLIAM W. PHELPS saw "the destroyer riding in power upon the waters." The next morning, the Prophet sought the Lord in prayer.

TEACHINGS

Travel by Water: The elders had been instructed to "preach by the way" as they traveled home (D&C 58:46–48). The Lord now reminded them that it was not necessary for the whole group to be sailing swiftly down the river while people on either side were "perishing in unbelief" (v. 3). Nevertheless, He had allowed them to have this experience so they could warn others about the dangers on the waters (v. 4, 18). While in the beginning the waters were blessed (Gen. 1:20) and the land cursed (Moses 4:23), in the latter days this will be reversed (v. 13–17; Rev. 8:8–10). Still, a person with sufficient faith not only can command the waters, but will know by the Spirit what to do (v. 27–28). Therefore, the Lord declared that it mattered not to Him whether the elders went by land or by water, "if it so be that they fill[ed] their mission" (v. 22). In conclusion, the Savior gave this assurance: "Be of good cheer, little children; for I am in your midst, and I have not forsaken you." He then urged the Saints to be humble, to watch for His Coming, and to pray always (v. 36–39).

Elder Franklin D. Richards explained, "To be diligent in our work also means to be effective and not just busy. The Lord recognized this difference between just being busy and being effective when in 1831 the elders were traveling down the Missouri River in canoes. Just as it was unnecessary for all of the elders to be moving swiftly upon the waters, so it is with us—it is not necessary to do many unessential things that keep us busy but result in little or no real benefit to anyone" (CR, Oct. 1964, 75–78).

Section 62

To Those Going to Zion

SETTING

By chance, the Prophet met Hyrum Smith, John Murdock, David Whitmer, and Harvey Whitlock, four of the missionaries called the previous June (see D&C 52:8, 25), who were still headed to Missouri. Wanting to know whether they should continue their journey, the Prophet inquired of the Lord.

TEACHINGS

A Spiritual Perspective (v. 1–3): The Savior understands our weaknesses and knows how best to help us (v. 1). The testimonies we bear are "recorded in heaven for the angels to look upon" (v. 3).

Testimony (v. 3): President Harold B. Lee testified, "For the strength of the Church is not in the numbers, nor in the amount of tithes and offerings paid by faithful members, nor in the magnitude of chapels and temple buildings, but because in the hearts of faithful members of the Church is the conviction that this is indeed the Church and kingdom of God on the earth" (*Ensign,* July 1973, 6).

Instructions on Travel (v. 4–9): The travelers should continue on to "the land of Zion." Then, on their way home, it didn't matter how they traveled as long as they shared the "glad tidings" of the gospel with "the inhabitants of the earth, or among the congregations of the wicked" (v. 4–5). They would be allowed to ride rather than walk if they did so "with a thankful heart in all things" and if they used their best judgment and sought the Lord's direction (v. 7–8).

Section 63

INSTRUCTIONS ABOUT GOING TO ZION

SETTING

Upon JOSEPH SMITH's return from Missouri, he found that the Saints in OHIO desired to know more about the land of ZION, as well as anything pertaining to their salvation. The PROPHET inquired of the Lord concerning these matters.

TEACHINGS

Instructions Concerning Zion (v. 24-48): The Lord again reminded His Saints that they should gather to Zion, but "not in haste" (v. 24). As the Lord withdraws His Spirit from the wicked world, wars will be poured out and fear will spread (v. 32–35). When the Saints gathered to Zion, they were to warn the wicked both by their words and by their example of fleeing from the world (v. 36–37). Still, not all were to go to Zion right away; Joseph Smith would have power to discern who should go and who should stay (v. 41). In our day, Elder Harold B. Lee declared: "The Lord has placed the responsibility for directing the work of gathering in the hands of the leaders of the church to whom he will reveal his will where and when such gatherings would take place in the future . . . the Saints in every land [should] prepare themselves and look forward to the instruction that shall come to them from the First Presidency of this Church" (CR, Apr. 1948, 55). All were to help raise money to buy land in Zion, and NEWEL K. WHITNEY was to become the AGENT in OHIO to handle these funds (v. 41). Those who sent "treasures unto the land of Zion" were to be blessed in this life and in "the world to come" (v. 48). In our day, those who devote their "treasures" of time, energy, and other resources to advancing the work of the Lord will similarly be blessed.

In addition to providing instructions for gathering to Zion, this revelation treats a number of other important doctrinal subjects.

Signs and Faith (v. 7-12): External "proofs" or miracles do not produce faith, because a person needs to have the Spirit to discern their significance; for example, even seeing the gold plates of the Book of Mormon would not necessarily convince a person of the plates' divine purpose (see D&C 5:7). On the other hand, such "SIGNS" follow FAITH, are a result of faith, and strengthen faith (v. 9–10; compare Mark 16:17–18). The wicked who seek signs may see them, "but not unto salvation" (v. 7); Korihor's experience is a well-known example (see Alma 30).

The Fruits of Sin: Verse 16 lists some of the rather serious negative consequences of immoral thoughts. Ponder how righteous living produces the opposite of each of these consequences.

Fate of the Righteous and the Wicked (v. 17-21, 49-54): Because they did not have a sure knowledge of Jesus Christ through the HOLY GHOST, most of the sinners described in verse 17 will not become SONS OF PERDITION, but rather will be heirs of the telestial kingdom (see D&C 76:81–83, 103). Nevertheless, their time in the SPIRIT WORLD, when they will be in spirit prison, might be described at least in part as the SECOND DEATH. Certainly they will not come forth in the First RESURRECTION (v. 18), when heirs of the celestial and terrestrial kingdoms will come forth. The promise that the faithful and obedient, including those who have died, will inherit the EARTH when it is TRANSFIGURED (v. 20–21, 49) will be fulfilled on at least two occasions: (1) when it receives its PARADISIACAL STATE at the beginning of the MILLENNIUM and only the righteous may remain, and (2) when it is ultimately celestialized and becomes the abode of those worthy of a CELESTIAL glory. Those who live during the Millennium will not die prematurely, and when they die, they will not sleep in the grave but will be resurrected immediately (v. 50–52).

Knowing the Mysteries (v. 22-23): A mystery is something that cannot be known through human reason or senses, but must be made known by revelation through the Spirit. This includes a testimony of gospel truths, which is like "a well of living water, which springs up unto everlasting life" (v. 23). In this particular case, the mystery to be made known is God's will (v. 22). Of course, these things can only be made known on condition of obedience to God's commandments.

Elder Joseph B. Wirthlin explained, "By living the gospel of Jesus Christ, we develop within ourselves a living spring that will quench eternally our thirst for happiness, peace, and everlasting life. The Lord explains clearly in the Doctrine and Covenants that only faithful obedience can tap the well of living water that refreshes and enlivens our souls: 'But unto him that keepeth my commandments I will give the mysteries of my kingdom, and the same shall be in him a well of living water, springing up unto everlasting life' [v. 23]" (*Ensign,* May 1995, 18).

A Day of Warning (v. 53–58): Because the Lord's Coming is nigh (v. 53), we should warn the world to prepare without wasting words (v. 57–58; compare D&C 19:31).

Taking the Name of God in Vain (v. 61–64): We should refer to Deity reverently (v. 61). Even the name of the PRIESTHOOD was changed to avoid repeating God's name too frequently (see D&C 107:3–4). Most people think of taking the name of God in vain only in terms of profanity, but verse 62 suggests another form of this offense. Still, if one speaks by the Spirit, there will be no condemnation (v. 64).

Section 64

FORGIVE ONE ANOTHER

SETTING

Influenced by the apostasy of EZRA BOOTH and others, some Saints began to question the character of the PROPHET. On behalf of several ELDERS, JOSEPH SMITH sought the Lord's guidance.

TEACHINGS

Forgiveness Essential: Unity is an essential quality of a ZION people (see Moses 7:18; D&C 38:27). Since all of us are imperfect, we must be willing to FORGIVE one another if the desired oneness is to be achieved. The Lord acknowledged Joseph Smith's weaknesses but still considered complaints about him to be "without cause" (v. 6–7). The Lord also regarded His ancient disciples' failure to forgive one another as "evil" (v. 8). While the Lord will forgive all those who REPENT (see D&C 1:32; 58:42), since we cannot always know who has repented, we must "forgive all men"; a failure to do so is "a greater sin" (v. 9–10). Nevertheless, there are times when offenders must be brought before Church DISCIPLINARY COUNCILS so that justice might be done (v. 11–14). There are also circumstances in which we are justified in protecting ourselves against offenders, but even this must be done in the right spirit (see D&C 98:23–41).

President Gordon B. Hinckley counseled, "Teach our people always to forgive and forget. Get it behind them. We carry the cankering evil of memories of little things that destroy us and destroy our feelings, whereas with just a little turnaround, a little kindness, we could bestow blessings upon people" (Pittsburgh Pennsylvania Regional Conference, Priesthood Leadership Session, Apr. 27, 1996).

Now Is the Time (v. 23–25): Amulek declared that now is the time for us to repent and prepare to meet God (see Alma 34:32–35). From the Lord's point of view, "tomorrow" is when He will come again (v. 24). Truly we must "improve each shining moment" and "prepare for tomorrow by working today" (*Hymns,* no. 226 and 229). Specifically, this is a time to sacrifice and to obey the law of TITHING. Verse 23 is one of the scriptural passages that links tithe paying with being spared from the burnings that will precede the SECOND COMING.

Avoid Debt (v. 27–28): The Saints were cautioned against being in debt to their enemies. Debt is a kind of bondage, and our goal should be to remain independent (see D&C 78:14).

Lofty Goals: Consider how the counsel in verses 29, 33, and 34 applied to the Saints in 1831 and how it applies to us today. Each of these verses is the kind of passage that could well be copied and placed in a prominent place where we could see it and make it a part of our daily lives. We should live so the Church might truly be a beacon on a hill for all to follow (v. 37–42; D&C 115:5).

SCRIPTURE HELPS

The word *ordinances* in verse 5 refers primarily to God's laws rather than to sacred ceremonies.

Stronghold in Kirtland: This revelation gave instructions to several individuals about selling or retaining their property. The Lord indicated that He would maintain His strength in KIRTLAND for five years (v. 21). The fall of 1836, just five years after this revelation was received, marked a shift from the marvelous spiritual experiences that accompanied the dedication of the KIRTLAND TEMPLE to the dark days of APOSTASY that would dominate the following year and eventually result in the faithful fleeing from that place.

"Terrible Ones" in Zion: Because Zion's inhabitants will be righteous, the Lord's power will be manifested among them. This will cause the wicked to tremble. Hence "terrible" in verse 43 might be understood to mean "terrifying" (compare D&C 45:70).

Section 65

THE KINGDOM OF GOD TO ROLL FORTH

SETTING

This section was given during the period when the PROPHET was preparing to recommence work on the JOSEPH SMITH TRANSLATION of the BIBLE.

TEACHINGS

Preparing for the Latter Days: The Lord commanded the Saints to prepare for His SECOND COMING (v. 1) and reminded them that they had already received the KEYS for doing so (v. 2; compare D&C 27:13). The Lord recalled several Biblical images related to this Latter-day preparation: the kingdom rolling forth (v. 2; compare Dan. 2:26–45); "prepare ye the way of the Lord" (v. 3; compare Matt. 3:3); the supper of the Lord (see Matt. 22:1–14; 26:17–29; D&C 27:5); and the coming of the Bridegroom (v. 3; compare Matt. 25:1–13). When the Lord instructed the Prophet to pray for "the kingdom of God [to] go forth, that the kingdom of heaven may come" (v. 4–6), He was not only suggesting what Joseph might pray for, but also what the Saints should be striving to accomplish. The phrases "kingdom of God" and "kingdom of heaven" are often used interchangeably to refer to God's work and organization. In this section, however, the "kingdom of God" refers to the Lord's Church on EARTH, which must roll forth to prepare the way for the "kingdom of heaven," which will come from the CELESTIAL realms to the earth at the beginning of the MILLENNIUM.

President Gordon B. Hinckley noted, "The Church has become one large family scattered across the earth. There are now more than 13 million of us in 176 nations and territories. A marvelous and wonderful thing is coming to pass. The Lord is fulfilling His promise that His gospel shall be as the stone cut out of the mountain without hands which would roll forth and fill the whole earth, as Daniel saw in vision [v. 2]. A great miracle is taking place right before our eyes" (*Ensign,* Nov. 2007, 83–86).

Section 66

WILLIAM E. MCLELLIN

SETTING

Twenty-five-year-old WILLIAM MCLELLIN, who had been baptized two months before, had asked the Lord to reveal the answers to five questions. He did not disclose them to the PROPHET, but all of them were answered in this REVELATION.

TEACHINGS

Hope Even for the Imperfect: William was assured that he was blessed because he had turned away from his iniquities (v. 1); he was clean, "but not all" (v. 3). He was specifically counseled not to be cumbered, or burdened, by the sin of adultery, "a temptation with which thou hast been troubled" (v. 10). Despite these concerns, William was called to proclaim the NEW AND EVERLASTING COVENANT—or gospel of Jesus Christ—in the eastern states with SAMUEL SMITH (v. 2, 5–9). Even though William was not personally to go to ZION at this time (v. 6), the Lord revealed that he would "push" many there (v. 11). Despite William's imperfections, he was promised that he might still inherit "a crown of eternal life at the right hand of my Father" (v. 12). William would become one of the original Twelve APOSTLES just over three years later.

Section 67

A CHALLENGE AND A PROMISE

SETTING

The November 1831 conference decided to publish a collection of REVELATIONS given through JOSEPH SMITH. The Lord revealed His "preface" (SECTION 1). Some of the brethren expressed feelings that the language of the revelations was inferior. The Lord's response and challenge to these doubters was given through the PROPHET.

TEACHINGS

The Lord's Challenge to the Critics (v. 4–9): After testifying that the revelations to be published were true (v. 4), the Lord challenged the critics to duplicate the least of them. Joseph Smith recorded, "WILLIAM E. McLELLIN, as the wisest man, in his own estimation, having more learning than sense," accepted the challenge but failed (*HC* 1:226). Some of the ELDERS present then signed a testimony that the Lord revealed to them that the revelations were true.

The Promise to See God (v. 10–13): The elders received a marvelous promise: "Ye shall see me and know that I am." They would need to overcome their jealousies, fears, and pride in order to be more united, full of faith, and humble. The Lord specified that this great blessing would not come through the "carnal neither natural mind" (v. 10). "Carnal" literally means pertaining to the flesh, but in the scriptures is often used to suggest worldliness or sinfulness in contrast to spirituality. "Natural" has a similar meaning. Paul wrote that the "natural man receiveth not the things of the spirit of God: for they are foolishness unto him" (1 Cor. 2:14). King Benjamin similarly contrasted the "natural man" with saints who "yield to the enticings of the Holy Spirit" (Mosiah 3:19). In the revelation now known as section 67, the Lord told the elders that no one "in the flesh" can see God "except quickened by the Spirit of God" (v. 11; compare Moses 1:11).

Elder Spencer W. Kimball remarked, "To know God, one must be aware of the person and attributes, power, and glory of God the Father and God the Christ. Moses declares he 'saw God face to face, and he talked with him' (Moses 1:2). This experience of Moses is in harmony with the scripture, which says: 'For no man has seen God at any time in the flesh, except quickened by the Spirit of God. Neither can any natural man abide the presence of God neither after the carnal mind' [v. 11–12]. It must be obvious then that to endure the glory of the Father or of the glorified Christ, a mortal being must be [transfigured] or otherwise fortified. Moses, a prophet of God, held the protecting Holy Priesthood: 'and the glory of God was upon Moses; therefore Moses could endure his presence' (Moses 1:2)" (CR, Apr. 1964, 94–95).

Section 68

The Saints' Responsibilities

SETTING

This REVELATION was given following the CONFERENCE where the decision was made to publish the Book of Commandments. (SECTION 133, "The Appendix," was also given at this time.) Four of the ELDERS desired to know the mind of the Lord concerning them. After giving them direction (v. 1–12), the Lord listed several items to be added to the forthcoming published revelations (v. 13); the balance of this section presents those additions.

TEACHINGS

Message to the Elders (v. 1-12): The Lord gave these elders the same commission He had given to His ancient APOSTLES (v. 8–10; compare Mark 16:15–17). They were also promised that they would understand the signs of His SECOND COMING (v. 11).

Selecting Bishops (v. 14-24): At the time this revelation was received, only one man, EDWARD PARTRIDGE, was serving as a BISHOP. The promise of "other bishops" began to be fulfilled the following month with the call of NEWEL K. WHITNEY as a bishop. The "legal right" of literal descendants of Aaron to this office is related to the organization of the lesser PRIESTHOOD during Old Testament times. Note that these verses contain the first reference to the "FIRST PRESIDENCY" in latter-day revelation. Provisions in verses 22–24 regarding the trial of bishops refer only to the Presiding Bishop.

Parents' Responsibility (v. 25-28): The prime responsibility of teaching children the gospel rests with their parents. Church leaders have frequently cited these verses in support of family home evening. Parents who fail to teach their children must assume responsibility for the children's transgressions (compare Jacob 1:18).

President James E. Faust emphasized, "Who are good parents? They are those who have lovingly, prayerfully, and earnestly tried to teach their children by example and precept 'to pray, and to walk uprightly before the Lord' [v. 28]. This is true even though some of their children are disobedient or worldly. Children come into this world with their own distinct spirits and personality traits. Some children would challenge any set of parents under any set of circumstances. Perhaps there are others who would bless the lives of, and be a joy to, almost any father or mother. Successful parents are those who have sacrificed and struggled to do the best they can in their own family circumstances. The depth of the love of parents for their children cannot be measured. It is like no other relationship. It exceeds concern for life itself. The love of a parent for a child is continuous and transcends heartbreak and disappointment. All parents hope and pray that their children will make wise decisions. Children who are obedient and responsible bring to their parents unending pride and satisfaction" (*Ensign,* May 2003, 61).

Here, for the first time, the Lord specifies the precise age of accountability when children should be BAPTIZED. Verse 25 contains the first Doctrine and Covenants reference to STAKES of ZION; the first stake was organized in KIRTLAND about two years later.

Other Admonitions (v. 29–31): The Saints were reminded to keep the SABBATH day holy (v. 29) and to avoid idleness (v. 30–31).

Section 69

Keeping a History

SETTING

OLIVER COWDERY had been appointed to carry Church monies and the manuscripts for the Book of Commandments through the often-hazardous wilderness to INDEPENDENCE.

TEACHINGS

The Importance of History: JOHN WHITMER, who earlier had been called as CHURCH HISTORIAN (D&C 47), was now appointed to accompany Oliver Cowdery to Missouri. In this same revelation, the Lord called for local histories to be collected at Church headquarters (v. 5–6), and gave John additional instructions about compiling his history "for the good of the church, and for the rising generation" (v. 7–8). Likewise, we should be diligent in compiling our own histories for the benefit of our families and for our descendants who will follow hereafter.

Section 70

Publishing the Commandments

SETTING

At the conclusion of the November 1831 CONFERENCE, the Lord gave stewardship of all official Church literature and its publication to JOSEPH SMITH, OLIVER COWDERY, SIDNEY RIGDON, JOHN WHITMER, and MARTIN HARRIS. These men in their stewardship were known as the LITERARY FIRM.

TEACHINGS

Source of Support: According to the principle of REMUNERATION for Church service, members of the Literary Firm were to receive an income from the Church because they were giving full-time service in their callings. Thus these men with spiritual stewardships would be treated the same way as those with temporal stewardships (v. 12; compare D&C 42:70–73). The published revelations were not to be given away free of charge, as proceeds from their sale could become a source of support for these men in their stewardships (v. 6–7, 14–16).

Section 71

Answering False Accusations

SETTING

EZRA BOOTH had APOSTATIZED and printed nine scandalous letters about the Church in a newspaper called the *OHIO Star*. These letters had inflamed the public against the Church, and JOSEPH SMITH and SIDNEY RIGDON were commanded to stem the tide of lies.

TEACHINGS

Missionary Methods: The two brethren were to set aside their work on the JOSEPH SMITH TRANSLATION only "for the space of a season" (v. 2). The MYSTERIES they were to expound were to be "my gospel . . . out of the scriptures" (v. 1). Their instruction to "confound your enemies" (v. 7) was unique; normally missionaries avoid contentious arguments (see D&C 19:30).

Success Assured (v. 7–9): Those in the Lord's service should be grateful for the promise that "no weapon that is formed against you shall prevail" (v. 9). Speaking of the tactics used by the Church's enemies, Elder Neal A. Maxwell observed, "True, the enemies and the critics of the Lord's work will not relent; they only regroup [v. 7]. Even among the flock, here and there and from time to time, are a few wolves, wearing various styles of sheep's clothing—ironically, just before the shearing season! A few defectors and 'highminded' traitors (2 Tim. 3:4) even go directly to the 'great and spacious building' to hire on (1 Ne. 8:26). There recruits are celebrated and feted until—like their predecessors—they have faded into the dark swamps of history. As President Heber C. Kimball said, divine justice will eventually require that they 'pay all the debt of [all] the trouble that they have brought upon the innocent'" (*Ensign,* May 1988, 7).

Section 72

A Second Bishop

SETTING

Several Church members and leaders gathered for instruction and edification. The discussion turned to the temporal and spiritual welfare of the Church and its members, resulting in a revelation. The first BISHOP, EDWARD PARTRIDGE, had moved to Missouri, so there was no longer a bishop in OHIO.

TEACHINGS

Role of a Bishop: NEWEL K. WHITNEY, the co-owner of the successful store in KIRTLAND, was called to be bishop in OHIO in order to receive an accounting of stewardships in that area (v. 2–8). Bishop Whitney's other responsibilities would include handling Church funds, operating a storehouse, and assisting those in need (v. 10–11). He was to send information to the bishop in Missouri about people who were moving there from OHIO (v. 13–14), much as membership records are transferred from one ward to another when people move today. Members moving from Ohio to Missouri were to obtain a certificate recommending them to the leaders in Zion (v. 16–19, 24–26); today, membership records are transferred electronically. The bishop was also to assist members of the Literary Firm (see D&C 70), as needed, in publishing the Book of Commandments (v. 20–23).

An Eternal Stewardship (v. 3): Elder Joseph B. Wirthlin instructed, "Each of you has an eternal calling from which no Church officer has authority to release you. This is a calling given you by our Heavenly Father Himself. In this eternal calling, as with all other callings, you have a stewardship, and 'it is required of the Lord, at the hand of every steward, to render an account of his stewardship, both in time and in eternity' [v. 3], This most important stewardship is the glorious responsibility your Father in Heaven has given you to watch over and care for your own soul" (*Ensign,* May 1997, 15).

Eternal Rewards: Those who are faithful stewards in time shall inherit mansions in eternity (v. 4; compare D&C 51:19).

Section 73

Instructions for the Elders

SETTING

The elders of the Church were desirous to know what they should do while waiting for the January 1832 conference in Amherst, Ohio.

TEACHINGS

Receiving Direction: While most of the elders were to continue preaching, Joseph Smith and Sidney Rigdon were to resume work on the Joseph Smith Translation of the Bible. All would receive further instructions at the upcoming conference. This is an illustration of receiving direction by revelation from the Lord and from His duly appointed servants.

Section 74

Paul's Teaching on Marriage

SETTING

This revelation was received in connection with work on the Joseph Smith Translation of the Bible as an explanation of 1 Corinthians 7:14.

TEACHINGS

Children in Interfaith Marriages: Verse 1, a copy of 1 Corinthians 7:14 in the King James Bible, suggests that Christian husbands or wives should convert their unbelieving spouses; otherwise, their children would be "unclean." The Apostle Paul recognized, however, that an unbelieving spouse could demand that his children comply with Jewish law and traditions, making them less apt to accept the gospel of Jesus Christ and leaving them therefore unrepentant and unclean (v. 3–4). This is why he counseled Christians against marriage with unbelievers (v. 5; see 2 Cor. 6:14). But as verse 7 reminds us, "little children are holy, being sanctified through the atonement of Jesus Christ" (see Moroni 8:8; D&C 93:38).

Interfaith Marriages: President Spencer W. Kimball explains, "Clearly, right marriage begins with right dating. A person generally marries someone from among those with whom he associates, with whom he goes to school, with whom he goes to church, with whom he socializes. Therefore, this warning comes with great emphasis. Do not take the chance of dating non-members or members who are untrained and faithless" (*MF,* 241–242).

Section 75

Rewards for Preaching

SETTING

This revelation was given at the January 25, 1832, conference held in Amherst, Ohio, where Joseph Smith was first sustained as president of the high Priesthood. The ELDERS present were anxious to know how they were to bring people to a knowledge of their fallen condition.

TEACHINGS

Missionary Work: Various elders received their assignments (v. 6–18, 30–36); those responsible for assigning missionaries to their fields of labor still seek to do so by revelation. The elders were told to work hard (v. 3, 29) and were promised great rewards, including ETERNAL LIFE (v. 5, 16). The promise that they would "be laden with many SHEAVES" (v. 5) recalls the image of a wheat field being "white already to harvest (D&C 4:4). The missionaries were reminded that the Holy Ghost would teach them and their investigators "all things that are expedient for them" to know (v. 10). The elders were to leave a blessing on those who received the gospel message, but were to shake the DUST off their feet against those who rejected the gospel (v. 19–22). They were to rejoice (v. 21), not because people would be condemned, but because they could rest assured that they had faithfully discharged their duties.

Family Responsibilities: Despite the importance of sharing the gospel, the elders needed to first care for their families (v. 24–28). President Ezra Taft Benson explained, "Early in the history of the restored Church, the Lord specifically charged men with the obligation to provide for their wives and family. In January of 1832 he said, 'Verily I say unto you, that every man who is obliged to provide for his own family, let him provide, and he shall in nowise lose his crown [v. 28].' Three months later the Lord said again, 'Women have claim on their husbands for their maintenance, until their husbands are taken (D&C 83:2).' This is the divine right of a wife and mother. While she cares for and nourishes her children at home, her husband earns the living for the family, which makes this nourishing possible. In a home where there is an able-bodied husband, he is expected to be the breadwinner. Sometimes we hear of husbands who, because of economic conditions, have lost their jobs and expect the wives to go out of the home and work, even though the husband is still capable of providing for his family. In these cases, we urge the husband to do all in his power to allow his wife to remain in the home caring for the children while he continues to provide for his family the best he can, even though the job he is able to secure may not be ideal and family budgeting may have to be tighter" (*Ensign*, Nov. 1987, 48).

Section 76

"THE VISION"

SETTING

The PROPHET and SIDNEY RIGDON were deeply involved with the JOSEPH SMITH TRANSLATION when they came to John 5:29, which raised questions about the concept of one heaven and one hell. The heavens were opened and this revelation was given to them. This section is actually a series of several glorious visions.

Section 76 was received in the home of JOHN JOHNSON in HIRAM, OHIO. Philo Dibble, a close associate of the Prophet who was in the room during much of the time while Joseph and Sidney saw the vision, wrote the following eyewitness account:

"Joseph would, at intervals, say: 'What do I see?' as one might say while looking out the window and beholding what all in the room could not see. Then he would relate what he had seen or what he was looking at. Then Sidney replied, 'I see the same.' Presently Sidney would say, 'What do I see?' and would repeat what he had seen or was seeing, and Joseph would reply, 'I see the same.' This manner of conversation was repeated for short intervals to the end of the vision. And during the whole time not a word was spoken by any other person . . . not a sound or motion made by anyone but Sidney, and it seemed to me that they never moved a joint or limb during the time I was there, which I think was over an hour, and to the end of the vision. Joseph sat firmly and calmly all the time, in the midst of a magnificent glory, but Sidney sat limp and pale, apparently as limp as a rag. Observing such at the close of the vision, Joseph remarked smilingly 'sidney is not used to it as I am'" (*Juvenile Instructor,* 27:303, quoted in *RR,* 513).

After the vision closed, Joseph Smith observed: "Nothing could be more pleasing to the Saints . . . than the light which burst upon the world through the foregoing vision. . . . Every honest man is constrained to exclaim: 'It came from God'" (*HC,* 1:252–53).

TEACHINGS

Inspired Revision of John 5:29 (v. 17): As the brethren were revising the BIBLE, they questioned the traditional doctrine of "one heaven and one hell" in general, and the meaning of John 5:29 in particular. The correct meaning of this verse was restored as follows (italics added):

John 5	**Section 76**
29. And shall come forth; they that have done good, *unto* the resurrection of *life,* and they that have done evil, *unto* the resurrection of *damnation.*	17. They who have done good *in* the resurrection of the *just,* and they who have done evil *in* the resurrection of the *unjust.*

Thus the inspired version of the verse shifts the emphasis from two ultimate conditions to the idea of two RESURRECTIONS. The remainder of the section then elaborates on this theme and gives an enlarged view of the four final kingdoms.

Testimony of Jesus Christ (v. 22–24): This testimony of the glory of the Father and the Son is a fitting introduction to the entire REVELATION, and it stands in marked contrast to the vision of the sons of perdition that immediately follows. Joseph and Sidney considered their witness to be a climax of all the testimonies that had been given because they were eyewitnesses. Their knowledge may be contrasted with the weak stand taken by those who argue that "God is dead" because they have never seen Him personally. Verse 24 echoes a truth earlier revealed to Moses—that innumerable worlds are peopled with the sons and daughters of God (compare Moses 1:33–34). The Prophet Joseph Smith later composed a poetic paraphrase of section 76. Expanding on the thought in verse 24, he declared that Christ is the Savior as well as the Creator of these worlds:

> And I heard a great voice bearing record from heav'n,
> He's the Savior and Only Begotten of God;
> By him, of him, and through him, the worlds were all made,
> Even all that career in the heavens so broad.
>
> Whose inhabitants, too, from the first to the last,
> Are sav'd by the very same Savior of ours;
> And, of course, are begotten God's daughters and sons
> By the very same truths and the very same powers.
>
> (*TS,* Feb. 1, 1843, 82–83)

The Four Final Kingdoms: The following chart organizes the information revealed in section 76 and related scriptures. You may wish to fill it in as you study this material.

The names and symbols of these kingdoms are intended to identify conditions rather than locations. For example, the celestial (meaning "heavenly") kingdoms will be located on this earth (D&C 88:17–20), while the terrestrial (meaning "earthly") kingdom will be located elsewhere. The name *telestial* is found only in writing based on latter-day revelation. Elder James E. Talmage suggested that its meaning might be linked to the Greek word *telos,* meaning "end" (*AF,* 521). The Apostle Paul stressed that each man will be resurrected "in his own order"—initially the "first fruits" (celestial), later those who are "Christ's at his coming" (terrestrial), and finally "then cometh the end (*telos* or telestial)"(1 Cor. 15:21–24). *Telestial* might also be related to the prefix *tele* in such words as telescope, television, etc., suggesting the idea of distance—perhaps, in this case, distance from the throne of God. The name *Perdition* connotes loss.

Symbols of the kingdoms of glory are based on our point of view. Even though some stars are actually brighter, our sun appears to us to be the brightest object in the heavens and hence is the symbol for the most glorious kingdom. Similarly, even though the moon originates no light of its own, to us it appears to be the second-brightest object in the sky. The number and varying brightness of the stars make them a fitting symbol for the telestial kingdom. In contrast to the symbols for the three degrees of glory, which all involve light, the symbol for perdition is darkness.

The kingdom we ultimately inherit is determined by the law we choose to live (see D&C 88: 21–24). Note particularly what those going to each kingdom do in regard to a testimony of Jesus Christ.

Perdition (v. 25-49): Various titles reflect Satan's status before and following his fall. He was "Lucifer" (meaning light bearer or morning star) and "*a* son of the morning" (not "*the* son of the morning"). For a time, he was "in authority in the presence of God." Nevertheless, he rebelled against the Father and became "Satan" (a Hebrew word meaning "enemy"—compare Moses 4:1–4), or the "devil" (from the Greek *diabolos,* meaning "slanderer"). He was also called *Perdition* (meaning complete loss or ruin). The description of his fall constitutes a solemn warning against departing from the path that leads to the celestial kingdom.

President James E. Faust taught, "In the Grand Council in Heaven, when the great plan of salvation for God's children was presented, Jesus responded, 'Here am I, send me' (Abr. 3:27), and 'Father, thy will be done, and the glory be thine forever' (Moses 4:2). And thus He became our Savior. In contrast, Satan, who had been highly regarded as 'a son of the morning' [v. 26], countered that he would come and 'redeem all mankind, that one soul shall not be lost (Moses 4:2).' Satan had two conditions: the first was the denial of agency, and the second, that he would have the honor. In other words, something had to be in it for him. And thus he became the father of lies and selfishness" (*Ensign,* Nov. 2002, 19).

One may qualify as a son of perdition only by denying and defying the Lord's Spirit and power after having known them (v. 31, 35), thus committing the UNPARDONABLE SIN. Sons of perdition are the only souls who will suffer the SECOND DEATH, or permanent separation from the Lord. They will "go away into the lake of fire and brimstone, with the devil and his angels" (v. 36–37). The Book of Mormon clarifies that references to such a place are only symbolic representations of the second death (see 2 Ne. 9:16; Alma 12:17). King Benjamin taught that their torment is a sense of anguish or guilt (Mosiah 2:38; 3:25–27). The Hebrew prophets wanted to compare eternal damnation to the worst possible place known to the people at that time. Gehenna, a sulfurous dump outside Jerusalem where garbage was continually consumed by fire, became a most fitting symbol.

While verse 39 may seem to suggest that the sons of perdition will not receive a resurrection, it actually reveals that they are the only ones who will not be redeemed from their personal sins, while all other souls receive a resurrection of glory. In fact, D&C 88:32 clarifies that even the sons of perdition will be quickened or resurrected. Furthermore, Alma taught that even though the wicked would suffer torment compared to a lake of fire, they cannot die because there is no physical corruption following the resurrection (see Alma 12:17–18).

Punishment of the Sons of Perdition (v. 44-48): Verse 44 states that the sons of perdition are one group who will actually suffer "eternal punishment" eternally (compare D&C 19:11–12). Verse 48 does not teach predestination when it speaks of sons being ordained into this condemnation. Everyone has his AGENCY, but it is "ordained" that all who choose to transgress God's laws must suffer the consequences (see Alma 42:22).

The Celestial Kingdom (v. 50-70, 92-96): "In the celestial glory there are three heavens or degrees" (D&C 131:1–4). Exaltation refers only to obtaining the highest of these three divisions. In addition to the requirements for entering the celestial kingdom itself, one must also be faithful to the covenants of celestial or eternal marriage. Those who are exalted become gods, and therefore must be prepared to carry out the works of a god—creating and populating worlds—hence, the need for an eternal marriage relationship. The material in section 76 appears to refer specifically to those who will be exalted rather than all who inherit the celestial kingdom in general (see especially v. 56–59, 92–95).

To attain exaltation, one must overcome all things through the Atonement of Jesus Christ. Mortal language is inadequate to fully communicate the transcendent glory to be enjoyed by those who are exalted. Compare the promises in section 76 with other descriptions of the celestial world in D&C 77:1; 130:9; 137:2–4.

Those who will inherit the celestial kingdom "are sealed by the Holy Spirit of Promise" (v. 53), meaning that they are worthy to receive the promise of eternal life (see D&C 88:3–4; 131:5). They become "the Church of the Firstborn" (v. 54). The Lord explained that because He is the Firstborn Son of God in the spirit, those who are begotten through Him partake of His glory and are members of the "church of the Firstborn" (see D&C 93:21–22).

The Terrestrial Kingdom (v. 71-80): The second degree of glory is for those who are "honorable" (v. 75), but "are not valiant in the testimony of Jesus" (v. 79). A casual reading of verses 72 through 74 may suggest that all those who receive the gospel in the spirit world will be heirs of the terrestrial kingdom. If this were true, there would be no point in performing temple ordinances for the dead, since those ordinances are designed to qualify people for the celestial kingdom. This statement may only be a generalization, and there are many exceptions. The Lord explained: "All who have died without a knowledge of this gospel, who would have received it if they had been permitted to tarry, shall be heirs of the celestial kingdom of God" (D&C 137:7–9). Those in this kingdom may receive visits from the Son, but do not enjoy "the fulness of the Father" (v. 77).

The Telestial Kingdom (v. 81–88, 98–112): Those who inherit the telestial kingdom will come forth in the second or last resurrection. Because everyone will be given an opportunity to accept the gospel, the statement that telestial candidates "receive not the gospel" (v. 82) actually means that they *reject* it. They should be distinguished from those who *do* receive the gospel and then *deny* it, thereby becoming sons of perdition (see v. 83). Even some who professed to be followers of Christ (v. 100) but who "received not the gospel, neither the testimony of Jesus" (v. 101), perhaps because of their generally sinful way of life (v. 103), shall inherit the telestial kingdom.

Room in the John Johnson home where Section 76 was received

When verses 84 and 85 are read together, the "hell" spoken of in verse 84 seems to refer to spirit prison rather than to Satan's permanent kingdom. Thus, the devil and his angels apparently will not dwell in the telestial kingdom. The Book of Mormon uses the term *hell* in the same sense as does D&C 76:84 (see, for example, 2 Ne. 9:11–13).

Progress from Kingdom to Kingdom? Heirs of the telestial kingdom can never go where God and Christ are (v. 112). Those who choose not to enter into celestial marriage during this mortal life cannot receive exaltation, but they can become ministering angels in the celestial kingdom. The possibility of progressing from kingdom to kingdom would destroy the emphasis on this life being "the time for men to prepare to meet God" (Alma 34:32–35).

Section 77

THE REVELATION OF JOHN

SETTING

While working on the JOSEPH SMITH TRANSLATION, the brethren had many questions about the Revelation of John.

TEACHINGS

History of the Earth: There are five distinct stages through which the EARTH has passed or will pass: (1) celestial spirit earth, (2) terrestrial or paradisiacal condition while ADAM and Eve were in the garden, (3) present telestial phase, (4) terrestrial or paradisiacal condition during the MILLENNIUM, (5) glorified CELESTIAL sphere. Its "temporal existence" (v. 6–7) includes the third and fourth of these stages. Elder Russell M. Nelson noted that the "scriptures foretell the final days of the earth's temporal existence as a telestial sphere. The earth will then be renewed and receive its paradisiacal, or terrestrial, glory. (See Article of Faith 1:10.) Ultimately, the earth will become celestialized" (*Ensign,* May 1990, 16). The "sea of glass" (v. 1) refers to this fifth or final phase.

We often speak of the seven major DISPENSATIONS, but these are not the same as the seven thousand-year periods mentioned in verse 7.

Timing of the Second Coming: Some have attempted to determine the precise time of the SECOND COMING based on the explanations given in this section. However, such an effort is fruitless, as the Lord has declared that no one will know the exact time until He actually comes (see D&C 49:7). Notice that verse 12 does not say that Christ will come *at* the beginning, but rather that "*in* the beginning of the seventh thousand years" there should be a "preparing of the way before his coming" (emphasis added). Verse 13 actually identifies events that are to happen after the beginning of the seventh thousand years and before the Lord's Coming. Furthermore, the precise date of Adam's FALL, when the clock presumably started ticking, is not known.

Two Prophets (v. 15): These will be official representatives sent by the Lord's Church to the Jews. Their identity is not known, but Elder Bruce R. McConkie believed they would be GENERAL AUTHORITIES (*MM,* 390). Elder Parley P. Pratt commented that these prophets would preach for three and a half years while Jerusalem was besieged by Gentiles. The prophets would then be killed and their enemies would rejoice, "sending gifts one to another." They would be left unburied three and a half days when, as Elder Pratt wrote, "after three days and a half on a sudden, the spirit of life from God enters them, and they will arise and stand upon their feet, and great fear will fall upon them that see them. And then they shall hear a voice from heaven saying, 'Come up hither,' and they will ascend up to heaven in a cloud, and their enemies beholding them." After this would follow the great earthquake prophesied of by Ezekiel, Zechariah, and John. Next would be heard a voice saying, 'The kingdoms of this world are become the kingdom of our Lord, and of his Christ; and he shall reign forever and ever'" (*Voice of Warning,* 49–50).

SCRIPTURE HELPS

Animals also have spirits (v. 2–3).

Angels' wings are a symbolic representation of their power (v. 4).

Angelic messengers, including ELIAS, are to come during the sixth thousand-year period (verses 8–10). In our day, near the end of the sixth thousand years, these messengers have participated in the restoration of all things.

144,000: The identity of this group mentioned in Revelation 7:4–8 has been the subject of much speculation, but is clarified here (v. 11).

Creation of Man: The accounts in Genesis, Moses, and Abraham all place the formation of man at the climax of the creation of animals on the sixth day. Some have suggested that verse 12 places this event on the seventh day, but the wording here is ambiguous (*CDC,* 2:346–47).

Section 78

THE UNITED ORDER

SETTING

This and the following three REVELATIONS were received by the PROPHET at HIRAM, OHIO, in March 1832. The law of CONSECRATION had been revealed just over a year earlier (SECTION 42). This revelation outlines the Lord's will in organizing and establishing a storehouse for the poor.

TEACHINGS

The United Order (v. 1–14): The Lord called a number of the leading brethren of the Church to unite by COVENANT and form the "UNITED ORDER," an administrative body sometimes called the "united firm," to coordinate and operate various business enterprises related to the law of consecration. Further instructions were given in D&C 82:11–24. Equality (v. 6) was necessary among those who would establish ZION (compare D&C 38:27 and Moses 7:18). Economic independence (v. 14) is still an objective of the Church's welfare program today.

The Storehouse (v. 3–4): Elder Robert D. Hales explained, "Unrestricted by programs and projects, bricks and mortar, the Lord's real storehouse is indeed in the homes and the hearts of His people. As the members of the Church follow the counsel to become self-reliant, they represent an immense pool of resources, knowledge, skills, and charity available to help one another. This storehouse, the Lord has said, is "for the poor of my people . . . to advance the cause, which ye have espoused, to the salvation of man, and to the glory of your Father who is in heaven" (*Ensign,* May 1986, 28).

Independence: Elder James E. Faust taught, "The Lord said that it is important for the Church to 'stand independent above all other creatures beneath the celestial world [v. 14].' Members of the Church are also counseled to be independent. Independence means many things. It means being free of drugs that addict, habits that bind, and diseases that curse. It also means being free of personal debt and of the interest and carrying charges required by debt the world over" (*Ensign,* May 1986, 20).

SCRIPTURE HELPS

Michael (v. 16) was the name by which ADAM was known in the PREMORTAL world. According to the PATRIARCHAL ORDER, he is our "prince" because he stands at the head of the human family. Still, he is not our God, because he functions under the direction of "the Holy One," or JESUS CHRIST. We know that Adam received PRIESTHOOD authority before the world was formed (*TPJS,* 157, 167–68).

Ahman is the name of God the Father in the pure language of Adam. Elder Orson Pratt suggested that "Son Ahman" would be the corresponding title for Jesus Christ and "sons Ahman" for the rest of God's children (*JD*, 2:342). The location of ADAM-ONDI-AHMAN (v. 15) would be revealed six years later (SECTION 116).

Section 79

Jared Carter's Call

SETTING

Jared Carter had come to inquire of the Lord through the PROPHET about where he should labor as a missionary.

TEACHINGS

Missionary Work: Key elements of missionary service were reflected in Carter's call: He was to serve in a specified area (v. 1). He was to teach by proper AUTHORITY (v. 1; compare D&C 42:11). The Holy Ghost would teach him the truth and direct him where to go (compare Moroni 10:5). He was promised success, symbolized by "many SHEAVES" (v. 3). Missionary work has been likened to harvesting a field (see D&C 4:4); as wheat is harvested, it is bound into sheaves, or bundles. Elder Carter was to rejoice and go forward without FEAR (v. 4).

Section 80

Calls to Preach

SETTING

Stephen Burnett, an eighteen-year-old convert, desired a missionary companion. Twenty-six-year-old Eden Smith joined him and they preached in eastern Ohio (*WWDC*, 39, 271).

TEACHINGS

Missionary Responsibility: The assignment of missionary companions by inspiration (v. 2) is still important today. Truly, opportunities for sharing the gospel are on every side (v. 3). We should have a testimony of that which we teach (v. 4; compare D&C 11:21).

Section 81

Counselor to the Prophet

SETTING

The call extended in this section was another step toward the organization of the FIRST PRESIDENCY, which would occur just a year later. Originally, the call was addressed to Jesse Gause, who, due to apostasy, was replaced by FREDERICK G. WILLIAMS, forty-four years old, who had been a member of the Church for a year and a half.

TEACHINGS

Keys of the Kingdom (v. 2): As head of the Church, JOSEPH SMITH held all the KEYS, including the right to receive REVELATION in directing the Church. President Joseph Fielding Smith testified, "May I now say—very plainly and very emphatically—that we have the holy priesthood and that the keys of the kingdom of God are here. They are found only in The Church of Jesus Christ of Latter-day Saints. By revelation to Joseph Smith, the Lord said that these keys 'belong always unto the Presidency of the High Priesthood' [v. 2], and also, 'Whosoever receiveth my word receiveth me, and whosoever receiveth me, receiveth those, the First Presidency, whom I have sent' (D&C 112:20)" (*Ensign,* July 1972, 87).

Role of a Counselor (v. 3–6): Frederick G. Williams' role was to seek revelation to advise the PROPHET and then to support his inspired decisions; hence, Frederick was to fulfill his calling in the attitude of prayer (v. 3). The charge in verse 5 applies to all of us who are in the Lord's service (compare Luke 22:32), and the promise of eternal life in verse 6 also applies to us all. President Dieter F. Uchtdorf, upon being called to the First Presidency, affirmed, "When the Lord called Frederick G. Williams to be a counselor to the Prophet Joseph Smith, He commanded him to 'be faithful; stand in the office which I have appointed unto you; succor the weak, lift up the hands which hang down, and strengthen the feeble knees' [v. 5]. I believe this counsel applies to all who accept callings to serve in the kingdom of God—and certainly to me in this season of my life" (*Ensign,* May 2008, 68–69, 75).

Section 82

"I THE LORD AM BOUND"

SETTING

In response to the Lord's directive (D&C 78:3), JOSEPH SMITH went to ZION and established the UNITED ORDER. At the same meeting, jealousies that had existed between some members in Zion and those in KIRTLAND were resolved. In addition, Joseph Smith was sustained in Missouri as the president of the HIGH PRIESTHOOD, just as he had been in OHIO.

TEACHINGS

God Lives According to Law (v. 1–10): The concept of justice is based on law. Obedience brings blessings (v. 10; see also D&C 130:20–21), while disobedience brings punishments (v. 4; Alma 42:22). Alma effectively taught his wayward son, Corianton, the consequences of his choices (see, in particular, chapters 41–42), and Alma's counsel is just as applicable to us today. Lehi also emphasized the ultimate results of our choices (see 2 Ne. 2:26–29).

God's Law and the Principle of Justice

Our choice:	Obedience	or	Disobedience
A Condition of:	Righteousness	or	Wickedness, Sin
Which Results In:	Blessings	or	Punishment, Cursings
Bringing Us:	Happiness, Joy	or	Suffering, Sorrow
Ultimately Brings	Liberty, Eternal Life	or	Captivity, Death

Understanding of the Law is a factor in determining the consequences of our actions (compare v. 3 with Luke 12:47–48).

Endurance to the End is Essential: We are grateful for the Lord's promise that He will FORGIVE sins of which we REPENT and remember them no more (see D&C 58:42–43). We often do not realize, however, that the opposite is also true—that if we slip back into SIN, our righteous deeds may be overlooked and our former guilt may return (v. 7). Ezekiel taught these points quite effectively (see Ezek. 18:21–24; 33:12–16). Hence, judgment will not be based merely on the total of our deeds, good and bad, but will also consider the direction we have chosen to go. We must therefore choose righteousness and then endure to the end (see 2 Ne. 31:19–21).

Forgiveness of Sin: President Harold B. Lee taught, "If the time comes when you have done all that you can to repent of your sins, whoever you are, wherever you are, and have made amends and restitution to the best of your ability; if it be something that will affect your standing in the Church and you have gone to the proper authorities, then you will want that confirming answer as to whether or not the Lord has accepted of you. In your soul-searching, if you seek for and you find that peace of conscience, by that token you may know that the Lord has accepted of your repentance. Satan would have you think otherwise and sometimes persuade you that now having made one mistake, you might go on and on with no turning back. That is one of the great falsehoods. The miracle of forgiveness is available to all of those who turn from their evil doings and return no more, because the Lord has said in a REVELATION to us in our day: 'go your ways and sin no more; but unto that soul who sinneth [meaning again] shall the former sins return, saith the Lord your God' [v. 7]. Have that in mind, all of you who may be troubled with a burden of sin" (*Ensign,* July 1973, 122).

Further Instructions to the United Order (v. 11–24): As instructed earlier (D&C 78:11), the members of the united order were to be united by an unbreakable covenant to supervise the work of the BISHOP in helping the poor, both in Zion and in Kirtland (v. 11–12). Only just wants were to be considered (v. 17). One objective of CONSECRATION was the development of each individual (v. 18), who in turn should seek "the interest of his neighbor" and the glory of God (v. 19).

SCRIPTURE HELPS

Stakes (v. 13–14): STAKES, which represented sources of strength for the Church, would be established at Kirtland and in Missouri during 1834.

Mammon (v. 22): The term *mammon* generally refers to the materialistic world (see, for example, Matt. 6:24). The injunction in verse 22 and in Luke 16:9 may suggest learning how to succeed in the world while still living the gospel.

Section 83

RESPONSIBILITIES FOR FAMILIES

SETTING

During his brief visit to ZION in April 1832, the PROPHET sought to organize the Saints in the law of CONSECRATION.

TEACHING

Family Responsibilities: The duties of husbands and parents set forth in this REVELATION have been taught before (see 1 Tim. 5:8; Mosiah 4:14–15). BISHOPS still have a particular responsibility to widows and orphans.

Father's Role: President Boyd K. Packer cautioned, "Your responsibility as a father and a husband transcends any other interest in life. It is unthinkable that a Latter-day Saint man would cheat on his wife or abandon the children he has fathered, or neglect or abuse them. The Lord has 'commanded you to bring up your children in light and truth' (D&C 93:40; see D&C 93:36–40). You are responsible, unless disabled, to provide temporal support for your wife and children (see D&C 83:2). You are to devote, even sacrifice yourself to the bringing up of your children in light and truth (see D&C 93:40). That requires perfect moral fidelity to your wife, with no reason ever for her to doubt your faithfulness. Never should there be a domineering or unworthy behavior in the tender, intimate relationship between husband and wife (D&C 121:41–43). Your wife is your partner in the leadership of the family and should have full knowledge of and full participation in all decisions relating to your home" (*Ensign,* May 1994, 19).

Section 84

Revelation on Priesthood

SETTING

Joseph Smith recorded the setting for this revelation: "The Elders during the month of September began to return from their missions to the Eastern States, and present the histories of their several stewardships in the Lord's vineyard; and while together in these seasons of joy, I inquired of the Lord, and received on the 22nd and 23rd of September [1832], the following revelation on Priesthood" (*HC,* 1:273, 286–87).

TEACHINGS

Priesthood and the Temple (v. 1-42): In his opening remarks, the Lord refers to the restoration of the gospel, to the building of the city of the New Jersusalem, and to the temple in which the sons of Moses and of Aaron would make an acceptable offering and sacrifice. When the Lord mentioned the sons of Moses in verse 6, he then inserted a lengthy explanation of the history and powers of the PriesthoodS (v. 6–30) before returning in verse 31 to the subject of the offering to be made in the temple.

Powers of the Two Priesthoods (v. 19-22): The Lord declared that the higher priesthood holds the "keys of the mysteries of the kingdom"—sacred truths that are known only by revelation, such as "the knowledge of God" (v. 19). The "power of godliness"—the ability to acquire godlike attributes and qualify to be in His presence—is made fully available only through the ordinances of the Melchizedek Priesthood (v. 20–21). In contrast, the lesser priesthood holds the keys of the "preparatory gospel" and the "ministering of angels" (v. 26). Concerning the powers of the higher priesthood, President James E. Faust said, "The greater priesthood administers the gospel and holds 'the key of the mysteries of the kingdom, even the key of the knowledge of God.' What is the key of the knowledge of God, and can anyone obtain it? Without the priesthood there can be no fulness of the knowledge of God. The Prophet Joseph Smith said that the 'Melchizedek Priesthood . . . is the channel through which all knowledge, doctrine, the plan of salvation and every important matter is revealed from heaven'" (*Ensign,* Nov. 2004, 52–55).

Oath and Covenant of the Priesthood (v. 33-42): Those who are faithful and who magnify their callings in the priesthood are promised both physical and spiritual blessings. The "renewing" of the body mentioned in verse 33 may refer to an unusual endowment of good health and strength during mortality, or to the resurrection, when the body will be quickened by the Spirit according to the individual's degree of worthiness (see D&C 88:25–32). Faithful bearers of the Melchizedek Priesthood and AARONIC PRIESTHOOD will become the sons of Moses and of Aaron, respectively, or, in other words, the sons of Levi (of whose tribe Moses and Aaron were members). All will be of the seed of Abraham and, therefore, heirs to the great blessings promised to his posterity. They are also described as the "ELECT of God" and are in line to receive His choicest blessings in time and in eternity. On the other hand, the Lord warns that those who do not honor their priesthood will bring serious condemnation unto themselves.

Priesthood Service: President Henry B. Eyring observed, "You may at times need reassurance, as I do, that you will have the strength to meet your obligations in this sacred priesthood. The Lord foresaw your need for reassurance. He said, 'For whoso is faithful unto the obtaining these two priesthoods of which I have spoken, and the magnifying their calling, are sanctified by the Spirit unto the renewing of their bodies' (v. 33). I have seen that promise fulfilled in my own life and in the lives of others. A friend of mine served as a mission president. He told me that at the end of every day while he was serving, he could barely make it upstairs to bed at night, wondering if he would have the strength to face another day. Then in the morning, he would find his strength and his courage restored. You have seen it in the lives of aged prophets who seemed to be renewed each time they stood to testify of the Lord Jesus Christ and the restored gospel. That is a promise for those who go forward in faith in their priesthood service" (*Ensign*, May 2008, 61–64).

Instruction to the Missionaries (v. 43-120): The Lord first counseled the elders to hearken to His words that represent the LIGHT OF CHRIST or spirit of truth (v. 45–46). Because of the wicked condition of the world (v. 49–52), the Lord commanded the missionaries to go out and proclaim the message of the gospel. Even the Saints were condemned because they had neglected the BOOK OF MORMON (v. 54–57). Going without purse or SCRIP (v. 78–86) meant that the missionaries were not to be overly concerned with material matters. The Lord promised the missionaries that if they were prepared, He would tell them what to say (v. 85). He called these missionaries His "friends" (v. 77), and tenderly described His close association with them (v. 88). If rejected, they were to wash the DUST from their feet as a testimony; nevertheless, they were to be diligent in proclaiming the gospel (v. 92–95). Aaronic Priesthood bearers were to assist the missionaries (v. 107); the role described in this verse is carried out by the Aaronic Priesthood and other Church members who refer interested individuals to the missionaries.

SCRIPTURE HELPS

The Temple to Be Built "in This Generation" (v. 4-5, 31): "Generation" is often used in the scriptures to refer to a general period of time. Hence, this phrase can be understood to mean "in this DISPENSATION."

The Office of Bishop as an Appendage to the High Priesthood (v. 29-30): The office of bishop is normally grouped with the Aaronic Priesthood. One might think of the entire Aaronic Priesthood with the bishop at its head (D&C 107:87–88) as being, like the office of elder, an appendage to the Melchizedek Priesthood (D&C 107:14). The offices of deacon, teacher, and priest, by contrast, are appendages *within* the lesser priesthood.

Offering and Sacrifice (v. 31): Because faithful priesthood bearers may be thought of as "the sons of Levi" (v. 33–34), their worthy service constitutes their offering. Specifically, the "offering" may include that mentioned in Doctrine and Covenants 128:24—an acceptable record of our dead. The "sacrifice" might refer to the offering of blood sacrifices on a very limited scale as part of the "restoration of all things" (*TPJS,* 172).

Zion from Above and from Beneath (v. 100): The missionaries were to look forward to the time when the Lord would bring "down ZION from above" (perhaps the city of Enoch, of which the return was prophesied in Moses 7:62–64) and also would bring "up Zion from beneath" (perhaps the city of Zion or NEW JERUSALEM, which is to be built on the American continent).

Priesthood Correlation (v. 108-110): Over the years, the Brethren have emphasized the central role of the priesthood. All unnecessary duplication in Church programs was to be eliminated, and each organization would then be helped to carry out its unique role more completely. In several of their talks on this subject, the General Authorities have used these verses as a basic text.

Section 85

The One Mighty and Strong

SETTING

William W. Phelps had been appointed to assist the bishop in administering the law of Consecration and had many concerns over the great responsibility that was placed on him. Section 85 is an extract from the letter the prophet wrote addressing these concerns.

TEACHINGS

Obedience: In Doctrine and Covenants 85:3–5, the Lord warned that individuals going to Zion who refused to live the law of consecration would not have their names recorded among the names of those worthy to receive blessings. Because Bishop Edward Partridge was lax in dealing with such individuals, the Lord threatened to send "one mighty and strong" to set his affairs in order (v. 7).

The Still Small Voice: Elder Gerald N. Lund explained, "The Holy Ghost is a personage of spirit, which allows Him to dwell in our hearts and communicate directly with our spirits (D&C 8:2). The voice of the Spirit is described as still and small and one that whispers [v. 6]. How can a voice be still? Why is it likened to a whisper? Because the Spirit almost always speaks to our minds and to our hearts rather than to our ears" (*Ensign,* May 2008, 32).

The Book of the Law of God (v. 5–11) was the book to be kept by the Lord's clerk. The Lord said, 'Their names [apostates] shall not be found, neither the names of the fathers, nor the names of the children written in the book of the law of God." There is also another book that is kept in heaven, and the one kept by the Lord's clerk should be accurately kept so that it would agree with the Lamb's book of life (also known as the book of remembrance). The book of life is a record kept in heaven that contains the names of the righteous and an account of their covenants with the

Lord and their righteous deeds. It is also referred to in the scriptures as the Lamb's book of life and the book of the names of the sanctified. It is possible for the names of righteous Saints yet living to be included in the book of life (see *TPJS,* 9), but such a name will be blotted out if the person reverts to wickedness (D&C 128:6–7).

SCRIPTURE HELPS

False Claims Refuted: Through the years, many apostates have come forward, claiming the right to lead the Church as "the one mighty and strong" the Lord had promised. In 1905, however, the FIRST PRESIDENCY noted that Bishop Partridge had repented, so the Lord's threat did not need to be carried out. "If, however, there are those who will still insist that the prophecy concerning the coming of 'one mighty and strong' is still to be regarded as relating to the future," the First Presidency instructed, "let the Latter-day Saints know that he will be a future bishop of the Church who will be with the Saints in Zion, Jackson County, Missouri" (*MFP,* 4:118). Some apostate groups profess to hold the "high priesthood" and therefore claim to be above the jurisdiction of the organized Church. Nevertheless, verse 11 makes even those bearing the "high priesthood" subject to the Church's discipline.

Section 86

PARABLE OF THE WHEAT AND THE TARES

SETTING

While working on the JOSEPH SMITH TRANSLATION, the PROPHET received this REVELATION to explain the parable of the wheat and tares.

TEACHINGS

Parable of the Wheat and Tares (v. 1–4): Doctrine and Covenants 86 places the Lord's parable of the wheat and tares (see Matt.13:24–30, 36–43) in the context of the LATTER DAYS (compare JS—M 13:41 with D&C 101:64–75). During the Savior's earthly ministry, He was the sower of the good seed (see Matt. 13:37), whereas in the latter days, this task is accomplished by His servants (see D&C 86:2). The Church being driven into the wilderness (see D&C 86:3) describes the APOSTASY; the Restoration is likened to the "the Church being called forth out of the wilderness" (D&C 33:5). President Joseph Fielding Smith pointed out that "even in the Church the tares are to be found. It is the tares which are to be gathered up and burned from all over the world, but those in the Church will also be gathered out and find their place in the fire" (D&C 112:23–26; see also *CHMR,* 1:354).

Angels are to "reap down the earth" (v. 5–7). The Lord declared that He was holding his angels back from cleansing out the wicked because His kingdom was still young. Years later, however, President Wilford Woodruff wrote that the time had come for the gathering out of the tares and that the Lord had released His angels to "reap down the earth" (General Conference, Oct. 1896, quoted in *Discourses of Wilford Woodruff,* 229–30).

Heirs to the Priesthood (v. 8–11): The Lord's statement that the Saints are heirs to the PRIESTHOOD "according to the flesh" may be related to His promise that Abraham's seed would "bear this ministry and Priesthood to all nations." In this way "all the families of the earth will be blessed, even with the blessings of the Gospel, which are the blessings of salvation, even of life eternal" (Abr. 2: 9–11).

Section 87

"PROPHECY ON WAR"

SETTING

The PROPHET was very conscious of "troubles among the nations," such as outbreaks of cholera and the plague. Specifically, he was concerned that the United States was "threatened with immediate dissolution." For some time the southern states, which depended heavily on imports from abroad, had resented the high tariffs passed primarily to protect manufacturing interests in New England. JOSEPH SMITH recorded in his history that in November 1832, the South Carolina legislature adopted an exposition that advanced the doctrine of the states' rights to nullify any act of the federal government that was not in their interest, and President Andrew Jackson called out a force to put down this "rebellion" (*HC,*

1:301). Joseph Smith's prophecy of wars beginning with the rebellion of South Carolina was given on Christmas Day, 1832, over twenty-eight years before the American Civil War began at Fort Sumter on Charleston Bay in South Carolina.

Some critics argue that anyone in 1832 could have guessed that difficulties would begin in South Carolina and that the so-called South Carolina prophecy is not evidence at all of divine appointment. Joseph Smith, however, made it clear in a later statement that the South Carolina rebellion mentioned in section 87 was not the nullification controversy of 1832 but was still future (see D&C 130:12–13).

TEACHINGS

War (v. 1–4): Specific elements of this prophecy have found fulfillment in the American Civil War and beyond: "War will be poured out upon all nations" (v. 2)—two "world wars" dominated events during the next century. The South would be divided against the North (v. 3)—in 1832, the division was not strictly North against South, but more specifically the manufacturing Northeast against the predominantly rural West and South. The South would call on Great Britain for help (v. 3)—a major diplomatic crisis arose during the Civil War when the Northern navy stopped a British ship and seized a Southern envoy on his way to England. Nations would call on other nations for help (v. 3)—competing systems of alliances contributed to the wars of the twentieth century. The "slaves" who would "rise up against their masters" (v. 4) would include not only those in the nineteenth-century American South, but also oppressed peoples behind the Iron Curtain of the twentieth century who were denied basic freedoms, including the right to worship God (see, for example, CR, Oct. 1958, 32).

The Remnant Will Vex the Gentiles (v. 5): The prophecy of the REMNANT vexing the GENTILES is not limited only to Native Americans within the United States. For example, Joseph Fielding Smith declared, "It was during our Civil War that the Indians in Mexico rose up and gained their freedom from the tyranny which Napoleon endeavored to inflict upon them . . . let us not think that this prophecy has completely been fulfilled" (*CHMR,* 1:363).

Calamities (v. 6–7): During the LATTER DAYS, tribulations will be poured out upon the wicked so that the Saints will no longer cry to the "Lord of SABAOTH."

Stand in Holy Places (v. 8): These HOLY PLACES may include our homes, chapels, or wherever we are, as they are made holy by our righteous living. Elder Dallin H. Oaks asked "Are we following the Lord's command? . . . What are those 'holy places'? Surely they include the TEMPLE and its COVENANTS faithfully kept. Surely they include a home where children are treasured and parents are respected. Surely the holy places include our posts of duty assigned by PRIESTHOOD authority, including missions and callings faithfully fulfilled in branches, wards, and stakes" (*Ensign,* May 2004, 7).

Section 88

"The Olive Leaf"

SETTING

At a meeting of HIGH PRIESTS two days after section 87 had been received, Joseph gave instructions on how to receive REVELATION and the blessing of heaven. Each of the brethren present in turn offered prayer that they might be of one heart and mind and receive the will of the Lord. This revelation followed. About two weeks later, the PROPHET wrote to the brethren in Missouri and sent a copy of this revelation, which he likened to "the olive leaf plucked from the tree of paradise." He hoped that its lofty concepts would help pacify the antagonisms that had been manifested among some of the brethren in ZION.

TEACHINGS

Promise of the Lord's Spirit (v. 3–13): The brethren's prayers had reached "the Lord of SABAOTH" (v. 2), who promised to send "another Comforter" or "THE HOLY SPIRIT OF PROMISE. Both of these are titles of the HOLY GHOST, which would promise the worthy that they would attain ETERNAL LIFE (v. 3–4; D&C 131:5). The brethren would also be illuminated by the LIGHT OF CHRIST, described as "the power of God" that fills "the immensity of space"; it is in the light of the sun, moon, and stars, and it is the power by which they were created (v. 6–13).

Resurrection (v. 14–16): As an individual enters mortality, the spirit and body, the two component parts of the soul of man (v. 15), are brought together. At death they are separated, which may be thought of as a temporary dissolution of the soul as a unit. The RESURRECTION, then, is the "redemption of the soul" (v. 16), because through it the spirit and body are inseparably joined together. Only then can one experience a fulness of joy (see D&C 93:33), because both spirit and body are essential to an individual's total development. Note that section 88 uses the term *soul* in a very special sense; in other scriptural passages, *soul* is used in a more general sense as a synonym for *spirit* (see Alma 11:40–45; 40:23; Abr. 3:23).

Kingdoms and Law (v. 17–40): The Lord stated that each kingdom is governed by law and that each person receiving a kingdom must abide by its respective law. The law pertaining to the CELESTIAL kingdom is the GOSPEL of Jesus Christ. God the Father, knowing through His own experience what course one must take in order to attain maximum fulfillment, has given laws to mark the path. Therefore, His laws should not be thought of as restrictive, but as showing the way to maximum achievement. Thus, "that which is governed by law is also preserved by law and perfected and sanctified by the same" (D&C 88:34). The Lord spoke of keeping the law as abiding "in the liberty wherewith ye are made free" and of breaking the law as becoming entangled in sin (v. 86).

Evidence for God's Existence (v. 41–50): These verses suggest that the principle of order in nature (such as the regular motions of the planets) is an evidence of God's existence, and hence that those who have seen these things have, in a sense, seen Him (see, in particular, v. 47; compare Alma 30:44). The only ultimate proof of His existence comes to each individual personally through the witness of the Holy Ghost and as prayers are answered. On the other hand, note that even many who associated with JESUS CHRIST in the flesh did not acknowledge His divinity (v. 48); apparently they lacked the convincing witness of the Spirit.

Instructions to the Elders (v. 62–86): The Lord gave his "friends" significant instructions and beautiful promises related to personal preparation (see, in particular, v. 63–69). He then directed the ELDERS to convene a "solemn assembly" in order that they might be prepared and sanctified (v. 70, 74). This commandment is the underlying theme for the remainder of section 88.

Seek Knowledge (v. 76–80, 118): The elders were directed to gather together in order to "teach one another." These verses, sometimes called "the charter of Church education," continue to guide the Church's educational programs. The elders were to seek learning by study as well as by faith. We should acknowledge that God knows all things about all branches of learning and that He can reveal these truths to us through the Holy Ghost (see Mor. 10:5). Nevertheless, we must prepare ourselves through effective study to receive and be able to comprehend that which He may reveal. The Spirit, in turn, provides an absolute standard by which we may judge the truth of ideas we study. Not only were the elders to learn "the doctrine of the kingdom" (v. 77), but they were to become familiar with a variety of other subjects as well (v. 79; see also D&C 90:15; 93:53). This knowledge would help the elders to be better prepared when called to serve, and it is an important lesson for us today. In consequence of these verses, the Church has always highly valued EDUCATION. President Gordon B. Hinckley encouraged, "Get all the schooling you can. Education is the key that unlocks the door of opportunity. God has placed upon this people a mandate to acquire knowledge 'even by study and also by faith'" [v. 118] (*Ensign,* Nov. 1997, 49).

Responsibility to Warn Neighbors (v. 81–82): Church leaders have often quoted verse 81 to emphasize Latter-day Saints' responsibility to share the gospel. The following verse implies that if we fail to do so, our neighbors might be able to excuse themselves for breaking commandments they did not know. Even as parents must assume responsibility when they fail to teach their children (see D&C 68:25), perhaps the Saints must also bear some responsibility for the lives of their neighbors whom they fail to warn. The BOOK OF MORMON records that Jacob and Joseph reached this same conclusion (see Jacob 1:18–19).

The Last Days (v. 87–116): To emphasize the importance of the ministry for which the elders were to prepare, the Lord inserted this lengthy discourse on LATTER-DAY events that were soon to occur. While section 45 gives an overview of the last days in general, these verses emphasize those events that are more particularly linked with Christ's SECOND COMING. The Lord warned that after the elders' testimony, there would follow "the testimony of earthquakes," hurricanes, tsunamis, etc. (v. 87–91).

Sign of the Son of Man (v. 93): All mankind together shall see "a great sign in heaven" (see JS—M 1:24–26, 36). Although the world will explain it away as being nothing more than an astronomical phenomenon (*TPJS,*

287), Elder Orson Pratt said that the prophets will declare that the sign is a warning to the Saints to prepare for the Lord's coming (*JD,* 8:50).

What Will Happen to the Living and the Dead? (v. 96–102): At the time of Christ's Second Coming, "the earth will be renewed and receive its paradisiacal [or terrestrial] glory" (Article of Faith 10; see SECTION 77). Those not worthy of at least a terrestrial condition will be removed—burned as "stubble" (see Mal. 4:1). Those worthy to remain will be quickened, like the earth, to a terrestrial condition. Those worthy of a celestial glory will not only be quickened, but they will also be "caught up." At this same time, those who have died and are worthy of a celestial RESURRECTION will come forth from their graves. All these will join Christ in His glorious Advent (v. 96–98). Then, the dead who are worthy of a terrestrial glory will come forth (v. 99; compare D&C 76:72–74). On the other hand, "the rest of the dead" who are not worthy of at least a terrestrial resurrection must wait until the MILLENIUM has ended (v. 100–102; D&C 43:18).

Further Instructions to the Elders (v. 117–141): In verse 117, the Lord returned to the subject of the solemn assembly to be held by the elders. The command to "establish a house" (v. 119) was fulfilled with the erection of the KIRTLAND TEMPLE. Notice how verses 117 through 120 were repeated in the dedicatory prayer for that structure (see D&C 109:6–9). In verses 118 through 126, the Lord gave further instructions about personal preparation that are as meaningful and relevant today as ever. The command to cease from "all laughter" should be understood in the light of the prohibition against an "excess of laughter" (v. 69). The instructions on sleep (v. 124) have often been linked with the Word of Wisdom (see SECTION 89).

The School of the Prophets (v. 127–141): The concluding portion of section 88 sets forth the order and procedures to be observed in the School of the Prophets. Some of these instructions anticipated temple worship, which had not yet been restored. Several important events happened in the School of the Prophets, including the reception of the "Word of Wisdom" (D&C 89) and the organization of the FIRST PRESIDENCY (see section 90).

Section 89

"A Word of Wisdom"

SETTING

According to Brigham Young, this was the first revelation given to the brethren assembled in the school of the prophets. He described the specific circumstances as follows: "The first school of the prophets was held in a small room situated over the Prophet Joseph's kitchen, in a house which belonged to Bishop Whitney. . . . The brethren came to that place for hundreds of miles to attend school in a little room probably no larger than eleven by fourteen. When they assembled together in this room after breakfast, the first they did was to light their pipes, and, while smoking, talk about the great things of the kingdom, and spit all over the room, and as soon as the pipe was out of their mouths, a large chew of tobacco would then be taken. Often when the Prophet entered the room to give the school instructions he would find himself in a cloud of tobacco smoke. This, and the complaints of his wife at having to clean so filthy a floor, made the Prophet think upon the matter, and he inquired of the Lord relating to the conduct of the Elders in using tobacco, and the revelation known as the Word of Wisdom was the result of his inquiry" (*JD,* 12:158). The widespread temperance movement at the time helped provide a receptive climate for the principles revealed in this section.

TEACHINGS

Introduction (v. 1–3): In early editions of the Doctrine and Covenants, these verses appeared as introductory material with the text of the revelation beginning with verse 4. This is a "word of wisdom" for the Saints both in Kirtland and Zion (v. 1). Although it was given "not by commandment or constraint," it nevertheless was identified as a "revelation . . . showing forth the order and will of God" (v. 2). Because we have been commanded to "live by every word that proceedeth forth from the mouth of God" (D&C 84:44), there should be no question about its importance to us. Although it obviously impacts our "temporal salvation" (v. 2), it is surely a spiritual commandment (see D&C 29:34) that teaches obedience and offers important spiritual promises. President Gordon B. Hinckley testified, "The so-called Mormon code of health, widely praised in these days of cancer and heart research, is in reality a revelation given to

Joseph Smith in 1833 as a 'Word of Wisdom' from the Lord [v 1]. In no conceivable way could it have come of the dietary literature of the time, nor from the mind of the man who announced it. Today, in terms of medical research, it is a miracle, whose observance has saved incalculable suffering and premature death for uncounted tens of thousands" (*Ensign,* May 1977, 64).

Specific Prohibitions (v. 5–9): This revelation specifically prohibits liquor, tobacco, and hot drinks, but does not specifically define what is meant by hot drinks. The Prophet Joseph Smith declared that "tea and coffee are what the Lord meant when he said 'hot drinks'" (in Widtsoe and Widtsoe, *Word of Wisdom,* 85–86). The Lord has described as "slothful" servants those who wait to be "commanded in all things" (D&C 58:26). "Members write in asking if this thing or that is against the Word of Wisdom," observed President Boyd K. Packer. "It's well known that tea, coffee, liquor, and tobacco are against it. It has not been spelled out in more detail. Rather, we teach the principle together with the promised blessings. There are many habit-forming, addictive things that one can drink or chew or inhale or inject which injure both body and spirit which are not mentioned in the revelation" (*Ensign,* May 1996, 17). We should be cautious in sharing our own conclusions and opinions with others. Only the prophet has the stewardship to define what is or is not "against the Word of Wisdom."

Positive Counsel (v. 10–17): After listing substances that should not be used, the Lord reviewed items that would be good "for the use of man." These include fresh fruits and vegetables, grains, and the sparing use of meat.

Promised Blessings (v. 18–21): The positive health benefits of living the Word of Wisdom have been widely discussed. Benefits from obedience, however, also include spiritual blessings—"hidden treasures of knowledge" that can be made known only by the Holy Ghost. President Gordon B. Hinckley promised, "There is nothing the Lord expects of us that we cannot do. His requirements are essentially so easy. For instance, He said concerning the Word of Wisdom that it is 'a principle with promise, adapted to the capacity of the weak and the weakest of all saints, who are or can be called saints' [v. 3]. We *can* observe that Word of Wisdom. We receive numerous letters inquiring whether this item or that item is proscribed by the Word of Wisdom. If we will avoid those things which are definitely and specifically defined, and beyond this observe the spirit of that great revelation, it will not involve a burden. It will, rather, bring a blessing. Do not forget: it is the Lord who has made the promise" (*Ensign,* Nov. 1985, 83).

Section 90

THE FIRST PRESIDENCY

SETTING

Earlier REVELATIONS had called both SIDNEY RIGDON and FREDERICK G. WILLIAMS to work with JOSEPH SMITH (SECTIONS 35 and 81). This present revelation was given as an answer to the petitions of the PROPHET and the brethren through prayer.

TEACHINGS

The First Presidency Formed: Because of his faithfulness, Joseph Smith received the promise that the keys of this DISPENSATION would never be taken from him (v. 3; contrast the conditional statement in D&C 43:4). Sidney Rigdon and Frederick G. Williams were now called to join the PROPHET to compose the FIRST PRESIDENCY, which was organized ten days after this revelation was given. The counselors were to be "equal" with the Prophet in holding the KEYS—the right to preside and direct—but were to function under his "administration" (v. 6–7). The Church was to receive ORACLES or revelations through Joseph, and the Saints were warned not to hold them lightly (v. 5). The Lord upheld the Prophet's right to preside not only in OHIO, but also in ZION, thus refuting rival claims to authority that

Joseph Smith Jr.

had arisen in Missouri (v. 32–33). This word was to be sent to the brethren in Missouri in the spirit of love and greeting. (Compare the language in verse 32 with the similar instruction in D&C 89:2.)

SCRIPTURE HELPS

"In His Own Language" (v. 11): The promise in this verse provides a foundation for the important work being done by more than a dozen missionary training centers around the world.

"Work Together for Your Good" (v. 24): This comforting promise spells out conditions by which even negative experiences can benefit us (compare Ether 12:27).

"Let Your Families Be Small" (v. 25): The term "family" had been used among Sidney Rigdon's Campbellite congregation to mean a cooperative group consisting of several conventional families. The practice had developed among the Saints to extend hospitality to the numerous visitors and newcomers arriving in Kirtland. Verse 26 specifically warned them not to dissipate their goods on "those that are not worthy," who might take advantage of such hospitality. The injunction in verse 25 has nothing to do with limiting the number of children in a family, since the Lord was speaking of "those who do not belong to your families." In particular, the Lord addressed his "aged servant," Joseph Smith Sr., who was sixty-one years old, well beyond the usual age of having children.

Section 91

The Apocrypha

SETTING

"The Apocrypha" is a collection of writings included in Catholic Bibles but not in most Protestant Bibles; it comes from the periods of Hebrew history roughly between the Old and New Testaments. The Bible used for the Joseph Smith Translation included the Apocrypha, so the prophet wondered if it should be translated.

TEACHINGS

The Lord indicated that the Apocrypha contains many things that are true, but also other things that are not, so the Prophet was instructed not to translate it. Still, those who read it with the SPIRIT may derive some benefit. This counsel can be applied to almost anything we might read. The related adjective *apocryphal* means "of doubtful or questionable origin"; this term is also used to refer in general to noncanonical or nonscriptural writings.

Section 92

FREDERICK G. WILLIAMS TO BE A LIVELY MEMBER

SETTING

FREDERICK G. WILLIAMS had been called to the FIRST PRESIDENCY just one week earlier (see D&C 90:6–7). This revelation was given to leaders of the Church who were members of the UNITED ORDER.

TEACHINGS

Williams's Role (v. 1–2): As a member of the new First Presidency, Frederick G. Williams was added to the united order and was told that he would be a "lively" or active member. Speaking of activity in the Church, President Harold B Lee taught, "One of the mission presidents, with a group of his missionaries back in the Eastern States some years ago, was meeting in a hall with pillars that ran down the center of the hall, and he said to one of the missionaries, 'Get up and push that pillar over.' 'Well,' said the missionary, 'I can't.' 'Why?' 'Because the weight of that ceiling is all on top of the pillar.' Then the president asked, 'suppose that weight were lifted off. Could you push the pillar over then?' The missionary replied, 'Why, sure, I think I could.' Then the president said, 'Now, brethren, you and I are just like one of those pillars. As long as we have a weight of responsibility in this church, all hell can't push us over; but as soon as that weight is lifted off, most of us are easy marks by the powers that drag us down" (CR, Oct. 1971, 129).

Section 93

The Glory of God

SETTING

No historical records give any indication as to what preceded this revelation.

TEACHINGS

Receiving a Fulness of God's Glory: Verse 29 equates intelligence, light, and truth with man in the beginning, while verse 36 equates them with God's glory. The difference is that we had those qualities only to a small degree, while God has them in full. Verse 12 affirms that even the Savior did not have these powers in full at first but afterwards received them "grace for grace." The dictionary in the LDS edition of the Bible defines *grace* as "divine means of help or strength."

John affirmed that we too may receive of God's fulness "grace for grace" (John 1:16). Other Bible translations may shed light on the meaning of this phrase: "We have, all of us, received—one gift replacing another" (Jerusalem Bible); "We have all received one blessing after another" (New International Version); "And from His fullness have we all received, grace upon grace" (Revised Standard Version). Latter-day Saint scholar Richard Draper has suggested another possibility: "To receive grace for grace is to receive assistance on the condition of giving assistance. . . . Apparently, it was necessary for the Lord to grow through this process. In order to do so, he first received grace, or divine assistance from the Father. This grace he extended to his brethren. As he did so he received even more grace. The process continued until he eventually received a fullness of the glory of the Father" (*DE,* 37–38*).

Significantly, we too must receive "grace for grace" (v. 20). Once we have begun receiving God's gifts, our challenge is to ascend "from grace to grace" or from one gift to another. Through continued righteousness we progress from one level of holiness to another until we receive a fulness of godlike attributes. The message of section 93 is that through Jesus Christ we too can receive a fulness of truth and light by keeping the commandments (see v. 19–20, 28). On the other hand, Satan seeks to take away these qualities from us by tempting us to disobey (see v. 39).

"The Glory of God Is Intelligence" and Education (v. 36): It is evident that this passage has a broader meaning than just supporting EDUCATION. However, applying this verse to gaining an education is appropriate because "truth," one of the attributes characterizing God's glory, is defined in this same revelation as a "knowledge of things as they are, and as they were, and as they are to come" (v. 24). Elder John A. Widtsoe distinguished between intelligence and mere learning: "It often happens that a person of limited knowledge but who earnestly and prayerfully obeys the law, rises to a higher intelligence or wisdom, than one of vast Gospel learning who does not comply in his daily life with the requirements of the Gospel. Obedience to law is a mark of intelligence" (CR, Apr. 1938, 50).

SCRIPTURE HELPS

The Record of John (v. 6–18): In the opening chapter of his gospel, John the Apostle bore witness of Christ's glorious role since the beginning (see John 1:1–14). He also quoted the testimony or "record" of John the Baptist (John 1:15, 19–34). Doctrine and Covenants 93 seems to be quoting from both John the Apostle (see verses 8–10) and from John the Baptist (see verses 15–16).

Section 94

THREE BUILDINGS IN KIRTLAND

SETTING

Four months had passed since the Lord had commanded the Saints to build a sacred house (D&C 88:119). In a meeting, a committee was appointed for raising funds to build a place for the SCHOOL OF THE PROPHETS to meet. Shortly afterwards, the revelation in section 94 was given.

TEACHINGS

Three Sacred Buildings were to be at the heart of the city of KIRTLAND—the TEMPLE and two others. On the first lot south of the temple, a house for the presidency was to be built, and on the second lot a house for the publication of God's word was to stand (see D&C 94:3, 10). All three of these buildings were to have the same dimensions (compare v. 4 and 11 with D&C 95:15). All were to be regarded as sacred (v. 8–9, 12). These latter two structures were not to be built until the Lord gave further instruction (see D&C 94:16). This direction was not given before the Saints were forced to flee from Kirtland, so these structures were never built. On the other hand, less than a month after Doctrine and Covenants 94 had been received, the Lord gave further instruction concerning the design and building of His temple (see D&C 95:8–17). Within a few weeks of receiving these revelations, the Prophet drew up his plan for the city of Zion, in which he called for not three but twenty-four sacred structures to serve as "houses of worship, schools, etc." at the city's center (*HC,* 1:358).

Section 95

The Temple to be Built

SETTING

Hyrum Smith, Jared Carter, and Reynolds Cahoon were the committee that had been appointed to gather funds for the Church's building projects. They issued a circular encouraging the Saints to fulfill the divine command given six months previously to build the house of the Lord. Section 95 was given the same day the circular was issued.

TEACHINGS

Design and Functions of the Temple: The Lord described the TEMPLE as a place where He would prepare His "Apostles" to go forth (v. 4), where the Saints might worship "the Lord of SABAOTH" (v. 7), and where He would "endow" those whom He had chosen "with power from on high" (v. 8). The Saints would have power to build the temple only if they were worthy (v. 11–12). It was to be designed "not after the manner of the world," but according to a pattern the Lord would reveal to three appointed brethren (v. 13–14). It would have two main halls measuring fifty-five by sixty-five feet; the one on the ground floor would be a chapel, while the one above would be for instruction (v. 15–17). The three chosen to receive the design of the temple were JOSEPH SMITH, SIDNEY

RIGDON, and FREDERICK G. WILLIAMS, the recently organized FIRST PRESIDENCY (SECTION 90). Shortly afterwards, these three saw in vision the exterior and interior of the future temple (*TDE,* 25–26). Frederick G. Williams recalled, "We went upon our knees, called on the Lord, and the Building appeared within viewing distant: I being the first to discover it. Then all of us viewed it together. After we had taken a good look at the exterior, the building seemed to come right over us, and the makeup of this Hall seems to coincide with what I there saw to a minutia" (Truman O. Angell Journal, BYU Library, Special Collections).

SCRIPTURE HELPS

Apostles (v. 4): Because the Quorum of the Twelve would not be organized until 1835 (SECTION 107), the reference to Apostles in this revelation probably had reference to all who would be sent out as official representatives of the Church rather than just to the priesthood office of APOSTLE.

Strange Act (v. 4): This phrase comes from the Old Testament (Isaiah 28:21–22). *Strange act* conveys the idea that "the gospel will appear 'strange,' and the things the Lord does or has his people do will appear as a 'strange act' to those so given up to the things of the world that they have lost all spiritual discernment or sensitivity" (*RR,* 690).

Section 96

DISPOSITION OF LANDS

SETTING

In a meeting of HIGH PRIESTS, the brethren were not able to decide who should be in charge of the lands that had been acquired by the Church. They decided to ask the Lord what to do.

TEACHINGS

Temporal Affairs were to be managed by the BISHOP, NEWEL K. WHITNEY (v. 1–5). The STAKE at KIRTLAND would be organized eight months later (SECTION 102). As a new member of the UNITED ORDER, JOHN JOHNSON was to pay debts arising from building the KIRTLAND TEMPLE (v. 9).

Section 97

Difficulties in Zion

SETTING

This revelation came exactly two years after the land of Zion had been dedicated in 1831. During this period, many Latter-day Saints had gathered to the area, but unfortunately there was ill will between them and their non-Mormon neighbors. For several months, tensions between Mormons and non-Mormons grew in Jackson County, culminating in the destruction of the Latter-day Saints' press on July 20, 1833. It was in this attack that most of the printed sheets for the Book of Commandments were lost. Some of the causes of this friction included the following:

1. The Latter-day Saints belonged to what was thought of as a strange religion, and their cultural background was not the same as that of the majority.
2. The 1820 Missouri Compromise had made Missouri a slave state, while the Latter-day Saints had come from the anti-slave North.
3. By 1833 there were enough Mormons to dominate Jackson County politics and to wield quite an influence throughout the state as well.
4. Some of the Saints lacked good judgment and boasted that Jackson County was their Zion by divine decree.

These and other factors antagonized the earlier settlers in the area. Because the lawless element tended to flock to the frontier, the hostile feelings resulted in mob violence against the Saints. Following the mob attack, Oliver Cowdery left for Kirtland to consult with Joseph Smith, but did not arrive until mid-August—after sections 97 and 98 gave counsel to the beleaguered Missouri Saints. Thus the Prophet could have known about these difficulties only by revelation.

TEACHINGS

A Temple in Zion (v. 10–17): The location of the temple at Independence had been revealed two years earlier (see D&C 57:3). Preliminary sketches for this temple indicate that it would have been built "like unto the pattern" that the Lord had given for the Kirtland Temple (see D&C 97:10). The temple would have been a source of temporal as well as spiritual salvation for the Saints in Zion. By means of a parable in a subsequent revelation, the Lord spoke of his servants' failure to build a tower (or the temple) as He had commanded in order to provide defense (see D&C 101:43–62). In Section 97, verses 13 and 14 list functions of temples, and verses 15 and 17 set forth a marvelous promise that may be applied to these sacred structures today as well as to the projected temple in Zion.

Warning to the Saints in Zion (v. 18-26): Since Zion is the "pure in heart" (v. 21), the Lord was pleased with the humble, righteous Saints in Missouri but chastened those in need of repentance. He stressed that righteous Zion would be protected during the time when scourges would sweep over the wicked. Nevertheless, if the inhabitants of Zion failed to keep the Lord's commandments, they too would partake of the afflictions to come upon the disobedient.

Section 98

WAR AND FORGIVENESS

SETTING

The Saints in Missouri had been experiencing severe persecutions. This revelation was given in answer to their prayers.

TEACHINGS

Obedience to the Law of the Land (v. 4-10): The Lord requires His Saints to obey "constitutional" laws that uphold basic rights (v. 5–6). The Lord subsequently testified that the United States Constitution had been established by men whom He had "raised up unto this very purpose" (D&C 101:80). Because "when the wicked rule, the people mourn," we must seek and uphold "good men and wise men" (v. 9–10).

"Renounce War" (v. 16): Although pacifists refuse to participate in any kind of military action, the Lord indicates that there are circumstances in which we are justified in going to war (see v. 33–36). Still, He prefers us to "renounce war and proclaim peace" (v. 16). The Nephites were instructed anciently that they should not start wars for selfish gain but to fight "even to the shedding of blood if it were necessary" in defense of their homes, their freedoms, and their religion (Alma 48:14; see also Alma 43:45–47).

Only a few weeks after the outbreak of World War II, the First Presidency reminded Church members to obey constitutional law (see D&C 98:4–7): "When, therefore, constitutional law, obedient to these principles, calls the manhood of the church into the armed service of any country to which they owe allegiance, their highest civic duty requires that they meet that call. If, harkening to that call and obeying those in command over them, they shall take the lives of those who fight against them, that will not make of them murderers, nor subject them to the penalty that God has prescribed for those who kill . . . For it would be a cruel God that would punish His children as moral sinners for acts done by them as the innocent instrumentalities of a sovereign whom He had told them to obey and whose will they were powerless to resist" (CR, Apr. 1942, 94–95).

President Gordon B. Hinckley speaks of the Church's position on war, "One of our Articles of Faith, which represent an expression of our doctrine, states, 'We believe in being subject to kings, presidents, rulers, and magistrates, in obeying, honoring, and sustaining the law' (Article of Faith 1:12). But modern revelation states that we are to 'renounce war and proclaim peace' (D&C 98:16). In a democracy we can renounce war and proclaim peace. There is opportunity for dissent. Many have been speaking out and doing so emphatically. That is their privilege. That is their right, so long as they do so legally. However, we all must also be mindful of another overriding responsibility, which I may add, governs my personal feelings and dictates my personal loyalties in the present situation. When war raged between the Nephites and the Lamanites, the record states that 'the Nephites were inspired by a better cause, for they were not fighting for . . . power but they were fighting for their homes and their liberties, their wives and their children, and their all, yea, for their rites of worship and their church. And they were doing that which they felt was the duty which they owed to their God' (Alma 43:45–46). It is clear from these and other writings that there are times and circumstances when nations are justified, in fact have an obligation, to fight for family, for liberty, and against tyranny, threat, and oppression. When all is said and done, we of this Church are people of peace. We are followers of our Redeemer, the Lord Jesus Christ, who was the Prince of Peace. But even He said, 'Think not that I am come to send peace on earth: I came not to send peace, but a sword' (Matt. 10:34). This places us in the position of those who long for peace, who teach peace, who work for peace, but who also are citizens of nations and are subject to the laws of our governments. Furthermore, we are a freedom-loving people, committed to the defense of liberty wherever it is in jeopardy" (*Ensign,* May 2003, 78).

How Many Times Are We Expected to Forgive? (v. 23-48): The Savior instructed Peter that he should FORGIVE those who offended him "until seventy times seven" (Matt. 18:21–22). Latter-day Saint scholar Sidney B. Sperry said: "The Master's answer to Peter, uttered in the form of common Oriental overstatement, did not mean that one was to forgive his brother exactly four hundred and ninety times. The spirit of it was that a man should have a lot of forgiveness in his heart" (*Doctrine and Covenants Compendium,* 500), meaning that we should forgive indefinitely. A latter-day revelation tells us that we should forgive always (see D&C 64:9–10).

A superficial reading of Doctrine and Covenants 98, however, may give the impression that we are expected to forgive only three times. Verses 23 through 27 require that we forgive our enemies at least three times and emphasize that we should do so "patiently." If our enemy comes against us a fourth time, he is in our hands; but, even then, "if thou wilt spare him, thou shalt be rewarded for thy righteousness" (v. 30). Such forbearance would give offenders time to reconsider their actions and perhaps repent.

This revelation was given to the Saints at the time they were being violently driven from Jackson County, Missouri. Even though they would be blessed for maintaining an attitude of forgiveness, they were not expected to stand by without seeking to defend themselves. "If [thine enemy] has sought thy life, and thy life is endangered by him, thine enemy is in thine hands and thou art justified" (v. 31).

In the revelation in Doctrine and Covenants 98, the Lord likewise admonishes all of us not to limit the number of times we are willing to work with transgressors even when they are not seeking forgiveness (see v. 39–45). When action must be taken against the unrepentant, it should be done in the Lord's way (see v. 44; compare D&C 42:88–92).

Section 99

JOHN MURDOCK

SETTING

If this revelation were in chronological order, it would come just before section 84. The revelation is addressed to John Murdock, who was baptized in November 1830 by PARLEY P. PRATT. (Elder Pratt had come to KIRTLAND as part of the LAMANITE MISSION.) When John Murdock's wife died after giving birth to twins in April 1831, John gave the babies to JOSEPH and EMMA SMITH to raise. Three older children remained with John.

TEACHINGS

Priorities: Brother Murdock was called to preach the gospel. If he was rejected, he was to cleanse the DUST off his feet privately (v. 4). Nevertheless, he was not to leave for his mission until his children were properly provided for (v. 6–8). He would fill a mission with Zebedee Coltrin from April 1833 to April 1834, mostly in NEW YORK. He later participated in ZION'S CAMP and was a faithful member of the Church for many years (*WWDC,* 202).

Section 100

SIDNEY RIGDON TO BE A SPOKESMAN

SETTING

While on a mission in the company of SIDNEY RIGDON and Freeman Nickerson, the PROPHET was worried about the welfare of his family. He was also concerned about ORSON HYDE and John Gould, who had been dispatched several weeks before with encouragement and counsel to the Saints in ZION. This revelation was received at Nickerson's home in Perrysburg, in western NEW YORK, near the shore of Lake Erie.

TEACHINGS

Missionary Work (v. 5–8): After assuring the brethren that their families and the envoys to Zion were well, the Lord reminded the brethren why they had come on this mission. He commanded them to lift up their voices and promised to give them the words they should say (v. 5–6; compare D&C 84:85). He promised that if they would teach with "solemnity of heart" and "in the spirit of meekness," the HOLY GHOST would bear testimony that their words were true (v. 7–8).

President Ezra Taft Benson remarked, "One of the greatest secrets of missionary work is work! If a missionary works, he will get the Spirit; if he gets the Spirit, he will teach by the Spirit; and if he teaches by the Spirit, he will touch the hearts of the people; and he will be happy. There will be no homesickness, no worrying about families, for all time and talents and interests are centered on the work of the ministry. That's the secret—work, work, work. There is no satisfactory substitute, especially in missionary work" (quoted in *PMG,* 121).

The Spirit Testifies: President James E. Faust recounted, "A lonely young Persian student was in Munich, struggling to find meaning to life in postwar Europe. He heard a knock at the door one day, and two Mormon missionaries stood before him. He was not the least interested in religion. The only thing that interested him about these two young men was their accent. He had mastered four languages, but English was not one of them. He invited them in, but as soon as they began their discussion, he cautioned, 'I don't want to hear about God, nor how your religion got started. I only want to know one thing: what do you people do for one another?' He waited as the elders exchanged glances. Finally, one of them said softly, 'We love one another.' Nothing the missionary could have said would have been more electrifying than this simple utterance, for the Holy Ghost immediately bore witness that these missionaries were true servants of the Lord. Shortly thereafter, he was baptized into the Church" (*Ensign,* May 1996, 40).

SCRIPTURE HELPS

Relative Roles of Joseph and Sidney (v. 9–11): While JOSEPH SMITH was to be a revelator "mighty in testimony," Sidney was to use his background as a Campbellite minister in serving as "a spokesman unto this people"; he was promised that he would be "mighty in expounding all scriptures" (compare D&C 35:23).

Section 101

Instructions for the Saints in Zion

SETTING

Just six days before, the PROPHET had received news of the expulsion of the Saints from JACKSON COUNTY.

TEACHINGS

Cause of the Saints' Suffering (v. 1–8): The Saints' own failings were to blame for their suffering. Their transgressions, disunity, lustfulness, and slowness in hearkening to the Lord were in marked contrast to the ideals that must characterize a ZION people—unity and righteousness (see D&C 97:21–26; Moses 7:18–19). The Saints needed further chastening and purifying, and the Lord promised he would be merciful toward them (compare D&C 103:1–4; 105:2–6).

Be Still and Know That I am God (v. 16): President Gordon B. Hinckley testified, "Recently while wrestling in my mind with a problem I thought to be of serious consequence I went to my knees in prayer. There came into my mind a feeling of peace and the words of the Lord, 'Be still and know that I am God.' I turned to the scripture and read this reassuring statement spoken to the Prophet Joseph Smith 150 years ago: 'Let your hearts be comforted concerning Zion; for all flesh is in mine hands; be still and know that I am God.' God is weaving his tapestry according to his own grand design. All flesh is in his hands. It is not our prerogative to counsel him. It is our responsibility and our opportunity to be at peace in our minds and in our hearts, and to know that he is God, that this is his work, and that he will not permit it to fail" (*Ensign,* May 1983, 5).

Two Phases of Gathering (v. 17–22): Despite the Saints' difficulties, the appointed place of GATHERING would not be changed. Nevertheless, a time would come when there would be no more gathering to one central location and when STAKES would be designated as other places for gathering. These two phases have been reflected in Church History: During most of the nineteenth century, Latter-day Saint converts gathered to the Rocky Mountains, while in the twentieth century, they were counseled to remain in their own lands and to build up the kingdom there. Hundreds of "stakes of Zion" have been set up around the world (compare D&C 115:5–6, 17–18).

The Millennium (v. 24-34): In the midst of these difficulties, the Lord explained that His Saints should gather in preparation for the glorious events, especially those associated with the inauguration of the MILLENNIUM when Christ will reign personally upon the earth. The earth itself will be cleansed by fire, all corruptible things being done away (v. 24–25), and Satan will be bound (v. 28). Those who are alive when the Millennium begins or who are born during the thousand years will live in a terrestrial mortal state and will not die prematurely; there will be no death as we know it, but they will pass through a change equivalent to death and instantaneous resurrection (v. 29–31). The Lord will reveal to the righteous "all things" (v. 32–34).

Instructions through Parables (v. 42-101): In the parable of the vineyard (v. 43–62), a certain nobleman (the Lord Jesus Christ) commanded His servants to go and plant a vineyard (establish Zion) on a choice piece of ground (the American continent in general or Jackson County in particular). The servants were to erect a tower, the temple (compare D&C 97:12), as a means to see their enemies while they were still far away and thereby still have time to defend themselves (received by revelation in the temple—the Lord's warning for the future). The servants failed to build the tower as commanded, so when the enemies came the servants were scattered and the vineyard was destroyed. The Lord then directed another servant, Joseph Smith (see D&C 103:21), to take the strong and young from among His servants (ZION'S CAMP) and drive the enemy out of the vineyard. Then "after many days" (v. 62), the Lord and His people would again possess the land and all things would be fulfilled.

The parable of the good wheat being gathered and the tares being burned (v. 64–75) was compared to the righteous gathering of the Saints. In connection with this gathering, the Lord directed His people to continue purchasing land in and around Jackson County, and commanded them not to sell the land they already possessed there (v. 96–101).

The Saints were to continue importuning or petitioning government officials for redress, even as did the widow in the Savior's parable (see v. 76–89; compare Luke 18:1–8). While introducing this counsel, the Lord revealed the significant fact that He had established the Constitution of the United States "by the hands of wise men whom I raised up unto this very purpose" (v. 80).

Section 102

The Original High Council

SETTING

This section is composed of minutes (notes) from the organization of the first High Council. The PROPHET set forth the ancient pattern for Church councils revealed to him in vision. This occasion marks the formation of the first STAKE.

TEACHINGS

The High Council as a Disciplinary Council: At this early stage of the Church's growth, the First Presidency also served as the presidency of the stake in Kirtland (v. 3). High councils today generally function as administrative bodies. This section, however, focuses on their less frequent yet important role as a DISCIPLINARY COUNCIL. They would settle matters beyond the jurisdiction of the BISHOP'S council (v. 2). The procedures outlined in verses 12 through 23 are followed by high councils when they are functioning in their disciplinary capacity. In this capacity, the members are divided into two equal groups. One group represents the interests of the Church, while the other represents the interests of the accused. This arrangement is unique in that neither of these two groups constitutes a prosecution, defense, or jury. Instead, their function is to prevent insult and injustice to either the Church or the accused.

Special Disciplinary Councils (v. 24–34): These councils have been convened only rarely, typically to handle matters in areas where no stakes have jurisdiction. The reference to the "general authorities" (verse 32) is the first usage of this term in the standard works.

Section 103

ZION'S CAMP

SETTING

The dispossessed Saints in Missouri sent PARLEY P. PRATT and LYMAN WIGHT to find out by what means they would be restored to their inheritances in ZION.

TEACHINGS

Accountability: The Lord again commented on the cause of the Saints' difficulties. He had respected the AGENCY even of the wicked, allowing them to "fill up the measure of their iniquities." Nevertheless, this "sore and grievous chastisement" had come upon the Saints because of their own failure to keep the commandments (v. 1–4; compare 101:1–8; 105:2–6).

Speaking of the Saints in Missouri, President Marion G. Romney stated that they "did not demonstrate the necessary dedication and commitment to establish Zion at that time. On February 24, 1834, after they had been 'driven and smitten by the hands of [their] enemies [v. 2]' the Lord told the Prophet Joseph that the reason he had permitted their expulsion was so 'that those who call themselves after my name might be

Zion's Camp on the march

chastened for a little season with a sore and grievous chastisement, because they did not hearken altogether unto the precepts and commandments which I gave unto them' [v. 4]. They were not yet his disciples in the true sense of the term" (*Ensign,* Nov. 1978, 38).

Formation of Zion's Camp: The Lord called on the brethren to respond to the Missouri governor's invitation to cooperate in restoring the Saints to their lost properties in JACKSON COUNTY. Eventually, 205 men responded, and during the late spring of 1834, ZION'S CAMP made the march of over 900 miles from the Great Lakes area to western Missouri.

Section 104

SETTING

In order to stabilize the financial situation of the Church before the members of ZION'S CAMP departed, the UNITED ORDER was divided into individual stewardships. The Lord confirmed the action in this revelation.

TEACHINGS

Economic Counsel: Because of persecution and because some of the Saints themselves had transgressed (v. 1–10), the united order in KIRTLAND was reorganized. Each individual was given his own stewardship for which he would be accountable (v. 11–13). Specific properties were assigned to each individual; each was promised "a multiplicity of blessings" if he would be faithful (v. 19–46). The beleaguered united order in Missouri was also to be separated from that in Kirtland "in consequence of their being driven out and that which is to come," for the "salvation" of both groups (v. 51). The Lord reminded the brethren of their responsibility to publish the scriptures He had given them and to build up His Church "to prepare my people for the time when I shall dwell with them, which is nigh at hand" (v. 57–59). For this purpose they were to establish "the sacred treasury of the Lord" (v. 60–66). Another treasury was set up to help individuals with their stewardships as long as they were faithful (v. 67–76).

The Lord Can Take Care of the Poor (v. 14-18): The Lord reminded the Saints that He had created the earth, so "all the things therein are mine." He indicated that it was His purpose to provide for them, "but it must needs be done in mine own way." He explained that the rich must be willing to take of their abundance to help the poor. He testified that "the earth is full, and there is enough and to spare." Elder Joseph B. Wirthlin explained, "The Lord's way consists of helping people help themselves. The poor are exalted because they work for the temporary assistance they receive, they are taught correct principles, and they are able to lift themselves from poverty to self-reliance. The rich are made low because they humble themselves to give generously of their means to those in need. We teach members to be self-reliant, to do everything possible to sustain themselves, and to seek help from their families for needed assistance. When members and their families are doing all they can to provide necessities but still cannot meet basic needs, the Church stands ready to help" (*Ensign,* May 1999, 76).

Pay Your Debts (v. 78-83): Finally, the brethren were directed to pay their DEBTS, and the Lord promised to help them. President Gordon B. Hinckley cautioned, "We have been counseled again and again concerning self-reliance, concerning debt, concerning thrift. So many of our people are heavily in debt for things that are not entirely necessary. When I was a young man, my father counseled me to build a modest home, sufficient for the needs of my family, and make it beautiful and attractive and pleasant and secure. He counseled me to pay off the mortgage as quickly as I could so that, come what may, there would be a roof over the heads of my wife and children. I was reared on that kind of doctrine. I urge you as members of this Church to get free of debt where possible and to have a little laid aside against a rainy day" (*Ensign,* Nov. 2001).

Section 105

Requirements for Establishing Zion

SETTING

After Zion's Camp arrived in Clay County, Missouri, the aid promised by the governor was rescinded, as he hoped to avoid bloodshed and to find a peaceful solution. Hence the efforts of the brethren to restore the Saints to their inheritances were frustrated. Concerning the contributions of Zion's Camp, President James E. Faust observed, "Although Zion's Camp failed in its stated purpose of restoring the Saints to their lands in JACKSON COUNTY, Missouri, it was invaluable as a stern schooling. They learned that faith is more important than life itself. At a [CONFERENCE] held February 14, 1835, the Quorum of the Twelve Apostles and the Seventy were chosen from the ranks of those who had served in Zion's Camp. These valiant brethren led the Church for the next 50 years" (*Ensign*, Nov. 1998, 45).

TEACHINGS

What Must Be Accomplished Before Redeeming Zion? The Lord reminded the Saints that ZION could have been redeemed already except for their own "transgressions"; notice that He spoke collectively and not individually, just as He had done earlier when praising the Church (v. 2; compare D&C 1:30). They had not learned obedience, did not help the poor, and were not sufficiently united as required by the law of CONSECRATION (compare v. 3–4 with D&C 101:1–8; 103:1–4). Because Zion can be established only by CELESTIAL law, the Saints needed to be chastened in order to learn obedience to that higher law (v. 5–6). For these reasons, the ELDERS needed to "wait for a little season for the redemption of Zion" (v. 9).

Several things needed to be accomplished. The Saints needed to be prepared by being taught more perfectly and having additional experience (v. 10); participation in Church programs can help us meet these requirements. The Lord counseled His people not to boast of judgments, etc., but to consider the feelings of others regarding the gathering of the Saints (v. 24). For the present, the elders were to continue purchasing land in the area (v. 28–29), but the redemption of Zion had to wait until the Lord's people themselves were prepared (v. 10). The Lord's "army" or people needed to become more numerous and "sanctified" or worthy (v. 31). Recent worldwide growth and temple activity suggest that we are approaching these goals. In addition, the Lord indicated that the elders of the Church needed to receive an endowment of power from on high in the KIRTLAND TEMPLE (v. 11–12, 33).

Section 106

Warren A. Cowdery

SETTING

This REVELATION was given while JOSEPH SMITH was preparing for the beginning of another session of the SCHOOL OF THE PROPHETS.

TEACHINGS

Blessings for Faithful Service (v. 1–3, 6–8): Warren A. Cowdery was called to preside over the Church in the small town of Freedom (about forty miles southeast of Buffalo) and surrounding areas. He was promised earthly as well as eternal blessings as a reward for his faithful service.

SCRIPTURE HELPS

"The Children of Light" (v. 4–5): While the SECOND COMING of Christ will overtake the world as "a thief in the night," Paul insisted that the faithful disciples were "the children of light," so should not be caught off guard (1 Thes. 5:2–5).

Section 107

"Revelation on Priesthood"

SETTING

The original quorums of the Twelve APOSTLES and SEVENTY were formed in February 1835. The following month, in preparation for their mission to the eastern states, the Twelve requested a written revelation from the Lord to guide and comfort them in their labors. Section 107 is actually a composite of at least two major revelations. Verses 1 through 58 were dated March 1835. Notice how verse 58 introduces a separate revelation that had been received earlier; the earliest known manuscript of this portion of section 107 is dated November 1831. The earlier revelation did not include verses 93 through 98; the date of this "vision showing the order of the Seventy" (v. 93) is not known, but it must have been received before that quorum was organized in February 1835.

TEACHINGS

Both section 84 and 107 have been designated "Revelation on Priesthood."

Power of the Holy Priesthood: Elder Jeffrey R. Holland testified, "I have beheld the power of God manifest in my home and in my ministry. I have seen evil rebuked and the elements controlled. I know what it means to have mountains of difficulty move and ominous Red Seas part. I know what it means to have the destroying angel 'pass by them' (D&C 89:21). To have received the authority and to have exercised the power of 'the Holy Priesthood, after the Order of the Son of God' [v. 1–3], is as great a blessing for me and for my family as I could ever hope for in this world. And that, in the end, is the meaning of the priesthood in everyday terms—its unequaled, unending, constant capacity to bless" (*Ensign,* May 2005, 43).

Priesthood Orders (v. 1-20): There are two orders of PRIESTHOOD: The higher administers "spiritual things" (v. 18–19; compare D&C 84:19–22), while the lesser administers the "outward ordinances" of the "preparatory gospel" and "temporal things" (v. 14, 20, 68; compare D&C 13, 84:26–27). The name of the higher order was changed to show greater respect for the name of Deity (v. 1–4; compare D&C 63:61–62).

Presiding Quorums (v. 21-38): Section 107 outlines an administrative structure based on three presiding QUORUMS—the FIRST PRESIDENCY, the Quorum of the Twelve Apostles, and the Seventy. This organization, revealed in 1835 when the Church had only a few hundred members, mostly in northeastern OHIO and western Missouri, is the same today in the worldwide Church with millions of members. The revelation speaks of the First Presidency, the Twelve Apostles, and the Seventy as being "equal in authority" (v. 24, 26). This means they are potentially equal, having authority to preside over the Church whenever the higher quorum or quorums are dissolved. Still, the Twelve work under the direction of the First Presidency, and the Seventy labor under the direction of the Twelve (v. 33–34, 38). President Joseph F. Smith stated: "The duty of the Twelve Apostles of the Church is to preach the gospel to the world, to send it to the inhabitants of the earth and to bear testimony of Jesus

Christ the Son of God, as living witnesses of his divine mission. That is their special calling and they are always under the direction of the Presidency of The Church of Jesus Christ of Latter-day Saints when that presidency is intact, and there is never at the same time two equal heads in the Church—never. The Lord never ordained any such thing, nor designed it. There is always a head in the Church, and if the Presidency of the Church are removed by death or other cause, then the next head of the Church is the Twelve Apostles, until a presidency is again organized of three presiding high priests who have the right to hold the office of First Presidency over the Church." (*GD,* 177–78). President James E. Faust proclaimed, "By revelation in our day the Seventies have been given an expanded role as members of Area Presidencies and in general Church administration, helping the First Presidency and the Twelve 'in building up the church and regulating all the affairs of the same in all nations' [v. 34]" (*Ensign,* Nov 1989, 8).

Other Presiding Quorums (v. 36-37): At the time section 107 was revealed, there were only two stake high councils in the Church. Elder John Taylor later explained that they had unusual powers not generally accorded to such bodies. The high council in Kirtland, for example, was unique in that it was headed by the First Presidency of the Church (*JD,* 19:241).

Early Patriarchs (v. 39-57): After stating that the Twelve should ordain "evangelical ministers" or PATRIARCHS, this revelation reviews the history of early patriarchs from Adam to Noah (v. 40–52), including the great meeting at ADAM-ONDI-AHMAN shortly before Adam's death (v. 53–57).

Other Offices and Quorums (v. 58-98): After reviewing the history of early patriarchs, section 107 returns to the duty of the Twelve to regulate the Church (compare v. 39, 58). This is also the point at which the earlier (1831) revelation is introduced and incorporated. Presiding officers are to be appointed over quorums of deacons, teachers, priests, and ELDERS (v. 60–63). These leaders are to teach quorum members their duties (v. 85–89). The "President of the High Priesthood" is to "preside over the whole church." He is to be "like unto Moses" and to serve as a SEER, revelator, translator, and PROPHET (v. 65–67, 91–92). The BISHOP has a distinct calling. He is a "judge in Israel" with the assistance of his counselors (v. 68–75). The First Presidency, with the assistance of the Twelve, is the DISCIPLINARY COUNCIL having final jurisdiction. If the President of the

Church were to transgress, his case would be heard by the Presiding Bishopric (v. 76–84). The Seventies have a unique organization; their seven presidents can form additional quorums as required by Church growth (v. 93–97).

Conclusion (v. 99–100): This great revelation on priesthood and Church administration concludes with an admonition that each member should learn his respective duties and serve diligently therein, thus making his contribution to the overall success of the kingdom of God on earth.

SCRIPTURE HELPS

"Covenants and Commandments" (v. 20, 63): In the manuscript of the original 1831 revelation, the phrase "according to the covenants and commandments of the church" in verse 63 read, "according to the Church Articles and Covenants" (*RR*, 801). This is the title under which SECTION 20 was accepted by vote at the Church's first CONFERENCE, June 9, 1830. "Covenants" as mentioned in verses 85 through 89 undoubtedly again refers to section 20 because the offices mentioned in these verses are the same as those whose duties are explained in that revelation.

Section 108

Strengthen Your Brethren

SETTING

Under the influence of the Spirit, Lyman Sherman, one of the seven Presidents of the SEVENTY, came to the PROPHET to express his feelings and desires and to receive a REVELATION teaching him his duty.

TEACHINGS

Proper Perspective: In 1837, Lyman Sherman was released as a President of the Seventy and as a General Authority because he had been ordained a HIGH PRIEST. This revelation, given over two years before, undoubtedly put into perspective any loss he may have felt following his release. "Let your soul be at rest concerning your spiritual standing," the Lord counseled (v. 2). Lyman was promised "exceeding great blessings"

(v. 3). He was counseled to be patient and was assured that he would "be remembered with the first of mine ELDERS" (v. 4). Finally, he was exhorted to "strengthen [his] brethren" through his prayers and by everything he said and did (v. 7; compare Luke 22:32).

Section 109

DEDICATORY PRAYER FOR THE KIRTLAND TEMPLE

SETTING

This dedicatory prayer of the KIRTLAND TEMPLE was composed and copied under the direction of the Spirit by JOSEPH SMITH, SIDNEY RIGDON, OLIVER COWDERY, Warren Cowdery, and Warren Parrish. Hence like section 65, this is a prayer given by revelation.

TEACHINGS

Dedicating Temples: President Joseph Fielding Smith taught, "When we dedicate a house to the Lord, what we really do is dedicate ourselves to the Lord's service, with a covenant that we shall use the house in the way He intends that it shall be used. . . . Dedicatory prayers for temples, however, are formal and long and cover many matters of doctrine and petition. This pattern was set by the Prophet Joseph Smith in the dedication of the Kirtland Temple. The prayer given on that occasion was revealed to him by the Lord; all prayers used since then have been written by the spirit of inspiration and have been read by such of the Brethren as have been appointed to do so" (*Church News,* Feb. 12, 1972).

Elder Dallin H. Oaks observed, "The prayer offered at the dedication of the Kirtland Temple in 1836 is another model that illustrates the language of prayer used by the Prophet Joseph Smith: 'And now, Holy Father, we ask thee to assist us, thy people, with thy grace, in calling our solemn assembly . . . that thy glory may rest down upon thy people, and upon this thy house, which we now dedicate to thee, that it may be sanctified and consecrated to be holy, and that thy holy presence may be continually in this house' [v. 10, 12]. This prophetic model of the language of prayer has been faithfully followed in all of the sacred petitions by which the prophets have dedicated temples to the Lord" (*Ensign,* May 1993, 15).

Functions of Temples (v. 5): This verse refers to the function of TEMPLES as a place where the Lord may reveal Himself. The other major function, priesthood ORDINANCES, would be restored more fully beginning at NAUVOO.

Blessings Petitioned: The Lord inspired the PROPHET to pray for the fulfillment of earlier instructions and promises concerning the temple (compare v. 6–9, 19–20 with D&C 88:117–120; 132–134). The Prophet asked the Lord to sanctify the temple with His presence, that all who entered might feel His power and holiness, and that those who would go forth from it would do so armed with testimony (v. 12–13, 22–23). This prayer petitions blessings not only for the Church, but also for many other worthy purposes, such as the GATHERING of the Jews, the Lamanites, and other scattered remnants of Israel (v. 61–67). There was even a prayer for members of "the wicked mob," that they might repent (v. 50). The

The Kirtland Temple

Lord was also asked to bless the leaders of the Church and their "immediate connections" or relatives (v. 68–72). Section 109 set the pattern for subsequent temple dedicatory prayers. They are generally quite lengthy, and their inspired content reflects a review of the greatest concerns to Church leaders at the time they are given.

The Sacred Hosanna Shout (v. 79–80): The "Hosanna Shout" has been a part of every temple dedication. This sacred ceremony has also been part of other special occasions, including the centennial General Conference in 1930 and the dedication of the Conference Center in 2000. The hymn "The Spirit of God Like a Fire Is Burning" had been written earlier in anticipation of the glorious experiences especially to be associated with the Kirtland Temple. It has been sung at the dedication of all Latter-day Saint temples since that time; its chorus reflects this sacred rite.

SCRIPTURE HELPS

To Whom Was the Prayer Addressed? It seemed to be directed to the Father but also to Jehovah, the Son, whose house was here being dedicated. Both are addressed almost interchangeably (see, for example, v. 4, 34, 42, 47, 56, and 68). Recent Church Presidents have typically addressed dedicatory prayers to God the Father, but have said that the temple was being dedicated "to Thee and to Thy Son."

Section 110

The Restoration of Keys

SETTING

One week after the Kirtland Temple was dedicated, a general meeting was held. In that meeting Joseph Smith and Oliver Cowdery, separated from the congregation by a veil, offered silent prayer at the pulpit. When they had finished, this glorious vision was given to them. (Statements in the heading and in this section itself suggest that this revelation came by vision. It is also true, however, that at least Moses, Elias, and Elijah had to appear in person because they conferred keys, which is done by the laying on of hands.)

TEACHINGS

Christ Accepts His Temple (v. 1–10): JESUS CHRIST appeared as a glorious, resurrected Being to accept the TEMPLE that had been dedicated to Him just one week earlier. The Lord repeated His earlier promise to manifest Himself in His house if no unclean person is permitted to pollute it (compare verses 7–8 with D&C 97:15, 17). The prophecy that "the fame of this house" would "spread to foreign lands" (v. 9–10) certainly has been fulfilled with the recent construction of temples worldwide.

Keys Restored (v. 11–16): Moses, who gathered the ancient children of Israel and led them to the promised land, restored the keys for the latter-day GATHERING (v. 11).

Elias restored authority related to the DISPENSATION of Abraham (v. 12). Available sources do not clarify the exact nature of the keys Elias brought.

Elijah's appearance (v. 13–16) fulfilled Malachi's prophecy (compare Malachi 4:5–6 with MORONI's clarified version in SECTION 2). The SEALING KEYS he restored are the power by which ordinances performed on earth are acknowledged or "bound" in heaven. The sudden increase in genealogical work around the world beginning about the time these keys were restored is often attributed to the "spirit of Elijah."

Concerning these events, President James E. Faust taught, "In the Kirtland Temple on April 3, 1836, Moses appeared and gave the Prophet Joseph Smith and Oliver Cowdery the keys of the gathering of Israel. After this, Elias appeared and committed the gospel of Abraham, that in 'our seed all generations after us should be blessed' [v. 12]. After this, Elijah the prophet appeared and gave to them the keys of this dispensation, including the sealing power, to bind in heaven that which is bound on earth within the temples [v. 13–16]. Thus, prophets of previous gospel dispensations presented their keys to the Prophet Joseph Smith in this, the 'dispensation of the fulness of times' spoken of by the Apostle Paul to the Ephesians [Eph. 1:10]" (*Ensign,* May 2006, 62).

Elder Jeffrey R. Holland said: "Then when a temple had been built to which other heavenly messengers might come, there unfolded on April 3, 1836, a modern-day equivalent of that earlier Mount of Transfiguration, part of something President Hinckley once called the 'Kirtland cascade' of revelation in which the Savior Himself, plus Moses, Elijah, and Elias, appeared in glory to the Prophet Joseph Smith and Oliver Cowdery and conferred keys and powers from their respective dispensations upon these men. That visit was then concluded with this thunderous declaration, 'Therefore, the keys of this dispensation are committed into your hands' [v. 16]" (*Ensign,* May 2005, 43).

President Joseph Fielding Smith wrote, "It is interesting to know that on the third day of April 1836, the Jews were celebrating the feast of the Passover, and were leaving the doors of their homes open for the coming of Elijah. On that day Elijah came, but not to the Jewish homes, but to the Temple in the village of Kirtland near the banks of Lake Erie, to two humble servants of the Lord who were appointed by divine decree to receive him" (*CHMR,* 3:78, 84).

Jesus Christ appears to Joseph Smith and Oliver Cowdery in the Kirtland Temple

Section 111

REVELATION IN SALEM

SETTING

The year 1836 was a period of economic distress throughout the United States, and the Saints in OHIO were not immune. Several thousand dollars were still owed for construction of the KIRTLAND TEMPLE, so JOSEPH SMITH, SIDNEY RIGDON, HYRUM SMITH, and OLIVER COWDERY went to New York City to seek financing. When an individual in KIRTLAND claimed to know the location of some hidden treasure in Salem, Massachusetts, Joseph decided to visit that city as well. At that time there was widespread interest in locating old treasures. Upon reaching Salem, their informant was unable to locate the anticipated treasure (for a further discussion, see (B.H. Roberts, *Comprehensive History of the Church,* 1:410–12). While they were there, this revelation was given.

TEACHINGS

Other Treasures: After reproving the PROPHET for his "follies" (v. 1), the Lord admonished the brethren not to be concerned about the DEBT (v. 5). Even though He promised that riches would eventually come from the city of Salem (v. 4), He reminded the Prophet that there were more treasures than one for him in the city (v. 10). Joseph Smith was therefore to hire a place where he could stay and preach to the people. He was also encouraged to inquire about the former inhabitants of the area (v. 9). In light of these instructions, Joseph Smith and his associates spent about a month in Salem preaching the gospel and visiting historic sites. The Prophet also looked into the Smith family genealogy, much of which was found in the immediate area.

Section 112

THE DUTY OF THE TWELVE

SETTING

This revelation delineated the roles of the FIRST PRESIDENCY and the Quorum of the Twelve APOSTLES and their relationship to one another. Early the previous month JOSEPH SMITH had called Heber C. Kimball and others on a mission to England, stating that this would be for the salvation of the Church.

TEACHINGS

Instructions to the Twelve: Thomas B. Marsh had become the original President of the Twelve when that group was organized in February 1835. The Twelve were to carry the gospel into the world under the direction of the First Presidency (v. 16–19); the Apostles in turn were to have authority to send out others (v. 21; compare D&C 107:34–35). The counsel given to Marsh and the Twelve in verse 10 is relevant to all who strive to serve the Lord.

Apostasy in Kirtland (v. 23–25): The years 1836 and 1837 were one of the darkest periods in Church history. Many blamed Joseph Smith personally for the failure of the Saints' bank (the Kirtland Safety Society), and a wave of APOSTASY affected even some leaders. For example, during 1837, FREDERICK G. WILLIAMS apostatized, and therefore HYRUM was called to take his place as second counselor in the First Presidency. This change was reflected in verse 17. Furthermore, on one occasion the Prophet's enemies, with pistols and knives drawn, sought to disrupt a worship service and to take possession of the KIRTLAND TEMPLE. Section 112 seems to have anticipated these developments. The mission in Great Britain, which opened on the very day this revelation was given, brought converts into the Church who brought new faith and vitality at this critical time.

Section 113

ISAIAH EXPLAINED

SETTING

Soon after the arrival of JOSEPH SMITH in FAR WEST, MISSOURI, Elias Higbee and other Church members inquired about particular passages from the book of Isaiah.

TEACHINGS

Stem, Rod, and Root of Jesse (v. 1–6): Like section 77, this revelation includes answers to the Prophet's questions on scripture. Jesse was the father of King David. Even though the "stem of Jesse" is clearly identified as Jesus Christ, it is not known for certain who the "root" and "rod of Jesse" are. However, many scholars identify the "servant in the hands of Christ" (v. 4) as Joseph Smith (see *RR,* 910–12; *CDC,* 4:97–100).

Zion's Strength (v. 7–8): Reference to latter-day ZION putting on her strength through the PRIESTHOOD has been fulfilled in part in Church programs that have placed greater responsibilities on priesthood leaders and quorums and by individual priesthood bearers who magnify their callings.

Section 114

David W. Patten

SETTING

During the summer of 1837, the citizens of Clay County, Missouri, asked the Mormons to leave in peace, citing differences over slavery and Indian policy. As a result, most of the Saints left the area during the fall of that year. About the same time, economic difficulties throughout the nation brought a real crisis in Kirtland. During the opening weeks of 1838, Joseph Smith and the faithful who were loyal to him fled from Ohio to Missouri. Both groups began settling at Far West in Caldwell County; David W. Patten, who ranked second among the Twelve Apostles, was a leader in this settlement.

TEACHINGS

David Patten, a member of the first Quorum of Twelve Apostles and a leader in the Church at Far West, was given counsel to prepare for his mission to Great Britain with other members of the Twelve. The group was scheduled to depart the following spring, 1839 (v. 1). David was unable to accompany the quorum on its overseas mission because he was killed in the Battle of Crooked River on October 25, 1838. Church historians often refer to him as the first martyr of this dispensation.

According to Wilford Woodruff, Elder Patten had requested such a privilege from the Lord: "David made known to the Prophet that he had asked the Lord to let him die the death of a martyr, at which the Prophet, greatly moved, expressed extreme sorrow, 'For,' said he to David, 'when a man of your faith asks the Lord for anything, he generally gets it'" (*Life of David W. Patten,* 53; see also *Wilford Woodruff, History of His Life and Labors,* 352).

Elder Heber C. Kimball remembered David W. Patten's concern for those who were not steadfast in the gospel: "Speaking of those who had fallen from their steadfastness, he exclaimed, 'O that they were in my situation! For I feel that I have kept the faith, I have finished my course, henceforth there is laid up for me a crown, which the Lord, the righteous Judge, will give me.' Speaking to his beloved wife, he said, 'whatever you do else, Oh do not deny the faith'" (*LHCK,* 213–14).

SCRIPTURE HELPS

"Bishopric" (v. 2): Here this term is used in a broader sense than we typically understand now, and means "office" or "calling" (note a similar usage in Acts 1:20 and Psalm 109:8).

Section 115

A Stake at Far West

SETTING

The PROPHET needed instructions concerning establishing the settlement at FAR WEST.

TEACHINGS

Church's Name (v. 4): The full NAME OF THE CHURCH was here specified by REVELATION.

Functions of Stakes (v. 5–6): The Saints were to be a light or example to the world, and their GATHERING into STAKES was to provide a refuge from the world's corruption, which would bring the judgments of God.

A Gathering Place (v. 7–19): The Lord directed His Saints to gather to CALDWELL COUNTY in northern Missouri. They were to gather not only at Far West, but at other stakes that the Lord would identify (v. 17–18). The Church was to build a TEMPLE according to the pattern the Lord would reveal. They were to begin construction July 4, 1838, and resume work after the winter season, on April 26, 1839, just one year after this revelation was given. In verse 13, the Lord cautioned the FIRST PRESIDENCY against going into DEBT as they had done while building the KIRTLAND TEMPLE. This counsel may have contributed to the Church's policy of not dedicating buildings until they are fully paid for.

Gathering Is a Defense for the Stakes of Zion: Elder Dallin H. Oaks testified, "Another sign of the times is the gathering of the faithful [v. 6]. In the early years of this last dispensation, a gathering to Zion involved various locations in the United States: to Kirtland, to Missouri, to Nauvoo, and to the tops of the mountains. Always these were gatherings to prospective temples. With the creation of stakes and the construction of temples in most nations with sizeable populations of the faithful, the current commandment is not to gather to one place but to gather in stakes in our own homelands. There the faithful can enjoy the full blessings of eternity in a house of the Lord. There, in their own homelands, they can obey the Lord's command to enlarge the borders of His people and strengthen her stakes (see D&C 101:21; 133:9, 14). In this way, the stakes of Zion are 'for a defense, and for a refuge from the storm, and from wrath when it shall be poured out without mixture upon the whole earth' [v. 6]" (*Ensign,* May 2004, 7).

Section 116

ADAM-ONDI-AHMAN

SETTING

This section was an extract from the journal of JOSEPH SMITH regarding his visit to various sites for settlement, including Spring Hill, about thirty miles north of FAR WEST.

TEACHINGS

Site of Important Conferences: This, the shortest section in the Doctrine and Covenants, records the fact that the Lord named a site several miles north of Far West ADAM-ONDI-AHMAN because of the great events that had occurred there and that will yet take place there (see D&C 107:53–57; Dan. 7:13–14).

Section 117

THE EXODUS FROM KIRTLAND

SETTING

Apostasy and bitterness resulted in a mass exodus of faithful Latter-day Saints from OHIO in 1838. JOSEPH SMITH left in January and the "KIRTLAND Camp," consisting of more than five hundred individuals, headed for Missouri in June. William Marks and NEWEL K. WHITNEY, who had been left behind to settle the Saints' financial affairs, had been negligent in their duties and needed instruction. After section 117 was given, Joseph Smith sent Oliver Granger, whom he had appointed to settle his own personal affairs, back to Kirtland with a copy of this REVELATION. Granger's integrity was respected even among non-Mormon creditors (see *HC,* 3:164–65). William Marks did move west as this revelation directed, and later became STAKE president in Nauvoo. Section 117 was the first of three revelations given at FAR WEST on this same day.

TEACHINGS

Oliver Granger Remembered: President Boyd K. Packer observed, "There is a message for Latter-day Saints in a seldom quoted revelation given to the Prophet Joseph Smith in 1838. 'I remember my servant Oliver Granger; behold, verily I say unto him that his name shall be had in sacred remembrance from generation to generation, forever and ever, saith the Lord' [v. 2]. Oliver Granger was a very ordinary man. He was mostly blind having 'lost his sight by cold and exposure' (*HC,* 4:408). The First Presidency described him as 'a man of the most strict integrity and moral virtue; and in fine, to be a man of God' (*HC,* 3:350). When the Saints were driven from Kirtland, OHIO, in a scene that would be repeated in Independence, Far West, and in Nauvoo, Oliver was left behind to sell their properties for what little he could. There was not much chance that he could succeed. And, really, he did not succeed! But the Lord said, 'Let him contend earnestly for the redemption of the First Presidency of my Church, saith the Lord; and when he falls he shall rise again, for his sacrifice shall be more sacred unto me than his increase, saith the Lord' (D&C 117:13). What did Oliver Granger do that his name should be held in sacred remembrance? Nothing much, really. It was not so much what he did as what he was. When we honor Oliver, much, perhaps even most, of the honor should go to Lydia Dibble Granger, his wife. Oliver and Lydia finally left Kirtland to join the Saints in Far West, Missouri. They had gone but a few miles from Kirtland when they were turned back by a mob. Only later did they join the Saints at Nauvoo. Oliver died at age 47, leaving Lydia to look after their children. The Lord did not expect Oliver to be perfect, perhaps not even to succeed. 'When he falls he shall rise again, for his sacrifice shall be more sacred unto me than his increase, saith the Lord' (D&C 117:13). We cannot always expect to succeed, but we should try the best we can" (*Ensign,* Nov. 2004, 86).

Temporal Concerns in Perspective: The Lord reminded the brethren who were settling affairs in Kirtland that He had created the earth and had power to help them with their temporal concerns. Oliver Granger, whom the Lord appointed particularly to protect the sanctity of the Kirtland Temple, was promised that his reputation "would be had in sacred remembrance" forever (v. 12). The Savior affirmed that Oliver's sacrifice would be more important than possible financial gains, "for what is property unto me?" (v. 4, 13).

SCRIPTURE HELPS

Olaha Shinehah (v. 8): The book of Abraham identifies "Shinehah" as the sun and "Olea" (perhaps related to Olaha) as the moon. The intent of using these words in section 117 may have been to remind the Saints that the Lord had created these heavenly bodies, so He had power to help them. This verse also emphasizes that there is ample room for the Lord's Saints in the plains named for these heavenly objects and in the hills of Adam-ondi-Ahman, which is the land where Adam dwelled, in present-day Missouri.

Nicolaitane Band (v. 11): John the Beloved declared that the Lord hated the doctrines of the Nicolaitanes (see Rev. 2:15). This ancient apostate group rejected the counsel of Church leaders, as did a similar group in Kirtland who wanted to profit from the Saints' distress (*CDC,* 126–27; *RR,* 930).

Section 118

Overseas Mission of the Twelve

SETTING

Earlier revelations had called the APOSTLES to perform an overseas mission beginning in the spring of 1839 (D&C 114:1), but a wave of APOSTASY had affected even the Twelve. There were now four vacancies in the quorum, so the PROPHET sought guidance in regards to filling them.

TEACHINGS

The Apostles' Assignment: The Lord had directed that construction on the TEMPLE in FAR WEST be renewed on April 26, 1839 (D&C 115:8–11). He now instructed the Twelve to leave for their mission from Far West on that date (v. 5–6). Of the four men called in this section to fill the vacancies (v. 6), two—JOHN TAYLOR and WILFORD WOODRUFF—later became PRESIDENTS OF THE CHURCH, while a third—WILLARD RICHARDS—became a counselor in the FIRST PRESIDENCY.

During the winter of 1838–39, the Latter-day Saints fled from Missouri under Governor Boggs' threat of extermination if they remained in the state. Non-Mormons openly boasted that these circumstances would prevent the Twelve from keeping the above commandment and, thus prove that Joseph Smith was a false prophet. But the Apostles returned to Far West at great personal risk, and early in the morning of April 26, 1839, they laid the cornerstone of the temple and then prepared to depart for their missions. It was on this occasion that Wilford Woodruff was ordained an Apostle.

Elder David B. Haight noted, "There is a spirit moving upon our people to want to live their lives in harmony with truth that they may someday respond to an opportunity to serve. This is the same spirit and heavenly influence that directed John Taylor, Wilford Woodruff, and others to take leave of the Saints from the city of Far West early on the morning of April 26, 1839, before departing for their missions to Great Britain [v. 4–5]. On that occasion each prayed in turn at the temple site and bore testimony. Then, after a song, they took leave, directed by revelation, filled with the blessings of heaven and the confirming influence of the Holy Ghost. These early Apostles departed for their missions having been spiritually fed and blessed in a manner that would sustain them and their families throughout their many hardships and inspire their powerful testimonies of the truthfulness of the message of the restored Church upon the earth" (*Ensign,* Nov. 1993, 61).

Section 119

THE LAW OF TITHING

SETTING

The financial troubles of the Church and the failure of the Saints to keep the law of CONSECRATION, led to this REVELATION on TITHING.

TEACHINGS

Tithing Defined: Those to whom this revelation was originally given had been living the law of consecration. For them, the "beginning of the tithing" consisted of giving their surpluses to the BISHOP as they had been doing under consecration (v. 1, 3). Since then, the law of tithing has consisted of giving one-tenth of one's "interest" annually or as earned (v. 4). The FIRST PRESIDENCY has explained that interest "is understood to mean income" (First Presidency circular letter, March 19, 1970). Elder Howard W. Hunter added: "Interest means profit, compensation, increase. It is the wage of one employed, the profit from the operation of a business, the increase of one who grows or produces, or the income of a person from any other source" (CR, Apr. 1964, 33–36).

President James E. Faust taught, "The law of tithing is simple: we pay one-tenth of our individual increase annually (v. 4). Increase has been interpreted by the First Presidency to mean income. What amounts to 10 percent of our individual income is between each of us and our Maker. There are no legalistic rules. As a convert in Korea once said: 'With tithing, it doesn't matter whether you are rich or poor. You pay 10 percent, and you don't have to be ashamed if you haven't earned very much. If you make lots of money, you pay 10 percent. If you make very little, you still pay 10 percent. Heavenly Father will love you for it. You can hold your head up proud' . . . Members of the Church who do not tithe do not lose their membership; they only lose blessings" (*Ensign,* Nov. 1998, 54).

An acquaintance of President George Albert Smith described how he planned to take the money he would normally pay in tithing and use it for various charitable purposes of his own choice, President Smith responded, "I think you are a very generous man with someone else's property. . . . You have told me what you have done with the Lord's money but you have not told me that you have given anyone a penny of your own. He is the best partner you have in the world. He gives you everything you have, even the air you breathe. He has said you should take one-tenth of what comes to you and give it to the Church as directed by the Lord. You haven't done that; you have taken your best partner's money, and have given it away" (*Sharing the Gospel with Others,* sel. Preston Nibley [1948], 46; see also 44–47).

The Lord's Law of Revenue: Verse 2 lists some of the purposes for which the tithes could be spent. In our day, tithing continues to be the dominant source of the Church's income; it funds the building of chapels and TEMPLES; operating expenses of wards, STAKES, and missions; the Church's educational program; and many other activities.

Blessings Promised: The Lord has promised great blessings to those who keep this law (see Mal. 3:8–10; D&C 64:23). Latter-day PROPHETS have taught that those who pay an honest tithing will always prosper. This does not necessarily mean immediate financial return, but it does mean that the Lord will bless the faithful with those things most important to their overall well-being. Because tithing is the Lord's law of revenue, those who pay are helping to build the kingdom and thereby share more fully in the blessings that His Church can bring. Despite these promised blessings, one should pay tithing primarily because he loves the Lord (see John 14:15).

Section 120

The Disposition of Tithes

SETTING

The brethren wished to know how to dispense the properties given through TITHING.

TEACHINGS

The Council on the Disposition of Tithes consists of the FIRST PRESIDENCY, the Twelve APOSTLES, and the Presiding Bishopric. These leaders are to handle sacred tithing funds as they are inspired by the Lord. Currently, the Budget and Appropriations subcommittees, consisting of the First Presidency, selected members of the Twelve, and the Presiding Bishopric, make specific decisions within general guidelines set forth by the Council on the Disposition of Tithes (see *EM,* 2:508).

Elder Robert D. Hales described how this council functions: "Then, as revealed by the Lord, the use of tithing is determined by a council comprised of the First Presidency, the Quorum of the Twelve Apostles, and the Presiding Bishopric. The Lord specifically states that the council's work be directed 'by mine own voice unto them' [v. 1]. . . . It is remarkable to witness this council heed the Lord's voice. Each member is aware of and participates in all the council's decisions. No decision is made until the council is unanimous. All tithing funds are spent for the purposes of the Church, including welfare—care for the poor and needy—temples, buildings and upkeep of meetinghouses, education, curriculum—in short, the work of the Lord. . . . The tithing of the members of the Church belongs to the Lord. He decides, through a council of His servants, how it should be used" (*Ensign,* Nov. 2002, 26).

Section 121

WORDS FROM LIBERTY JAIL

SETTING

The persecutions against and sufferings of the Saints led JOSEPH SMITH to plead with the Lord in their behalf while he was in Liberty Jail. For several years, Latter-day Saint settlement in MISSOURI had met intense opposition, and during the fall of 1838, difficulties flared anew. A series of attacks on outlying Mormon settlements led on October 25 to a clash between the Saints and their enemies on the banks of Crooked River; several lost their lives, including Apostle David W. Patten. Two days later, Governor Lilburn Boggs ordered that "the Mormons must be treated as enemies and must be exterminated or driven from the state." In this climate, a mob attacked Haun's Mill on October 30 and killed seventeen

Saints. The following day, Far West itself surrendered, and Joseph Smith and other Church leaders were taken as prisoners. That winter some 12,000 to 15,000 Saints were forced to flee from Missouri.

Meanwhile, the prisoners were "exhibited" at Independence, and were then taken to Richmond to await trial. Elder Parley P. Pratt described how one night the guards boasted obscenely of evils committed against the Latter-day Saints. Although chained, Joseph Smith suddenly arose and thundered: "Silence, ye fiends of the infernal pit. In the name of Jesus Christ I rebuke you, and command you to be still; I will not live another minute and hear such language. Cease such talk, or you or I die this instant!" The guards immediately ceased their boastings and begged the Prophet's pardon. Elder Pratt, in recalling his experiences with the leaders of the world, concluded, "Dignity and majesty have I seen but *once,* as it stood in chains, at midnight, in a dungeon in an obscure village in Missouri" (*PPP,* 211).

Following a preliminary hearing in November 1838, the prisoners (Joseph Smith, Hyrum Smith, Sydney Rigdon, Lyman Wight, Alexander McRae, and Caleb Baldwin) were transferred to the jail in Liberty, Missouri, to await a trial that never came. Throughout the winter the brethren suffered from inadequate ventilation, lack of heating, and poor sanitation; their food was grossly inferior, and they had nothing but the rough stone floor for a bed. It was in these circumstances that the Prophet wrote a letter to the Saints dated March 25, 1839, from which the material in sections 121, 122, and 123 was selected.

TEACHINGS

Joseph's Prayer and the Lord's Response (v. 1–25): The Prophet's prayer reflects the months of suffering that he and his associates had endured in Liberty Jail (v. 1–6). The Lord's answer put their suffering into perspective by comparing it to the greater suffering of Job and by assuring them that the reward for enduring these tribulations well would be exaltation in the celestial kingdom (v. 7–10; compare D&C 122:5–7). The Lord asserted that those who falsely accuse His righteous servants of sin are themselves guilty and will be cut off from the blessings of His temple and Priesthood (v. 17–22). Robert D. Hales affirmed, "There is meaning and purpose in our earthly challenges. Consider the Prophet Joseph Smith: throughout his life he faced daunting opposition—illness, accident, poverty, misunderstanding, false accusation, and even persecution. One might be tempted to ask, 'Why didn't the Lord protect His prophet from such obstacles, provide him with unlimited resources, and stop up the mouths of his accusers?' The answer is, each of us must go through certain experiences to become more like our Savior. In the school of mortality, the tutor is often pain and tribulation, but the lessons are meant to refine and bless us and strengthen us, not to destroy us. Said the Lord to the faithful Joseph Smith, 'My son, peace be unto thy soul; thine adversity and thine afflictions shall be but a small moment' [v. 6]" (*Ensign,* May 2003, 15).

The Prophet's Reflections (v. 26-46): Joseph Smith next shared inspired insights as he meditated on the Lord's response. Though written in a Missouri dungeon, the profound ideas and beauty of expression in these verses make these passages truly great literature. Joseph could see that the Saints had been blessed with unprecedented revelations through the HOLY GHOST, ranging from an understanding of the nature of God to insights regarding the motions of heavenly bodies (v. 26–32). One need only realize that the means of transportation and communication were essentially the same in Joseph Smith's day as they had been in the time of the Savior, and then consider the remarkable developments during the DISPENSATION of the fulness of times (compare Joel 2:28–29). In verse 33, the Prophet expressed the idea that it would be as impossible for men to prevent the Lord from blessing His people as it would be for them to stop the Missouri River or divert it from its course. Verses 34 through 40 warn that pride, materialism, and sin undermine priesthood power, hence "many are called, but few are chosen." Elder David A. Bednar explained, "To be or to become chosen is not an exclusive status conferred upon us. Rather, you and I ultimately determine if we are chosen. . . . God does not have a list of favorites to which we must hope our names will someday be added. He does not limit 'the chosen' to a restricted few. Rather, it is *our* hearts and *our* aspirations and *our* obedience which definitively determine whether we are counted as one of God's chosen" (*Ensign,* May 2005, 99).

Virtuous Thoughts (v. 45-46): These verses promise that the virtuous will not be ashamed of their lives, but that their "confidence [shall] wax strong in the presence of God," and that the Holy Ghost shall be their constant companion. Elder Boyd K. Packer suggests "If you can control your thoughts, you can overcome habits, even degrading personal habits. If you can learn to master them you will have a happy life. . . . Choose from among the sacred music of the Church a favorite hymn, . . . one that makes you feel something akin to inspiration. . . . Go over it in your mind carefully. Memorize it. . . . Now, use this hymn as the place for your thoughts to go. Make it your emergency channel. Whenever you find these shady actors have slipped from the sidelines of your thinking onto the stage of your mind, put on this record, as it were (*Ensign,* Jan. 1974, 25)."

President Henry B. Erying testified, "No priesthood holder who wants to succeed will be careless about where his eyes may go. Choosing to look at images which incite lust will cause the Spirit to withdraw. You have been warned . . . about the dangers of the Internet and the media in putting pornographic images before us. But immodesty is now so common that everyday life requires discipline—a conscious choice not to linger watching whatever might create in us feelings which would repel the Spirit. The same care is required in what we say. We cannot hope to speak for the Lord unless we are careful with our speech. Vulgarity and profanity offend the Spirit. Just as immodesty seems to be more common, so does vulgar and profane language . . . God helps the faithful priesthood holder who decides to see and say no evil, even in a wicked world" (*Ensign,* Nov. 2007, 55–58).

SCRIPTURE HELPS

Sheol (v. 4): Hebrew name for the dwelling place of the dead in the depths of the EARTH, often translated "hell."

Amen to the Priesthood (v. 37): If a man becomes unrighteous, his priesthood that he does not magnify will become a source of personal condemnation rather than a blessing for him. His ability to bless others through his priesthood will be impaired, and he will not normally be called to represent the Lord or the Church in performing sacred ordinances. If one's unworthiness is not known and those in authority should call him to perform an ordinance, the ordinance is still valid because the person performs it not so much by his own authority but, rather, acts as a duly appointed agent for the Church. The efficacy of ordinances depends more on the worthiness of those receiving than upon the worthiness of those performing them.

Betimes (v. 43): This infrequently used word means "promptly." When the Spirit directs us to do something, we should act without hesitation. Only in this way can needs be met or problems resolved in a timely manner.

Section 122

Trials for Our Good

SETTING

This section is another extract from the PROPHET's March 1839 letter to the Saints from Liberty Jail (see SECTION 121, "Setting").

TEACHINGS

Helpful perspective: The Lord's words recorded in this section build on those cited earlier in the Prophet's letter (see D&C 121:7–25). The Lord's words in verses 1 and 2 echo Moroni's declaration that Joseph's name "should be had for good and evil" (JS—H 1:33). The reference in verse 4 to the Prophet's righteous voice being more terrible than a lion recalls the experience in the Richmond Jail just a few months earlier (see heading for section 121). Joseph Smith had actually experienced all the trials the Lord enumerated in verses 5 through 7, and the Prophet was told that such trials would "give thee experience, and shall be for thy good" (v. 7; compare D&C 90:24). Elder Neal A. Maxwell taught, "Thus within the discipleship allotted to us, we are to overcome the world (1 Jn. 5:3–4); to finish the work we personally have been given to do; to be able to partake of a bitter cup without becoming bitter; to experience pouring out our souls; to let our wills increasingly be swallowed up in the will of the Father; to acknowledge—tough though the tutoring trials—that, indeed, 'All these things shall give thee experience, and shall be for thy good'" (*Ensign,* May 2001, 59).

The statement and pointed question in verse 8 once again put Joseph's trials in perspective as the Lord referred to Himself in the third person ("The Son of Man hath descended below them all. Art thou greater than he?"). The concluding verse in this section provided the ultimate perspective and hopeful assurance.

Section 123

PERSECUTIONS TO BE RECORDED

SETTING

This section is another extract from the Prophet's March 1839 letter to the Saints from Liberty Jail (see SECTION 121, "Setting").

TEACHINGS

A Record to Be Compiled: The PROPHET directed the Saints to collect accounts of their persecutions and the names of those responsible as a basis for petitions of redress (v. 1–6). He emphasized that this was the Saints' duty to those who had suffered and to future generations (v. 7–16). Eventually, these petitions for redress were submitted and now fill a volume of over 800 pages (see Clark V. Johnson, ed., *Mormon Redress Petitions* [Provo, UT: BYU Religious Studies Center, 1992]). Joseph blamed the persecutions on the spirit of the devil (v. 7) and on the "craftiness of men" (v. 12). After compiling these accounts, the Saints were to leave the matter in God's hands (v. 17).

Sharing the Gospel (v. 12): The Prophet asserted that "there are many yet on the earth . . . who are only kept from the truth because they know not where to find it." This is still true today. It is our responsibility to help them find it (compare D&C 88:81). Elder Jeffrey R. Holland encouraged, "We can also pray daily for our own personal missionary experiences. Pray that under the divine management of such things, the missionary opportunity you want is already being prepared in the heart of someone who longs for and looks for what you have. 'There are many yet on the earth . . . who are only kept from the truth because they know not where to find it.' Pray that they will find you! And then be alert, because there are multitudes in your world who feel a famine in their lives, not a famine of bread, nor a thirst for water, but of hearing the word of the Lord (Amos 8:11). When the Lord delivers this person to your view, just chat—about anything. You can't miss. You don't have to have a prescribed missionary message. Your faith, your happiness, the very look on your face is enough to quicken the honest in heart. Haven't you ever heard a grandmother talk about her grandchildren? That's what I mean—minus the photographs! The gospel will just tumble out. You won't be able to contain yourself!" (*Ensign,* May 2001, 14).

Section 124

Establishing Nauvoo

SETTING

About two years had passed since the Saints had fled from Missouri and began settling at what was then the small village of Commerce, Illinois. They named their new settlement NAUVOO, a Hebrew word meaning "beautiful." This was the first Doctrine and Covenants revelation received in Nauvoo.

TEACHINGS

Proclamation to World Leaders (v. 2–11): The PROPHET was to announce the establishment of a STAKE of ZION and invite the leaders of governments to treat the Saints with favor. Because of many delays, this proclamation was issued by the Twelve after the Prophet's martyrdom and published in England (*MFP* 1:252–66; see also CR, Oct. 1975, 46–49).

Blessings Conditioned upon Faithfulness (v. 12–21): Various individuals were called to assist in the work and were promised great blessings. They were warned, however, that they must be meek, hearken to counsel, continue to be faithful, and that they would be accountable for their actions. Unfortunately, some of these brethren did not endure in faith. On the other hand, the Lord paid a high compliment to HYRUM SMITH for his integrity (v. 15) and affirmed the blessed status of DAVID W. PATTEN, EDWARD PARTRIDGE, and JOSEPH SMITH, SR., three faithful brethren who had died (v. 19).

The Nauvoo Temple (v. 25–55): After calling for the construction of an inn for travelers (v. 22–24), the Lord directed that a second and more sacred building be erected—the NAUVOO TEMPLE. He explained that those who do all that is possible to keep His commandments but are thwarted by the opposition of others will not be held accountable, but the penalties of the broken law will come upon those enemies who prevented it from being kept. In this spirit, the Lord would not hold the Saints responsible for failing to build His temple in Missouri, but because of their good faith He would give them another opportunity by commanding them to build a temple in Nauvoo (v. 49–55).

One of the major purposes of building this temple was to provide a place where the Lord could come and restore "the fulness of the priesthood" (v. 27–28). Verse 39 lists some of the specific functions of the temple, including BAPTISM for the dead, ENDOWMENTS, washings and anointing, memorials (or records/reminders) of certain Levitical offerings, and oracles in holy places by which revelation comes. All these things were for the building up of Zion and her "municipalities" or units, such as stakes and wards.

In particular, the Lord reminded the Church that there was no font where baptisms for the dead could be performed (v. 29–30). Joseph Smith had introduced this practice the previous summer, and these ordinances were performed in the Mississippi River until the temple font was completed. The Lord warned His Church that these ordinances would be rejected if they were not being performed in His house by the end of a reasonable period of time (v. 31–33).

The "fulness of the priesthood" was restored most completely through the instructions and ordinances belonging to the temple endowment. The Savior promised to reveal to Joseph Smith "things which have been kept hid from before the foundation of the world, things that pertain to the DISPENSATION of the fulness of time. And I will show unto my servant Joseph all things pertaining to this house, and the priesthood thereof" (v. 41–42).

The Nauvoo House (v. 22-24, 56-82, 119-122): This building was to fill the need in Nauvoo for a hotel or boarding house. It was not merely to be a commercial venture but was to provide the opportunity to share the gospel with travelers who might wish to stop there (see v. 23, 60); the "cornerstone" they were to observe was the Lord's stake in that place (compare v. 2). Therefore, investors had to meet not only the usual economic criteria but were also to have a testimony of the gospel (see v. 119). The brethren were to form a "quorum" (not a priesthood QUORUM) or building committee to supervise the project. The provision that Joseph Smith's heirs were to have their place in the house forever (v. 56–59) had nothing to do with the idea of lineal succession in the Presidency of the Church but merely conformed to the policy that applied to all others who invested in this venture. (Notice how verses 69, 74, 77–78, 80–82, and 117 use the same language in reference to others.) Nevertheless, the promise made in verses 57 and 58 should be taken as a personal challenge by anyone who may be among Joseph Smith's descendants.

The Nauvoo House was not finished before the Saints were forced to flee from ILLINOIS. Many years later, the partially completed building was finished on a smaller scale than originally planned, and presently is operated by the Community of Christ (formerly The Reorganized Church of Jesus Christ of Latter Day Saints) as a hostel.

Scourge on Kirtland (v. 83): This curse began with those who professed to be Saints but were not faithful (see D&C 112:23–26). In 1979, Ezra Taft Benson, President of the Quorum of the Twelve Apostles, specifically removed this scourge as he broke ground for a chapel in Kirtland (*CDC,* 4:193).

First Presidency Reorganized (v. 91-96): William Law had been directed to preach in nearby towns and to assist in publishing the JOSEPH SMITH TRANSLATION (v. 8889). He was now named second counselor to take the place of Hyrum Smith, who was being released to accept two other positions. Hyrum, being the eldest son of Joseph Smith Sr., who had died a few months earlier, was called to succeed his father as PATRIARCH to the Church, according to the pattern set in Doctrine and Covenants 107:40. Hyrum was also to occupy the office of Assistant or Associate President held by OLIVER COWDERY before his apostasy. Oliver had been sustained as the "second ELDER" next to Joseph Smith in authority when the Church was organized in 1830. On December 5, 1834, following the organization of the FIRST PRESIDENCY, Joseph Smith set Oliver apart as Assistant President (see *HC,* 2:176). Oliver was not only to assist the Prophet in administering the Church, but he was to stand with him as the second witness of the Restoration, having been with Joseph Smith when the KEYS of the priesthood were restored. The Lord now called Hyrum to assume this responsibility—promising to show him the things of which he was to bear record (v. 94–96). Thus, the two brothers who gave their lives at Carthage Jail stood as the two presidents and witnesses to seal their testimonies with their blood. Joseph Fielding Smith suggested that if Oliver had not fallen, perhaps he, rather than Hyrum, would have been at Carthage to seal his testimony with his blood (*DS,* 1:211–19).

Unfortunately, neither of the counselors in the First Presidency heeded the Lord's words in verses 97 through 110. In fact, William Law would be among those conspiring against Joseph Smith just before the Prophet's martyrdom three years later. Sidney Rigdon rejected the instruction to remain with the Saints in Nauvoo so that he might be of greater assistance to the Prophet. At the time of the martyrdom, Rigdon had moved from Nauvoo to Pittsburgh.

Church Organization Outlined (v. 123-145): In the concluding verses of section 124, the Lord listed the various offices that were to be filled and for which rooms were to be provided in the temple. Blessings given by the Patriarch would help the faithful withstand temptation (v. 124). The President of the Church is a Prophet, seer, revelator, and translator (v. 125). The Twelve Apostles are a traveling council with responsibility to carry the gospel to the ends of the earth (v. 127–128). The quorum of high priests was to qualify its members to be standing presidents (v. 133–135). Elders are identified as standing ministers (v. 137), while the seventy are traveling elders (v. 138–139). The prefix "standing" refers to local Church officers, while "traveling" suggests responsibilities to the world. These leaders were to hold keys by which they might give direction to those bearing the priesthood (v. 123). Because they were given for "helps and for governments, for the work of the ministry and the perfecting of my Saints," these positions were all to be filled (v. 143–144).

Section 125

Iowa Saints

SETTING

After plans for the Nauvoo Temple were revealed, the question arose whether the Saints in Iowa settlements across the Mississippi River should move to Nauvoo.

TEACHINGS

Gathering Places: The Iowa Saints were directed to build up a community named Zarahemla across the river from Nauvoo. Saints gathering from afar could then settle there or in any of the stakes (compare D&C 101:20–22). It was from this Iowa settlement that Brigham Young and other members of the Twelve Apostles left on their mission to Britain in 1840 (see D&C 114:1; 118:4–5).

Section 126

BRIGHAM YOUNG TO STAY WITH HIS FAMILY

SETTING

BRIGHAM YOUNG, President of the Quorum of the Twelve APOSTLES, had just spent a year with his QUORUM preaching the gospel in Great Britain.

TEACHINGS

Church and Family Responsibilities: Following his extended time away, Brigham was directed to stay home with his family. As President David O. McKay counseled, "No other success can compensate for failure in the home" (CR, Apr. 1964, 5). As different priorities compete for our time, the Lord can direct us through the HOLY GHOST where we need to be and what we need to be doing at any particular time. An advantage of Brigham Young's remaining time in NAUVOO was that he could be close to the PROPHET and prepare to succeed him.

Reflecting on the message of section 126, Elder Neal A. Maxwell noted, "Obviously, family values mirror our personal priorities. Given the gravity of current conditions, would parents be willing to give up just one outside thing, giving that time and talent instead to the family? Parents and grandparents, please scrutinize your schedules and priorities in order to ensure that life's prime relationships get more prime time! Even consecrated and devoted Brigham Young was once told by the Lord, 'Take especial care of your family' [v. 3]. Sometimes, it is the most conscientious who need this message the most" (*Ensign,* May 1994, 88).

Section 127

INSTRUCTIONS ON RECORDING TEMPLE ORDINANCES

SETTING

During May 1842, Governor Lilburn Boggs of Missouri, who issued the extermination order against the Mormons, was shot and wounded.

The Latter-day Saints were immediately suspected, and Joseph Smith was accused of being an accessory to the crime. During August, some Missourians threatened to cross the river into Illinois and seize him by force. At this point, the Prophet went into hiding for the safety of both the Church and himself. It was in this setting that he wrote the two letters dated September 1 and 6, which are now sections 127 and 128, respectively. Performance of ordinances for the dead without any organization or record-keeping led to instructions in this epistle concerning baptism for the dead.

TEACHINGS

After referring to his persecutions and reaffirming his faith in God (v. 1–3), Joseph encouraged the Saints to continue the work of building the Nauvoo Temple (v. 4).

The Need for a Recorder (v. 5–9): The Prophet insisted that whenever an ordinance is performed, there should be an eyewitness present who could testify that it had been done properly. The object was to have accurate records in the temple archives. This subject would be developed more fully in the Prophet's subsequent letter (see Section 128).

Elder Dallin H. Oaks stated, "Witnesses and witnessing are vital in God's plan for the salvation of His children. . . . The most important ordinances of salvation—baptism, marriage, and other ordinances of the temple—are required to have witnesses" (*Ensign,* May 1999, 35).

Section 128

Further Instructions on Temple Ordinances

SETTING

The Prophet remained in hiding to avoid being seized by the mob from Missouri (see Section 127, "Setting"). This letter reflected his continuing interest in temple ordinances and work for the dead.

TEACHINGS

General and Ward Recorders (v. 3–4): In his first letter (D&C 127:5–9), JOSEPH SMITH emphasized the importance of having a recorder present when baptisms for the dead were performed, not only to make a record but also to be a witness that the ordinance was done properly. The Prophet returned to this same theme in his second epistle. The reference in verse 3 is the first mention of the "ward" in the Doctrine and Covenants. The appointment of a general Church recorder (v. 4) marked the beginning of the Church Historian and Recorder as a formal office. WILLARD RICHARDS was the first to hold this position, although OLIVER COWDERY and JOHN WHITMER had been called earlier to keep histories.

Recording and Binding (v. 6–9): The Prophet linked record-keeping to the power of binding and sealing on EARTH and having these acts recognized in heaven. He specified that for an ordinance to be valid it must be performed by PRIESTHOOD authority, performed in the name of Jesus Christ, performed properly, and recorded accurately (v. 9).

Baptism for the Dead (v. 12–13): BAPTISM is a symbol of death, burial, and resurrection. Therefore, immersion is the proper mode, and the baptismal font is generally located on a lower level of a chapel or temple in similitude of the grave.

Importance of Work for the Dead (v. 15–18): In stressing the importance of vicarious work for the dead, Joseph Smith amplified the meaning of several biblical passages. For example, Paul taught that the dead cannot be made perfect without us (Heb. 11:40); Joseph Smith added that we cannot be made perfect without the dead (v. 15), as our ancestors form the needed "welding link" (see v. 18). The Prophet also cited Malachi's prophecy that ELIJAH would "turn" the hearts of the fathers and the children to one another (Mal. 4:5–6) and indicated that this was sufficiently clear. On another occasion, however, he suggested that "turn" might be understood to mean link, bind, or seal (*TPJS,* 330). Elder Russell M. Nelson asserted, "Any discussion of family responsibilities to prepare for exaltation would be incomplete if we included only mother, father, and children. What about grandparents and other ancestors? The Lord has revealed that we cannot become perfect without them; neither can they without us be made perfect [v. 15]. Sealing ordinances are essential to exaltation. A wife needs to be sealed to her husband; children need to be sealed to their parents; and we all need to be connected with our ancestors"

(*Ensign,* May 2008, 7–10). On another occasion, Elder Nelson said, "Now, we are mindful of those not of our faith who are concerned about or even offended by the practice of temple ordinances for the dead. To them we say, our Heavenly Father directed the restoration of keys of priesthood authority and surely intended no offense to any of His children. Quite to the contrary. He intended to bless them. This doctrine and its ordinances are laden with love and are intended to perpetuate the sweetest of all relationships—in families forever. Nevertheless, the Church is sensitive to these concerns. The First Presidency has asked that, as far as possible, individual rights of privacy be protected. In 1972, they wrote, 'Persons submitting names for other than direct ancestors [should] have obtained approval from the closest living relative of the deceased before submitting records of persons born within the last ninety-five years'" (*Ensign,* Nov. 1994, 84).

Restoration of the Gospel (v. 19–21): As the Prophet reviewed some of the glorious events that had been part of the Restoration, he called on the people to rejoice. In these verses, he gave information about certain events that is not found anywhere else. The exact area where the Melchizedek Priesthood was restored is specified here. The voice of God heard in the Whitmers' chamber was part of the circumstances leading to the reception of SECTION 18. There is no other information about appearances of Michael (Adam). Perhaps the coming of Gabriel refers to the appearance of ELIAS in the KIRTLAND TEMPLE. The exact identity of Raphael is unknown. In our own day, Church leaders have often quoted and renewed the challenge given by Joseph Smith in the first part of verse 22 to "go forward . . . to the victory"!

A Worthy Record (v. 24): The Prophet challenged us as "a church and a people" and as individual Latter-day Satins to compile an acceptable genealogical record. In recent years, the Church (as an organization) has provided an unprecedented array of databases, while we as individuals or families are still responsible to compile our own particular records.

SCRIPTURE HELPS

Origin of Wards: Wards were a common political subdivision. Nauvoo was divided into wards for both political and ecclesiastical purposes. Even though there had been BISHOPS in the Church since 1831, they were first associated with ward units in Nauvoo.

Section 129

Angels and Spirits

SETTING

Satan's continued efforts to deceive the Saints necessitated these instructions by the PROPHET on how to perceive if an angel was from God or the devil. Note that this and the following two sections are identified as instructions given by JOSEPH SMITH rather than as REVELATIONS.

TEACHINGS

Identifying Messengers: The Prophet offered "three grand keys" (v. 9) for discerning the nature and origin of supernatural messengers. This revelation indicates that two kinds of messengers may come from heaven: (1) spirits of "just men made perfect" (v. 6), who are future inhabitants of the CELESTIAL kingdom, and (2) ANGELS, who are RESURRECTED beings (v. 5). Joseph Smith later broadened the definition of angels to include TRANSLATED as well as resurrected beings. Although messengers from Satan would likely want to deceive us, something compels them to respond in the way described in this section.

Elder Wilford Woodruff recorded in his journal the circumstances of how this revelation was received: "I spend the day in Commerce in Council with the Presidency & Twelve. We had an interesting day. Joseph was president of the Council. Brother Orson Hyde was restored to the Church and the quorum of the Twelve was in full fellowship by a full vote of the Council, after making a humble confession & acknowledgement of his sins &c. Among the vast number of the Keys of the Kingdom of God Joseph presented the following one to the Twelve for their benefit in there experience & travels in the flesh which is as follows: In order to detect the devil when he transforms himself nigh unto an angel of light. When an angel of God appears unto man face to face in person & reaches out his hand unto the man & he takes hold of the angels hand & feels a substance the same as one man would in shaking hands with another he may then know that it is an angel of God & he should place all Confidence in him. Such personages or angels are Saints with there resurrected Bodies. But if a personage appears unto man & offers him his hand & the man takes hold of it & he feels nothing or does not sense any substance he may know it is the devil, for when a Saint whose body is not resurrected appears unto man in the flesh he will not offer him his hand for this is against the law given him & in keeping in mind these things we may detect the devil that he deceived us not" (*WWJ,* June 27, 1839; 1:341; original spelling and grammar retained).

Section 130

INSTRUCTIONS BY THE PROPHET

SETTING

While on a short trip to Ramus, ILLINOIS, with the PROPHET, Elder ORSON HYDE delivered a sermon on 1 John 3:2, suggesting that the Savior will come as a warrior and that we would be like Him, having some of that same spirit. Afterward, the Prophet offered some corrections about the SECOND COMING (see *HC,* 5:323). These and other items are included in this section.

TEACHINGS

Personal Nature of God (v. 1–3, 22): These verses emphasize the personal character of Christ at the Second Coming and suggest that we will be like the Savior because He is a person. Unlike us, however, He is a glorified, RESURRECTED, CELESTIAL being. In verse 22, the Prophet gave what is perhaps the clearest single statement about the bodily nature of Jesus Christ and God the Father. These teachings agree with numerous biblical passages in which persons describe Deity in bodily terms (see Gen. 1:27; Ex. 24:9–11; 33:11, 21–23; Acts 7:55–56; Heb. 1:1–3).

When Will He Come? (v. 4–11, 14–17): The Prophet taught that God, like us, reckons time according to the planet on which He resides (compare Abr. 3:3–4). In verses 6 through 11, the Prophet deviated from the theme of the Second Coming to comment on the nature of the world on which God resides and the nature of our EARTH when it becomes celestialized. The earth will be like a giant URIM AND THUMMIM by which its inhabitants can behold inferior kingdoms; in addition, each person will have his personal Urim and Thummim by which he can see greater kingdoms—other celestial worlds in a more advanced state of progression. In verses 14–17, the Lord answered a question about the timing of the

Second Coming, which the Prophet had persistently asked about. Some critics have asserted that in these verses Joseph Smith taught that the Second Coming would occur in 1890 (he having been born in 1805), and that the failure of this "prophecy" to be fulfilled proved him a false prophet. To the contrary, the Prophet himself questioned that this referred to the beginning of the MILLENNIUM. The fact is that he did not live to be eighty-five years old, so the required conditions were not met. Some have suggested that if the Prophet had lived that long, he might have been able to prepare the people to receive the Lord, but this is mere conjecture.

Civil War Prophecy (v. 12–13): Joseph Smith referred to the prophecy that had been given in 1832 (see SECTION 87) and indicated that its fulfillment was still future. Notice that the Prophet was "praying earnestly" when he received the earlier revelation.

Intelligence (v. 18–19): The intelligence and knowledge mentioned in these verses may include worldly learning, but they undoubtedly go far beyond. Intelligence and knowledge from the Lord can be acquired only through obedience and diligence. Elder Joseph B. Wirthlin affirmed, "Knowledge is very important and one of the few things that accompanies us into the next life. We should always be learning. However, we must be careful not to set aside our FAITH in the process, because faith actually enhances our ability to learn" (*Ensign,* Nov 2004, 101).

Law and Obedience (v. 20–21): In order for AGENCY to exist, there must be law with known consequences for obedience or disobedience, and one must have the freedom to choose. Here the Prophet teaches the direct relationship between obedience to law and the blessings received. Elder Richard G. Scott testified, "But our Eternal Father defined truth and established what is right and wrong before the creation of this earth. He also fixed the consequences of obedience and disobedience to those truths. He defended our right to choose our path in life so that we would grow, develop, and be happy, but *we do not have the right to choose the consequences of our acts.* Those who willfully, consistently disobey His commandments will inevitably learn that truth. Joseph Smith was inspired to record, 'When we obtain any blessing from God, it is by obedience to that law upon which it is predicated.' Please understand, no one has the privilege to choose what is right. God reserved that prerogative to Himself. Our agency does allow us to choose among alternate paths, but then we are bound to the consequence God has decreed. Later, if we don't like where the path takes us, the only out is through repentance" (*Ensign,* Nov. 1992, 60).

Section 131

FURTHER INSTRUCTIONS

SETTING

JOSEPH SMITH was back at Ramus, ILLINOIS, about a month and a half after the instructions in SECTION 130 were given. Before leaving Ramus, the PROPHET gave instructions on PRIESTHOOD.

TEACHINGS

Divisions within the Celestial Kingdom (v. 1-4): This is the clearest scriptural statement concerning the internal structure of the CELESTIAL kingdom. Only those who are in the highest of the three divisions are "exalted" (see D&C 76:50–70; 137:1–4). MARRIAGE is an appropriate requirement for this reward because marriage is at the heart of what exalted beings do—begat spirit children to populate the worlds they create. Elder Russell M. Nelson explained, "ETERNAL LIFE, or celestial glory or EXALTATION, is a conditional gift. Conditions of this gift have been established by the Lord, who said, 'If you keep my commandments and endure to the end you shall have eternal life, which gift is the greatest of all the gifts of God.' Those qualifying conditions include FAITH in the Lord, REPENTANCE, BAPTISM, receiving the HOLY GHOST, and remaining faithful to the ORDINANCES and COVENANTS of the TEMPLE. No man in this Church can obtain the highest degree of celestial glory without a worthy woman who is sealed to him. This temple ordinance enables eventual exaltation for both of them" (*Ensign,* May 2008, 7–10).

The New and Everlasting Covenant (v. 2): The "new and everlasting covenant" is the GOSPEL of Jesus Christ as a whole. It is "new" because it has been newly restored in the LATTER DAYS, and it is "everlasting" in its effects (see D&C 66:2). There are distinct branches of this covenant, such as baptism (see D&C 22:1) or the priesthood (see D&C 84:40). Here, the PROPHET is specifically referring to another facet of the gospel, the "new and everlasting covenant *of marriage,*" meaning marriage for eternity.

Man Cannot Be Saved in Ignorance (v. 5–6): Some have supposed that these verses teach that secular knowledge is essential to salvation. It is true that in order to become as God one must have all knowledge, but when taken together, these verses suggest that the knowledge necessary for entrance into the celestial kingdom is a spiritual knowledge. At some point during our progression, all who will eventually be exalted must reach the point at which they have so demonstrated their worthiness that the Lord is able through the Spirit to assure them that they will receive the highest glory in the celestial kingdom. It is possible through living the gospel to receive this "more sure word of prophecy" and make one's "calling and election sure" while still in mortality, but many will receive this assurance hereafter (see 2 Pet. 1:10; D&C 88:3–4).

Elder M. Russell Ballard stated, "We cannot be saved in ignorance, but the Lord can only reveal light and truth to us as we are prepared to receive it. And so it is incumbent upon each of us to do everything we can to increase our spiritual knowledge and understanding by studying the scriptures and the words of the living prophets. When we read and study the revelations, the Spirit can confirm in our hearts the truth of what we are learning; in this way, the voice of the Lord speaks to each one of us (D&C 18:34, 36). As we ponder the teachings of the gospel and apply them in daily living, we become better prepared to receive additional light and truth" (*Ensign,* May 1998, 31).

Spirit Is Matter (v. 7–8): Some philosophies hold that spirit and matter are opposites. These verses teach that spirit and matter are of similar substance but are of a different order or degree of refinement. A resurrected body, for example, is tangible and yet more refined than a mortal body (see Luke 24:36–39). The difference in refinement may account for the contrast drawn in the scriptures between the willing spirit and the relatively weaker flesh (see Matt. 26:41; 2 Ne. 2:28–29).

Section 132

Celestial Marriage

SETTING

The heading states that this REVELATION was "recorded" in 1843. Some of its teachings were received as early as the fall of 1831 when the PROPHET was preparing the JOSEPH SMITH TRANSLATION of the Bible. He had asked if the ancient PATRIARCHS committed adultery by having more than one wife (v. 1, 41). This revelation was recorded at the request of HYRUM SMITH to convince EMMA SMITH that the doctrine of PLURAL MARRIAGE was true.

TEACHINGS

Celestial or Eternal Marriage (v. 1–25): Latter-day Saints understand that in order to be exalted and obtain godhood in the CELESTIAL kingdom, one must abide all aspects of the gospel, including celestial marriage (see D&C 131:1–4). Some have thought that celestial marriage was the same as plural marriage, but this is not true. In order for an ordinance to be a valid celestial marriage, it must be (1) a COVENANT for eternity, (2) performed by the authority of the PRIESTHOOD, and (3) sealed by the HOLY SPIRIT OF PROMISE (v. 7, 15); in other words, those involved must be worthy to receive the promised blessings. Elder David A. Bednar taught, "The Holy Spirit of Promise is the ratifying power of the Holy Ghost. When sealed by the Holy Spirit of Promise, an ordinance, vow, or covenant is binding on earth and in heaven [v. 7]. Receiving this 'stamp of approval' from the Holy Ghost is the result of faithfulness, integrity, and steadfastness in honoring gospel covenants 'in [the] process of time' (Moses 7:21). However, this sealing can be forfeited through unrighteousness and transgression. Purifying and sealing by the Holy Spirit of Promise constitute the culminating steps in the process of being born again" (*Ensign,* May 2007, 19–22).

Those who are faithful to the celestial marriage covenant are promised the greatest of all blessings—they may become gods and share in the fulness of our Father's glory. They are assured that they will come forth in the first RESURRECTION, being able to pass by the angels set to guard the way to EXALTATION. They will receive the blessing of "eternal increase," "continuation of the seed," or "eternal lives," meaning that they alone will have the power of procreation by which they may bring forth spirit offspring to inhabit the worlds they may create (v. 19–24). On the other hand, those who do not abide this covenant cannot be gods, but rather are angels or "ministering servants" to those who are exalted; they must remain "separately and singly" and "cannot have an increase" (v. 16–17; compare D&C 131:4).

Promise Misunderstood (v. 26): Some have concluded that this verse promises that all who are married in the temple will be exalted regardless of what sins they commit, as long as they do not commit the UNPARDONABLE SIN. President Joseph Fielding Smith, however, described verse 26 as the most abused passage in scripture and pointed out that it does not promise exaltation unconditionally. He declared that setting this verse in the context of all other scriptural teachings shows that these blessings may come only on condition of genuine REPENTANCE. Furthermore, those who will be exalted must be worthy enough to be "sealed by the Holy Spirit of Promise," which requires a level of worthiness even higher than that needed to receive a temple recommend (see *DS,* 2:94–99). Any sins committed by such individuals may be overcome only by thorough repentance, including suffering the penalties demanded by justice—the extent of which we cannot fathom (see D&C 19:15).

Plural Marriage (v. 30-66): Plural marriages cannot be adultery because the husband receives his wives by recognized authority (see v. 61–62). The Lord therefore justified the ancient patriarchs in their plural marriage relationships. For example, He had given David and Solomon many wives and concubines and they sinned only when they took that which was not given them by the Lord (v. 38). A concubine was not a mistress, but rather a wife of lower social status, such as the "handmaids" who became wives of Abraham and Jacob (see Gen. 16:3; 30:4, 9). The Lord explained that He instituted plural marriage so that His people could "multiply and replenish the earth . . . that they may bear the souls of men" (v. 63).

Section 133

"THE APPENDIX"

SETTING

At the 1831 CONFERENCE where the decision was made to publish the Book of Commandments, the Lord gave this REVELATION as the book's appendix. It was received a day or so after SECTION 67—a section that responded to criticisms of JOSEPH SMITH's revelations—was received. SECTION 1, "The Lord's Preface," was given around the same time as section 133; note the similarity of ideas in these two revelations. Because this section is designated "The Appendix," the 1876 edition of the Doctrine and Covenants placed it at the end of the REVELATIONS given through Joseph Smith. However, the 1981 edition added SECTION 137, which had also been given through the Prophet).

TEACHINGS

The Command to Gather (v. 1–15): This revelation was given to answer the ELDERS' questions concerning what they should preach. Verses 7 through 9 directed that the missionaries' message should be a call for GATHERING. For several decades, converts "gathered to ZION," or, in other words, actually left home to join the main body of the Saints in America. Today, the missionaries' message is still "gather," but more in the sense suggested in verse 14. This is a spiritual gathering out of the wicked world into the community of Saints who are building strong branches of the Church in their respective homelands. To stress the urgency of the gathering, the Lord next reviewed some of the great events to be associated with His SECOND COMING.

Geographical Changes (v. 22–29): Massive changes in climate and topography will be part of the earth's receiving its paradisiacal glory as the MILLENNIUM begins. Verses 23 and 24 indicate that these changes will even include the relocation of continents. Recently discovered evidence has led scientists to consider more seriously the idea that our separate continents were originally one landmass. In the midst of these great changes, the LOST TRIBES of Israel will return (v. 26–28). This will take place as part of the gathering for which MOSES restored KEYS (see D&C 110:11).

The Lord's Appearance (v. 38–51): The Lord's Coming will be a time of rejoicing for the righteous, but it will be a time of judgment for the wicked. Verse 41 identifies the presence of the Lord's glory as the source of the fire that will consume the wicked. Even the red color of his clothing will be symbolic of the judgments upon the wicked and of His atoning blood (compare v. 46–48 with Isa. 63:2–3).

Others Resurrected with Christ (v. 54-55): This list of those "who were with Christ in his resurrection" includes several who originally were TRANSLATED BEINGS: Moses, Noah, and Enoch and his city. These individuals could not have been resurrected before the time of Christ because He was to be the "first fruits" of the resurrection. Moses and Elias (or Elijah) needed to retain their mortal bodies (through being translated) so that they could bestow keys at the Mount of Transfiguration by the laying on of hands, prior to the time of the Lord's Resurrection.

"These Commandments" (v. 60-64): The "commandments" were the Lord's revelations about to be published in the Book of Commandments, of which section 133 was to be the "Appendix." Those who receive these things were and are promised ETERNAL LIFE, while those who reject them will suffer the judgments outlined in this and preceding revelations. In His "Preface," revealed at about this same time, the Lord described this book as a "voice of warning . . . unto all people" (D&C 1:4). The degree to which we heed this warning will determine our eternal destiny.

Section 134

Declaration on Governments and Laws

SETTING

This section, written by Oliver Cowdery on behalf of the First Presidency, was a declaration approved at the same conference that authorized publication of the 1835 edition of the Doctrine and Covenants. Hence, it fits chronologically between sections 107 and 108. In light of persecution and the apparent ineffectiveness of civil government in protecting the Saints, the brethren felt the need for clarifying the Church's stand, in order that it would not be misinterpreted or misunderstood.

TEACHINGS

Responsibility to Obey the Law: Article of Faith 12 states: "We believe in being subject to kings, presidents, rulers, and magistrates, in obeying, honoring, and sustaining the law." This statement is qualified somewhat in two Doctrine and Covenants passages. Verse 5 in this section states that the Saints are "bound to sustain and uphold" their "respective governments . . . while protected in their inherent and inalienable rights by the laws of such governments." Section 98, verse 5, requires not only that the law support basic rights and privileges but that it must also be constitutional.

Church and State: Both civil governments and the Church were instituted by God for the good of mankind (v. 1, 4), yet neither of these institutions should unduly dominate the other (v. 9). Nevertheless, there is not total separation, because religion may appeal to the state for protection (v. 11), and Church members must also seek and uphold wise and good men in government (see D&C 98:10). On the other hand, the state may not interfere with religious beliefs unless they promote practices that infringe on the rights of others or result in crime (v. 4).

Elder Joseph B. Wirthlin affirmed, "The Church maintains a policy of strict political neutrality, favoring no party or candidate, but every member should take an active part in the political process. We should study the issues and the candidates to be sure our votes are based on knowledge rather than hearsay. We need to pray for our public officials and ask the Lord to help them in making momentous decisions that affect us. Our beliefs regarding earthly governments and laws are summarized in section 134 of the Doctrine and Covenants and the twelfth article of faith. We should support public policy that coincides with these moral beliefs" (*Ensign,* May 1992, 86).

The United States Constitution, which was drawn up by inspired men (see D&C 101:80), includes three provisions regarding religion: (1) Congress (the national government) cannot establish an official state church; (2) Congress cannot infringe upon freedom of worship; (3) There can be no religious qualifications or test for holding public office.

While the state may inflict punishment for murder, robbery, perjury, and other crimes, the Church is responsible for dealing with those guilty of adultery and other "iniquity" (see D&C 42:78–87). However, the Church may impose the penalties of excommunication or disfellowship, but may not deprive one of life liberty or property (v. 10).

Section 135

The Martyrdom

SETTING

The Saints wished to know the circumstances surrounding the PROPHET's martyrdom. This statement, written by JOHN TAYLOR, was added to the edition of the Doctrine and Covenants published shortly afterwards.

TEACHINGS

John Taylor, who had edited the *Times and Seasons* in NAUVOO, was the ideal person to write this announcement of the martyrdom of Joseph and HYRUM SMITH for at least two reasons: (1) he was an eyewitness to the martyrdom, and (2) as a member of the Twelve he was qualified to assess the spiritual significance of the Prophet's contributions (see, in particular, v. 3).

President Thomas S. Monson testified, "In Carthage Jail [Joseph] was incarcerated with his brother Hyrum and others. On June 27, 1844, Joseph, Hyrum, John Taylor, and Willard Richards were together there when an angry mob stormed the jail, ran up the stairway, and began firing through the door of the room they occupied. Hyrum was killed, and John Taylor was wounded. Joseph Smith's last great act here upon the earth was one of selflessness. He crossed the room, most likely 'thinking that it would save the lives of his brethren in the room if he could get out . . . and sprang into the window when two balls pierced him from the door, and one entered his right breast from without' (*HC,* 6:618). He gave his life; Willard Richards and John Taylor were spared. 'Greater love hath no man than this, that a man lay down his life for his friends' (John 15:13)" (*Ensign,* Nov. 2005, 7).

Carthage Jail

With their deaths, Joseph and Hyrum Smith sealed their testimonies with their blood (see Heb. 9:16–17). Hyrum Smith had replaced OLIVER COWDERY as the second witness of the Restoration (see D&C 124:91–96).

Section 136

THE PIONEERS

SETTING

The call of the Mormon Battalion during the summer of 1846 prompted the pioneers to spend the winter on the Missouri River rather than pushing on to the Rocky Mountains that year. In January of the following year, President BRIGHAM YOUNG was already thinking about organizing the Saints for the trek westward. This is the only Doctrine and Covenants REVELATION given to the Church's second President.

TEACHINGS

Organization of the Pioneers (v. 1-16): There were to be leaders of tens, fifties, and hundreds, all under the direction of the Twelve APOSTLES (v. 2); the FIRST PRESIDENCY would not be reorganized until December 1847. Certain men were to be selected as "Pioneers" to go ahead and prepare the way for the main body of Saints who would be coming later (v. 7, 9). Because they would need the Lord's blessings, they were told to keep all His commandments and be pure in heart (v. 1, 4, 11).

Specific Counsel to the Pioneers (v. 17-29): The practical directions given to the 1847 pioneers are still relevant today (v. 20–27). The pioneers certainly followed the counsel to use music and dance to bring a spirit of joy (v. 28–29).

Persecution in Perspective (v. 30-39): The Saints needed to be tested in order to be prepared for "the glory of ZION" (v. 31). Specifically, it was necessary for JOSEPH SMITH to give his life to seal his testimony with his blood; this also allowed the wicked to exercise their AGENCY to their condemnation (v. 39). President Spencer W. Kimball provided this perspective, "During the winter of 1846–47, when the Saints were at Winter Quarters preparing for their long and difficult trek across the plains, my grandfather, Heber C. Kimball, for twenty-one years a counselor to Brigham Young, was one of them. During that winter the Lord declared in a revelation to President Young, 'My people must be *tried* in all things, that they may be prepared to receive the glory that I have for them, even the glory of Zion; and he that will not bear chastisement is not worthy of my kingdom' [v. 31]. Few miracles in our history exceed that of establishing our settlements in a desolate land no one else wanted and then making the desert blossom as a rose. Our people not only survived but flourished because of their *f*aith *and their* family solidarity. Our pioneer character was molded in the crucible of hard work, sacrifice, pulling together, and depending upon the Lord" (*Ensign,* May 1981, 79).

Section 137

JOSEPH SMITH'S VISION OF THE CELESTIAL KINGDOM

SETTING

By January 1836, two months before the dedication of the KIRTLAND TEMPLE, it was completed to the point that meetings could be held on the attic story. Three days after the SCHOOL OF THE PROPHETS had moved into the temple, the FIRST PRESIDENCY and others met at "early candlelight." Concerning this occasion, the PROPHET testified that the heavens were opened and he saw the vision recorded in this section. He declared: "Many of my brethren who received the ordinance [of washing and anointing] with me saw glorious visions also. ANGELS ministered unto them as well as to myself, and the power of the Highest rested upon us, the house was filled with the glory of God, and we shouted Hosanna to God and the Lamb. . . . Some of them saw the face of the Savior, and . . . we all communed with the heavenly host" (*HC,* 2:381–82). This section was added to the Doctrine and Covenants in the 1981 edition and would fit chronologically between SECTIONS 108 and 109.

TEACHINGS

Glory of the Celestial Kingdom (v. 1–4): Descriptions of the "blazing" throne of God and of "circling flames of fire" are consistent with physical brilliance, a characteristic of celestial beings (see, for example, JS—H 1:16–17; 30—32.) Saying that even streets have the appearance of gold adds to the glorious description of this kingdom.

Salvation for the Dead (v. 5-9): When Joseph Smith saw his brother in the celestial kingdom, he wondered how this could be, since Alvin had died before the Priesthood was restored and therefore had not been baptized by proper authority. This was a vision of the future: Joseph's father and mother, whom he also saw in the celestial kingdom, were still alive. Vicarious baptisms, inaugurated just four years after this vision was received, would extend the opportunity of salvation to those who died without hearing the gospel. The Lord affirmed that those who died without the opportunity of hearing the gospel would still have the opportunity to inherit the celestial kingdom (v. 7—9). This confirms that many who receive the gospel in the spirit world will inherit the celestial kingdom, thus clarifying that many but not all of such people would go to the terrestrial kingdom.

Status of Little Children (v. 10): They will have the same opportunity to earn their exaltation as though they had lived to maturity. Elder Joseph Fielding Smith affirmed: "Every privilege to obtain the exaltation given to mortals will be given to those who die in infancy" (*AGQ,* 1:59). President Thomas S. Monson quoted the Prophet Joseph Smith as follows, "'The mother [and father] who laid down [their] little child[ren], being deprived of the privilege, the joy, and the satisfaction of bringing [them] up to manhood or womanhood in this world, would, after the resurrection, have all the joy, satisfaction and pleasure, and even more than it would have been possible to have had in mortality, in seeing [their] child[ren] grow to the full measure of the stature of [their] spirit[s]'(quoted in Joseph F. Smith, *Gospel Doctrine,* 5th ed. [1939], 453)" (*Ensign,* Nov. 1998, 17). Then President Monson added, "This is as the balm of Gilead to those who grieve, to those who have loved and lost precious children" (ibid).

Section 138

VISION OF THE REDEMPTION OF THE DEAD

SETTING

As World WAR I was drawing to its close, President Joseph F. Smith was well aware of the many who had died during that terrible conflict. His own son, Hyrum Mack Smith, one of the Twelve APOSTLES, died unexpectedly at age 45. Furthermore, President Smith himself had been ill for some time and would die the following year. All of these circumstances must have focused his attention on life after death and on what would take place in the post-earthly SPIRIT WORLD. He was studying the scriptures in order to understand our postmortal existence better. This revelation is the only numbered section in the Doctrine and Covenants that was received in the twentieth century or in Utah, where the headquarters of the Church are now located. Like section 137, this revelation was added to the Doctrine and Covenants in the 1981 edition. Both sections 137 and 138 shed light on salvation of the dead, so their addition to the scriptural cannon was timely, coming just before an era of unprecedented temple-building activity.

TEACHINGS

To Whom Did the Savior Preach? (v. 18–30): President Smith's vision shed further light on Peter's declaration that the Lord preached to those who had been "disobedient." The Savior did not go "in person" to the "ungodly" or "unrepentant" (v. 20, 29). Rather, President Smith learned, the Master "organized his forces," authorizing righteous spirits to carry the GOSPEL message to those to whom he could not personally go (v. 28–30). This work still goes on, and faithful ELDERS of the present dispensation can look forward to continuing their preaching of the gospel even after they have left mortality (see v. 37).

Concerning those who accept the gospel in the spirit world, President James E. Faust stated, "The process of finding our ancestors one by one can be challenging but also exciting and rewarding. We often feel spiritual guidance as we go to the sources which identify them. Because this is a very spiritual work, we can expect help from the other side of the veil. We feel a pull from our relatives who are waiting for us to find them so their ordinance work can be done. This is a Christlike service because we are doing something for them that they cannot do for themselves" (*Ensign,* Nov. 2003, 53).

Bondage in the Spirit World (v. 50–51): Although we generally identify "spirit prison" as the condition of only the wicked, in at least one sense all spirits—both good and evil—consider their existence in the spirit world as a bondage. Hence, when the Savior announced to them that they would soon be resurrected, he truly was "declaring liberty to the captives" who had eagerly been looking forward to "the hour of their deliverance from the chains of death" (v. 18).

Speaking of Joseph F. Smith's vision, Elder Henry B. Erying taught, "He saw in vision what happened in the spirit world when the Savior appeared there between the time of His death and His resurrection. President Smith saw the joy of the spirits when they learned that the Savior had broken the bands of death and because of His Atonement they could be resurrected. And he saw the Savior organize His servants among the spirits to preach His gospel to every spirit and offer the chance to choose the covenants and the blessings which are offered to you and which you want for your ancestors. All are to have that chance. President Smith also saw the leaders the Savior called to take the gospel to Heavenly Father's children in the spirit world. He named some of them: Father ADAM, Mother Eve, Noah, ABRAHAM, Ezekiel, ELIJAH, prophets we know from the BOOK OF MORMON, and some from the last days, including JOSEPH SMITH, BRIGHAM YOUNG, JOHN TAYLOR, and WILFORD WOODRUFF. Think of the power of those missionaries to teach the gospel and to touch the hearts of your ancestors. It is not surprising that Wilford Woodruff said while he lived that he believed few, if any, of the ancestors of the Latter-day Saints in the spirit world would choose to reject the message of salvation when they heard it" (*Ensign,* May 2005, 77).

SCRIPTURE HELPS

"The Acceptable Day of the Lord" (v. 31): This phrase is undoubtedly related to references in the King James Bible to "the acceptable year of the Lord" (Isa. 61:2; Luke 4:19). Other modern versions translate this phrase as the "the year of God's favor." Hence, the Lord's authorized representatives are declaring to the inhabitants of the spirit world that the time has come when they are to enjoy the Lord's favor and his full acceptance on condition of their repentance.

Elias or Elijah (v. 45–48): The "ELIAS" who appeared on the Mount of

Transfiguration was known as "Elijah" in the Old Testament, and was the same individual Malachi prophesied would come in the latter days (compare Mal. 4:5–6 with Moroni's paraphrase of this prophecy in SECTION 2). President Smith emphasized that Elijah's KEYS, like the Savior's mission in the spirit world, were closely related to the "the great work to be done in the TEMPLES" (v. 48).

Official Declaration 1

"The Manifesto"

SETTING

Congress passed the first anti-bigamy law in 1862, but concern over the Civil War and Reconstruction delayed enforcement. In 1882, the Edmunds Law made it a crime to marry a plural wife (new PLURAL MARRIAGE) or to live with one (polygamist cohabitation). The decade of the 1880s was a period of very bitter anti-Mormon persecution, leading to the passage of the Edmunds-Tucker Law in 1887, under which Church property was confiscated and many Latter-day Saints were prevented from voting and holding office. In May 1890, the Supreme Court upheld the constitutionality of this law, and members of Congress were considering even harsher measures.

In this setting, the President of the Church, Wilford Woodruff, had a most difficult decision. His choice was not between obeying a law of God or a law of man, but rather between two divine precepts, because the Lord had commanded obedience to the constitutional law of the land (see D&C 98:5; 58:21). President Woodruff received a revelation showing him that if plural marriage continued, not only some, but all Church leaders would be imprisoned, and all the temples would be seized. Therefore, under existing conditions it would be best to suspend the practice (read President Woodruff's statements that were added to the 1981 edition of the Doctrine and Covenants, on pages 292–93).

Consequently, the Endowment House, an adobe structure on Temple Square that had been built as a place where sacred ordinances could be performed until the Salt Lake Temple was finished, was torn down during November 1889 when President Woodruff learned that unauthorized marriages were being performed there. For nearly a year, charges persisted that the Church was still sanctioning polygamous marriages. To answer these attacks, President Woodruff issued this "Official Declaration" or "MANIFESTO" prior to the October Conference in 1890.

Church leaders and non-Mormon officials agreed that new polygamous marriages would not be allowed, but that those who had entered plural marriage before the Manifesto was issued could continue to live with their families without fear of prosecution. Under these terms, Utah was admitted as one of the United States in 1896. In 1904, President Joseph F. Smith again upheld the principles set forth in the Official Declaration and stressed that the Church would not sanction plural marriages anywhere in the world. Since that time, a few small groups have gained notoriety by their practice of polygamy, but such persons are subject to excommunication from the Church.

TEACHINGS

President Woodruff's Statement: He emphatically denied that the Church was still sanctioning plural marriages. He then declared his intention to obey the law against plural marriage that had been declared constitutional by the Supreme Court. Hence, his advice to the Saints was to "refrain from contracting any marriage forbidden by the law of the land" (final paragraph).

Official Declaration 2

PRIESTHOOD TO ALL RACES

SETTING

Perhaps nothing has had a greater impact on the worldwide spread of the Church than the 1978 REVELATION received through President Spencer W. Kimball that extended the PRIESTHOOD to worthy brethren of all races. For several months, the GENERAL AUTHORITIES had discussed this topic at length in their regular TEMPLE meetings. Then, on June 1, 1978, after a three-hour meeting in the temple, President Kimball invited his counselors and the Twelve to remain while the other General Authorities were excused. He again brought up the question of conferring the priesthood on worthy brethren of all races. During the two-hour discussion, a wonderful spirit of unity prevailed. Still, President Kimball desired to know the will of the Lord on this crucial matter.

He invited his brethren to join him in solemn and fervent prayer. President Gordon B. Hinckley recalled: "There was a hallowed and sanctified atmosphere in the room. For me, it felt as if a conduit opened between the heavenly throne and the kneeling, pleading PROPHET of God who was joined by his Brethren. The Spirit of God was there. And by the power of the HOLY GHOST there came to that prophet an assurance that the thing for which he prayed was right, that the time had come, and that now the wondrous blessings of the priesthood should be extended to worthy men everywhere regardless of lineage. Every man in that circle, by the power of the Holy Ghost, knew the same thing. It was a quiet and sublime occasion" (*Ensign,* Oct. 1988, 70).

Elder Bruce R. McConkie added, "The Spirit of the Lord rested mightily upon us all; we felt something akin to what happened on the day of Pentecost and at the dedication of the KIRTLAND TEMPLE" ("The New Revelation on Priesthood," *Priesthood* [Salt Lake City: Deseret Book Co., 1981], 128).

TEACHINGS

Priesthood Blessings Extended: Citing the worldwide growth of the Church, the FIRST PRESIDENCY acknowledged that they had "pleaded long and earnestly . . . spending many hours in the Upper Room of the Temple supplicating the Lord for divine guidance." The First Presidency reported, "He has heard our prayers, and by revelation has confirmed that the long-promised day has come when every faithful, worthy man in the Church may receive the holy priesthood."

Elder Helvécio Martins of the Seventy reflected the feelings of those impacted by this revelation: "June 8, 1978, is no doubt an unforgettable day. On this day, priesthood and temple blessings were extended to all worthy male members of the Church. Memorable indeed, its impact affected the lives of uncountable multitudes—of millions who had full knowledge of its meaning and of many others who have not yet arrived, perhaps, to the knowledge of the full extension of its effects. On that date, the First Presidency announced to the whole world a new and special revelation of the Lord, which revelation was preceded by many prayers and much supplication for his divine direction. What great changes that revelation promoted in the lives of so many children of our Father in Heaven, and among them, my humble family in the city of Rio de Janeiro, Brazil. It seemed unbelievable. It was an unexpected event, never before dreamed of by those whom the Father in his perfect wisdom preserved until this day when they would be best prepared to respond to the serious requirements of this truly honorable stewardship, which is the priesthood" (*Ensign,* May 1995, 43).

The impact of this revelation was felt on both sides of the veil. Missions were opened in such areas as the Caribbean and in new areas of Africa. At the same time, temple ordinances could be performed for those in the SPIRIT WORLD regardless of race.

Like President WILFORD WOODRUFF's "MANIFESTO," this document is an affirmation that a revelation had been received rather than being an account of the revelation itself. Perhaps this is why these documents are called Official Declarations rather than being numbered sections.

A to Z

— A —

Aaron: The brother and spokesman of Moses, the Old Testament leader for which the AARONIC PRIESTHOOD was named (D&C 84:18; 107:1). When the Lord took the Melchizedek Priesthood from the children of Israel, Aaron and his sons were given the lesser or Aaronic Priesthood (Ex. 28; 40:12–16). On May 15, 1829, JOHN THE BAPTIST restored the Aaronic Priesthood to JOSEPH SMITH and OLIVER COWDERY (D&C 13). In addition, Oliver Cowdery received the gift of Aaron (D&C 8:6–7). This refers to his role as spokesman for Joseph Smith and the Church (*CHMR,* 1:52). Aaron was the spokesman before Pharaoh in Egypt (Ex. 4:27–31), and in a similar manner Oliver Cowdery was the spokesman for the Church.

Aaronic Priesthood: The lesser order of priesthood. The Aaronic Priesthood has particular responsibility in the "preparatory gospel," dealing with "outward ordinances" and temporal affairs (D&C 13; 84:26–27; 107:13–14, 20). See PRIESTHOOD.

Abraham: The son of Terah of Ur. Abraham was the Old Testament PROPHET with whom the Lord first established His covenant to bless all the nations of the EARTH (D&C 84:33–34). Because Abraham walked uprightly before the Lord (see JST, Gen. 17:1), the Lord made His covenant with Abraham and promised specific blessings to him and his posterity. This is known as the Abrahamic covenant. Elder Bruce R. McConkie explained: "Abraham first received the gospel by baptism (which is the covenant of salvation); then he had conferred upon him the higher priesthood, and he entered into CELESTIAL MARRIAGE (which is the covenant of exaltation), gaining assurance thereby that he would have eternal increase; finally he received a promise that all of these blessings would be offered to all his mortal posterity [see Abr. 2:6–11; D&C 132:29–50]. Included in the divine promises to Abraham was the assurance that Christ would come through his lineage, and the assurance that Abraham's posterity would receive an internal inheritance" (*MD,* 13).

In vision, the Prophet Joseph Smith beheld Abraham in the celestial kingdom (see D&C 137:5). The Prophet was also informed that Abraham has received his exaltation and now sits on a throne as a god (see D&C 132:37).

Adam: The father of all mankind. Adam is also known as Michael, the prince, the archangel, and the Ancient of Days (D&C 27:11; 29:26; 78:15–16; 107:54). His transgression in the Garden of Eden brought about the Fall, a necessary act that enabled mankind to come to the EARTH, an essential step in our eternal progression (D&C 29:40–42). In the SPIRIT WORLD, Adam—known as Michael—led us in a battle against Lucifer and the one-third of the host of heaven who chose to fight against JEHOVAH and our Father in Heaven (D&C 29:36–37; Abr. 3:27–28). At a place called Adam-ondi-Ahman in northern Missouri, Adam, at the age of 927 years, gathered his posterity and called the HIGH PRIESTS together, and there bestowed upon them his last blessing before his death (D&C 107:53). Prior to the SECOND COMING of Jesus Christ, Adam will once again visit Adam-ondi-Ahman and give an accounting of his stewardship of all mankind and the earth (D&C 116; *TPJS,* 157). During the MILLENNIUM of the earth, he will bind the devil and cast him into outer darkness (D&C 88:110–115). JOSEPH SMITH testified that he had seen Father Adam, along with others, in the CELESTIAL kingdom (D&C 137:1–7).

Adam-ondi-Ahman: The place in northern MISSOURI where Adam gathered his posterity three years before his death and blessed them (see D&C 107:53–56; 116; Dan. 7:9–14). In addition, prior to the SECOND COMING, DISPENSATIONAL leaders will give an accounting of their stewardships to Adam at this location; he, in turn, will then deliver up his stewardship to Christ (*TPJS,* 157–58). Adam-ondi-Ahman means "the valley where God talked with Adam" (*MA,* 69–70). The name Adam-ondi-Ahman was revealed to JOSEPH SMITH when he visited the area known as Spring Hill, in Daviess County, Missouri (D&C 116).

Agency: The God-given right to choose, knowing that we are accountable for our choices (D&C 101:78). Agency existed even in the premortal world (D&C 29:36). Our choices bring predictable results because God operates according to law, obedience to which will always bring blessings (D&C 130:20–21; 82:10), but disobedience to which will always bring punishment (Alma 42:22; 2 Ne. 9:25–27).

God's Law and the Principle of Justice

Our choice:	Obedience	or	Disobedience
A Condition of:	Righteousness	or	Wickedness, Sin
Which Results In:	Blessings	or	Punishment, Cursings
Bringing Us:	Happiness, Joy	or	Suffering, Sorrow
Ultimately Brings	Liberty, Eternal Life	or	Captivity, Death

Mercy cannot rob justice (Alma 42:25), but rather operates within the context of God's law. Someone who is willing and able may pay the penalties resulting from our transgressions; this Person is our Savior JESUS CHRIST. His ATONEMENT was infinite, so it completely satisfies the demands of justice. The Lord, however, requires that we show good faith in our desire to improve; therefore, He requires our REPENTANCE as a condition for our receiving benefit from the payment He has made. In this way, His mercy is not robbing justice.

Agent: Early Church officer who handled business affairs, particularly in connection with the law of CONSECRATION, under the direction of the BISHOP. This position was called for by revelation in May 1831 (see D&C 51:8), and ALGERNON SIDNEY GILBERT, a successful business man and partner to NEWEL K. WHITNEY, was the first person called to this position. He received the calling by revelation (see D&C 53) in June 1831, just four months after the law of consecration had been revealed in SECTION 42. In August, the Lord specified that an agent was to be appointed in OHIO for receiving money to purchase land in Zion (D&C 58:49). Newel K. Whitney, Gilbert's former business partner, was subsequently called to this position (D&C 63:42–45). After Whitney was called as a bishop, he was directed to appoint an agent to "take charge and to do his secular business" under Whitney's direction (D&C 84:113).

Ahman: The name of God the Father in the pure language of ADAM. Elder Orson Pratt explained that "Son Ahman" (D&C 78:20; 95:15) is the name of the Son, and that "sons Ahman" is the designation for the remainder of God's children (see *JD,* 2:342).

Alpha and Omega: The first and last letters of the Greek alphabet.

When JESUS CHRIST is called "Alpha and Omega" (such as in D&C 19:1), this is equivalent to referring to Him as the first and the last, meaning that He has all divine attributes. In one REVELATION (see D&C 95:17), this title was altered to incorporate Latin masculine endings.

Angels: Heavenly beings typically sent to EARTH to accomplish specific purposes. Different classes of angels may be linked with the different stages in the life of a spirit: disembodied (in the pre-earthly existence), embodied (during mortality, including TRANSLATED BEINGS), disembodied (following death), and re-embodied (RESURRECTED).

In elaborating on the teachings in D&C 129, JOSEPH SMITH pointed out that there are two classes of beings in heaven (see *HC*, 4:425):

1. "Angels," which are heavenly beings possessing tangible bodies either translated or resurrected. (Note that this is a more precise usage of the term *angel*, which is often used to refer to all heavenly messengers in general.)
2. "Ministering spirits," which may be either unembodied or disembodied. Because those who became sons of perdition on earth will not be resurrected until after the MILLENNIUM, and because those who were cast out with SATAN will never receive bodies (D&C 29:36–38), at the present time all messengers from Satan's kingdom must be spirits. (See the chart below, which lists the various kinds of beings.)

Types of Messengers	Spirit Only	With Body
Heaven	Ministering spirits of just men made perfect (unembodied or disembodied)	Angels translated (embodied) and resurrected (re-embodied)
Hades	Satan and his emissaries (unembodied or disembodied)	

Apostasy: The abandonment of a formal loyalty or the turning away from truth. An apostate is one who follows the path of such a course. He is one who "will not hear the voice of the Lord, neither the voice of his servants, neither give heed to the words of the PROPHETS and APOSTLES"

(D&C 1:14). Apostasy results when "every man walketh in his own way, and after the image of his own god, whose image is in the likeness of the world and whose substance is that of an idol" (D&C 1:16).

In the early restored Church, the Lord warned many leaders about their tendencies toward apostasy and gave them counsel to help them avoid it. Oliver Cowdery was told to "seek not for riches but for wisdom," "do not murmur," and to "stand by my servant Joseph faithfully, in whatsoever difficult circumstances" (D&C 6:7, 18; 9:6). Thomas B. Marsh was told "not to revile against those that revile" and to "govern your house in meekness and be steadfast" (D&C 31:9). Sidney Rigdon was admonished to "forsake him [Joseph Smith] not" and to "keep all the commandments and covenants" (D&C 35:22, 24). James Covill was told that he had rejected the Lord "many times because of pride and the cares of the world" (D&C 39:9).

Brigham Young encountered a group of apostates who were plotting against the Prophet Joseph Smith within the very walls of the Kirtland Temple. He declared, "I rose up, and in a plain and forcible manner told them that Joseph was a Prophet, and I knew it, and they might rail and slander him as much as they pleased, they could not destroy the appointment of the Prophet of God, they could only destroy their own authority, cut the thread that bound them to the Prophet and to God and sink themselves to hell" ("History of Brigham Young," *DNW,* Feb. 10, 1858, 386).

The Church teaches that not long after Jesus Christ's mortal life, internal rebellions within the early Christian community caused the primitive Church, led by the Twelve Apostles, to disappear and be replaced by many factions, each of which had pieces of the truth but not a fulness. This is called the Great Apostasy. More importantly, this falling away (see 2 Thes. 2:3) resulted in a loss of Priesthood authority. During the Great Apostasy, people were without divine direction from living prophets. Many churches were established, but they did not have priesthood power to lead people to the true knowledge of God the Father and Jesus Christ. Parts of the holy scriptures were corrupted or lost, and no one had the authority to confer the gift of the Holy Ghost or to perform other priesthood ordinances. This apostasy lasted until Heavenly Father and His Beloved Son appeared to Joseph Smith in 1820 and initiated the Restoration of the fulness of the gospel. In these latter-days, the Lord has promised that The Church of Jesus Christ of Latter-day Saints will not be overcome by general apostasy or be destroyed (D&C 138:44).

Apostle: This the highest office in the Melchizedek PRIESTHOOD. Each member of the FIRST PRESIDENCY of the Church, as well as the Quorum of the Twelve Apostles, holds this high office. The PRESIDENT OF THE CHURCH is always the senior Apostle—the man who has held the office of Apostle for the greatest amount of time.

An Apostle is assigned to act as a special witness of JESUS CHRIST. "The word Apostle, in its origin, literally means 'one sent forth,'" explained President Gordon B. Hinckley. "If that definition were stated to say 'one sent forth with certain authority and responsibility,' it would properly describe the calling as it was given at the time our Lord walked the earth, and as it has been given in our time" (*Ensign,* May 1984, 50). From among His disciples or followers, Jesus chose twelve whom He called Apostles (Luke 6:12–13). He sent them forth to preach the gospel (Matt. 9:37–10:10).

In the present DISPENSATION, JOSEPH SMITH and OLIVER COWDERY received the authority of the apostleship in connection with the restoration of the Melchizedek Priesthood (see D&C 18:9; 20:2–3; 27:12). Oliver Cowdery and DAVID WHITMER were assigned in 1829 to "search out the Twelve" (D&C 18: 26–29, 37–38); later, MARTIN HARRIS was added, so that all Three Witnesses to the BOOK OF MORMON held this responsibility. The Quorum of the Twelve Apostles was officially organized on February 14, 1835, from among brethren who had taken part in ZION's CAMP. The following month, SECTION 107 was given to instruct them and other priesthood officers in their duty.

Apostles are "special witnesses of the name of Christ in all the world" (D&C 107:23; compare D&C 27:12), "particularly of his divinity and of his bodily resurrection from the dead" (BD, 612). Concerning the source of this witness, Elder Boyd K. Packer reported being asked a question: Usually it comes as a curious, almost an idle, question about the qualifications to stand as a witness for Christ. The question [asked] is, 'Have you seen Him?' . . . I have not asked that question of others, but I have heard them answer it—but not when they were asked. . . . I have heard one of my brethren declare: 'I know from experiences, too sacred to relate, that Jesus is the Christ.' I have heard another testify: 'I know that God lives; I know that the Lord lives. And more than that, I know the Lord.' It was not the words that held the meaning or power. It was the Spirit" (*Ensign,* June 1971, 87–88).

In addition to being special witnesses, members of this quorum work under the direction of the FIRST PRESIDENCY in building up the Lord's kingdom and regulating and setting in order the various officers thereof

(D&C 107:33, 58). In this capacity, the quorum is called a "traveling, presiding HIGH COUNCIL" in contrast to "standing high councils" in stakes (D&C 107:33).

Concerning how the Twelve carries out its work, President Packer explained, "We now have means by which we can teach and testify to leaders and members all over the world electronically. But in order to confer the keys of authority in that unbroken line upon the priesthood leaders, 'by the laying on of hands,' wherever they are in the world, one of us must be there every time [D&C 107:21]. I am no different from the Brethren of the Twelve and the Seventy and the Bishopric with whom I have served for these 47 years when I tell you that the records show I have been in Mexico and Central and South America more than 75 times, in Europe over 50 times, Canada 25 times, the islands of the Pacific 10 times, Asia 10 times, and Africa 4 times; also China twice; to Israel, Saudi Arabia, Bahrain, the Dominican Republic, India, Pakistan, Egypt, Indonesia, and many, many other places around the globe. Others have traveled even more than that" (*Ensign,* May 2008, 83–87).

When the President of the Church passes away, the First Presidency is dissolved and the Quorum of the Twelve Apostles automatically becomes the presiding quorum, with its senior member becoming the presiding officer of the Church (see D&C 107:23–24). President WILFORD WOODRUFF taught that this pattern was inspired; it brings to the office of President of the Church the man who has the longest experience in the Quorum of the Twelve (*WW,* 561).

Atonement: In the gospel sense, the act of atoning or suffering for an act of sin in order to remove sin from the sinner, thereby allowing the REPENTANT soul to be reconciled to God. This reconciliation is necessary because of the physical and SPIRITUAL DEATH (Alma 42:7) that resulted from the fall of ADAM. By appointment (2 Ne. 9:6–13), JESUS CHRIST became our Advocate with the Father, pleading our cause—if we repent—before Him (D&C 45:3–5). The Savior wrought the perfect Atonement through the shedding of His own blood (D&C 76:69). He was the Only Begotten of the Father, with power to either retain or lay down His life (D&C 49:5); therefore, He had power over physical death. Because He alone never succumbed to sin, He was a sinless sacrifice, giving Him power over spiritual death (D&C 20:22; 45:4). The Savior voluntarily shed His blood in Gethsemane for our sins, but if we fail to repent during our days of probation, justice will have its claim and we must suffer even as Christ suffered (D&C 19:16–19). Lastly, little children are redeemed through the Atonement, so those who die before the age of accountability will be automatically saved in the CELESTIAL kingdom (D&C 29:46–47).

Authority: The permission given from God to man to act in behalf of God the Father or JESUS CHRIST in doing Their work. This can be received either through ordination to the PRIESTHOOD or by being set apart to a particular calling. JOSEPH SMITH was called of God and ordained as a prophet, seer, revelator, translator, and Apostle (D&C 20:2; 21:1). No one within the Church may preach the gospel or build up the Church unless he is ordained and it is known to the Church that he has authority (D&C 42:11). The authority is necessary to perform any ordinance of salvation (D&C 50:26–27).

— B —

Babylon: An ancient kingdom used as a symbol for worldly wickedness (see D&C 1:16). The Lord commanded His Saints to go out from Babylon and to GATHER into ZION (see D&C 133:5–7, 14), promising that all who remained in Babylon would not be spared (see D&C 64:24).

Baptism: The necessary ordinance for all those seeking to obtain a remission of sins and to become a member of The Church of Jesus Christ of Latter-day Saints. The correct method for baptism was revealed to JOSEPH SMITH: it must be done with the proper authority by one who holds the PRIESTHOOD and it must involve complete immersion (D&C 20:73–74). Immersion is used to symbolize ending and burying one's old life of wickedness, and beginning one's new life in Christ. The first baptisms in this DISPENSATION were performed by Joseph Smith and OLIVER COWDERY (they baptized each other) in connection with the restoration of the Aaronic Priesthood (JS–H 1:68–71).

To qualify for baptism, one must have faith in the Lord and repent. When we are baptized, we make a covenant with God that we will take upon ourselves the name of Christ, keep His commandments, and have "a determination to serve him to the end" (Mosiah 18:8–10; D&C 20:37). The covenant made at baptism is renewed each time we partake of the sacrament during SACRAMENT MEETING. After baptism, we can receive the gift of the HOLY GHOST to guide us in our daily lives.

Baptisms for the dead are also performed in this dispensation, as they were anciently (1 Cor. 15:29). This practice was revealed to the PROPHET Joseph Smith while in NAUVOO and taught for the first time in the summer of 1840 (see also SECTIONS 127, 128). It is important that baptism is performed for those who did not have the opportunity to hear and accept the gospel while on the EARTH.

Bible: A book of scripture and one of the standard works of the Church. "We believe the Bible to be the word of God as far as it is translated correctly" (Articles of Faith 1: 8). REVELATIONS in the Doctrine and Covenants sometimes refer to the Bible as "the holy scriptures" (see, for example, D&C 20:11; 33:16) The elders of the Church were commanded to use the Bible as the basis for their teaching (see D&C 42:12). By inspiration, the PROPHET prepared what has come to be known as the JOSEPH SMITH TRANSLATION of the Bible.

Bishop: An office in the Aaronic Priesthood. The bishop presides in (or leads) a ward, as a high priest. A bishop has many responsibilities. While serving as Presiding Bishop, Robert D. Hales stated: "The mantle of the bishop includes being president of the Aaronic Priesthood and president of the priests quorum, being a common judge in Israel (D&C 58:17–18; 107:68–75), being presiding high priest, assisting in temporal matters, providing for the welfare of the Saints through auxiliaries and priesthood councils, and being responsible for tithes and offerings" (*Ensign,* May 1985, 28). In addition, a bishop often conducts funerals and performs civil marriages where legal. Even though he administers temporal things, the bishop is also a spiritual leader with a special ENDOWMENT of the gift of discernment (see D&C 46:27).

Several REVELATIONS in the Doctrine and Covenants throw light on various aspects of the bishop's work. Under the LAW OF CONSECRATION in the nineteenth century, the bishop received consecrations, assigned stewardships, and maintained the bishop's storehouse.

The firstborn or eldest among the literal descendants of Aaron has a "legal" right to the office of presiding bishop, because Aaron and his sons were appointed to hold the KEYS of the lesser PRIESTHOOD. In the absence of such a person, a high priest may be called to serve as a bishop (see D&C 68:14–24; 107:15–17, 71–73). According to section 107, a literal descendant of Aaron could serve without counselors (v. 76).

A bishop actually holds more than one office at a time. For example, if an elder were called and sustained to be a bishop, he would have to be ordained a high priest, and ordained a bishop (both of these are permanent priesthood offices). Then he would be set apart as "bishop" or as presiding high priest of the specific ward. Therefore, an acting bishop actually holds three offices. In this latter ecclesiastical capacity, the bishop corresponds at the local level to the president of the stake and the President of the Church at their respective levels. When released, a bishop would still be a high priest and bishop, but no longer bishop of the particular ward; if he were subsequently called again to be bishop, he would not have to be re-ordained, but merely set apart in his new calling.

Bishops were part of the New Testament Church. Paul instructed that bishops should be married, "vigilant, sober, of good behavior, given to hospitality, apt to teach," and patient (see 1 Tim. 3:1–7).

The first bishop ordained in the present DISPENSATION was EDWARD PARTRIDGE (see D&C 41:9–10). He was called on February 4, 1831, just five days before the law of consecration was revealed. After Bishop Partridge moved to MISSOURI, a second bishop, NEWEL K. WHITNEY, was called in December of that year to serve in OHIO. He was to function under the supervision of Bishop Partridge (see D&C 72:2–8). This established the pattern of a presiding bishop supervising the work of local bishops. Orson Pratt explained that each of these were "general bishops," Bishop Partridge having responsibility for the state of Missouri, and Bishop Whitney being responsible for OHIO, NEW YORK, and Pennsylvania. (Neither presided over the other.) "By and by, after the Church of God was driven from the State of Missouri," Elder Pratt continued, "it became necessary to have a Presiding Bishop; and the Lord gave a revelation, saying: 'Let my servant Vinson Knight, and my servant Shadrach Roundy, and my servant Samuel H. Smith, be appointed as Presidents over the bishopric of my church. Here, then, is the first intimation that we have of a Presiding Bishop. Neither Bishop Partridge nor Newel K. Whitney at that time was a presiding Bishop. . . . But when Vinson Knight, in years afterwards, was called, it was his duty to preside over all of the Bishops that were then appointed" (Oct. 10, 1880, *JD,* 22:34).

Book of Mormon: An abridgment by an ancient prophet named Mormon of the records of the ancient inhabitants of the Americas. The Book of Mormon, one of the four volumes of scripture canonized by The Church of Jesus Christ of Latter-day Saints, is a religious record of three groups of people who migrated from the Old World to the American continents. These groups were led by PROPHETS, who recorded their religious and secular histories on metal plates. Within the pages of the book "are all things written concerning the foundation of my church, my gospel, and my rock" (D&C 18:4). The Book of Mormon records the visit of JESUS CHRIST to the people in the Americas following His RESURRECTION (see

3 Nephi). The purpose of the book is to testify that Jesus is the Christ (see Title Page, Introduction, and other front matter of the Book of Mormon).

MORONI, the last of the Nephite prophet–historians, sealed up the abridged records of these people and hid them in about A.D. 421. In 1823, the resurrected Moroni visited JOSEPH SMITH and later delivered to him these ancient and sacred records (D&C 2).

Joseph explained that the records were translated by the gift and the power of God (D&C 1:29). In addition, to the gift of translation (D&C 21:1), Joseph was given two stones in a silver bow—these stones fastened to a breastplate and were called the URIM AND THUMMIM. They were given to the Prophet to assist in the purpose of translating the records. The Urim and Thummim was also used to receive revelations in the Doctrine and Covenants—these included sections 3 and 6.

Joseph Smith was assisted with the translation by several scribes. The first person to act as scribe was MARTIN HARRIS from PALMYRA, NEW YORK. Before scribing for Joseph, Martin made a memorable trip to the East to show characters from the plates to several noted linguists of the time. This fulfilled the prophecy of Isaiah 29:11–12 about a "sealed book." By June 14, 1828, the translation had progressed to fill 116 foolscap (legal size) pages. Martin convinced Joseph to allow him to take the manuscript home to Palmyra to show to his wife Lucy, resulting in the loss of the 116 pages (see D&C 3, 10). Joseph and Martin were chastened by the Lord as follows: "How oft you have transgressed the commandments and the laws of God, and have gone on in the persuasions of men. For behold, you should have feared man more than God" (D&C 3:6–7). Joseph lost the gift to translate for a short time, and Martin lost the privilege to write for Joseph. In the mean time, the Lord had prepared another to replace Martin—his name was OLIVER COWDERY. Oliver proved a faithful and reliable scribe until the completion of the translation in July 1829 (D&C 6, 8, 9).

As a testimony of the truthfulness of the Book of Mormon the Lord called witnesses to testify of the book. Three men, Oliver Cowdery, DAVID WHITMER, and Martin Harris, were given a special witness of the Book of Mormon (2 Ne. 27:12–14; D&C 5:11; 17:1–9). In addition, to the Three Witnesses, eight other witnesses—faithful men who were close to the Prophet during the translation—were chosen to see the plates. These witnesses' testimonies can be read in the front matter of the Book of Mormon.

Certain events associated with the publication of the Book of Mormon are a testimony of the tender mercies of the Lord, who prepared many of the individuals involved. After contacting publishers in Rochester, New York, and upper Canada, Joseph contracted E. B. Grandin of Palmyra, New York, to publish five thousand copies for $3,000. After the printing of the Book of Mormon began, many citizens of Palmyra protested, promising to boycott (refuse to buy) the book. Fearing that he would not be paid for his work, Grandin halted the printing process. A revelation from the Lord commanded Martin Harris to impart freely of his property for the printing of the Book of Mormon (D&C 19:26). Martin gave a promissory note to Grandin that mortgaged one-third of his three-hundred-acre farm, and the printing of the book resumed. On March 26, 1830, the Book of Mormon was posted for public sale.

Concerning this record, the Prophet Joseph Smith, who translated it by the gift and power of God, said: "I told the brethren that the Book of Mormon was the most correct of any book on earth, and the keystone of our religion, and a man would get nearer to God by abiding by its precepts, than by any other book" (see Introduction, Book of Mormon).

President Gordon B. Hinckley declared: "I believe in the Book of Mormon as another witness of the Son of God. This book has come forth as an added testimony to the world of the great truths concerning the Master as set forth in the Bible. The Bible is the testament of the Old World. The Book of Mormon is the testament of the New World, and they go hand in hand in testimony of the Lord Jesus Christ. I can't understand why those of other faiths cannot accept the Book of Mormon. One would think that they would be looking for additional witnesses to the great and solemn truths of the Bible. We have that witness, my brothers and sisters, this marvelous book of inspiration which affirms the validity and the truth of the divine nature of the Son of God. God be thanked for this precious and wonderful testimony. Let us read it. Let us dwell upon its truths. Let us learn its message and be blessed accordingly" (*Ensign,* June 2000, 18–19).

President James E. Faust testified, "A keystone keeps an arch in place; without a keystone the whole arch will collapse. Why is the Book of Mormon the keystone of our religion? Because it is central to our history and theology. It is the text for this dispensation. Nothing took priority over getting the Book of Mormon translated and published. Everything was held until that was accomplished. There were no Apostles until it came into being. Ten days after the book's publication the Church was organized. Publication of the Book of Mormon preceded missionary work because Samuel Smith needed to have it in hand before he could go forward as the first missionary of the Church. Sections 17 and 20 of the

Doctrine and Covenants indicate that the Brethren could not fully know the divinity of the latter-day work until the Book of Mormon was translated. . . . May our testimonies ring forth with power and authority and conviction concerning Joseph Smith, the greatest prophet who has ever lived, and concerning the Book of Mormon, which he brought forth" (*Ensign,* Jan. 1996, 7).

Lastly, Jesus Christ Himself bore testimony that the Book of Mormon is true: "And he [Joseph Smith] has translated the book even that part which I have commanded him, and as your Lord and your God liveth it is true" (D&C 17:6).

Booth, Ezra: An early apostate. He was one of several ELDERS called to preach the gospel as he traveled to the land of MISSOURI to be an eyewitness to the establishment of the Church in JACKSON COUNTY (D&C 52:23). Unfortunately, soon after his mission, Booth lost his FAITH. He was rebuked by the Lord for failure to keep the law and the commandments (D&C 64:15) and later APOSTATIZED and turned against the Church. Booth was rebuked by the Lord for failure to keep the law and the commandments (D&C 64:15). He was responsible for liable articles published in a local paper that created a bitter spirit against the Church. To prevent Booth's slanderous attacks from hindering the Church and the preaching of the true gospel, JOSEPH SMITH and SIDNEY RIGDON were called on a mission to refute the falsehoods (D&C 71).

Branch: A small, local congregation of the Church. As the term suggests, a *branch* is often an offshoot of a larger entity. When members in one congregation share the gospel with friends or family members in nearby areas, the latter eventually break off and form a separate unit of their own. In some early revelations, these branches were called "churches"; see for example SECTION 24:3 and 51:10–11. Today *branch* is the designation for a congregation in a mission district. In STAKES, *branch* designates a congregation that is less completely organized and typically smaller than a ward. A branch is led by a branch president, who is a Melchizedek PRIESTHOOD holder.

— C —

Caldwell County, Missouri: Created in the mid 1830s for the homeless Saints expelled from JACKSON COUNTY in 1833. By 1838, 4,000 to 5,000 members of the Church lived in the community of FAR WEST, making this the largest community in Caldwell County. Far West was the headquarters for the Church for a brief period of time in 1838. In addition, seven Doctrine and Covenants revelations (D&C 113–115, 117–120) were received here and a temple site was dedicated. Shortly after the Saints' expulsion from Caldwell County in 1839, members of the Quorum of the Twelve Apostles returned at great personal risk, met at the temple site, and departed on their missions to England from this county (D&C 118:4–5).

Carter, Jared: An early convert who served as a member of the high councils in Kirtland, Ohio, and Far West, Missouri (D&C 102:3). Carter is mentioned several times in the Doctrine and Covenants. Born January 14, 1801, in Benson, Vermont, he was baptized in February 1831 by Hyrum Smith. His ordination as a priest was directed in D&C 52:38. In the revelation now known as section 79, Carter was called on a mission to the "eastern countries," where he was quite successful, establishing the Church's first branches in Vermont and Michigan. He served on the Kirtland building committee (D&C 94:14–15) but eventually fell away from the Church and died in Illinois during the 1850s (*WWDC,* 51–54).

Celestial: A word that means "heavenly," suggesting the highest or best. The celestial kingdom is where God dwells and is therefore the goal of all who want to return to His presence. Its glory is compared to the dazzling light of the sun (D&C 76:70). The earth will ultimately be a celestial sphere, which John the Revelator likened to a "sea of glass" (Rev. 4:6; D&C 77:1). The celestialized earth has also been referred to as a giant Urim and Thummim (D&C 130:8–10). Joseph Smith saw the celestial kingdom in vision and described its gates as "circling flames of fire" and its streets as having the "appearance of being paved with gold." In its midst was the "blazing throne of God" (D&C 137:2–4).

"In the celestial glory there are three heavens or degrees" (D&C 131:1). In the highest of these are found those who have attained exaltation. To achieve exaltation, one must be valiant in the testimony of Christ and in keeping all the commandments, including that of celestial or eternal marriage (D&C 131:2–4). The descriptions of celestial glory in section 76 seem to focus on this highest level. Those who receive exaltation are gods, and all things are theirs. Having received of God's fulness, they are equal in power and dominion (see 78:58–59, 94–95).

"In contrast to traditional Christianity," noted Elder Dallin H. Oaks, "we join with Paul in affirming the existence of a third or higher heaven. Modern revelation describes it as the celestial kingdom—the abode of those 'whose bodies are celestial, whose glory is that of the sun, even the glory of God' (D&C 76:70). Those who qualify for this kingdom of glory 'shall dwell in the presence of God and his Christ forever and ever' (D&C 76:62). Those who have met the highest requirements for this kingdom, including faithfulness to covenants made in a temple of God and marriage for eternity, will be exalted to the godlike state referred to as the 'fulness' of the Father or eternal life (D&C 76:56, 94; see also D&C 131:1–4; 132:19–20). For us, eternal life is not a mystical union with an incomprehensible spirit-god. Eternal life is family life with a loving Father in Heaven and with our progenitors and our posterity" (*Ensign,* May 1995, 84).

Those who will enter the celestial kingdom must abide a celestial law even as the earth itself is doing (see D&C 88:22, 25–26). Those who live this law will receive a celestial body in the RESURRECTION (D&C 88:28–29). They will come forth in the morning of the first resurrection (D&C 88:97–98). The nature of the celestial law was suggested by the Master in His Sermon on the Mount when He contrasted the traditional standards of no killing and no adultery with His higher expectations of no anger and no lustful thoughts (see Matt. 5:21–22, 27–28). The celestial law is also the basis for establishing ZION (D&C 105:5).

Church Discipline: Designed to help sinners REPENT and at the same time protect the Church's reputation and members. The Lord commanded that Church discipline be done confidentially wherever possible (see D&C 42:88–92). Often, this involves convening DISCIPLINARY COUNCILS. Elder Neal and Maxwell taught, "All sins are to be confessed to the Lord, some to a Church official, some to others, and some to all of these. A few may require public confession. Confessing aids forsaking. We cannot expect to sin publicly and extensively and then expect to be rescued privately and quickly, being beaten 'with only a few stripes'" *(Ensign,* Nov. 1991, 30).

Church Historian: Responsible for keeping an accurate record of events and developments, as well as of ordinances performed. The first commandment the Lord gave the Church was to keep a history. Elder Marlin K. Jensen, Church historian, taught, "I suggest that the history of the Church of Jesus Christ and its people deserves our remembrance. The scriptures give the Church's history high priority. In fact, much of scripture is Church history. On the very day the Church was organized, God commanded Joseph Smith, 'Behold, there shall be a record kept among you' [D&C 21:1]. Joseph acted on this command by appointing Oliver Cowdery, the second elder in the Church and his chief assistant, as the first Church historian" (*Ensign,* May 2007, 36–38).

As Oliver's other duties increased, this calling was given to John Whitmer. He was promised that if he was faithful, the Comforter would direct him in what he should write (D&C 47:4). The history was to be written "for the good of the Church, and for the rising generations" (D&C 69:8).

When temple ordinances were introduced, Joseph Smith instructed that there should be a recorder present. He was to "testify" as an "eye-witness" so that the ordinances could be recorded and bound in heaven as well as on earth (D&C 127:6–7). The prophet also specified that there should be such a recorder in each ward as well as a general recorder for the whole Church (D&C 128:3–4). Eventually the responsibilities of recorder and historian were combined in the office of Church historian and general Church recorder. The first person to occupy this office was Willard Richards.

Elder Marlin K. Jensen stated, "We keep records to help us remember, and a record of the Church's rise and progress has been kept from Oliver Cowdery's time to the present day. This extraordinary historical record reminds us that God has again opened the heavens and revealed truths that call our generation to action" (*Ensign,* May 2007, 36–38).

Church, Name of: See name of the Church.

Clay County, Missouri: Where the beleaguered Saints were harbored for two and a half years in the early 1830s, as they tried to negotiate a return to their homes in Jackson County. Failing to be reestablished in their homes, the Saints moved north to Daviess and Caldwell Counties. In 1838 at Liberty, the county seat, Joseph Smith and others languished in jail for several months. While in Liberty Jail, Joseph Smith received three revelations (D&C 121, 122, and 123).

Colesville, New York: The home of Joseph Knight Sr., an early convert. Colesville, now known as Nineveh, together with Fayette and Palmyra, New York, were the three most important branches in the early Church. Consequently, Colesville was a place where a number of firsts occurred in the Church. Here, the first branch of the Church was organized. The first miracle of the Church took place in Colesville when an evil spirit was cast out of Newel Knight by the Prophet JOSEPH SMITH. In Colesville, for the first time of many, Joseph Smith was arrested, charged, tried, and acquitted for disorderly conduct. EMMA SMITH and others were baptized at this location. When the revelation was give to gather the Church to OHIO (D&C 37), the Colesville branch, under the direction of Newel Knight, responded en masse and settled at Thompson (just east of KIRTLAND).

Comforter: A title by which the HOLY GHOST is known. This is an appropriate title because "the Holy Ghost, even the Comforter . . . [showeth] all things and teacheth the peaceable things of the kingdom" (D&C 39:6). Furthermore, the testimony we have of Heavenly Father's plan and our place in it is a source of assurance and comfort (see HOLY GHOST).

Common Consent: The means by which Church officers are appointed and decisions made in the Church. There are three steps to this process: first, an individual is called through prayerful revelation to a position within the Church (Articles of Faith 5). Second, Church members are presented with the name and asked to sustain that person in the calling (D&C 20:65). Finally, if the sustaining vote is unanimous in the affirmative, the individual is ordained or set apart to that calling by one holding the proper PRIESTHOOD authority. Notice how all three of these steps were to be incorporated into the calling of EDWARD PARTRIDGE as the Church's first BISHOP (D&C 41:9). Unlike worldly elections, we don't have time to research all the candidates for Church office, so sustaining votes should be made "by much prayer and faith" (D&C 26:2; compare 28:13). When we vote to sustain a person, we should commit ourselves to actually support the individual in the calling. Common consent represents the order the Lord would have in His Church and promotes unity among Church members. President Boyd K. Packer explained: "This common procedure occurs whenever leaders or teachers are called or released from office or whenever there is reorganization in a stake or a ward or a quorum or in the auxiliaries. It is unique to The Church of Jesus Christ of Latter-day Saints. We always know who is called to lead or to teach and have the opportunity to sustain or to oppose the action. It did not come as an invention of man but was set out in the revelations: 'It shall not be given to any one to go forth to preach my gospel, or to build up my church, except he be ordained by someone who has authority, and *it is known to the Church* that he has authority and has been regularly ordained by the heads of the Church.' In this way, the Church is protected from any imposter who would take over a quorum, a ward, a stake, or the Church" (*Ensign,* Nov. 2007, 6–9).

Confer: To bestow or give. The word *confer* is used when bestowing the Aaronic or Melchizedek PRIESTHOOD (see D&C 13). *Confer* should be distinguished from *confirm,* which refers to Church membership following BAPTISM; *confer* is also distinct from *ordain,* which today refers to installing one in a particular priesthood office. For example, the following is said when a young man first receives the priesthood: "We confer upon you the Aaronic Priesthood and ordain you a deacon." When he later receives the offices of teacher and priest, no additional priesthood is conferred. Upon reaching maturity, the following may be said to a brother: "We confer the Melchizedek Priesthood and ordain you an elder." In the early history of the Church, some of these terms were used less precisely and more interchangeably than at present. Whether conferring, confirming, or ordaining, the "laying on of hands" is used (D&C 33:15).

Conference: A term that, in the restored Church, originally referred to key meetings convened to transact business (see D&C 20:61–62). Other REVELATIONS mentioned conferences as times when key decisions or assignments would be made (see, for example, D&C 73:1–2; 124:88).

Today, conferences are held at various levels—ward (annually), STAKE (semiannually), regional, and general (semiannually), etc. President David O. McKay listed four reasons for holding conferences: "First, to transact current Church business; second, to hear reports and general Church statistics; third, to 'approve of those names which I (the Lord) have appointed, or to disapprove of them' (D&C 124:144); fourth, to worship the Lord in sincerity and reverence, and to give and to receive encouragement, exhortation, and instruction" (CR, Oct. 1938, 130–31).

A second usage of the term *conference* was common during the Church's first century but is not used today. Local BRANCHES or congregations within a particular geographical area met together for their conferences. This cluster of branches came to be identified as a *conference.* Hence this became a geographical designation, such as the "Scottish Conference." More recently the designation *district* has been used instead.

Consecration, Law of: The voluntary work or contribution of men and women who dedicate their time, talents, and material wealth for the establishment of the kingdom of God. This law was an important part of the restoration of all things. In addition, it was given to acquaint the Saints

The Law of Consecration

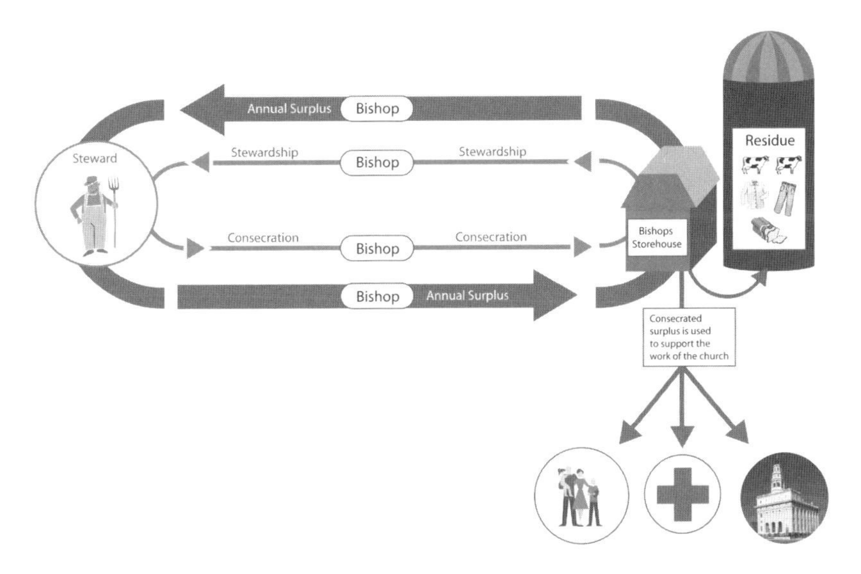

with what will be expected if they are to build Zion. Furthermore, the Lord had commanded His people to "be one" (D&C 38:27), for, as He subsequently explained, "if ye are not equal in earthly things ye cannot be equal in obtaining heavenly things" (D&C 78:6).

An individual who recognized that everything on this earth was actually the Lord's (Ps. 24:1) and who had the desire to build the kingdom of God would consecrate all his property and legally deed it to the Lord's authorized representative, the BISHOP (see D&C 42:30–32). This property was placed in a storehouse from which the bishop could create stewardships and help the poor. A stewardship, also called an inheritance or portion, was to be based not only on the individual's or the family's needs, but also on their "circumstances" (including abilities, talents, etc.) and on their "wants" (see D&C 51:3; 82:17). The bishop was not to accept a consecration unless he and the individual could agree on the size and nature of the stewardship. Even though everyone thought of this property as being the Lord's, the stewardship was nevertheless given to the individual by formal deed; thus, even if the individual left the Church, he would retain title to his stewardship (see D&C 51:4–5) but could not reclaim his original consecration (see D&C 42:37). President J. Reuben Clark Jr. stated, "The fundamental principle of this system was the private ownership of property. Each man owned his portion, or inheritance, or stewardship, with an absolute title, which he could alienate, or hypothecate, or otherwise treat as his own. The Church did not own all of the property, and the life under the United Order was not a communal life, as the Prophet Joseph, himself, said. The United Order is an individualistic system, not a communal system" (CR, Oct. 1942, 55–57).

An individual living the law of consecration felt not only the usual economic pressures, but also a religious or spiritual obligation to develop or magnify his stewardship. That which he produced above his family's needs or wants was designated a "surplus" and was transferred to the bishop's storehouse (see D&C 42:55). From this source, as well as from the "residue" resulting from an excess of consecration over property needed for stewardships, the bishop could help the poor, buy land, erect Church buildings, and establish Zion on earth (see D&C 42:34–35). In addition, this property could be used to expand all existing stewardships or to improve community conditions; thus, there would be an economic profit motive of a sort, but rather than being on an individual and purely selfish basis, it would be broadened to include the well-being of the whole group.

Features of the law of consecration during the 1830s became important in the welfare program of the 1930s, and they still apply today: Members are encouraged to be economically independent, thrifty, and to avoid debt; the bishop and storehouse play a key role in temporal well-being; individuals work for what they get and receive according to their needs; each person is still accountable for his or her stewardships; and rather than contributing surpluses, Saints now pay tithes and offerings.

President Clark declared that "when the Welfare Plan gets thoroughly into operation . . . we shall not be so very far from carrying out the great fundamentals of the United Order" (CR, Oct. 1942, 57).

Fundamental similarities exist between the law of consecration and the tithing, fast offering, and welfare programs of the Church. Elder Marion G. Romney explained that tithing "implements to a degree at least the United Order principle of stewardships, for it leaves in the hands of each person the ownership and management of the property for which he produces the needs of himself and family" ("Socialism and the United Order Compared," *Improvement Era,* June 1966, 537). In place of the residues and surpluses of the law of consecration, today Church members contribute tithes, fast offerings, and other donations to be used for similar purposes—aiding those in need and building the kingdom of God on earth. The bishop's storehouse is a key institution, and at present time it fulfills a function similar to its function under the law of consecration. "Through these practices," Elder Romney concluded, "we could as individuals, if we were of a mind to do so, implement in our lives all the basic principles of the United Order" (ibid).

Some have confused the ideals of the law of consecration with communism as it was practiced in the Soviet Union. Although both sought the temporal well-being of mankind by eliminating economic inequalities and selfishness, there were still fundamental differences: While God was the author of consecration, Soviet communism was openly atheistic; consecration was based on free agency, while communism depended on external coercion; while communism was collective, consecration preserved private ownership of property and individual accountability.

Copley, Leman: An early convert from the "Shaking Quakers" and a controversial member of the Church in OHIO. Born in 1781 in Connecticut and baptized in KIRTLAND, OHIO, in 1831, Copley and his wife joined the Shaker community in North Union, OHIO. Still partial to his former faith, he asked Joseph Smith to inquire of the Lord about the particulars of the Shaker teachings and practices. The result was the REVELATION in SECTION 49, which corrected many of the Shaker doctrines and which called Copley, along with SIDNEY RIGDON and PARLEY P. PRATT, on a mission to that group. The mission proved unsuccessful.

Copley owned 759 acres in Thompson, OHIO, and under the spirit of consecration had invited the SAINTS who had gathered to OHIO from COLESVILLE, NEW YORK, to live on his land. Unfortunately, Copley's unsuccessful mission to the Shakers brought a change of heart. The Colesville Saints, who had made improvements on the land, were now asked to vacate the property. This action brought a scathing rebuke from the Lord to Copley for breaking his covenant. The Lord said, "Wo to him by whom this offence cometh, for it had been better for him that he had been drowned in the depths of the sea" (D&C 54:5). Subsequently, Copley left the Church. In March 1836, however, he asked for forgiveness and requested to be rebaptized. The Prophet received him back into the Church in full fellowship. Copley remained in the Thompson area and died in 1862.

Covenant: A two-way promise most often made between the Lord and an individual or a group of people. When a gospel covenant is made, the conditions are set by the Lord and are accompanied by promised blessings that will be granted according to the faithfulness of the covenant-keeper in meeting the assigned conditions. Today, as in every dispensation, members of the Church are expected to make and keep covenants. In order to remain faithful, we must keep the covenants made at BAPTISM (D&C 20:37; Mosiah 18:8–10). Men must uphold the oath and covenant of the PRIESTHOOD (D&C 84:33–41), and in order to return to live with and live like our Heavenly Father, we must enter into the new and everlasting covenant of marriage (D&C 131:2–3).

Covill, James: An investigator into the early Church, who had been a Baptist minister for about forty years. Two sections in the Doctrine and Covenants are directed to Covill. He was commanded to "arise and be baptized" (D&C 39:10), and though this command was received "with gladness," SATAN tempted Covill and led him to reject it (D&C 40:1–3).

Cowdery, Oliver: The second ELDER in the Church. He was instructed to "be diligent: stand by my servant Joseph, faithfully, in whatsoever difficult circumstances he may be for the word's sake" (D&C 6:18). This call included being a second witness to many of the important events of the Restoration. Born October 5, 1806, Oliver met Joseph on April 5, 1829, and their names were intertwined in the early period of the Church. Just two days following their initial meeting, Cowdery took over the scribal duties for the translation of the Book of Mormon (D&C 9:3–4). While translating, Joseph and Oliver received the Aaronic Priesthood from JOHN the Baptist on May 15, 1829, and later the Melchizedek Priesthood from Apostles PETER, JAMES, AND JOHN (D&C 13; 27:12). Oliver also assisted with the preparation of the Book of Mormon manuscript for printing, being one of the Three Witnesses to the book as well (D&C 5:2, 11; 17). At the organization of the Church, Oliver was sustained as the second elder and shortly thereafter took on the role as the first Church Historian (D&C 21). Within months, Oliver had been called to lead the LAMANITE MISSION, the first official mission of the Church (D&C 28:14). On April 3, 1836, in the Kirtland Temple, Oliver and the PROPHET received visitations from JESUS CHRIST, MOSES, ELIAS and ELIJAH.

Oliver Cowdery

Despite the miraculous events that Oliver experienced and witnessed, he fell away from the Church in 1838 due to pride and to greed over land. Charges were presented against him, and when he did not show up at the HIGH COUNCIL meeting in which the charges were to be discussed, Oliver was excommunicated. Joseph continued to inquire after his friend through letters and encouraged other faithful members in the high council to do the same. Then in the fall of 1848, after years of sickness and financial hardship, Oliver came back to the Church, requesting to be fellowshipped. The Saints were at that time moving to the West. At a conference held in Kanesville on October 24, 1848, Oliver stood and said:

"Friends and Brethren:

"My name is Cowdery—Oliver Cowdery. In the history of the Church I stood . . . in her councils. Not because I was better than other men was I called . . . to fill the purposes of God. He called me to a high and holy calling. I wrote with my own pen the entire Book of Mormon (save a few pages) as it fell from the lips of the Prophet Joseph Smith, and he translated it by the power and gift of God, by means of the Urim and Thummim, or as it is called by that book, 'Holy Interpreter.'

"I beheld with my eyes and handled with my hands, the gold plates from which it was translated. . . . That book is true, Sidney Rigdon did not write it; Mr. Spaulding did not write it; I wrote it myself as it fell from the lips of the Prophet. . . .

"I was present with Joseph when an Holy Angel from Heaven came down and conferred upon us . . . the Aaronic Priesthood, and said to us, at the same time, that it should remain on earth while the earth stands. I was also present with Joseph when the Higher or Melchizedek Priesthood was conferred by the Holy Angels from on high. . . .

"Brethren, for a number of years, I have been separated from you. I now desire to come back. I wish to come humble and be one in your midst. I seek no station. I only wish to be identified with you. I am out of the Church, but I wish to become a member. I wish to come in at the door: I know the door, I have not come here to seek precedence. I come humbly and throw myself upon the decision of the body, knowing as I do, that its decisions are right" (Stanley R. Gunn, *Oliver Cowdery* [Salt Lake City: Bookcraft, 1962], 203–4).

Oliver was rebaptized by ORSON HYDE. His intent was to join BRIGHAM YOUNG and the Saints in the westward trek to the Great Basin. Unfortunately, before he was able to go west, Oliver died of consumption, on March 3, 1850, at DAVID WHITMER'S home, bearing his testimony of the truthfulness of the Book of Mormon with his dying words.

— D —

Damnation: The condition of being stopped in one's eternal progression and denied access to the presence of God. The revelations teach that the disobedient and rebellious are in impending danger of damnation (D&C 42:60; 132:4, 6, 27). Unbelievers, including those who reject the saving ordinances, are also in danger of damnation (D&C 49:5; 68:9; 84:74; 112:29).

The term *eternal damnation* is mentioned in D&C 19:7. Eternal damnation is the opposite of eternal life. Those who fail to obtain eternal life, or exaltation in the highest degree within the celestial kingdom, are said to be receive eternal damnation. Their condemnation is to have limits imposed upon them. Their kingdom or progression has an end and they cannot have an "increase" (D&C 131:4). They remain "separately and singly," without exaltation, and will never become gods (D&C 132:17).

Dead, Baptism for: See BAPTISM and TEMPLES.

Death: The ending of life. The scriptures speak of two kinds of death, physical and spiritual. Physical death occurs when the spirit leaves the body, which dies and is placed in the grave. The GOSPEL OF JESUS CHRIST assures us that this death is not the end of our existence. In fact, it represents a necessary step from MORTALITY to the next stage of our eternal progression. Death is the transition into the post-earthly SPIRIT WORLD. Physical death was overcome through the ATONEMENT of JESUS CHRIST. All who die will be RESURRECTED—the spirit and the body being reunited, never again to be separated. "O death where is thy sting? O grave, where is thy victory?" (1 Cor. 15:55). Elder Russell M. Nelson testified, "Death is a necessary component of our eternal existence. No one knows when it will come, but it is essential to God's great plan of happiness. Thanks to the Atonement of the Lord, eventual resurrection is a reality and eternal life is a possibility for all humankind. That possibility becomes a reality as we obey God's law. He said, 'Except ye shall keep my commandments . . . ye shall in no case enter into the kingdom of heaven.' One day we will be judged by the Lord and go to our own mansion prepared in our Father's heavenly house. Celestial glory awaits those who have been faithful to God's gentle commands. Brothers and sisters, we live to die and we die to live—in another realm. If we are well prepared, death brings no terror. From an eternal perspective, death is premature only for those who are not prepared to meet God. Now is the time to prepare. Then, when death comes, we can move toward the celestial glory that Heavenly Father has prepared for His faithful children" (*Ensign,* May 2005, 16).

SPIRITUAL DEATH is a different matter. It is an estrangement from God caused by SIN. It too is overcome through the Atonement; all will be brought back into the presence of God to be judged. Only the SONS OF PERDITION will once again be completely cut off from God's presence and thereby suffer the SECOND DEATH, which is also a spiritual death (D&C 29:41–42).

Debt: Church leaders have repeatedly warned against the bondage of debt and counseled us to live within our means (see D&C 19:35). President Ezra Taft Benson testified that there are some times when it may be necessary to go into debt, particularly for a home or an education. Even in those cases, however, he counseled, "Resist the temptation to plunge into property far more pretentious or spacious than you really need. Buy within your means and use credit wisely. Save now and buy later, and you will be much further ahead. You will spare yourselves high interest" (*Ensign,* June 1987, 4).

Disciplinary Councils: Bodies responsible for considering action to be taken in cases of violation of Church laws. These "are not courts of retribution," declared Bishop Robert L. Simpson, "they are courts of love" (CR, Apr. 1972, 31–33). Their purpose is to help the transgressor to take "the first giant step back" (ibid). Church councils do not have the authority to deprive one of life, liberty, or property, but can only withdraw Church membership or fellowship (D&C 134:10). A person who is disfellowshipped retains his membership and PRIESTHOOD but is forbidden to take an active part; he is encouraged to attend Church meetings but is not called upon to speak or pray and should not partake of the sacrament. Excommunication is the most extreme penalty; it actually removes a person from membership in the Church, making it necessary for him to reenter by BAPTISM when he REPENTS. Excommunicated individuals may attend Church meetings but may not take an active part in them or pay TITHING.

Ward bishop's court or disciplinary council is the first of the three "regular courts" (see D&C 107:72–75). It has "original jurisdiction" in most matters. It may disfellowship anyone found guilty of sufficiently serious violation of Church standards. The BISHOP's court may also excommunicate anyone except a bearer of the Melchizedek Priesthood.

The STAKE Presidency and HIGH COUNCIL handle matters beyond

the scope of the ward bishop (D&C 102:2), and they may hear appeals from the bishop's court. SECTION 102 (verses 12–23) outlines the procedures followed by this council when sitting as a judicial body.

The FIRST PRESIDENCY is the regular disciplinary council having final jurisdiction in all matters (see D&C 107:78–81). This court holds the specific responsibility of trying a Presiding Bishop in case of the latter's transgression (see D&C 68:22–24). The "special councils" described in Doctrine and Covenants 102:24–34 have been convened only rarely, typically in areas where there were no stakes to assume jurisdiction.

Dispensation of the Gospel: A time when the gospel of JESUS CHRIST is on the EARTH, wherein the Lord's word and power are dispensed or sent forth anew from heaven. "Dispensation" may also refer to the period of time that elapses from one such restoration to another, and generally bears the name of the PROPHET who stood at its head. Hence, the first of these periods is known as the dispensation of Adam. Other dispensations are associated with Enoch, Noah, Abraham, and Moses. The dispensation opened by the Savior's earthly ministry is known as the dispensation of the meridian of time because it was approximately at the midpoint of the earth's temporal existence (see SECTION 77) and because years are numbered before and since His birth. The present and last dispensation, headed by the Prophet JOSEPH SMITH, is known as the dispensation of the fulness of times. Unlike all earlier dispensations, it will not be followed by an APOSTASY, but will lead directly to the establishment of ZION in preparation for the Savior's SECOND COMING.

Doctrine: Principles, precepts, and teachings of the GOSPEL of JESUS CHRIST. Understanding and living according to true doctrine brings saving power and affects our present lives for good. President Boyd K. Packer declared, "True doctrine understood, changes attitudes and behavior. The study of doctrines of the gospel will improve behavior quicker than a study of behavior will improve behavior" (*MEL,* 307). Hence, in these latter days we are to "teach one another the doctrine of the kingdom" (D&C 88:77–78; see also D&C 68:25) and maintain its purity.

Elder Dallin H. Oaks testified, "Well-taught doctrines and principles have a more powerful influence on behavior than rules. When we teach gospel doctrine and principles, we can qualify for the witness and guidance of the Spirit to reinforce our teaching, and we enlist the faith of our students in seeking the guidance of that same Spirit in applying those teachings in their personal lives (*Ensign,* Nov. 1999, 78)."

Doctrine and Covenants, Coming Forth of: See introductory material before SECTION 1 herein.

Dust from Feet: A symbol of removing responsibility for others' SINS. When the Lord sent out His early APOSTLES, He instructed them to "shake off the dust of your feet" wherever they were rejected (Matt. 10:14). Early missionaries in the present DISPENSATION received similar instructions (see D&C 24:15). The notion that this was done to motivate people to listen rather than be cursed is false, as the missionaries were directed to perform this ritual "not in their presence, lest thou provoke them, but in secret" (D&C 60:15). In a sense, missionaries assume the responsibility for the sins of those they are called to teach and may discharge that only when they have taught them (see Jacob 1:19). Shaking dust off one's feet may be thought of as a visible representation of freeing oneself from the sins of those who had been taught but who chose to reject the message. Even in such circumstances, missionaries may be "filled with joy" (D&C 75:20–21) because they know that they have faithfully carried out their responsibility. Because the purpose of this ritual has been misunderstood, it is performed rarely today, and only with the authorization of presiding mission authorities.

Earth: The planet on which we live, which was created by God the Father through Jesus Christ (Moses 2; Heb. 1:2; D&C 14:9) as the place where we as God's spirit children could gain additional experience and prove ourselves worthy to return to His presence (see Abr. 3:24–26; D&C 49:15–17). During its existence, the earth passes through five distinct stages:

1. The earth was first created as a spirit earth in heaven (Moses 3:5), so was in a CELESTIAL state.
2. The earth was created physically just before ADAM was placed in the Garden of Eden. It came into a terrestrial or PARADISICAL STATE that lasted during the time Adam and Eve lived in the Garden. Even though the earth was *physical* during this stage, it was *spiritual* rather than *fallen,* and Adam and Eve were in this same condition.
3. BRIGHAM YOUNG taught that with the FALL of Adam, the earth also fell (see *JD,* 17:143).
4. Christ's SECOND COMING at the beginning of the seventh thousand years is to usher in His MILLENNIAL reign (see D&C 77:12). The earth

will return to the condition that existed while Adam and Eve were in the Garden. The term *paradise* has been used in some theological writing to refer to Eden; hence, the statement in the tenth Article of Faith: "We believe . . . that the earth will be renewed and receive its paradisiacal glory." This thousand-year period will complete the seven thousand years of the earth's "temporal existence" (see D&C 77:6–7).

5. After the Millennium ends, the earth will be *consumed* by fire, in contrast to the beginning of the Millennium when it will be superficially *cleansed* by fire. It will become a celestial physical earth but will be spiritual rather than mortal or fallen in its nature. In this sanctified state it has been described as a "sea of glass" (D&C 77:1) or a "great URIM AND THUMMIM" (D&C 130:6–9). JOSEPH SMITH saw the celestialized earth in vision and described its glorious appearance (see D&C 137:1–4). President Brigham Young gave the following insight: "This Earth will become a celestial body—be like a sea of glass, or like a Urim and Thummim; and when you wish to know anything, you can look in this Earth and see all the eternities of God" (*JD,* 8:200; see also D&C 88:17–20, 25–26; 130:6–9).

Even though the earth is presently in a telestial state, it abides a celestial law; hence, it will one day become a celestial sphere. Similarly, in our own telestial condition, we need to abide a celestial law if we hope to inherit a celestial glory (see D&C 88:25–29).

Education: The process of gaining knowledge and understanding. God has commanded us to "seek ye out of the best books words of wisdom; seek learning, even by study and also by faith" (D&C 88:118). He directed the SAINTS to gain an understanding of "the doctrine of the Kingdom" (D&C 88:77). He also admonished them to gain a knowledge of "things both in heaven and in the earth, and under the earth; things which have been, things which are, things which must shortly come to pass; things which are at home, things which are abroad; the wars and the perplexities of the nations, and the judgments which are on the land; and a knowledge also of countries and of kingdoms" (D&C 88:79), of "languages, tongues, and people" (D&C 90:15), and of histories, countries, and laws (D&C 93:53). We need this knowledge to be better prepared to serve Him and to fulfill our callings (D&C 88:80). Other Doctrine and Covenants passages speak of gaining intelligence (D&C 93:36; 130:18–19) and affirm that we cannot be saved in ignorance (D&C 131:6); although these passages may be used in support of gaining an education, they seem to be speaking in broader and more spiritual terms (see SECTION 93).

The Church has promoted education almost from the beginning. In 1831, W. W. PHELPS was instructed to gather school books for the use of children (D&C 55:4). The instructions in section 88 resulted in the SCHOOL OF THE PROPHETS being organized, beginning in January 1833. At NAUVOO, the Saints chartered a university. As the pioneers settled in the Rocky Mountains, they established schools as one of the first institutions in each community. The growth of BRIGHAM YOUNG University and the far-flung seminary and institute programs of the Church Educational System are demonstrations of the Church's commitment to education.

Elder: Title of one bearing the Melchizedek PRIESTHOOD. The word *elder* is an archaic form of *older*, so this title refers to one who is regarded as more seasoned or mature. Elders have leadership and spiritual responsibilities (see D&C 20:38–45) in contrast to the lesser and more temporal duties assigned to bearers of the Aaronic Priesthood. The elders are described as "standing ministers" (D&C 124:137), their principal responsibility being to minister in spiritual things at the local level (see D&C 20:38–45; 107:11–12). It should be noted, however, that elders may also be asked to "travel" as missionaries (see D&C 84:111).

When the Church was officially organized April 6, 1830, JOSEPH SMITH and OLIVER COWDERY were sustained as the first and second elders, respectively. Others were subsequently ordained to this office and frequently served as local leaders and as missionaries. A QUORUM of elders consists of up to 96 members (D&C 107:89). The title "elder" is also held by members of the Quorum of the Twelve APOSTLES (see D&C 20:38).

Elect: Those who are to be exalted in the CELESTIAL kingdom. There is no predestination, because we can and must qualify for EXALTATION by FAITH in the Savior, by keeping His commandments, and by doing other good works (see D&C 5:35; 51:19; 52:43–44; 59:23). REVELATIONS speak of the GATHERING of the elect if the elect harden not their hearts but hear the voice of the Savior (D&C 29:7–8). One of the promises made to those who are faithful and MAGNIFY their callings is that they will become the "elect of God" (D&C 84:33–34). PETER challenges us to "make [our] calling and election sure" (1 Pet. 1:10) by faithfully living the gospel.

Elias: One of the messengers who restored KEYS on April 3, 1836, in the KIRTLAND TEMPLE (D&C 110:12). The name or title *Elias* is used in the scriptures in at least three different senses:

1. Elias and ELIJAH are two forms of the same name, the former coming

from the Greek and the latter from the Hebrew. Hence many references to *Elias* in the New Testament actually mean *Elijah*. For example, it was Elijah who appeared with Moses on the Mount of Transfiguration (see Matt. 17:1–3; *TPJS*, 158). JOSEPH SMITH used the two forms of this name in his discussion of the powers of the Aaronic and Melchizedek PRIESTHOODS (*TPJS*, 335–41). However, the Elias who came to the Kirtland Temple in 1836 could not have been Elijah, because Elijah also appeared directly afterwards (see D&C 110:12–13).

2. *Elias* is the title of a messenger or forerunner. Perhaps JOHN THE BAPTIST is the best known of those who have come in this role. Sidney Rigdon was also identified as a forerunner for the PROPHET Joseph Smith (D&C 35:4) by teaching his congregation that there needed to be a restoration of New Testament Christianity.
3. There was a great prophet who lived in the days of Abraham who was known as Elias. This is the person whose appearance is recorded in D&C 110:12. Joseph Fielding Smith suggested this was the same person as Noah, because Doctrine and Covenants 27:7 identified Elias as the person who visited Zacharias, and because Luke 1:19 identifies this visitor as Gabriel. Joseph Smith taught that Gabriel is Noah, who stood next to Adam in holding the keys (*TPJS*, 157). Available sources, however, do not confirm the identity of this Elias or the exact nature of the keys he brought.

Elijah: A PROPHET who has ministered in three DISPENSATIONS. He lived in the 9th century before Christ and demonstrated remarkable PRIESTHOOD power as he sealed the heavens and performed other miracles (see 1 Kgs. 17–18). He was taken into heaven without tasting of death (2 Kgs. 2:11). Latter-day REVELATION clarifies that he became a TRANSLATED BEING; this enabled him to retain his mortal body which he needed to bestow KEYS on PETER, James, and John on the Mount of TRANSFIGURATION (Matt. 17:1–3; *TPJS*, 158). Malachi prophesied that Elijah would return to the earth once again "before the great and dreadful day of the Lord" (Mal. 4:5–6; compare D&C 2). This prophecy was fulfilled when Elijah bestowed his sealing keys on Joseph Smith and OLIVER COWDERY in the KIRTLAND TEMPLE (D&C 110:13–16). Elder Henry B. Erying taught, "It is important to know why the Lord promised to send Elijah. Elijah was a great prophet with great power given him by God. He held the greatest power God gives to His children: he held the sealing power, the power to bind on earth and have it bound in heaven. God gave it to the

Apostle Peter. And the Lord kept His promise to send Elijah. Elijah came to the Prophet Joseph Smith on April 3, 1836, just after the dedication of the Kirtland Temple, the first temple built after the Restoration of the gospel" (*Ensign,* May 2005, 77). Elijah was to "turn the hearts of the children to the fathers and the fathers to the children" (Mal. 4:6). Within a few years of Elijah's coming, there was a marked increase in interest in genealogy and family history; this has been attributed to "the spirit of Elijah.

Endowment: A gift promised to the faithful. This term has been used in two senses, both related to the TEMPLE:

1. The Lord promised to endow the faithful "with power from on high" (see D&C 38:32; 95:8). This promise was fulfilled with the marvelous spiritual outpourings associated with the dedication of the KIRTLAND TEMPLE in 1836.
2. The temple endowment is a sacred ordinance administered only in holy sanctuaries. Elder James E. Talmage described it as a "course of instruction" that traces the events of the Creation and the FALL, depicts our present condition on EARTH, and emphasizes the "absolute and indispensable condition of personal purity and devotion to the right in present life, and a strict compliance with Gospel requirements" (*HL,* 100). Referring to the washings and anointings that occurred in the Kirtland Temple, Elder Boyd K. Packer explained that "in 1836 certain ordinances had been introduced in a limited way which later would form part of the regular temple ordinances" (*HT,* 129). President Brigham Young declared that in Kirtland the "first Elders" received only a "portion of their first endowments, or we might say more clearly, some of the first, or introductory, or initiatory ordinances, preparatory to an endowment" (*JD,* 2:31). In preparation for giving the endowment in the temple when completed, JOSEPH SMITH gave this ordinance to a select group in his office on May 4, 1842. He recorded that he had spent the day with these men "instructing them in the principles and order of the PRIESTHOOD, attending to washings, anointings, endowments and the communication of keys pertaining to the Aaronic priesthood, and so on to the highest order of the Melchesedek [sic] Priesthood, setting forth the order pertaining to the Ancient of Days, and all those plans and principles by which any one is enables to secure the fulness of those blessings which have been prepared for the Church of the First Born, and come up and abide in the presence of the Eloheim in the eternal worlds" (*HC,* 5:1–2).

While endowments for the living were given in Nauvoo, this ordinance in behalf of the dead was administered for the first time in this dispensation at St. George in 1877. The privilege of receiving this ordinance in behalf of our deceased loved ones enables us to return to the temple time after time to refresh our understanding of the endowment's teachings and to renew our covenants.

Eternal Life: Also known as exaltation. It is "the greatest of all the gifts of God" (D&C 14:7). The adjective *eternal* not only refers to the endless duration of this reward but it also describes its nature. "Eternal" is one of the titles of God. Just as we are told that "eternal punishment is God's punishment" (D&C 19:11), we should understand that eternal life is God's life. Those who inherit this highest reward have the privilege of becoming like our Heavenly Father.

Exaltation: eternal life, the highest reward promised to the faithful. The prophet taught that "in the celestial glory there are three heavens or degrees." To attain this lofty state, we must keep all of God's commandments, specifically including the new and everlasting covenant of marriage. Others may inherit one of the lower two divisions of the celestial kingdom, but there will be an "end" to their kingdom (D&C 131:1–4). They will "remain separately and singly" and will be ministering "angels" (D&C 132:17). On the other hand, those who qualify for exaltation are promised that they shall inherit thrones, kingdoms, principalities, and powers, dominions, all heights and depths . . . Then shall they be gods, because they have all power" (D&C 132:19–20). Elder Russell M. Nelson explained, "Eternal life, or celestial glory or exaltation, is a conditional gift. Conditions of this gift have been established by the Lord . . . Those qualifying conditions include faith in the Lord, repentance, baptism, receiving the Holy Ghost, and remaining faithful to the ordinances and covenants of the temple. No man in this Church can obtain the highest degree of celestial glory without a worthy woman who is sealed to him (D&C 131:1–3) This temple ordinance enables eventual exaltation for both of them" (*Ensign,* May 2008, 7–10).

Faith: A hope for things not seen (see Ether 12:6). Faith in the Lord Jesus Christ is the first principle of the gospel (Article of Faith 1) and a basic requirement for those who wish to serve the Lord (D&C 4:5–6). It is the "assurance of things hoped for, the evidence of things not seen" (JST, Heb. 11:1).

Alma declared that faith is not to have a perfect knowledge (Alma 32:21). He then likened developing faith to planting a seed, cultivating it, and then enjoying the fruit that it produces (Alma 32: 27–43). FEAR, on the other hand, impedes our ability to receive blessings from God and is the opposite of faith. JOSEPH SMITH taught that faith is a principle of power. If we believe in Jesus Christ, His atoning power, and His love for us, we will find the motivation to keep the commandments. This, in turn, strengthens our faith. Our faith cannot be greater than our obedience because faith is a measure of how willing we are to be obedient. President Hinckley observed, "When I discuss faith, I do not mean it in an abstract sense. I mean it as a living, vital force with recognition of God as our Father and Jesus Christ as our Savior. When we accept this basic premise, there will come an acceptance of their teachings and an obedience which will bring peace and joy in this life and exaltation in the life to come" (*Ensign,* Aug. 1988, 5).

Fall: An act of ADAM and Eve that brought to mankind MORTALITY, or physical DEATH, and separation from the presence of God, or spiritual death (1 Cor. 15:22; D&C 29:41). When placed in the Garden of Eden, our first parents were given two directives: first, to multiply and replenish the earth, and second, not to partake of the tree of knowledge of good and evil (Gen. 2:17; Moses 3:16–17). In the garden, there was no death; that is, Adam and Eve were not mortal. They were in the presence of God, yet they had no knowledge of good and evil. They were commanded to "multiply and replenish the earth," but in their condition, "they would have had no children" (2 Ne. 2:22–26). In the garden, SATAN beguiled mother Eve, who then enticed Adam, and they partook of fruit of the tree of knowledge of good and evil. Because they did so without knowledge of good and evil, their act is referred to as a transgression rather than a SIN (D&C 20:20). Both Adam and Eve rejoiced in the decision they had made. Eve said, "Were it not for our transgression we never should have had seed, and never should have known good and evil, and the joy of our redemption, and the eternal life which God giveth unto the obedient" (Moses 5:11). The Fall brought death to all mankind and separation from God. In D&C 29:40–41, we read: "Wherefore, I, the Lord God caused that he should be cast out from the Garden of Eden, from my presence, because of his transgression, wherein he became spiritually dead, which is the first death, even that death which is the last death, which is spiritual, which shall be pronounced upon the wicked when I shall say: Depart, ye cursed." (See also Hel. 14:16).

Elder Dallin H. Oaks provided valuable perspective: "To the first man and woman on earth, the Lord said, 'Be fruitful, and multiply' (Moses 2:28; see Gen. 1:28; Abr. 4:28). This commandment was first in sequence and first in importance. It was essential that God's spirit children have mortal birth and an opportunity to progress toward eternal life. Consequently, all things related to procreation are prime targets for the adversary's efforts to thwart the plan of God. When Adam and Eve received the first commandment, they were in a transitional state, no longer in the spirit world but with physical bodies not yet subject to death and not yet capable of procreation. They could not fulfill the Father's first commandment without transgressing the barrier between the bliss of the Garden of Eden and the terrible trials and wonderful opportunities of mortal life. For reasons that have not been revealed, this transition, or 'fall,' could not happen without a transgression—an exercise of moral agency amounting to a willful breaking of a law (see Moses 6:59). This would be a planned offense, a formality to serve an eternal purpose. The Prophet Lehi explained that 'if Adam had not transgressed he would not have fallen' (2 Ne. 2:22), but would have remained in the same state in which he was created. 'And they would have had no children; wherefore they would have remained in a state of innocence, having no joy, for they knew no misery; doing no good, for they knew no sin' (2 Ne. 2:23)" (*Ensign,* Nov. 1993, 72).

The Fall was a necessary step in man's progress. Because God knew that the Fall would occur, He had planned in the premortal life for a Savior (2 Ne. 2:4; D&C 124:33, 41; D&C 128:5). JESUS CHRIST came in the meridian of time to ATONE for the fall of Adam and also for man's individual sins on condition of man's REPENTANCE (2 Ne. 2:6; 9:21).

Far West, Missouri: A town near the center of CALDWELL COUNTY that was the headquarters of the Church from March to November 1838. When the faithful SAINTS had to leave KIRTLAND in 1838, JOSEPH SMITH and his family were welcomed by the MISSOURI Saints at FAR WEST. The area had been settled in 1836 and was no more than a wilderness. WILLIAM W. PHELPS and JOHN WHITMER were responsible for surveying and setting out the town on the 640-acre site, which was also designated as the Caldwell County seat. Over the next two years, the township was enlarged to two miles, nearly 200 homes were built, and 250,000 acres were pur-

Temple site in Far West, Missouri

chased in the area. The city grew to a population of about 5,000 by the fall of 1838.

The Lord said, "Let the city, Far West, be a holy consecrated land unto me" (D&C 115:7). This included the building of the Far West Temple in the town center (D&C 115:8). However, construction was postponed because the FIRST PRESIDENCY did not want to incur debt for this temple as had been done in Kirtland. Revelations received in Far West designated the official name of the Church (D&C 115:4). The doctrine of tithing was emphasized and clarified (D&C 119, 120).

In the fall of 1838, the city of Far West was besieged by a hostile Missouri militia, and many Church leaders, including Joseph Smith, were seized. Members of the Church were forced to flee the city because of the extermination order issued by Governor Lilburn W. Boggs.

Fasting: Abstaining from eating and drinking for two consecutive meals. We should always fast with a purpose, such as seeking answers or help from our Heavenly Father, or asking for blessings for an individual who is sick or otherwise afflicted (D&C 95:7). When fasting is done prayerfully, members will find that their prayers are enhanced and they can obtain greater spiritual power and knowledge through personal revelation (see D&C 88:76). When Christ's disciples asked how He was able to perform certain miraculous deeds, He responded that they were done through prayer and fasting (Matt. 17:21). Such a fast can be done at any time; however, Saints are asked to fast on the first Sunday of every month, at which time Church members pay an offering to the BISHOP for the care of the poor and attend a SACRAMENT MEETING at which testimonies are borne.

Fayette, New York: Location of the home and farm of Peter Whitmer Sr., where the Church of Christ was organized on April 6, 1830 (D&C 21). The Whitmers moved to this town in Seneca County in 1808 and acquired a 100-acre farm. The Whitmers were introduced to Joseph Smith by their son David Whitmer, who was a friend of Oliver Cowdery.

The latter part of the Book of Mormon was translated at the Whitmer home by Joseph Smith, with Oliver Cowdery serving as the scribe. At the Whitmer farm, David Whitmer, Martin Harris, and Oliver Cowdery were shown the gold plates by an angel, thereby becoming the Three Witnesses to the Book of Mormon (D&C 17). The first three conferences of the Church were held at the Whitmer home. The elders called to the Lamanite Mission departed from the Whitmer farm on their 2000-mile journey to Jackson County, Missouri (D&C 32).

Fear: The opposite of faith. Fear may prevent spiritual progress. In section 9, the Lord declares that Oliver Cowdery lost the power to translate because he "feared," much as Peter feared when he was walking on the Sea of Galilee (D&C 9:11; Matt. 14:28–31). Similarly, several elders of the early Church were counseled by the Lord, "Strip yourselves from . . . fears . . . the veil shall be rent and you shall see me and know that I am" (D&C 67:10).When our faith is overcome, fear becomes a barrier that keeps us from receiving appointed blessings.

Final Judgment: See Judgment.

First Presidency: The highest presiding quorum in the Church. The Presidency of the Church is composed of "three presiding high priests" (D&C 107:22). The President of the Church is sustained as a "prophet, seer and revelator" (compare D&C 21:1; 107:9; 124:125), and he is assisted by two counselors. The President stands at the head of the priesthood structure and is known as the presiding high priest or president of the high priesthood (D&C 107:65–66). As head of the ecclesiastical structure, he is called the President of the Church. He holds the keys of spiritual blessings and may officiate in all other offices in the Church (see D&C 107:9, 65–67, 91–92; D&C 21:1). On January 25, 1832, at a conference in Amherst, Ohio, Joseph Smith was sustained and ordained "by the will of the Lord, as President of the High Priesthood (*CHMR,* 1:174). This was a necessary step towards the organization of the First Presidency.

The original First Presidency consisted of Joseph Smith, Sidney Rigdon, and Frederick G. Williams. In December 1830, the Lord called

Sidney to work closely with Joseph Smith (D&C 35:18–22). Then in March 1832, Frederick was called to be a "counselor" to Joseph, "unto whom I have given the keys of the kingdom, which belong always unto the Presidency of the High Priesthood" (D&C 81:2). On March 8, 1833, the Lord declared that Sidney and Frederick would be "equal" with Joseph "in holding the keys," although they would function under his administration (D&C 90:6–7). Ten days later, the Presidency was formally organized. In a meeting of the SCHOOL OF THE PROPHETS, Elders Rigdon and Williams desired to be ordained. "Accordingly," Joseph Smith recorded, "I laid my hands on Brothers Sidney and Frederick, and ordained them to take part with me in holding the keys of this last kingdom, and to assist in the Presidency of the High Priesthood, as my Counselors; after which I exhorted the brethren to faithfulness and diligence in keeping the commandments of God, and gave much instruction for the benefit of the Saints" (*HC,* 1:334–35).

From time to time, the structure of the First Presidency has been expanded. OLIVER COWDERY was sustained in 1834 as the second or associate President of the Church; this recognized his position as the second witness to the restoration of the Aaronic and Melchizedek Priesthoods. Following his apostasy however, HYRUM SMITH was called to replace him (see D&C 124:91–96). After Joseph and Hyrum, the two witnesses of the Restoration, had sealed their testimonies with their blood (see D&C 135:3), this office had fulfilled its purpose, so was discontinued. Joseph Smith, BRIGHAM YOUNG, David O. McKay, and Spencer W. Kimball each had, for a time, three or more counselors.

Even though only a simple majority is generally necessary for a quorum to function (see D&C 107:28), the Quorum of the First Presidency is dissolved with the death of the President because the counselors are set apart as counselors to the particular President. With his death, they are automatically released and return to their former quorums—often, but not always, the Quorum of the Twelve.

President Gordon B. Hinckley stated, "When the President is ill or not able to function fully in all of the duties of his office, his two Counselors together comprise a Quorum of the First Presidency. They carry on with the day-to-day work of the Presidency. In exceptional circumstances, when only one may be able to function, he may act in the authority of the office of the Presidency as set forth in the Doctrine and Covenants, section 102, verses 10–11. . . . Under these specific and plenary delegations of authority, the Counselors in the First Presidency carry on with the regular work of this office. But any major questions of policy, procedures, programs, or doctrine are considered deliberately and prayerfully by the First Presidency and the Twelve together. These two quorums, the Quorum of the First Presidency and the Quorum of the Twelve, meeting together, with every man having total freedom to express himself, consider every major question" (*Ensign,* May 1994, 53).

First Vision: The appearance of the Father and the Son to JOSEPH SMITH in 1820, opening the present DISPENSATION. In the midst of religious revivals, young Joseph had wondered which church to join. After reading James 1:5 in the Bible, he was prompted to ask God for guidance. He left several accounts of the event, each throwing light on different aspects of his experience. Joseph's history of the First Vision, written in 1838, is included in the Pearl of Great Price (see JS–H 1:5–20). He learned several vital truths: Satan's power is real, but God's is greater; prayers are answered; God lives; the Father and the Son are two distinct, glorious Beings. The 1842 account, written as part of a letter to newspaper

The Sacred Grove, Manchester, New York

editor John Wentworth, adds that Joseph was told that the fulness of the gospel would be restored through him (*HC* 4:536). The term VISION may refer to something which may not be physically present but is nevertheless seen by the power of the HOLY GHOST; on this occasion, however, the Father and Son were actually present in the Sacred Grove. Hence, this might more appropriately be known as a personal visitation. The First Vision is not recorded in the Doctrine and Covenants (although it is alluded to in D&C 20:5); still, it should be regarded as the foundation underlying all subsequent divine REVELATIONS contained in this volume of scripture. President David O. McKay summarized, "That one revelation answers all the queries of science regarding God and his divine personality. Don't you see what that means? What God is, is answered. His relation to his children is clear. His interest in humanity through authority delegated to man is apparent. The future of the work is assured. These and other glorious truths are clarified by that glorious first vision" (*Gospel Ideals* [Salt Lake City: Improvement Era], 1957, 85).

Forgiveness: The withdrawing of blame and the reaffirmation of love. The Lord promised, "He that repents and does the commandments of the Lord shall be forgiven" (D&C 1:32). He also gave this reassuring promise: "He who has repented of his sins, the same is forgiven, and I, the Lord, remember them no more" (D&C 58:42). FAITH, repentance, and BAPTISM bring the REMISSION OF SINS, or a pardon. The word *forgiveness* is similar to the term *pardon,* but *forgiveness* suggests that penalties for sin have been paid with the help of the Savior's ATONEMENT. In addition, the Savior teaches, "I will forgive whom I will forgive, but of you it is required to forgive all men" (D&C 64: 10). Elder Dallin H. Oaks explained, "One of the most Godlike expressions of the human soul is the act of forgiveness. Everyone is wronged at some point by someone, and many suffer serious wrongs. Christians everywhere stand in awe of those pioneers who have climbed that steep slope to the spiritual summit attained by those who have heeded the Savior's command to forgive all men. Forgiveness is mortality's mirror image of the mercy of God" (*Ensign,* Nov. 1989, 64).

Only one sin is UNPARDONABLE—the sin against the HOLY GHOST. Alma made a distinction between this sin and murder and immorality, which are pardonable but "not easy to be forgiven" (Alma 39:6), probably because making restitution is impossible or extremely difficult. We should ever be grateful for the power of the Lord's atoning blood and determine to sincerely repent of our sins in order to claim His marvelous gift of forgiveness.

— G —

Gathering: Bringin together from a spread-out or scattered state (www.merriam-webster.com). The Lord commanded His servants to gather His elect from the four corners of the earth (D&C 29:7; 33:6; 39:11). The keys to the gathering were delivered by Moses on April 3, 1836, in the KIRTLAND TEMPLE (D&C 110:11). Gathering is an important responsibility of the faithful in preparation for the Lord's SECOND COMING.

The Doctrine and Covenants identifies different stages in the gathering. First, the Saints were to gather "in one place" (D&C 29:8). This would give the Church a strong nucleus from which it could spread its influence abroad. Later, STAKES would be identified as other places of gathering (D&C 101:20–22; 115:17–18). Thus, at first there was a gathering to a single "center place of ZION," while more recently there has been a gathering into an ever-expanding number of "stakes of Zion." The gathering can also be understood in a strictly spiritual sense—without moving geographically, faithful Saints leave the wicked world and associate with the Church (D&C 133:7, 14). Joseph Smith taught, "The main object [of gathering] was to build unto the Lord a house [or TEMPLE] whereby He could reveal unto His people the ordinances of His house and the glories of His kingdom, and teach the people the way of salvation" (*HC*, 5:423).

Elder Russell M. Nelson reported, "This doctrine of the gathering is one of the important teachings of The Church of Jesus Christ of Latter-day Saints. The Lord has declared: 'I give unto you a sign . . . that I shall gather in, from their long dispersion, my people, O house of Israel, and shall establish again among them my Zion' (3 Ne. 21:1). The coming forth of the Book of Mormon is a sign to the entire world that the Lord has commenced to gather Israel and fulfill covenants he made to Abraham, Isaac, and Jacob. We not only teach this doctrine, but we participate in it. We do so as we help to gather the elect of the Lord on both sides of the veil" (Ensign, Nov. 2006, 79–82).

General Authorities: The Brethren who preside over the whole Church (see D&C 102:32). The General Authorities consist of the FIRST PRESIDENCY, the QUORUM of the Twelve APOSTLES, the First and Second Quorums of the SEVENTY, and the Presiding BISHOPRIC. Before the organization of General Authority Quorums of the Seventy, beginning in 1975, only the Seven Presidents of the Seventy, known as the First Council of the Seventy, were sustained among the General Authorities. Prior to 1979, a PATRIARCH to the Church was also one of the General Authorities, having the responsibility to give blessings in areas where no STAKE patriarchs were available; since that time, this responsibility has been divided among several brethren, some speaking other languages, who are called to serve for limited periods of time and in specific parts of the world.

One individual, the PRESIDENT OF THE CHURCH, is acknowledged as *the* PROPHET, SEER, and revelator, entitled to receive REVELATION for the Church. His counselors and the Twelve Apostles are also sustained as prophets, seers, and revelators, meaning that they have a special spiritual endowment with their teachings. The common title of a General Authority is "ELDER," unless he is serving as a president.

Gentiles: "All those not of the house of Israel. [The word Gentile] is first used in Genesis with reference to the descendants of Japheth [Gen. 10:2–5]" (BD, 679). In the world today, the term *Gentile* commonly refers to a non-Jewish person. For Latter-day SAINTS, it has a more specific meaning. Elder Marion G. Romney said: "*Gentiles* is the term used by the Book of Mormon PROPHETS to refer to the present inhabitants of America and to the peoples of the old world from which they came" (CR, Oct. 1975, 54). The Gentiles were to play a key role in the latter days. Nephi foresaw that a Gentile would cross "the many waters" and that other Gentiles would follow, establish a country, and fight for their independence from their "mother Gentiles" across the sea. These Gentiles would have a book containing the words of prophets, but from which many "plain and precious" things had been taken (1 Ne. 13:12–23, 34). The "times of the Gentiles" began with the latter-day Restoration and refers to the time when the GOSPEL would go to the great gentile nations of the earth (see D&C 45:28–30).

Gift of the Holy Ghost: See HOLY GHOST.

Gilbert, Algernon Sidney: Agent to the early Church and co-owner with NEWEL K. WHITNEY of the general store in KIRTLAND, OHIO. Sidney was BAPTIZED in 1830 at the age of 40. In 1831, Sidney accompanied the PROPHET on his way to INDEPENDENCE, MISSOURI, where he was directed to stay as an agent and establish a storehouse for the Saints (D&C 57:8–10; 64:18–19). In 1833, the Lord indicated that He was "not well pleased" with Sidney (D&C 90:35) because of a letter he had written to Church officials. Despite the rebuke, Sidney remained and repented of his transgression. He also allowed members of ZION'S CAMP to live on his land. This act of kindness led to his death from cholera on June 29, 1834.

Gospel: The good news that the plan of salvation, made possible through Adam's FALL and Christ's Atonement, is available to all mankind. The gospel is our Heavenly Father's plan of happiness. Its central DOCTRINE is the ATONEMENT of JESUS CHRIST. The Prophet JOSEPH SMITH explained, "The first principles and ordinances of the GOSPEL are: first, FAITH in the Lord Jesus Christ; second, REPENTANCE; third, BAPTISM by immersion for the remission of sins; fourth, Laying on of hands for the gift of the HOLY GHOST" (Articles of Faith 1:4).

In its fulness, the gospel includes all the doctrines, principles, laws, ordinances, and covenants necessary for us to be exalted in the celestial kingdom. The Savior has promised that if we endure to the end, faithfully living the gospel, He will hold us guiltless before the Father at the Final JUDGMENt (see 3 Ne. 27:16).

The fulness of the gospel has been preached in all ages when God's children have been prepared to receive it. In the present DISPENSATION, the gospel was restored through Joseph Smith. Preaching the gospel to the world is one of the main responsibilities of members of the restored Church.

Grace: The help that God gives to men and women to obtain blessings in this life and to gain ETERNAL LIFE and EXALTATION in the world to come (D&C 138:14; Eph. 2:8). We are saved by grace after we have done all that we can do, including living by every precept of the GOSPEL of JESUS CHRIST (2 Ne. 25:23; Hel. 12:24). Such divine help or strength is given through the mercy and love of God (2 Ne. 2:8). It is a gift of our Heavenly Father. Because of SIN and physical DEATH, no one can return to live with God without the grace of JESUS CHRIST. Because of Christ, all can be forgiven of sin and resurrected to eternal life. Elder Dieter F. Uchtdorf clarified, "It is not repentance per se that saves man. It is the blood of Jesus Christ that saves us. It is not by our sincere and honest change of behavior alone that we are saved, but 'by grace that we are saved, after all we can do' (2 Ne. 25:23). True REPENTANCE, however, is the condition required so that God's FORGIVENESS can come into our lives. True repentance makes a brilliant day [out] of the darkest night" (*Ensign,* May 2007, 99–101).

— H —

Harmony, Pennsylvania: The residence of JOSEPH and EMMA SMITH from December 1827 to August 1830. HARMONY is located in the northeast corner of PENNSYLVANIA on the banks of the Susquehanna River. Isaac and Elizabeth Hale, Emma's parents, ran a tavern in Harmony in which JOSEPH SMITH SR. and Joseph Smith Jr. boarded in November 1825. The Smiths had come to Harmony to work for Josiah Stowell to hunt for a rumored Spanish treasure. Though the treasure hunting proved a failure, Joseph had made the acquaintance of Emma Hale, his future wife. In spite of Isaac Hale's disapproval of Joseph, he and Emma married on January 18, 1827, in South Bainbridge, NEW YORK, and traveled to MANCHESTER, New York, to live with Joseph's family. That fall, Joseph received the plates from the angel Moroni.

At the invitation of Isaac Hale, Joseph and Emma took up residence in Harmony, hoping this would be place where Joseph could begin the translation of the plates. Therefore, after their arrival in Harmony, Joseph and Emma purchased from Isaac a small home with some land where Joseph commenced translation. During the two and a half years the Smiths lived in Harmony, many important events took place: the Priesthoods, both Aaronic and Melchizedek, were restored; fifteen revelations now in the Doctrine and Covenants were received; the first baptisms were

Joseph Smith Jr. home in Harmony, Pennsylvania (center structure)

performed; most of the Book of Mormon was translated; the Prophet began work on what came to be known as the Joseph Smith Translation of the Bible; and Emma gave birth to her first child, who died the same day. As persecution mounted in Harmony against the Smiths, largely due to many false rumors, they found it necessary to move. Hearing of their difficulties, the Peter Whitmer family in Fayette, New York, extended an invitation for the Smiths to live with them.

Harris, Martin: One of the Three Witnesses to the Book of Mormon (D&C 5:2, 11) and scribe to Joseph Smith during the early days of translation. Martin, well known for being a patriot, served in the War of 1812. At age 25, Martin married his 16-year-old cousin Lucy, and the couple settled in Palmyra, New York, as farmers. Martin assisted the Prophet financially to his move from Manchester, New York, to Harmony, Pennsylvania, in December 1827. In 1828, due to carelessness, Martin lost part of the manuscript he had helped Joseph translate. However, after Martin repented he was forgiven and allowed to see the plates so that he could testify of them. Martin mortgaged a portion of his farm to help pay for the publication of the Book of Mormon (D&C 19:26). In 1835, Martin was called to be part of the first High Council in Kirtland, but in 1837 he was rejected "for speaking against the Prophet." He separated himself from the Church and did not return until he was 86 years old. Martin was rebaptized in Salt Lake City in 1870 and died July 9, 1875.

Martin Harris

Hell: The abode of Satan and his angels. The word *hell* is an English translation of the Hebrew term *sheol,* and signifies an abode of departed spirits, corresponding to the Greek *hades*. In common speech, *hell* generally denotes the place of torment for the wicked (BD, *699).* "Hell" is used in two senses in the scriptures: First, it may refer to spirit prison, the portion of the post-earthly spirit world to which the wicked are consigned (see D&C 76:84–85). This usage is common in the Book of Mormon (see 2 Ne. 9:11–13). This concept is also taught in section 19. At the JUDGMENT, those found on the "left hand" of God (D&C 19:5) are taken to hell in order to be cleansed of unrepentant sins; they must suffer even as the Savior suffered (D&C 19:16–18). Even though this state may be called "endless torment" and the result is "eternal damnation" (D&C 19:6–7), one will not be compelled to suffer forever in hell. After paying the price of and being cleansed from sin, one will in due time depart from hell and receive a kingdom of glory. One consequence of going to hell is eternal damnation—limitations being imposed that prevent progression to godhood. Elder Richard G. Scott explained, "The painful consequences of sin were purposely put in His plan of happiness by a compassionate Father in Heaven so that you need not follow that tragic path in life. A sinner will not only suffer in this life, but sins that have not been forgiven through true repentance will cause anguish beyond the veil" (*Ensign,* Nov. 2002, 86).

Hell, then, may also refer to the ultimate place for the wicked, specifically those who have committed the UNPARDONABLE SIN. It is known as PERDITION, meaning loss. Those who inherit this state—the sons of perdition—have lost all contact with God's glory, hence their dwelling place is called "outer darkness" (D&C 101:91). This realm is also described as "a kingdom which is not a kingdom of glory" (D&C 88:24).

High Council: An important administrative body in the Church. At the general Church level, the QUORUM of the Twelve APOSTLES is identified as a "traveling presiding high council" (D&C 107:33). A "standing high council" is organized in each STAKE of ZION. The Church's first stake was established February 17, 1834, with the organization of the high council at KIRTLAND. SECTION 102 outlines the procedures to be followed when a high council functions as a DISCIPLINARY COUNCIL.

High Priest: An office in the Melchizedek PRIESTHOOD. Brethren holding this office administer spiritual things and may function in any lesser office (see D&C 107:10–12). They are called "standing presidents," as the purpose of a high priests QUORUM is to prepare those who may be called to preside (see D&C 124:133–135).

In Old Testament times, the title of high priest was given to the one who presided over other priests, but who was a bearer of the Aaronic rather than Melchizedek PRIESTHOOD. In the present DISPENSATION, BISHOPS have been called to preside over the lesser priesthood (see D&C 107:87–88). High priests in the Melchizedek Priesthood may serve as bishops without being literal descendants of Aaron (see D&C 68:14–19; 107:73). The first high priests in this dispensation were called at a CONFERENCE held June 3–6, 1831, in KIRTLAND, OHIO. Statements at this time that brethren "received the high priesthood" typically meant that they had been ordained to the office of high priest. JESUS CHRIST Himself has been called the great High Priest (see Heb. 6:20; 9:11).

Hiram, OHIO: The home of JOSEPH and EMMA SMITH from September 12, 1831, to April 1, 1832. During this time, a number of important events transpired. In November, a CONFERENCE planned the publication of many of the REVELATIONS received by the PROPHET. This publication had 65 revelations, and in 1833 became known as the Book of Commandments, the predecessor to the 1835 edition of the Doctrine and Covenants. During this conference, four revelations were received (sections 1, 67, 68, and 133).

While at Hiram, Joseph was engaged in the revision of the BIBLE. SIDNEY RIGDON, his scribe for the revision, had also moved to Hiram from Kirtland to continue work on what became known as the JOSEPH SMITH TRANSLATION of the Bible. During their revisions in February 1832, Joseph and Sidney received a series of several visions on the kingdoms of glory, recorded as SECTION 76. This revelation was one of 15 revelations

John Johnson farm home in Hiram, Ohio

received by the Prophet in Hiram. Soon after these visions, on March 24, Joseph and Sidney were tarred and feathered by a mob. While Joseph and Sidney barely escaped this beating with their lives, the Smith's ten-month-old son, Joseph Murdock Smith, died of exposure resulting from the attack.

Holy Ghost: A male personage of spirit and the third member of the Godhead. The Holy Ghost—also known as the Holy Spirit, the Spirit of God, the Comforter, and the Testator—is the communicator between God and man. Being a spirit allows the Holy Ghost to carry out this assignment (see D&C 130:22). Because the Holy Ghost has a definite form and size, He cannot be everywhere at once, but His influence can be felt everywhere by the honest in heart. When we speak of feeling the Spirit, we are usually referring to receiving His influence and power rather than recognizing His actual presence. The messages of the Holy Ghost may be communicated in a more general way through the LIGHT OF CHRIST or more specifically when He acts directly upon our spirits.

The *gift* of the Holy Ghost is the *right,* if one is worthy, to have the constant companionship of the third member of the Godhead. The Holy Ghost does manifest Himself on a limited basis as necessary to unbaptized persons, but only with the laying on of hands following baptism can one have the right to this influence on a continuing basis. The words "receive the Holy Ghost" are a command, making it the individual's responsibility rather than merely his privilege to receive the Spirit (compare D&C 46:8).

Elder Robert D. Hales testified, "We are able to receive this spiritual manifestation because the Holy Ghost is 'a personage of Spirit' who can 'dwell in us' (D&C 130:22). His mission is to witness of the Father and the Son, convey Their will to us, and teach us 'all things what [we] should do' (2 Ne. 32:5). People everywhere may feel the influence of the Holy Ghost from time to time in their lives. But only those who have been baptized and confirmed can receive the gift of the Holy Ghost by the laying on of hands by one in authority, which makes His constant companionship possible. Retaining that companionship requires an earnest effort on the part of Church members. If we are not obedient to the laws, principles, and ordinances of the gospel, the Holy Ghost will withdraw. He cannot be with us if we are angry in our hearts, contentious with our companions, or critical of the Lord's anointed. He departs whenever we are rebellious, are immoral, dress or act immodestly, are unclean or profane in mind or body, are slothful in priesthood callings and duties, or commit other sins, for 'the Spirit of the Lord doth not dwell in unholy temples (Hel. 4:24)'" (*Liahona,* Nov. 2003, 28–31).

Holy Places: In preparation for the LATTER DAYS, the Saints are counseled to "stand in holy places"—places of spiritual refuge (see D&C 45:32). The "Prophecy on War" ended with this same counsel (D&C 87:8). We should make wherever we are a "holy place" by our own worthiness. President James E. Faust mentioned temples and chapels as holy places and encouraged the Saints to be a holy people (see *Ensign,* May 2005, 67–68). ELDER David A. Bednar insisted that we must have both clean hands and a pure heart to stand in holy places (see *Ensign,* Nov. 2007, 80–83).

Elder Dennis B. Neuenschwander of the SEVENTY provided an additional perspective: "Holy places have always been essential to the proper worship of God. For Latter-day Saints, such holy places include venues of historic significance, our homes, sacrament meetings, and temples. Much of what we reverence, and what we teach our children to reverence as holy and sacred, is reflected in these places. The faith and reverence associated with them and the respect we have for what transpires or has transpired in them make them holy. The importance of holy places and sacred space in our worship can hardly be overestimated" (*Ensign,* May 2003, 71).

Holy Spirit of Promise: The HOLY GHOST in His role as the one who "seals" or ratifies ordinances that are received worthily. This may take place at the time the ordinance is received, or later on if a person, through repentance, qualifies for the promised blessings. Furthermore, when an individual has sufficiently proven himself, he may receive "the promise of eternal life" (see D&C 76:53–54, 88:3–4, 131:5–6).

Hyde, Orson: An APOSTLE who dedicated the Holy Land for the return of the Jews. Born January 8, 1805, Orson became a Campbellite pastor in Florence, OHIO. While he was preaching against the BOOK OF MORMON, he had a thought that the "Mormon Bible" might be true and came to the personal conclusion that he was doing wrong. Orson was baptized on October 30, 1831. He served as the clerk to JOSEPH SMITH from 1831 to 1834, in which time he recorded the Kirtland REVELATIONS. He also served on the HIGH COUNCIL in KIRTLAND and became a member of the original member of the QUORUM of the Twelve. After his first mission in Britain, Hyde fell away from the Church from October 1838 to the spring of 1839. He repented and returned and was called to preach the gospel to those in England and Palestine. Atop the Mount of Olives, Elder Hyde dedicated the land and prophesied the erection of a TEMPLE in Jerusalem. In 1852, he moved to Salt Lake City, where he served in the Quorum of the Twelve Apostles. He died November 28, 1878.

— I —

Idumea or Edom: An ancient kingdom, like BABYLON, used as a symbol for worldly wickedness (see D&C 1:36).

Illinois: Headquarters of the Church from 1839 to 1846, and the site of the martyrdoms of JOSEPH and HYRUM SMITH in 1844 (D&C 124, 135). From 1830 through 1839, ILLINOIS was a thoroughfare state between the two official gathering places of the Church—OHIO and MISSOURI. In the fall of 1830, Lamanite MISSIONARIES were the first to travel this route (D&C 28, 32). The next group of members who traveled through ILLINOIS were several pairs of missionaries who were called by revelation (D&C 52:3) to journey from OHIO to the land of Missouri, the promised New Jerusalem (D&C 57; 58). In 1834, ZION'S CAMP traversed the state of ILLINOIS. By 1835, missionaries had labored in nearly every county in ILLINOIS, establishing many important settlements with branches along the thoroughfare trails. In 1838, hundreds of faithful members of the Church fled OHIO as a result of the Apostasy in KIRTLAND. They organized into what was referred to as the "Kirtland Camp," and traveled through ILLINOIS destined for Far West, Missouri. An incredible episode in the pre-Nauvoo period took place in 1838 and 1839. Literally thousands of Mormons flooded into Quincy, ILLINOIS, from Missouri, following Governor Boggs' Extermination Order. The citizens of ILLINOIS opened their doors and hearts to the weary Saints, who were temporarily leaderless and homeless.

The era of the Church's strongest influence in ILLINOIS was the Saints' time in Nauvoo. The city rose from the swamps to become a thriving river-town community along the Mississippi River. The NAUVOO TEMPLE was the centerpiece of the community, and missionaries were dispersed to foreign countries and every state in the nation. Joseph and his brother Hyrum were martyred at Carthage, ILLINOIS, on June 27, 1844. Persecutions continued, and in 1846, Church members in and around Nauvoo, no longer safe, were forced to flee their homes as they crossed the frozen Mississippi River to a safer haven in Iowa.

Independence, Missouri: See Jackson County, Missouri.

Israel: The Lord's COVENANT people. ABRAHAM's grandson Jacob was given the name "Israel" (Gen. 25:12), meaning "one who prevails with God" (BD, 708). Israel's twelve sons became the heads of tribes, and his descendants are often called the children or house of Israel. They are heirs of the covenant the Lord made with Abraham (see Abr. 2:9–11). Individuals may either be blood descendants of Jacob, or they may be adopted into the house of Israel through faithful living (see 3 Ne. 21: 22; compare Luke 3:8). PATRIARCHS declare through which tribe of Israel individuals will receive blessings. As heirs to the Lord's covenant with Abraham, our responsibility is to share the GOSPEL with the world.

Israel, Lost Tribes of: See LOST TEN TRIBES.

— J —

Jackson County, Missouri: The land of promise, with Independence as the "the center Place" of ZION, the site for the temple being just west of town (D&C 57:2–3). As early as September 1830, a revelation indicated that the City of Zion, the New Jerusalem, was to be built by the Latter-day Saints "on the borders of the Lamanites" (D&C 28:9).

JOSEPH SMITH and other Church leaders were directed to journey to the land of Missouri so that it could "be made known unto them the land of their inheritance" (D&C 52:3–4). Arriving in the summer of 1831 at Independence, the PROPHET was informed that Missouri was the land of promise, that Independence was the future city of Zion, and that a temple was to be built west of the city (D&C 57:2–3). The land was to be purchased and the SAINTS were to gather there "speedily." SIDNEY GILBERT was to establish a store, W. W. PHELPS was to be a printer, and OLIVER COWDERY was to edit material for publication. Before Joseph returned to KIRTLAND, he presided over the dedication of the land and dedicated the temple site (D&C 58:57).

Despite the Saints' enthusiasm for Jackson County, it proved to be a troublesome place for them. Differences in religion, politics, economics, and social concerns drove wedges between the Missourians and the Mormons. As part of the 1820 Missouri Compromise, Missouri became a slave state. The Latter-day Saints, predominantly from the North, opposed slavery. Violence erupted in the summer of 1833, and by November over a thousand members were driven from the county across the Missouri River into CLAY COUNTY for a temporary place of refuge.

Jehovah: The name by which JESUS CHRIST was known in the Old Testament. "It denotes the 'Unchangeable One,' 'the eternal I AM' (Ex. 6: 3; Ps. 83: 18; Isa. 12: 2, 26: 4)" (BD, 710). In the King James translation, Jehovah is rendered "Lord" or "God" and is printed in capital letters. A comparison of statements in the Old and New Testaments confirms that Jehovah is Jesus Christ; Jehovah and Jesus Christ are identified as the Creator of heaven and earth (compare Isa. 44:24, 45:11–12 with John 1:1–3 and Heb. 1:1–3). Similarly, both are identified as the only Savior (compare Isa. 12:2; 43:3, 11 and Hosea 13:4 with Acts 4:12). The Doctrine and Covenants clearly identifies Jesus Christ as the God of the Old Testament (see D&C 38:1–4). The dedicatory prayer for the KIRTLAND TEMPLE addressed the Lord as Jehovah (D&C 109:34, 56), and He was identified as Jehovah when He appeared in the temple one week later (see D&C 110:3).

Jesus Christ: The Son of God, the Creator of worlds, the Firstborn of the Father, the God of the Old Testament, the Light of the World, and the voice of the Doctrine and Covenants. Speaking of the role of Jesus Christ in the Doctrine and Covenants, the book's "Explanatory Introduction" states, "Finally, the testimony that is given of Jesus Christ—his divinity, his majesty, his perfection, his love, and his redeeming power—makes this book of great value to the human family and of more worth than the riches of the whole earth." Unique to the Doctrine and Covenants is the autobiographical information given by the post-resurrected Lord and Savior Jesus Christ. His role, His divine attributes, His mission, and His SECOND COMING in glory are all taught in a clear, concise way in this book. In addition, this volume of scripture also teaches our relationship to Christ and our responsibility to seek after His greatest gift—ETERNAL LIFE.

Jesus Christ

The Role of Jesus Christ. Elohim is the Father of the spirits of all those who have ever lived or will yet live upon the earth. His spirit offspring are innumerable. Among this mighty throng in the pre-earth life stood one like unto God the Father (see Abr. 3:24) who was known by the name of JEHOVAH or the Great I AM (D&C 29:1; 39:1; 109:34, 42, 56; 110:3–4; 128:9). It was He who would come to earth as Jesus, the Savior of mankind. The Doctrine and Covenants gives a clear understanding of the eternal role of the Savior.

Because He merited it, Jehovah was the Firstborn of the spirit offspring of Elohim (D&C 93:21), and as such, He became the legal heir to all the Father owned. Thus, the responsibility fell upon Jehovah to carry out the plan of salvation ordained by the Father whereby the rest of His spirit children might have the opportunity, through obedience, to become joint heirs with the Firstborn.

The Savior is the Creator of all things. The Doctrine and Covenants teaches this principle (D&C 14:9; 29:31; 38:3; 45:1; 76:24; 93:10; 95:7). Because He is the Creator of all things on EARTH, its elements respond to His commands.

The Savior is the Light of the World. Through the LIGHT OF CHRIST, He governs and controls the universe and gives life to all that is therein (D&C 88:6–10). By this same immensity-filling light—and also, to certain faithful ones, by the power of the Holy Ghost—He enlightens the mind and quickens the understanding (D&C 88:11). By His own upright, sinless, and perfect course in the premortal life, in mortality, and in resurrected glory, He sets a perfect example and is able to say to all men: "Follow thou me" (2 Ne. 31:10; D&C 45:4).

The Attributes of Jesus Christ. The inherent characteristics of the Savior are referred to throughout the scriptures as attributes. These divine qualities are held in fulness and perfection by the Savior because of His total obedience to the mind and will of the Father (D&C 93:11–17). It is important that we understand these attributes so that we can exercise FAITH in God. The *Lectures on Faith,* compiled under the direction of the JOSEPH SMITH, declares: "The real design which the God of heaven had in view in making the human family acquainted with his attributes, was, that they, through the idea of the existence of his attributes, might be enabled to exercise faith in him, and through the exercise of faith in him, might obtain eternal life; for without the idea of the existence of the attributes which belong to God, the minds of men could not have power to exercise faith in him so as to lay hold upon eternal life" (4:2).

Some of the attributes of the Lord are knowledge; faith, or power; justice; judgment; mercy; and truth (*Lectures on Faith,* 4:41–43). The Doctrine and Covenants testifies of these attributes and helps to increase our understanding of many of them.

Some have taught that the Savior and even God the Father are ever learning. This notion is inconsistent with the teaching of the scriptures that God knows all things (D&C 38:2). The knowledge that God possesses includes an understanding of the past, present, and future (D&C 130:7). The story of the loss of the 116-page manuscript by MARTIN HARRIS at the time the PROPHET was translating the BOOK OF MORMON is an example of the foreknowledge of God (D&C 3, 10; W of M 1:3–7).

By being perfectly obedient to the will of the Father, Jesus brought about the ATONEMENT and retains "all power" (D&C 19:3; see 49:6; 61:1). The Doctrine and Covenants, like the other standard works, bears witness that in the Godhead resides all power. There is nothing in the universe with sufficient power to stay the Lord's hand (see D&C 38:33). The word *power* is used over two hundred times in the Doctrine and Covenants, and in most of those usages it bears witness of God's power and His use of it for the benefit of His people.

One of the most comforting things derived from faith in the Savior is the knowledge that at some time everything will be made right—that justice will be done. There is something inherent in virtually every person that cries out for the righting of wrongs, the squaring of accounts, the giving of just dues, whether those dues be blessings for obedience or punishments for disobedience. In numerous instances in the Doctrine and Covenants, the Lord bears witness that He is a just God and that all people will be brought to judgment, receiving blessings for obedience, and punishments for all unrepented-of transgressions (D&C 3:4; 10:28; 39:16–18; 82:4; 84:102; 107:84; 109:77).

Knowing of God's awesome powers and of His continual promises to bring individuals to judgment would be a frightening and discouraging thing if one did not know that He also has a perfection and fulness of love and mercy. In addition to many promises of mercy and FORGIVENESS for the repentant (D&C 3:10; 29:1; 38:14; 54:6; 61:2; 76:5; 88:40), the Doctrine and Covenants contains some of the most tender and endearing expressions of the Savior to His servants and His people:

"Be faithful and diligent . . . and I will encircle thee in the arms of my love" (D&C 6:20).

"Fear not to do good, my sons" (D&C 6:33).

"Fear not, little flock" (D&C 6:34).

"From henceforth I shall call you friends" (D&C 84:77).

"I will call you friends, for you are my friends" (D&C 93:45).

"Whom I love I also chasten . . . and I have loved you" (D&C 95:1).

Understanding of the attribute of truth comes primarily from the Doctrine and Covenants, where it is revealed that truth is light (D&C 84:45; 88:6–7); truth is eternal (D&C 88:66); truth is knowledge of things as they are, and as they were, and as they are to come (see D&C 93:24). If the Savior is the Light of the World and the Light of Christ lights every person who comes into the world, and if truth is light, then it follows that not only is the Savior the source of truth but His very nature is truth.

All scriptures bear witness and teach of the attributes of deity, and the Doctrine and Covenants joins the other standard works as a powerful voice in this testimony.

The Mission of Jesus Christ. Only through Christ is salvation possible. Because He is God, and was God even in mortality, Jesus Christ possesses inherent powers and abilities that no other person has ever possessed. He is God's Only Begotten Son and thus possesses the powers and intelligence of God Himself. He is perfect in nature, so He was able to assume the sins of all other beings, to suffer for them so that, on condition of their REPENTANCE, they would not have to suffer.

Not only was Jesus *able* to bear the sins of His brothers and sisters, He was also *willing* to do so. He thereby demonstrated His great love (D&C 34:1–3) for every living soul. He accomplished this redemption by a voluntary act called the Atonement, in which He took upon Himself the sins of all mankind. The intense suffering of the Savior commenced in the Garden of Gethsemane and continued at Calvary. Luke described the suffering in the garden as being so intense that Christ's "sweat was as it were great drops of blood" (Luke 22:44.) Some scholars have tried to explain this passage as metaphorical and not literal; that is, they say that Jesus perspired heavily but did not actually bleed from His pores. The Doctrine and Covenants shows that this loss of blood was literal, describing in some detail His unfathomable suffering (D&C 19:15–19; 76:69).

Christ suffered as only a God could suffer, in both body and spirit. He took the cup willingly. In that solitary garden, made sacred by His presence, He "suffered the pain of all men, that all men might repent and come unto him" (D&C 18:11).

The Doctrine and Covenants testifies that Jesus, in bringing about the Atonement, descended below all things—meaning that He suffered the pains of HELL for all people if they would repent (D&C 88:6; 122:8). Because He suffered to this extent, there is no sin, no pain, no suffering that He cannot comprehend. He knows each individual's weaknesses. He understands each of us better than we understand ourselves, and thus the Savior knows "how to succor them who are tempted" (D&C 62:1).

Our Relationship to Christ. Through the Atonement of Christ, salvation is extended to every child of God. The responsibility rests upon each individual to repent, to believe in Christ, and then to endure faithfully to the end (see D&C 20:29). The Savior's Atonement, combined with a willing obedience to His GOSPEL, qualifies one to become His son or daughter (see D&C 39:4–6; 11:30; 25:1).

Thus, by keeping all commandments pertaining to Christ's gospel, we may receive His power and attributes and become His children. Eventually, through the grace of God, we may receive the fulness of godly power and attributes "*made perfect* through Jesus . . . who wrought out this perfect atonement through the shedding of his own blood" (D&C 76:69; italics added).

The Doctrine and Covenants commands all people to take upon themselves Christ's name, for in His name only is there salvation: "Take upon you the name of Christ, and speak the truth in soberness. And as many as repent and are baptized in my name, which is Jesus Christ, and endure to the end, the same shall be saved. Behold, Jesus Christ is the name which is given of the Father, and there is none other name given whereby men can be saved. . . . Wherefore, if they know not the name by which they are called, they cannot have place in the kingdom of my Father" (D&C 18:21–25). Those who believe in His name and keep His commandments shall find rest (see D&C 38:4), which is everlasting life in His presence (see D&C 45:3–5).

Christ's Coming. On April 3, 1836, ELIJAH appeared in the KIRTLAND TEMPLE to Joseph Smith and OLIVER COWDERY in fulfillment of the prophecy made by Malachi (Mal. 4:5–6; D&C 110:13–16). The prophet Elijah testified that He had come so that members of the Church might "know that the great and dreadful day of the Lord is near, even at the doors" (D&C 110:16). Christ's SECOND COMING in glory (D&C 34:7–8), to reign with the righteous for a thousand years (D&C 29:11, 17), is an event longed for by all Saints in all dispensations. This DISPENSATION has the privilege to make final preparation for His coming and to see that the kingdom of God is prepared to meet Him (D&C 65:6). Prior to His coming, however, there will be some who are members of His Church who will say that Christ delays His coming, and as a result, they will not be prepared (see D&C 45:26). It behooves all to live as though the Savior will come tomorrow (D&C 64:23), for those who are prepared need not fear (D&C 38:30).

The Doctrine and Covenants is a handbook on the Second Coming. It is replete with prophecies, promises, clarifications, and new revelations on the JUDGMENTS that precede this coming in glory, on the Second Coming itself, and on the conditions that will prevail during the Savior's MILLENNIAL reign.

The Doctrine and Covenants bears testimony of Christ. Just as the Book of Mormon is called a second witness for Christ, so, and with equal validity, could the Doctrine and Covenants be described as a witness for the Savior. It affirms that He was the Firstborn of Heavenly Father; that by Him the worlds were created; that He came to earth as God's Only Begotten Son in the flesh; that He suffered temptations, wrought miracles, proclaimed His gospel, and invited all to come to Him, repent, and receive the saving ordinances of the gospel. In the Doctrine and Covenants, the Savior witnesses that He suffered the pains of all and accomplished the perfect Atonement; that He was crucified, buried, and went into the world of spirits (D&C 138), where He declared His everlasting gospel and the doctrine of resurrection to an innumerable company of righteous spirits; and appointed and commissioned messengers to go to the wicked and disobedient spirits and teach them.

In the Doctrine and Covenants, the Lord says that on the third day after His death He rose again and He appeared to many, including the Nephites on the American continent and the Ten Tribes; that He ascended into heaven, where He sits in glory on the right hand of His Father; and that He has promised to come to earth again to reign with the righteous Saints for one thousand years.

The Doctrine and Covenants is a source of great strength in increasing our knowledge of the Savior in every aspect. It contributes many new insights to an understanding of the Holy One of Israel. It is a book of scripture that must be read and studied diligently by all Latter-day Saints.

President Gordon B. Hinckley testified, "It is He, Jesus Christ, who stands at the head of this Church which bears His sacred name. He is watching over it. He is guiding it. Standing at the right hand of His Father, He directs this work. Unitedly, as His Apostles, authorized and commissioned by Him to do so, we bear our witness that He lives and that He will come again to claim His kingdom and rule as King of Kings and Lord of Lords. Of this we are certain and bear apostolic testimony in His holy name, even the name of Jesus Christ, amen" (*Ensign,* Apr. 2001, 4).

Johnson, John: An early convert most remembered for the hospitality he showed JOSEPH SMITH and his wife, EMMA, when they needed a place to stay when they first arrived in Hiram, OHIO. John was born April 11, 1778, in Cheshire County, New Hampshire. In 1818, he and his Methodist family moved to Hiram, where they came in contact with the Latter-day SAINTS. After a small group conversation about the power to heal, the Prophet Joseph Smith took Elsa by the arm and healed her of her chronic rheumatism, which led to the baptism of the Johnson family. John was a member of the original HIGH COUNCIL (D&C 102:3). He also had one of the stewardships of land that were reassigned when the UNITED ORDER was dissolved in KIRTLAND (D&C 104: 24, 34). John was promised that if he kept the commandments he would receive eternal life (D&C 96:6). Unfortunately, John fell away from the Church in 1837 due to financial problems and a loss of commitment. His inn at Kirtland is one of the buildings that has been restored and can be visited today.

John the Baptist: The forerunner to JESUS CHRIST in preparing the way for His ministry. JOSEPH SMITH called John the Baptist the greatest prophet because he was entrusted with the "divine mission of preparing the way before the face of the Lord" and was given the honor of baptizing the Son of Man (*HC,* 6:316). During this dispensation, John restored the Aaronic PRIESTHOOD to Joseph Smith and OLIVER COWDERY on May 15, 1829 (D&C 13:1).

SIDNEY RIGDON was told by the Lord that he "wast sent forth, even as John, to prepare the way for me," because he had taught his congregation about the restoration of the New Testament Church, preparing them for the missionaries who would later teach them the restored gospel (D&C 35: 3–4).

John the Beloved: One of Christ's APOSTLES who has assisted in the Restoration of the GOSPEL during the LATTER DAYS. He was one of the chief Apostles, along with Peter and James. SECTION 7 is the translation of a parchment record John had made and records that he asked the RESURRECTED Lord to give him "power over death" so he could continue his work as an Apostle until Christ would come again. Therefore, John did not die, but rather remained on the EARTH as a TRANSLATED BEING. In 1831, Joseph Smith learned that John is laboring among the LOST TRIBES of Israel (*HC,* 1:76, footnote).

PETER, JAMES, AND JOHN ordained JOSEPH SMITH and OLIVER COWDERY to be Apostles in this last DISPENSATION (D&C 27:12). The Lord indicated that by the mouth of John, He cursed the waters (D&C 61:14). John is also referred to as "John the Revelator" because he is the author of the book of Revelation. While working on the Joseph Smith Translation of the Bible, the PROPHET received SECTION 77, which clarified some of the writings of John.

Joseph Smith Translation (JST): A revision of biblical texts made by the PROPHET through inspiration, known earlier as the Inspired Version of the Bible. Statements about the Prophet "translating" the Bible during the early years of the Church actually referred to this inspired revision. This was not a "translation" in the usual sense because no foreign language texts were involved. Instead, the Prophet received, through revelation, revisions that clarified the meaning of the King James Version in English. Still, the JST is more than merely commentary on the meaning of biblical passages; it appears in many instances to be a restoration of the original, or, strictly speaking, an inspired English translation of the original Hebrew, Aramaic, and Greek writings. In this latter sense, the Inspired Version might be called a "translation."

This Prophet's inspired revision of Genesis begins with what we know as the Book of Moses in the Pearl of Great Price, received by revelation in June and December of 1830. By September of that year, Joseph had started revising the Old Testament. The following March, the Lord directed the Prophet to work on the New Testament (see D&C 45:60–61). He completed this phase of the project by February 2, 1833. Roughly a month later, the Lord spoke to the Prophet about finishing "the translation of the prophets," that is, the Old Testament (D&C 90:13), and also counseled him not to revise the Apocrypha (see SECTION 91). On July 2, 1833, Joseph Smith recorded, "We this day finished the translating of the Scriptures, for which we returned gratitude to our Heavenly Father" (*HC,* 1:368).

The revisions in the JST help clarify biblical passages and gospel doctrines. These changes are most numerous in the books of Genesis and Matthew. The Church continues to use the King James Version as its official Bible, as do many other Christian churches; the most important insights from the JST are included in footnotes and in a special appendix.

The Joseph Smith Translation of the Bible has contributed to our knowledge of gospel doctrines in still another way. Questions about the meaning of specific biblical passages became the occasion for receiving several revelations now in the Doctrine and Covenants (sections 74, 76, 77, 86, 91, and 113, for example).

Judgment: One's opportunity, after this life, to account for his or her life.

We will actually pass through a series of judgments. We were not cast out with SATAN and his followers in the PRE-MORTAL existence, but were judged worthy to come to EARTH and receive our physical bodies. Our assignment to come to earth at a time when we could hear and accept the gospel is a form of judgment. Upon leaving this MORTAL life, a judgment will determine our status in the post-earthly SPIRIT WORLD (see Alma 40:11–14). The RESURRECTION will be a judgment as we are given a body suited for the particular kingdom we are to inherit (see D&C 88:28–32). At last, the Final Judgment will determine our place in either the CELESTIAL, terrestrial, or telestial kingdom, or in the "kingdom which is not a kingdom of glory" (D&C 88:22–24).

We will be judged under the direction of the Savior (see John 5: 22), who not only understands all of our circumstances but loves us (D&C 137:9). Others, such as the Twelve APOSTLES, will assist (see D&C 29:12). Alma taught that not just our deeds but our words and even our thoughts will be considered (Alma 12:14). The Lord has promised that if we REPENT of our sins, He will "remember them no more" (D&C 58:42). Nevertheless, if we return to these sins, "the former sins return" (D&C 82:7). We will not be surprised by the outcome of the judgment, because we will have a "bright recollection" of all our deeds (Alma 11:43). According to the principle of restoration, we will inherit the state consistent with what we will have become (2 Ne. 9:16). Whatever the outcome of the final judgment, we will be in the place that is best for us; for example, a sinner would be more miserable in the presence of God than "to dwell with the damned souls in hell" (Morm. 8:4). Elder Russell M. Nelson affirmed, "Each of you will be judged according to your individual works and the desires of your hearts. You will not be required to pay the debt of any other. Your eventual placement in the celestial, terrestrial, or telestial kingdom will not be determined by chance. The Lord has prescribed unchanging requirements for each. You can know what the scriptures teach, and pattern your lives accordingly (see John 14:2; 1 Cor. 15:40–41; D&C 76:50–119; D&C 98:18)" (*Ensign,* Nov. 1993, 33).

Justification: A necessary step on our way to salvation. This key step has been defined in different ways. One commentary states: "Justification is a judicial or legal term, and it means being acquitted or being declared innocent of all charges" (*CDC,* 1:136). This is made possible following REPENTANCE, BAPTISM, and obedience to God's law (D&C 88:39) through the ATONEMENT of Christ (Rom. 5:9). Elder Bruce R. McConkie relates justification to the role of the HOLY GHOST, or HOLY SPIRIT OF

Promise, in ratifying ordinances that are received worthily (*MD*, 408). Justification should lead to the further qualifying step of SANCTIFICATION. SECTION 20, given at the time the Church was organized, affirmed that "justification through the grace of our Lord and Savior Jesus Christ is just and true" (v. 30). Elder Bruce R. McConkie explained, "We believe in the law of justification. By virtue of this law, if a man walks, acts, and lives in this life in such a manner that his conduct is justified by the Spirit, he eventually will attain an inheritance in the celestial world. . . . Now let us take a simple illustration. If an individual is to gain an inheritance in the celestial world, he has to enter in at the gate of baptism, that ordinance being performed under the hands of a legal administrator. If he comes forward prepared by worthiness . . . it is ratified by the Holy Ghost, or it is sealed by the Holy Spirit of Promise. As a result it is of full force and validity in this life and in the life to come" (CR, Apr. 1956, 64–66).

K

Keys: The right to preside and the power to direct in the Lord's work. STAKE presidents, BISHOPs, and ELDERS QUORUM presidents—but not their counselors—hold keys. Elder Spencer W. Kimball taught that each member of the Quorum of the Twelve Apostles receives all the keys, which are held "in suspension, pending a time when he might become the senior Apostle and the President" (CR, Apr. 1970, 118). The President of the Church is the only one who is authorized to exercise the keys in full (see D&C 132:7). Counselors in the First Presidency are equal in holding the keys, but they are still subject to the administration and direction of the President of the Church (see D&C 90:6–7). Leaders receive keys when they are set apart, but then lose them when they are released.

President Joseph Fielding Smith said that keys are "the right of presidency; they are the power and authority to govern and direct all of the Lord's affairs on earth. Those who hold them have power to govern and control the manner in which all others may serve in the priesthood. All of us may hold the priesthood, but we can only use it as authorized and directed so to do by those who hold the keys. This priesthood and these keys were conferred upon Joseph Smith and Oliver Cowdery by Peter, James, and John and by Moses and Elijah and others of the ancient prophets. . . . May I now say—very plainly and very emphatically—that we have the holy priesthood and that the keys of the kingdom of God are here. They are found only in The Church of Jesus Christ of Latter-day Saints" (*Ensign*, July 1972, 87). Elder Russell M. Nelson used this analogy, "You know something about keys. In your pocket there might be a key to your home or car. Priesthood keys, on the other hand, are intangible and invisible. They 'switch on' the authority of the priesthood. Some keys even convey power to bind in heaven as well as on earth" (*Ensign,* Nov. 2003, 44).

Kirtland, OHIO: Headquarters of the Church from 1831 to 1838, and site of the first Latter-day temple. This small town in northeast OHIO first heard of the restored gospel when four elders serving in the LAMANITE MISSION stopped there in route to MISSOURI (D&C 28:32). One of the missionaries, PARLEY P. PRATT, was acquainted with a Campbellite minister named SIDNEY RIGDON, and therefore sought him out. Within a month's time, the membership of the Church nearly doubled as Rigdon and many other notable future leaders were converted. Sections 37 and 38 called for the NEW YORK and PENNSYLVANIA SAINTS to "gather to the OHIO," where the Lord could give them additional blessings.

A significant blessing in Kirtland, OHIO, was the building of the temple, which served as a spiritual center for the Church and as a house of learning. Around and during the time of its dedication, an unparalleled Pentecostal outpouring occurred (D&C 109). The appearance of JESUS CHRIST and of several biblical PROPHETS, who restored KEYS, was extraordinary (D&C 110). Sixty-five revelations published in the Doctrine and Covenants were received in Kirtland—the most in any single location. The 1835 edition of the Doctrine and Covenants was compiled, published, and sustained as canonized scripture during this era. In addition, the first LDS hymnal was published (D&C 25:11–12). Also in Kirtland, the Prophet completed the JOSEPH SMITH TRANSLATION of the Bible, and the book of Abraham was translated from papyrus scrolls.

Important aspects of the Church's organizational structure were put into place in Kirtland. This included the establishment of the First Presidency, the Quorum of the Twelve APOSTLES, the Seventy, patriarchs, and high priests (D&C 107). The first stake of the Church was organized in Kirtland, along with a high council, and the Church's first BISHOP was called there (D&C 102; 41).

Kirtland Temple: The first TEMPLE dedicated in this DISPENSATION. In December 1832, the Church was commanded to "establish a house" where the SCHOOL OF THE PROPHETS could meet (D&C 88:119). The following May, the Lord described a complex of three sacred buildings at the center of KIRTLAND, the first being the temple (D&C 94). In June, He chastised the Saints for not having begun work on His house, explaining that He wanted to ENDOW them with power there (D&C 95:1–8). He instructed that the temple be built "not after the manner of the world," but according to a design He promised to reveal to three appointed brethren (D&C 95:13–17). Soon afterwards, the FIRST PRESIDENCY received a vision in which they saw the temple's exterior and then its interior (*TDE*, 25–26).

Cornerstones were laid for the temple three weeks later on June 23, 1833. JOSEPH SMITH personally led the work in the quarry. Progress was hampered by the Saints' poverty and by persecution from their enemies. The departure of many able-bodied men with ZION'S CAMP the following year also slowed the work. As construction moved forward in 1835, women assisted by sewing clothing for the workmen and by preparing carpets and draperies for the temple.

As the building neared completion, meetings commenced in the small rooms in the attic story, starting in January 1836. At one of these early meetings, the PROPHET saw a VISION of the CELESTIAL kingdom as recorded in SECTION 137. During the next two months, meetings in the

The Kirtland Temple

temple were accompanied by marvelous spiritual outpourings. Joseph declared that "this was a time of rejoicing long to be remembered" (*HC,* 2:392). The temple's dedication on Sunday, March 27, was a climax. In the day-long service, the Prophet read the dedicatory prayer, which was given by REVELATION (see SECTION 109). The following week in meetings held in the temple, Church members witnessed remarkable spiritual experiences (*TDE,* 28–33). On Easter Sunday, April 3, 1836, the Savior appeared and accepted the temple, promising to speak to His servants there if it was kept unpolluted. MOSES, ELIAS, and ELIJAH then appeared and restored special KEYS (see SECTION 110).

Being the only building the Church had, the temple served a variety of purposes. The large room on the ground floor was a chapel. A similar room on the second floor was for instruction. There were no facilities for temple ordinances because these were not yet revealed. "The design and construction of the Kirtland Temple," Elder Boyd K. Packer explained, "was different from that of all other latter-day temples because its purpose was different. While already in 1836 certain ordinances had been introduced in a limited way which later would form part of the regular temple ordinances, the sacred ordinances and ceremonies performed in today's temples were not done in this first temple" (*HT,* 129). President Brigham Young noted that in Kirtland the first ELDERS received only a "portion of their first ENDOWMENTS, or we might say more clearly, some of the first, or introductory, or initiatory ordinances, preparatory to an endowment" (*JD,* 2:31).

In 1838, the Saints were forced to flee from Kirtland and leave their temple behind. Eventually, it became property of the Reorganized Church of Jesus Christ of Latter Day Saints (now known as the Community of Christ), who care for it and use it for special meetings.

Reflecting on the significance of the Kirtland Temple, Elder Harold B. Lee declared that it provided the setting "that there could be restored the keys, the effective keys necessary for the carrying on of the Lord's work." He concluded that the events of April 3, 1836 (as recorded in D&C 110), were "sufficient justification for the building of [this] temple" ("Correlation and Priesthood Genealogy," address at Priesthood Genealogical Research Seminar, 1968 [Provo: BYU Press, 1969], 60).

Knight, Joseph Sr.: An early convert to the Church who gave material assistance to JOSEPH SMITH and his scribes that enabled them to continue the translation of the plates. Joseph and Polly Knight, the parents of a large family, sacrificed a great deal for the restored gospel. Joseph Knight, a respected citizen of Colesville, New York, and a successful businessman, owned a card mill, a lumber mill, and a large grain farm. Joseph Smith was a hired hand at the Knight farm during the time he courted Emma Hale. Said Knight, "I paid him the money and I furnished him with a horse and cutter [sled] to go and see his girl" (Joseph Knight History).

Joseph Knight and his friend Josiah Stowell believed in Joseph Smith and his prophetic calling. Both Knight and Stowell were on hand in Manchester in September 1827 when Joseph received the plates. Joseph and Emma borrowed the Knight wagon and horse as transportation to and from the Hill Cumorah on that occasion. The first branch of the Church was organized on the Knight farm and several baptisms took place there, including Emma Smith's. Joseph Knight was admonished by the Lord to "unite with the true Church" (D&C 23:7). He was baptized June 28, 1830, along with Polly and their seven children and their spouses. The Knights gathered to Ohio and later to Jackson County. While traveling to Independence, Polly died. She was the first to be buried in Zion, and Joseph Smith spoke at her funeral. During the exodus from Nauvoo, Joseph Knight died at Mt. Pisgah, Iowa, on February 2, 1847.

Knight, Newel: Leader of the branch in Colesville, New York. Newel was a devout member of the Church and a dear friend of Joseph Smith. The son of Joseph and Polly Knight, Newel was born on September 13, 1800. He was baptized into the Church in May 1830. Shortly after Newel's baptism, an evil spirit was cast from him by the Prophet Joseph Smith; this came to be known as the first miracle of the restored Church. After moving with the Saints to Thompson, Ohio, near Kirtland, the Lord instructed Newel to move his branch of Saints to Missouri (D&C 54:7–9). They moved first to Jackson County and then, after countless persecutions, to Clay County. Newel remained a faithful member of the Church and died from lung inflammation on January 11, 1847, during the exodus from Nauvoo.

— L —

Lamanites: The designation given to those descended from the peoples of the Book of Mormon. This record initially identified them as descendants of Laman, Lehi's eldest son. For about five centuries, the Lamanites were described as being more wicked than the Nephites (see, for example, 2 Ne. 5:20–25). In about 24 b.c., however, this situation had

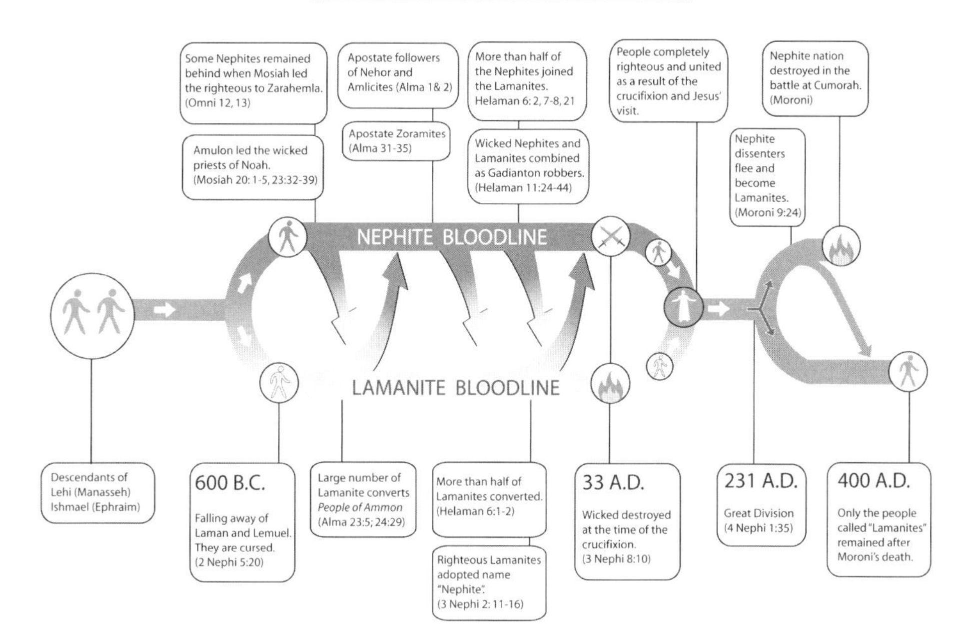

reversed (see Hel. 6:35–40); in fact, it was Samuel the Lamanite who was sent to call the Nephites to REPENTANCE (see Hel. 13–15). Following the Savior's visit to ancient America, about two hundred years passed in which there were no divisions among the people (see 4 Ne. 1:17). Later, when "Nephites" and "Lamanites" again emerged, both of these groups were of mixed blood—being descendants of both Nephi and Laman.

As the Book of Mormon record closed, the more wicked Nephites were destroyed in the final battle at Cumorah; only the Lamanites survived. These are among the ancestors of today's indigenous Americans. Hence, present-day Lamanites have such great PROPHETS as Nephi, Benjamin, Alma, Helaman, and others among their ancestors.

The scriptures speak of a glorious destiny for the Lamanites: "The Lamanites shall blossom as the rose" (D&C 49:24); "And the gospel of Jesus Christ shall be declared among them . . . and their scales of darkness shall begin to fall from their eyes; and many generations shall not pass away among them, save they shall be a pure and a delightsome people" (2 Ne. 30:5–6). Latter-day Saints have a particular responsibility to assist the Lamanites (see SECTION 28:8–9; compare Alma 17:11).

Lamanite Mission: The Church's first organized mission. The Lamanite Mission represented a commitment to assist these descendants of peoples in the BOOK OF MORMON. The first missionary to be called to serve in this mission was OLIVER COWDERY (D&C 28:9). Three others were soon called to join him—PETER WHITMER Jr. (D&C 30:5), PARLEY P. PRATT (D&C 32:1–2), and Ziba Peterson (D&C 32:3). Although these missionaries attempted to preach to Native Americans, they did not enjoy much success among them. The main significance of this mission was providing the Church's first contacts with SIDNEY RIGDON's congregation in the KIRTLAND area of northeastern OHIO. Soon there were about a thousand Church members in this region as a direct result of their preaching. The missionaries to the Lamanites were also the first Latter-day Saints to reach JACKSON COUNTY, MISSOURI, which would shortly be designated as the location for the future city of ZION (D&C 57:1–3).

Latter Days: The final DISPENSATION beginning with the Restoration of the GOSPEL and leading up to the SECOND COMING of Christ. SECTION 45 gives a helpful overview of the events prophesied to occur during this period. The "times of the GENTILES" began with the Restoration when the light of the GOSPEL burst over the earth (D&C 45:28). While in the Savior's day the gospel went first to the Jews and then to the Gentiles, in the present dispensation, the gospel is to go first to the Gentiles (D&C 90:9; 133:8). During the opening decades of the Church's history, the gospel was taken in power to the great gentile nations of northern Europe—Great Britain and Scandinavia. The Lord declared that the time would come when men would "receive it not; for they perceive not the light, and they turn their hearts from me because of the precepts of men" and the "times of the Gentiles will be fulfilled" (D&C 45:29–30).

The gathering of Israel would accelerate following the times of the Gentiles. As part of the dedicatory prayer for the KIRTLAND TEMPLE in 1836, the PROPHET prayed, "And may all the scattered remnants of Israel, who have been driven to the ends of the earth, come to a knowledge of the truth, believe in the Messiah, and be redeemed from oppression, and rejoice before thee" (D&C 109:67). One week later, MOSES restored the KEYS for this gathering and for "the leading of the ten tribes from the land of the north" (D&C 110:11). Especially during the second half of the twentieth century, such Israelite groups as the LAMANTIES have been particularly receptive to the gospel. The Jews have also gathered to the Holy Land and have established their own nation there. The Arabs, also descendants of ABRAHAM, have likewise become a major element in that part of the world.

Section 45 suggests that there would be wars and rumors of wars (D&C 45:26; see also D&C 87:1–4), and that iniquity would abound following the times of the Gentiles (D&C 45:27). There would also be "an overflowing scourge; for a desolating sickness shall cover the land," and "earthquakes also in divers places" (D&C 45:31–33).

One bright spot in this otherwise dismal picture is the rolling forth of the Lord's kingdom as prophesied by Daniel (see Dan. 2:26–45; compare D&C 65:2). The Church reached one million members in 1947, and reached the ten million mark just fifty years later. STAKES and TEMPLES can now be found on every continent. The Lord declared that His "army" must become "very great" and "sanctified" before ZION could be established (D&C 105:31).

As we read in D&C 88, calamities will intensify as the Second Coming draws closer: "The EARTH shall tremble and reel to and fro as a drunken man," so "men shall fall upon the ground and shall not be able to stand." In addition, "The sun shall hide his face, and shall refuse to give light; and the moon shall be bathed in blood; and the stars shall become exceedingly angry, and shall cast themselves down." People will hear "the voice of thunderings, and the voice of lightnings, and the voice of tempests and the voice of the waves of the sea heaving themselves beyond their bounds" (v. 87–90).

The basic message of the Doctrine and Covenants is a "voice of warning," urging us, "Prepare ye, prepare ye for that which is to come, for the Lord is nigh" (D&C 1:4, 12). The theme of many of our GENERAL AUTHORITIES' messages is preparing to withstand the challenges of the latter days and at the same time preparing to establish Zion.

Elder M. Russell Ballard said, "These are the last days. As has been foretold by God's holy prophets since the world began, they are challenging times, and they are going to become even more challenging. So wherein is our safety? Where is our peace? Where is our joy? Where is our inner security? My testimony is that safety, peace, joy, and security are found only in the life and mission of JESUS CHRIST, the Son of Almighty God. Bringing people to Him is the sum and substance of our ministry. So we embrace His teachings, we give up all of our SINS, we REPENT, we do all that is in our power to do to come unto Him in a true spirit of discipleship, knowing perfectly well that it is through His GRACE that we are saved, even after all that we can do (see 2 Ne. 25:23). And as we give ourselves to Christ, fully and completely, we find safety, peace, joy and security in Him.

"Does that mean we will not have turmoil or personal problems or sickness or family challenges or employment difficulties? Not at all. But it does mean that if our FAITH is anchored securely in our testimonies of Christ, we will be able to cope with whatever adversity comes our way, and we will be able to do so in a positive, faith-promoting manner. If we keep the eye of faith focused on Christ, we gain a broader view and an eternal perspective, and with that we can understand adversity from within the context of Heavenly Father's eternal plan for all of His children. And we can find comfort in this life in the eternal safety, peace, joy and security that He promises" (*Ensign,* Dec. 1996, 56).

Light of Christ: The power or influence of the Godhead that radiates throughout the universe. It is manifest in a variety of ways. God's power is in physical light and also enlightens men's minds (see D&C 88:6–13). Mormon describes it as the gift by which one can discern good from evil (see Moro. 7:15–19). Unlike the HOLY GHOST, "whom the world cannot receive" (see John 14:17) and whose influence is felt only on a limited basis, except by those who have received the laying on of hands, the Light of Christ "enlighteneth every man through the world" (D&C 84:45–46). The influence that comes through the Light of Christ is less specific or intense than that of the Holy Ghost. The Light of Christ is one of the channels by which the Holy Ghost may communicate even secular knowledge to the world. Through it, artists have been inspired and scientists have been guided to new discoveries. Often people are led through the Light of Christ to the point where they are ready to receive a surer witness of the gospel directly through the Holy Ghost. Both the Holy Ghost and Light of Christ may be known as "the Spirit of God," "light of truth," etc. So the context must determine which meaning is intended.

Elder Joseph B. Wirthlin explained, "As the sun gives life and light to the earth, a spiritual light gives nourishment to our spirits. We call this the Light of Christ. The scriptures teach us that it 'lighteth every man that cometh into the world' (John 1:9; see also Moro. 7:16; D&C 84:46). Thus, all mankind can enjoy its blessings. The Light of Christ is the divine influence that allows every man, woman, and child to distinguish between good and evil. It encourages all to choose the right, to seek eternal truth, and to learn again the truths that we knew in our premortal existence but have forgotten in mortality. The Light of Christ should not be confused with the personage of the Holy Ghost, for the Light of Christ is not a personage at all. Its influence is preliminary to and preparatory to one's receiving the Holy Ghost. The Light of Christ will lead the honest soul to 'hearkeneth to the voice' [v. 46] to find the true gospel and the true Church and thereby receive the Holy Ghost" (*Ensign,* May 2003, 26).

Literary Firm: A group of Church leaders who published the 1835 edition of the Doctrine and Covenants and EMMA SMITH's hymnbook. The proceeds of these sales were to support the temporal affairs of Church leaders (D&C 70:1–3).

Lost Ten Tribes of Israel: A group whose return will be associated with Christ's SECOND COMING. Originally, the kingdom of Israel included all twelve tribes, but in about 930 b.c. the ten northern tribes split off and formed their own kingdom. In about 722 b.c., the northern kingdom was conquered and most of the population was carried captive into Assyria. Later, the members of these ten tribes escaped from the Assyrians and departed toward the north. From that time onward, information about many of these people has been lost to history. When the Savior visited ancient America, He told his listeners that He would visit yet "other sheep" whom He identified as the "other tribes" of Israel (3 Ne. 16:1–5). At a conference held in June 1831, "The spirit fell upon Joseph in an unusual manner and he prophesied that JOHN the Revelator was then among the Ten Tribes of Israel who had been led away by Shalmaneser, king of Assyria, to prepare them for their return from their long dispersion, to again possess the land of their fathers" (*HC,* 1:176, footnote). While some of these tribes may have remained together as a body, many remnants, particularly of Ephraim, have been scattered widely, especially in northern Europe.

When MOSES appeared in the KIRTLAND TEMPLE in 1836, he bestowed "the keys of the gathering of Israel from the four parts of the earth and the leading of the ten tribes from the land of the north" (D&C 110:11). Many remnants of the lost tribes have been gathered into the Church as they respond to the gospel message when they hear it preached. The Lord declared that He would gather Ephraim first, that they might share the gospel with their fellow men, and in fact, a large percentage of modern Church membership hails from the lineage of either Ephraim or Manasseh, both among the "lost" ten tribes.

As the Savior reviewed events to be associated with His Second Coming, He declared, "They who are in the north countries shall come in remembrance before the Lord; and their prophets shall hear his word," the ice will melt, "and an highway shall be cast up in the midst of the great deep" (D&C 133:26–27). The circumstances of their return will be considered even more miraculous than Moses' parting of the Red Sea (see Isa. 35:8–10; Jer. 16:14–15). When the lost tribes return, they will bring scripture with them, which will provide evidence that God kept His covenant to remember the seed of Abraham (2 Ne. 29:12–14). The returning tribes will bring their treasures and then be "crowned with glory, even in Zion, by the hands of the servants of the Lord, even the children of Ephraim" (D&C 133:32).

— M —

Magnify: To enlarge or to increase in significance. The scriptures direct us to magnify our office or calling (D&C 24:3; 24:9; 84:33) rather than our own reputation. We should labor in such a way that our calling seems important to those whom it is our privilege to serve. JOSEPH SMITH was directed to magnify his calling by leaving his fields to devote full time to his service in the Church. As part of the "oath and covenant that belongeth to the PRIESTHOOD," we are promised great blessings if we are faithful and magnify our callings (see SECTION 84).

Manchester, New York: Location of many of the earliest events of the Restoration. The Joseph Smith Sr. farm, the Sacred Grove, the Smith's frame house, and the Hill Cumorah are all located in or near Manchester, New York. (See PALMYRA, NEW YORK.)

Manifesto: See OFFICIAL DECLARATION 1, first section of this book.

Marriage: The lawful union of a man and woman as husband and wife. President Joseph F. Smith once declared "that no man can be saved and exalted in the kingdom of God without the woman, and no woman can reach perfection and exaltation in the kingdom of God, alone. . . . God instituted marriage in the beginning. He made man in His own image and likeness, male and female, and in their creation it was designed that they should be united together in sacred bonds of marriage, and one is not perfect without the other" (CR, Apr. 1913, 118).

Elder Russell M. Nelson explained, "Scripture further reaffirms that 'the man [is not] without the woman, neither the woman without the man, in the Lord' (1 Cor. 11:11). Marriage is the foundry for social order, the fountain of virtue, and the foundation for eternal exaltation. Marriage has been divinely designated as an eternal and everlasting covenant. Marriage is sanctified when it is cherished and honored in holiness. That union is not merely between husband and wife; it embraces a partnership with God (Matt. 19:6). 'Husband and wife have a solemn responsibility to love and care for each other' (The Family: A Proclamation to the World). Children born of that marital union are 'an heritage of the Lord' (Ps. 127:3). Marriage is but the beginning bud of family life; parenthood is its flower. And that bouquet becomes even more beautiful when graced with grandchildren. Families may become as eternal as the kingdom of God itself" (*Ensign,* May 2006, 36–38).

Marsh, Thomas B.: The first President of the QUORUM of the Twelve APOSTLES. Born November 1, 1799, in Massachusetts, Thomas joined the Church in September 1830 after a long search for the truth. Soon thereafter, he was called to serve a mission. In 1835, Thomas became a member of the original Quorum of the Twelve and because all were called at the same time, he, being the oldest, became the President of the Quorum. He stayed faithful to the Church for three more years until his wife and a neighbor had a dispute over milk strippings (used for cheese). Elizabeth Marsh had greedily kept more than her share of strippings, and soon the dispute spiraled into a Church trial in which Sister Marsh was found guilty. Thomas, taking the side of his wife, was excommunicated and later became an enemy to the Church. Thomas had been told that his family was the cause of many of his afflictions and was cautioned to "pray always lest [he] enter into temptation" (D&C 31:12). Had he heeded this counsel, he might have been able to resist the temptations that eventually led to his excommunication. It was not until July 1857 that he made the trek across the plains to the Salt Lake Valley to ask forgiveness from BRIGHAM YOUNG. Thomas was rebaptized a few days later and returned to full fellowship in the Church. He died in Ogden, Utah, in January 1866.

McLellin, William E.: A member of the original QUORUM of the Twelve APOSTLES, an early missionary with a convincing testimony of the BOOK OF MORMON. He was born January 18, 1806, in Smith County, Tennessee, and was baptized by HYRUM SMITH after gaining a testimony of the Book of Mormon. Section 66 of the Doctrine and Covenants, revealed to the Prophet JOSEPH SMITH in HIRAM, OHIO, was addressed to William. Prior to the REVELATION, William had posed five questions that he hoped the Lord would answer in the revelation, and to William's satisfaction all five questions were answered. William was present at the conference in Hiram,

OHIO, as leaders of the Church prepared many of the revelations received by Joseph Smith, to be published in the Book of Commandments (D&C 67).

From time to time, William's relationships with other Church leaders were troubling, and in 1838 he apostatized and was excommunicated. He turned against the Church during the Missouri period, and was an active member of the mobs that drove the Saints out of the state. He had some affiliation with the Church of Christ and later the Reorganized Church of Jesus Christ of Latter Day Saints, but when he died on April 24, 1883, he was aloof in his religious beliefs. Although William persecuted the Church, he never denounced the truthfulness of the Book of Mormon, swearing to its purity until the day he died.

Melchizedek Priesthood: The higher order of PRIESTHOOD, which has the right of presidency and holds the KEYS of all spiritual blessings. From the days of ADAM, the Melchizedek Priesthood was known as "the Holy Priesthood After the Order of the Son of God," but in the days of Abraham this name was changed to avoid the repetition of the name of Deity (D&C 107:2–4). At that time, this higher order of the priesthood was named for Melchizedek, a great HIGH PRIEST in Salem to whom Abraham paid his TITHING (Gen. 14:18–20). In the present DISPENSATION, the Melchizedek Priesthood was restored by PETER, JAMES, AND JOHN. This priesthood includes the offices of ELDER, high priest, PATRIARCH, SEVENTY, and APOSTLE.

Messiah: One of the titles of JESUS CHRIST. The Hebrew word *Mashiah* and the Greek word *Christos* both mean "the anointed one." Hence, the titles Messiah and Christ have the same meaning. Over the centuries, people have thought of the Messiah as a deliverer who would help them overcome their enemies and usher in an era of righteousness and peace. We know that through the ATONEMENT of Christ, we can be delivered from sin and death, and that through living His GOSPEL we can qualify for an eternal inheritance in the CELESTIAL kingdom, the ultimate place of everlasting righteousness and peace.

Millennium: The thousand years when Christ will reign personally upon the EARTH. One of the major purposes of this glorious period is to enable all of God's children to prove themselves and to receive necessary ordinances. For this reason, TEMPLE work will be accelerated during the Millennium. At the time of Christ's SECOND COMING, the EARTH will be cleansed by fire and raised from its present telestial state to a higher terrestrial or paradisiacal condition (see D&C 63:20; 101:24–25; Article of Faith 10). The Millennium is like the earth's Sabbath (see D&C 77:12). There will be no enmity among humans or animals (D&C 101:26, compare Isa. 11:6–9). SATAN will not be able to tempt inhabitants of the earth during the Millennium (see D&C 101:28) due to: (1) the righteousness of the people (see 1 Ne. 22:26); (2) the power of Jesus Christ, who will reign personally on the earth (see D&C 43:29–30); and (3) the fact that the earth itself will have been elevated to a higher plane, further removed from Satan's realm. During this period, the Lord will "reveal all things," including how the world was created (D&C 101:32–34). During the Millennium, "Christ will reign personally upon the earth" (Article of Faith 1:10).

At the beginning of the Millennium, the living who are worthy of the CELESTIAL kingdom will be "quickened and be caught up to meet" Christ in the clouds of heaven and then descend with Him as He comes in glory (see D&C 88:96). Those worthy of the terrestrial kingdom will be "quickened but not caught up." The "quickening" refers to the individual's being changed (like the earth) from a telestial to terrestrial mortal state. Those living on a telestial level or lower will not be worthy to remain on earth in its terrestrial condition, so they will be burned as stubble (see Mal. 4:1). Hence, only those worthy of the celestial or terrestrial kingdoms will be on the earth during the Millennium. Those who are alive when the Millennium begins or who are born during the thousand years will live in a terrestrial mortal state until they reach the "age of a tree" (D&C 101:30), "the age of man" (D&C 63:49–50), or, as Isaiah specified, the age of 100 years (see Isa. 65:20). At that point, they will be "changed in a twinkling of an eye," or, in other words, pass through a change equal to death and an instantaneous RESURRECTION to an immortal state, either celestial or terrestrial, depending on the individual's worthiness. Thus, during the Millennium, there will be a step equal to death, but there will be no death as we know it in that none will sleep, "that is to say in the earth" (D&C 101:29, 31). Complete righteousness and peace will continue until the end of the thousand years, when Satan "shall be loosed for a little season, that he may gather together his armies." They will fight against the hosts of heaven, who will be led by Michael, or ADAM. Satan and his followers will be defeated and cast out forever (see D&C 88:111–115).

Ministering of Angels: One of the KEYS associated with the AARONIC PRIESTHOOD (see D&C 13:1; 84:26; 107:20). The Lord has promised those in His service that His angels will be "round about you, to bear you up" (D&C 84:88). An angel is generally thought of as a glorious messenger from God. Elder Dallin H. Oaks explained, "The ministering of angels can also be unseen. Angelic messages can be delivered by a voice or merely by thoughts or feelings communicated to the mind" (*Ensign,* Nov. 1998, 37). President JOHN TAYLOR described these ministrations as "the action of the angels, or messengers of God, upon our minds, so that the heart can conceive . . . revelations from the eternal world" (*GK,* 31).

Elder Jeffrey R. Holland suggested yet another possible meaning of "angels": "But when we speak of those who are instruments in the hand of God, we are reminded that not all angels are from the other side of the veil. Some of them we walk with and talk with—here, now, every day" (*Ensign,* Nov. 2008). They may be family members, close associates, or even perhaps complete strangers.

Missionary Work: The means by which the Church and its members share the GOSPEL with others. Along with perfecting the Saints and redeeming the dead, proclaiming the gospel is one of the three major responsibilities of the Lord's Church. When early associates asked JOSEPH SMITH how they could serve in the kingdom, the Lord's answer was typically a call to share the gospel. Their message was to be a call to REPENTANCE (see D&C 6:9). The Lord told two of the WHITMER brothers that "the thing which will be of the most worth unto you will be to declare repentance" (D&C 15:6; 16:6). Missionaries were promised that if they brought even just one soul to the Lord, they would have great joy with him in the kingdom of God (D&C 18:15–16). After the Church was organized, many other revelations now in the Doctrine and Covenants were calls to preach the gospel. Missionaries were instructed to go two by two, and to teach basic gospel principles from the scriptures (see D&C 19:29–31; 52:9–10). Their mission was not to be taught by the world, but rather to teach that which they received through the HOLY GHOST (see D&C 43:15). Some elders went without purse or SCRIP, depending on the Lord and the kindness of those whom they visited to provide food and lodging (see D&C 24:18; 84:78,86). The Lord promised to help them know what to say (see D&C 84:85) and to be with them in their labors (see D&C 84:88).

Blessings were promised to those who shared the gospel. After declaring that the field was "white already to harvest," the Lord promised that those who thrust in their sickle with their might would bring salvation to their souls (D&C 4:4). Continuing the imagery of the field, the Lord promised the faithful missionaries would "be laden with many SHEAVES, and crowned with honor, and glory, and immortality, and eternal life" (D&C 75:5).

Samuel H. Smith acted as one of the Church's first missionaries when he distributed copies of the Book of Mormon in neighboring communities. In October 1830, the Lamanite Mission was the first organized group called to share the gospel. Missionaries in "upper Canada" during 1833 were the first to leave the boundaries of the United States. Elder Heber C. Kimball and others opened the first overseas mission in 1837 when they carried the restored gospel to Great Britain.

Missionary activity continues today. Elder Russell M. Nelson reported: "Assignments this year have taken me to many nations of the earth. In some of those countries, the Church is relatively new. No matter where I go, I meet our missionaries. They are remarkably resilient and ever effective. They give visible and tangible evidence that the Church of Jesus Christ has been restored in its fulness. It was He who said, 'Go ye into all the world, and preach the gospel to every creature.' This commandment throbs in the heart of every missionary who testifies of Jesus Christ and teaches His message. When we think of missionaries, we generally picture in our minds young men with shirts and ties and young women dressed modestly. But along with them are marvelous senior missionaries who have answered the pleadings of prophets and Apostles for more missionary couples. I express gratitude for our senior missionaries" (*Ensign,* Nov. 2004, 40–43)

Morley, Isaac: A convert who allowed many early Saints, including the Prophet Joseph Smith and his wife Emma, to live on his large farm when they first relocated to Kirtland. Isaac was born in Massachusetts on March 11, 1786. After participating in the War of 1812, Isaac moved with his wife to Ohio. He joined Sidney Rigdon's Campbellite congregation and even offered his farm as a refuge to other members of the group. When Isaac was forty-four, he and his wife heard the gospel preached by Latter-day Saints serving in the Lamanite Mission, and were converted along with a large group of Campbellites. At the fourth general conference in 1831, Isaac was called as a counselor to Bishop Edward Partridge, and was commanded to sell his farm (D&C 64:20) and consecrate the money. Isaac remained faithful through much persecution and followed the Saints from Kirtland to Independence to Nauvoo, each time being run out by mobs. Isaac Morley was also among those who crossed the plains with Brigham Young. He helped settle many parts of Utah and soon after arriving was called as PATRIARCH in Sanpete Valley. Isaac died on June 24, 1865, in Fairview, Utah.

Moroni: The last historian in the BOOK OF MORMON, who eventually delivered this ancient record to JOSEPH SMITH. He first appeared to the young PROPHET on Sunday evening, September 21, 1823, three years after the FIRST VISION. He told Joseph about the Book of Mormon record, and cited biblical prophecies about the LATTER DAYS (see JS—H 1:27–47). He paraphrased Malachi's prophecy to emphasize that ELIJAH would restore PRIESTHOOD before "the great and dreadful day of the Lord" (compare SECTION 2 with Mal. 4:5–6). After a series of annual visits in which he taught the young PROPHET, Moroni delivered the plates to Joseph Smith, giving him strict instructions regarding their care. Following the loss of the manuscript in 1828, Moroni took the plates and other sacred objects from Joseph. Following a period of REPENTANCE and soul-searching on the part of Joseph Smith, Moroni returned these objects so the work of translation could proceed (see SECTIONS 3 and 10). Moroni may have been the ANGEL who showed the plates and the other sacred objects to the Three Witnesses, but the record does not identify him by name (see "The Testimony of Three Witnesses," Book of Mormon).

Latter-day Saints regard the coming of Moroni as one fulfillment of JOHN's prophecy of "another angel flying in the midst of heaven having the everlasting gospel to preach unto them that dwell on the earth" (Rev. 14:6). Statues of the angel Moroni on Latter-day Saint TEMPLES depict a herald sounding his trumpet, announcing the Restoration of the gospel, calling us to repentance, and warning us to prepare for Christ's SECOND COMING

Mortal: The state of being subject to physical death. ADAM and Eve became mortal when they partook of the forbidden fruit (Gen. 2:16–17; Moses 3:16–17). We entered mortality when we were born, and we will leave it when we die. Our mortal life is also called the second estate (Abr. 3:26). Its blessings include the marvelous physical body with which our spirits are now clothed. At death, the spirit returns to God and the body to the dust of the earth (Eccl. 12:7). Learning to overcome the weaknesses of the flesh gives us valuable experience and is an important element in our probationary state.

Translated beings and those who live on EARTH during the MILLENNIUM are still mortals, but their physical death will be followed by an immediate RESURRECTION. Thus they will not sleep in the grave, but "shall be changed in the twinkling of an eye" (D&C 101:30–31).

Moses: The Old Testament PROPHET who restored the KEYS of GATHERING. Anciently, he gave the law, including the Ten Commandments, to the children of ISRAEL. The first five books of the Old Testament, or books of the law, are also known as the "Five Books of Moses." At the end of his ministry, Moses did not die, but became a TRANSLATED BEING, enabling him to bestow PRIESTHOOD keys upon PETER, JAMES, AND JOHN on the Mount of TRANSFIGURATION (see Matt. 17:1–3; *TPJS*, 158). Moses was among those resurrected with Christ (see D&C 133:55). Having gathered ancient Israel from Egypt and led them to the promised land, Moses was the appropriate person to restore the keys of the gathering of Israel in the LATTER DAYS. He appeared to JOSEPH SMITH and OLIVER COWDERY for this purpose in the KIRTLAND TEMPLE on April 3, 1836 (see D&C 110:11). The Lord has promised that faithful bearers of the Melchizedek Priesthood may become "the sons of Moses" (D&C 84:33).

Mysteries: Sacred truths that cannot be known through human senses or reason but must be learned through REVELATION. The Lord indicated that these sacred mysteries may include "my will concerning all things pertaining to my kingdom," the "wonders of eternity," and "things to come" (D&C 76:7–8). In the two great revelations on PRIESTHOOD, the Lord declares that the higher priesthood holds the "keys of the mysteries of the kingdom." These include "the knowledge of God" (D&C 84:19), "to have the heavens opened," and to "enjoy the communion and presence of God the Father and Jesus" (D&C 107:19). The Savior testified that these mysteries are known only by those who know and follow His commandments and that a knowledge of these mysteries would be "a well of living water, springing up unto everlasting life" (D&C 63:23, see D&C 43:13). Other "mysteries" have not been revealed, such as the precise date of Christ's SECOND COMING and the location of the greater part of the LOST TRIBES OF ISRAEL. In such cases, we should follow Alma's example: "Now these mysteries are not yet fully made known unto me; therefore I shall forbear" (Alma 37:11).

— N —

Name of the Church: The title that identifies its unique status as Christ's true Church (see 3 Ne. 27:8; D&C 1:30). During the first years of its existence, the Church was generally called, by its members, the Church of Christ (see D&C 20:1). The 1831 title page for the published revelations identified the volume as "A Book of Commandments for the Government of the Church of Christ." Detractors, on the other hand, often referred to Church members as "Mormonites." In order to avoid this label, at a CONFERENCE held May 3, 1834, the Church adopted the official title The Church of the Latter-day Saints. The title page of the 1835 edition of the Doctrine and Covenants used this name. It is clear from many contemporary sources, however, that the brethren still regarded the Church as being the Church of Jesus Christ. (See *HC,* 1:392–93.) In 1838, section 115 instructed the members to use the full title of the Church as follows: "The Church of Jesus Christ of Latter-day Saints." The first phrase, "The Church of Jesus Christ," is certainly the key part of the title (see 1 Cor. 1:10–13). In 1996, the Church adopted an official logo that highlights the name Jesus Christ. The term *SAINTS* generally refers to those who are sanctified or holy, so the use of this term should be a constant challenge to all Church members. The word *Saints* is also used in a more general sense to refer to members of the Church, all of whom should be seeking sanctification through living the gospel of Jesus Christ. Paul addressed his epistles to the "Saints" or Church members in various places, yet he acknowledged that one purpose of the Church was the "perfecting of the Saints" (see Eph. 4:11–13). The definite article at the beginning of the name attests that this is not just one of several Christian churches, but *The* Church.

Speaking of the name of the Church, Elder Russell M. Nelson declared, "Today I would like to speak about a name. We are all pleased when our names are pronounced and spelled correctly. Sometimes a nickname is used instead of the real name. But a nickname may offend either the one named or the parents who gave the name. The name of which I shall speak is not a personal name, yet the same principles apply. I refer to a name given by the Lord: 'Thus shall my church be called in the last days, even The Church of Jesus Christ of Latter-day Saints' (D&C 115:4). Note carefully the language of the Lord. He did not say, 'Thus shall my church be *named.*' He said, 'Thus shall my church be *called.*' Years ago, its members were cautioned by the Brethren who wrote: 'We feel that some may be misled by the too frequent use of the term "Mormon Church."' (*Member-Missionary Class—Instructor's Guide* [Salt Lake City: The Church of Jesus Christ of Latter-day Saints], 1982, 2). Before any other name is considered to be a legitimate substitute, the thoughtful person might reverently consider the feelings of the Heavenly Parent who

Nauvoo, Illinois

bestowed that name. Surely every word that proceeds from the mouth of the Lord is precious. So each word in this name must be important—divinely designated for a reason" (*Ensign,* May 1990, 16).

Nauvoo, Illinois: Headquarters of the Church from 1839 through 1846. Following their expulsion from Missouri, the SAINTS began settling along the banks of the Mississippi River near the village of Commerce, ILLINOIS. Soon they named their settlement *Nauvoo,* a Hebrew word meaning "beautiful." Within a few years, the population reached nearly fifteen thousand, making Nauvoo even larger than Chicago at that time. Here the Saints were directed to build their second temple and an inn known as the Nauvoo House (see SECTION 124). In connection with the NAUVOO TEMPLE, important ORDINANCES, including BAPTISMS for the dead, the ENDOWMENT, and eternal MARRIAGE were restored. During the Nauvoo period, the Twelve APOSTLES served as a group in Great Britain, and the Relief Society was organized. The PROPHET unfolded many important doctrines in Nauvoo, including the eventual destiny of the children of God. JOSEPH and HYRUM SMITH were martyred June 27, 1844, at nearby Carthage, ILLINOIS. Persecution intensified again, and in 1846 the Saints were forced to flee to the west.

Nauvoo Temple: The second TEMPLE dedicated by the Church. Following their expulsion from Missouri, the SAINTS began establishing the city of NAUVOO in 1839. Here temple ordinances including BAPTISMS for the dead, the ENDOWMENT, and sealings were restored. Late in 1840, a committee was formed to plan the construction of the temple in Nauvoo. On January 19 of the following year, a REVELATION indicated that the new structure would serve two major purposes. Like the KIRTLAND TEMPLE, it would be a place "for the Most High to dwell therein" and "restore again that which was lost." It would also be a place for sacred ordinances such as baptisms for the dead (see D&C 124:27–30).

Cornerstones were laid on April 5, 1841, and at great sacrifice, construction moved forward on this million-dollar temple. A stone quarry was located nearby, but timbers had to be brought from Wisconsin. By November of that same year, a temporary font was completed and enclosed so that baptisms for the dead could be performed in the partially completed structure rather than in the Mississippi River. The Nauvoo Temple was only partly finished when JOSEPH SMITH was martyred in 1844. As per-

The reconstructed Nauvoo Temple

secution mounted and the Saints prepared for their westward exodus, they felt a compelling need to finish the temple and to receive the sacred blessings available only in the house of the Lord. Like the Kirtland Temple, the Nauvoo Temple contained two large meeting halls, one above the other, but it also had facilities for ordinances—a baptismal font in the basement, and rooms for the endowment and sealings on the attic level.

The temple was sufficiently completed by December 1845 that the endowment could be given there. About five thousand Saints received their temple blessings before heading west. The temple was not formally dedicated until April 30 and May 1, 1846, several weeks after most of the Saints had been forced to flee from their "City Beautiful." The temple was subsequently burned by a mob, and its remaining stone walls were toppled by a tornado several years later. In 1999, President Gordon B. Hinckley announced plans to rebuild the Nauvoo Temple. The reconstructed temple was dedicated in 2002.

New and Everlasting Covenant: The fulness of the GOSPEL of Jesus Christ (D&C 66:2). Jeremiah prophesied that in the LATTER DAYS there would be a "new COVENANT" (Jer. 31:31). Other PROPHETS referred to it as an "everlasting covenant" (Ezekiel 37:26; Isa. 24:5). It is new because it has been newly restored in our day, and it is everlasting because God is everlasting. The covenant does not change and its effects are everlasting (*MD*, 529–30). There are various branches of the "new and everlasting covenant" of the gospel of Jesus Christ, such as baptism (D&C 22:1–2), priesthood (D&C 84:33–39,) and marriage (D&C 131:2).

New Jerusalem: The Lord's Western Hemisphere capital in the LATTER DAYS. The Old Jerusalem in the Holy Land will also be rebuilt, but the New Jerusalem, also known as ZION, will be located at JACKSON COUNTY, MISSOURI (D&C 57:1–3). Thus the Lord will have two capitals during the MILLENNIUM. Isaiah declared, "Out of Zion shall go forth the law, and the word of the Lord from Jerusalem" (Isa. 2:3). There will be a great TEMPLE in the New Jerusalem. Elder Orson Pratt described the visible manifestation of God's glory at this future temple: "A cloud of glory [will] rest upon that temple by day, the same as the cloud rested upon the tabernacle of Moses. . . . Not only that, but a flaming fire will rest upon the temple by night . . . You will have no need of any artificial light, for the Lord God will be the light thereof, and his glory will be there, and you will see it and you will hear his voice" (*JD*, 21:330–31). The dream of this future glorious city motivated the SAINTS who attempted to settle in Jackson County during the 1830s, and it continues to give us hope today.

New York State: The location of the first three branches of the Church: PALMYRA-MANCHESTER, FAYETTE, and COLESVILLE (D&C 25:3). This was the home state to several of the first families to join the Church—the Smiths, Jollys, Kimballs, Knights, Rockwells, Youngs, and Whitmers, to mention just a few. The early events of the Restoration occurred in New York State; these include the First Vision, Moroni's visits, the translation and printing of the BOOK OF MORMON (D&C 3, 5–10, 17), the restoration of the AARONIC and MELCHIZEDEK PRIESTHOOD (D&C 13), and the organization of the Church (D&C 21).

— O —

Ohio: The first place of GATHERING for the Saints and the headquarters of the Church from 1831 to 1838. Section 37 directed the New York members to gather to the OHIO. Earlier, in the revelation now known as SECTION 29, the Lord had spoken about the importance of the doctrine of gathering—a principle that covenant Israel followed. Section 38 gives the reasons why the Saints were to make the move: (1) to escape the enemy (v. 31), (2) to receive the Lord's law (v. 32), (3) to be endowed with power from on high (v. 32), and (4) to look to the poor and needy and administer to their relief (v. 35). While KIRTLAND was the center place for the Saints in OHIO, many members settled in outlying towns; this is evident from the various locations mentioned in the sixty-five revelations given in the state, including Amherst, Cincinnati, HIRAM, Orange, North Union, and Thompson. (See also Kirtland, Ohio.)

Oracles: Communications from God or the means by which they come. Places where divine communications were received were also called oracles, such as the temple at Delphi in ancient Greece. The name of the holy of holies in Solomon's Temple is translated as "oracle" in the King James Bible (see 1 Kgs. 6:16). Oracles are among the functions of latter-day TEMPLES (see D&C 124:39). The PROPHETS are often identified as "the living oracles." The Saints were cautioned not to take the oracles lightly (D&C 90:4–5).

Ordinance: Literally means "a religious or ceremonial observance." In the restored Church, ordinances are the ceremonies we must participate in to qualify for ETERNAL LIFE. In secular terms, "ordinance" refers to laws, which help keep order. Elder Boyd K. Packer pointed out, "The word *ordinance* comes from the word *order,* which means, 'a rank, a row, a series'" (*HT,* 144). Thus, an ordinance aligns the powers of God in our behalf. Also, we need to be sure that our lives are in order to qualify us to receive the blessings promised in the ordinances.

The third Article of Faith states, "We believe that through the Atonement of Christ, all mankind may be saved, by obedience to the laws and ordinances of the Gospel." This means that it is not enough just to keep the commandments. We must receive certain ordinances and keep the covenants associated with them; if we do so, the Lord has promised us certain blessings (D&C 52:15–16). Ordinances must be performed with proper PRIESTHOOD authority in order to be acceptable to the Lord (D&C 84:20–21, compare Article of Faith 5). Those who hold the Aaronic Priesthood have the power to "administer in outward ordinances" (D&C 107:20), including BAPTISM, while the higher priesthood is required for bestowing the gift of the HOLY GHOST. These are the first two ordinances members of the Church must receive in order to attain eventual eternal glory. Many of the other required ordinances take place in the TEMPLE, namely the endowment and sealings of couples and children to parents. We are also commanded to perform these saving ordinances for those who are dead (D&C 138:54).

There are also ordinances that benefit those who receive them but are not prerequisites for CELESTIAL glory. Some of those include the consecration of oil, the dedication of buildings, blessing the sick, being setting apart for Church callings, and blessing of children.

— P —

Page, Hiram: One of the Eight Witnesses to the BOOK OF MORMON. After joining the Church on April 11, 1830, Hiram found a stone that he said allowed him to receive revelations. In SECTION 28 the Lord counseled OLIVER COWDERY to "tell him that those things which he hath written from that stone are not of me and that Satan deceiveth him (v.11)." Hiram was born in 1800, and in 1825 married Catherine Whitmer, daughter of PETER WHITMER. After hearing of the coming forth of the BOOK OF MORMON, Hiram was converted to the Church. After the SEER STONE incident, Hiram remained faithful for a few more years before he was excommunicated for denouncing JOSEPH SMITH as a PROPHET. Hiram did not, however, denounce the Book of Mormon at any time during his life. He died on August 12, 1852, near Excelsior Springs, Missouri.

Palmyra-Manchester, New York: The location of the earliest events in the Restoration of the gospel, including the FIRST VISION, MORONI'S visits, and the publication of the BOOK OF MORMON. In 1816, JOSEPH SMITH SR. moved his family from Norwich, Vermont, to the village of Palmyra, New York. For the next three years Palmyra, an Erie Canal town, was the home of the Smiths.

Some time in 1819, the Smiths relocated south on Stafford Road to a 100-acre parcel in the adjoining Manchester Township. The Smiths began building a log cabin but were unaware the cabin was not a part of the 100 acres but was just across the line from Manchester in Palmyra Township. In the early spring of 1820, Joseph Smith, then 14 years of age, went into the woods nearby and knelt in prayer to ask God which of the various churches was correct. The result was his First Vision of God the Father and His Son Jesus Christ. Three years later, in September 1823, Joseph's prayers were again answered, this time by an angel named Moroni, who visited him five times during the night and following morning (D&C 2). In addition, Lucy, the youngest of the Smith children, was born in the cabin in Palmyra, and Alvin, Joseph's oldest brother, died an untimely death there. In the summer of 1829, the Eight Witnesses to the Book of Mormon viewed the plates in this area.

The Smiths improved their farm and lived in the cabin until the spring of 1825, when they moved south into the frame home begun by Alvin and completed by Hyrum and his brothers. Joseph and Emma Hale Smith lived in this house with his parents' family. It is here Joseph brought the gold plates and URIM AND THUMMIM, which he received from Moroni at the Hill Cumorah in September 1827. Because the Smiths were not able to meet their annual mortgage payment on their farm, they lost the farm and home, returning to live in the log cabin, where HYRUM SMITH and OLIVER COWDERY prepared the Book of Mormon manuscript for publication.

Paradisiacal State: The EARTH in its terrestrial condition as during the time ADAM and Eve were in the Garden of Eden (a popular meaning of the word "paradise"), and as it will be during the MILLENNIUM.

Partridge, Edward: Called as the first BISHOP in the Church only a few days after his baptism (D&C 41:9). Edward was born in Massachusetts

The village of Palmyra, New York

on August 27, 1793. He moved to OHIO and became a hat maker in Painesville. After researching many different religions, he and his wife were taught by the LAMANITE MISSIONARIES came to know the BOOK OF MORMON was true. Edward, along with SIDNEY RIGDON, traveled from OHIO to NEW YORK in order to meet the PROPHET. After listening to Joseph's discourse, Edward desired to be baptized. After his call as bishop, he helped establish the LAW OF CONSECRATION (see sections 42, 48, and 51). Despite much persecution, Edward remained faithful throughout his life and died in Nauvoo on May 27, 1840.

Patriarch: An officer in the Melchizedek PRIESTHOOD responsible for giving special blessings to Church members. This title is a combination of the Latin word *pater,* meaning father and the suffix *arch,* referring to the chief one. Patriarchs are ordained to pronounce special blessings upon the faithful (see D&C 124:124). An "evangelical minister" or "evangelist," as patriarchs are also called, is appointed in each STAKE of the Church (see D&C 107:39). The word *evangel* means "gospel"; thus, a patriarchal blessing is an inspired application of specific teachings and promises of the gospel to an individual

ABRAHAM, Isaac, and Jacob are among Old Testament leaders who presided over large families and are called patriarchs. The first patriarch in this DISPENSATION was Joseph Smith Sr. Following his death, HYRUM SMITH was appointed to fill this position (D&C 124:91–93). A Patriarch to the Church was sustained until 1979, when worldwide growth made it necessary to distribute his duties among various brethren, including those who speak different languages, who were called to serve on a short-term basis. The office of Patriarch to the Church was passed down from father to son (D&C 107:40), but the patriarchs ordained in the various stakes are not chosen on that basis.

Patriarchal Order: A family-centered organization in the PRIESTHOOD. It existed in past DISPENSATIONS, and it will be the way EXALTED beings are organized in the CELESTIAL kingdom. Today, couples enter the patriarchal order when they are sealed in the TEMPLE. This name underscores the responsibility of fathers to give righteous leadership to their family in conjunction with their eternal companions.

Pennsylvania: The girlhood home of Emma Hale Smith and the residence of JOSEPH and Emma from December 1827 to August 1830. (See also HARMONY, PENNSYLVANIA.)

Peter, James, and John: Christ's three chief APOSTLES during His mortal ministry. James and John were brothers, and together with Peter and his brother Andrew were fishermen on the Sea of Galilee. Peter, James, and John were singled out by the Master to accompany Him on at least three sacred occasions: when He was TRANSFIGURED on the mountain (Matt. 17:1–2), when the daughter of Jairus was raised from the dead (Luke 8:51), and when He prayed in the Garden of Gethsemane in preparation for His atoning sacrifice (Matt. 26:36–37). On the Mount of Transfiguration, Peter, James, and John received KEYS from MOSES and ELIAS, or ELIJAH (*JPJS,* 158). Following Christ's ascension, they served as the FIRST PRESIDENCY of the New Testament Church. While Peter and James both suffered martyr's deaths, John did not die, but became a TRANSLATED BEING in order to remain on EARTH and continue the Lord's work here (D&C 7).

When JOHN THE BAPTIST restored the Aaronic PRIESTHOOD, he indicated that he did so under the direction of Peter, James, and John (JS–H 1:72). Shortly afterwards, they appeared to JOSEPH SMITH and OLIVER COWDERY in the country between HARMONY, Pennsylvania and COLESVILLE, New York (D&C 128:20). They conferred the Melchizedek Priesthood, including the Holy Apostleship and the "keys of [the] kingdom" of "the gospel for the last times" (D&C 27:12–13). Peter and James are among the few who died after the time of Christ and are known to be RESURRECTED already. John was still a translated being.

Perdition, Sons of: Those who will go into outer darkness. Perdition literally means "loss." The sons of perdition have lost all contact with God's glory, hence their state is appropriately described as darkness. It is also known as HELL or eternal DAMNATION. To become a son of perdition, one must commit the UNPARDONABLE SIN—receive a sure witness of Jesus Christ through the HOLY GHOST and then knowingly deny it and fight against God (D&C 76:31; Alma 39:6). It is fruitless to try to determine whether a given person has or has not qualified as a son of perdition. Rather, we who profess testimonies of the GOSPEL should concentrate on enhancing our own righteousness and spirituality that we might endure faithful to the end and thereby avoid this fate.

Phelps, William Wines: A printer for the Church in MISSOURI and a counselor in the first stake presidency in Missouri. William was born February 17, 1792, in Hanover, New Jersey. In section 55 of the Doctrine and Covenants, he was directed to assist Oliver Cowdery in Missouri in the work of printing. A printer by trade, William helped Oliver select and print books for the Church's schools, edited the *Evening and Morning Star,* prepared and printed the Book of Commandments, assisted in compilation of the 1835 Doctrine and Covenants, and joined with EMMA SMITH in selecting and publishing the first Church hymnbook. An accomplished author, he wrote the words to over a dozen hymns in our modern hymnal, including "The Spirit of God," "Now Let Us Rejoice," Redeemer of Israel," and "Praise to the Man." William donated a large sum of money to the building of the KIRTLAND TEMPLE. Caught up in the Missouri APOSTASY, William left the Church for a time but returned in humility and received a pardon from JOSEPH SMITH. After speaking at the PROPHET's funeral, William moved with the Saints to Iowa and then to Salt Lake, where he died on March 6, 1872.

Plural Marriage: The practice of a man being authorized by God to have more than one wife. Plural marriage was practiced in Old Testament times, the PATRIARCHS typically having more than one wife. There have been other times when the divinely mandated pattern was to have only one wife (see Jacob 2:27; 1 Tim. 3:2). The faithful Latter-day Saints who entered the challenging plural marriage relationship did so because of their faith that it was a divinely appointed institution. As had been the case with the LAW OF CONSECRATION, the Lord revealed plural marriage as an essential part of the restoration of all things (D&C 132:45).

This form of MARRIAGE was revealed to the PROPHET as early as 1831 when he was working on what became the JOSEPH SMITH TRANSLATION. In the course of the revisions of the Bible, Joseph asked the Lord why He had justified ABRAHAM, MOSES, and others in having more than one wife (D&C 132:1, 41). The "doctrines and principles" revealed at this time eventually became a part of SECTION 132. The Lord emphasized that plural marriage was not adultery because the wives were married to their husbands by acknowledged authority (D&C 132:61). The practice of plural marriage was designed to facilitate fulfillment of the commandment "to multiply and replenish the EARTH . . . that they may bear the souls of men" (D&C 132:63). The Lord affirmed that He had given Abraham, Isaac, Jacob, Moses, David, Solomon, and others their wives and concubines, and that they did not sin unless they took what He had not given them (D&C 132:37–39). A concubine was not an immoral mistress, but rather she was a wife having a lower social status (see Gen. 16:3; 30:4, 9).

Joseph Smith married his first plural wife as early as 1835. The principle of plural marriage was taught to selected leaders at NAUVOO during the 1840s, but the practice was kept confidential to avoid anticipated persecution.

In the relative isolation of the Rocky Mountains, about 15 to 20 percent of the Utah Saints participated in plural marriage. Church leaders enforced strict standards in connection with authorizing plural marriages. Following the first public announcement in 1852, Congress passed a series of anti-bigamy laws, resulting in intense persecution of the Saints during the 1880s. Finally, the U.S. Supreme Court in 1890 upheld the last (and most severe) of these laws as constitutional.

The Lord had authorized the practice of plural marriage, but He had also directed the Saints to obey the constitutional law of the land (see D&C 98:5). Therefore President WILFORD WOODRUFF prayed for guidance. He was shown in vision that under existing conditions it would be best to suspend the practice of plural marriage (read President Woodruff's statements added to the 1981 edition of the Doctrine and Covenants, on pages 292–93). He therefore issued his "MANIFESTO" (Official Declaration 1) in September 1890. This statement directed the Saints to "refrain from contracting any marriage forbidden by the law of the land." Men who had married plural wives before that time were permitted to retain them, but new plural marriages were strictly forbidden. In 1904, President Joseph F. Smith issued a statement, often called the "Second Manifesto," emphasizing that Church members performing or participating in new plural marriages were subject to excommunication.

Parley P. Pratt

Pratt, Parley P.: A member of the original QUORUM of the Twelve APOSTLES who was imprisoned in Richmond with JOSEPH SMITH. Parley was one of the most influential early missionaries in the Church. He was born April 12, 1807, in Burlington, New York. He married Thankful Halsey and traveled to northern OHIO searching for religious truth. He associated with Sidney Rigdon and the Campbellities in the Mentor area. While traveling back to New York, he obtained a copy of the Book of Mormon. He read it in one day and was convinced that its message was true. In PALMYRA, he met HYRUM SMITH and shortly thereafter was BAPTIZED by Oliver Cowdery in Seneca Lake. In 1830, Pratt was called as one of the missionaries to the Lamanites, along with Oliver Cowdery, PETER WHITMER JR., and Ziba Peterson (D&C 32). In the FAR WEST period, Parley was imprisoned in Richmond in 1838 for over eight months. While serving several missions, including two outside of the United States (to England and Chile), he wrote a number of significant missionary tracts. As he preached in the States, he was impressed by the Spirit to go home early. On his way back to Missouri, he heard of the deaths of Joseph and Hyrum Smith. He was overcome with grief for his beloved friends, but was comforted by the HOLY GHOST and inspired to return home and wait for the Quorum of the Twelve to gather. While traveling through Arkansas on May 13, 1857, he was murdered by the former husband of one of his plural wives. He is viewed as a martyr of the Church.

Premortal or Pre-Earthly Existence: Our life before being born into MORTALITY. Known as our "first estate," this portion of our eternal existence had two stages. First, we existed as intelligence: "Man was also in the beginning with God. Intelligence, or the light of truth, was not created or made, neither indeed can be" (D&C 93:29). Next, this intelligence became "organized" when each of us was begotten a spirit son or daughter of our Heavenly Parents. We lived with them, growing and progressing as much as we could in that condition. Finally, there came the time when our Heavenly Father called us together in what has been called the Grand Council in heaven. There He announced plans to create this EARTH where we could come to gain further experience and prove ourselves (Abr. 3:23–25). At that time, our eldest spirit brother, JESUS CHRIST, was foreordained to be the Savior of mankind. We then had the privilege of participating in, or at least witnessing, the creation of this earth, after which we eagerly looked forward to our turn to come here. We were told that if we "kept our first estate," we would be "added upon" in this present "second estate" (Abr. 3:26). At this point, SATAN, one of the prominent members in God's spirit family, offered a counter plan that would force every soul to do what was necessary to return to God's presence. After this plan was rejected, Satan rebelled and drew away "a third part of the hosts of heaven" (Moses 4:1–4; Abr. 3:27–28; D&C 29:36). Those who remained faithful were given the opportunity of coming to earth and enjoying the opportunities of mortality.

Prayer: The means by which we can communicate with our Father in Heaven. We are counseled to "pray always" so that we can have the power to resist the temptations of the adversary and have the HOLY GHOST to guide us (D&C 8:10; 31:12). Elder David A. Bednar affirmed, "We are promised that if we pray sincerely for that which is right and good and in accordance with God's will, we can be blessed, protected, and directed" (*Ensign,* Nov. 2008).

Prayer is a tool that we can use to counsel with our Heavenly Father, to thank Him for our blessings, and to ask for that which we feel we need (D&C 46:7), but we must always pray in faith, believing that our prayers will be heard and answered (D&C 29:6). Our Father will always answer our prayers. The answer may not come when we want it to and it may not be the answer we want, but once we know the will of the Lord, we must be obedient to it. Elder Richard G. Scott counseled, "Consider changing from asking for the things you want to honestly seeking what He wants for you. Then as you learn His will, pray that you will be led to have the strength to fulfill it" (*Ensign,* May 2007, 8). Knowing what the Lord's will is for us and what to pray for is one of the gifts of the Spirit (D&C 46:30).

President of the Church: He who is sustained as a PROPHET, SEER, and revelator, and who holds all the KEYS of the PRIESTHOOD. The first to hold this position was JOSEPH SMITH, who was sustained as the "first ELDER" on April 6, 1830, at the meeting where the Church was organized. At a CONFERENCE held at Amherst, OHIO, on January 25, 1832, Joseph was sustained as President of the High Priesthood (see heading of SECTION 75; compare D&C 107:65–66). He officially became known as President of the Church with the organization of the FIRST PRESIDENCY on March 18, 1833, in a meeting of the SCHOOL OF THE PROPHETS. The President is to "preside over the whole church, and to be like unto Moses . . . having all the gifts of God which He bestows upon the head of the Church" (D&C 107:91–92). When the President of the Church dies, the QUORUM of the First Presidency is completely vacated, because the others in the Presidency had been *his* counselors. The Twelve APOSTLES then become the presiding quorum of the Church (D&C 107:23–24), and their President, the senior Apostle, becomes the new President of the Church.

Priesthood: God's power delegated to man by which the ORDINANCES of salvation are performed on EARTH. It is the power by which the heavens and earth were created and continue to be governed by. Through this power, God redeems and exalts His children, bringing to pass "the immortality and eternal life of man" (Moses 1:39). Priesthood holders can be authorized to preach the gospel and govern the kingdom of God on the earth.

From the beginning of God's dealings with His children on earth to the LATTER DAYS, the priesthood has been a vital force. The first mortals placed on earth were Adam and Eve. They had direct, personal contact with God while in the Garden of Eden. After their SPIRITUAL DEATH (due to transgression) and their subsequent expulsion from the garden, Adam and Eve could no longer receive God's instructions directly (D&C 29:40–41). In God's absence, Adam continued to receive REVELATIONS from God. Adam functioned as God's PROPHET, declaring His word to his posterity. Because God is a God of order, those who minister for Him on earth must do so by His authority or PRIESTHOOD. As a prophet, Adam held the priesthood. The authority was the same as that which we know today as the Melchizedek Priesthood. In the days of Adam, this authority was known as "the Holy Priesthood, after the Order of the Son of God" (D&C 107:3).

The force of God's revelation and inspiration given through the prophets has always been opposed by the force of evil that spreads as mortals succumb to Satan's temptations. During the days of Adam, Satan was successful in leading astray a part of Adam's posterity. The scriptures refer to such a falling away into darkness as an "APOSTASY."

Because one of God's purposes in sending His children to the earth was to see how faithful they would be in keeping his commandments, it was not pleasing to Him that they should remain in a state of spiritual darkness and ignorance. For this reason, He has always sent prophets to "restore" men to a knowledge of His word. These acts of sending the gospel to the earth again are called "DISPENSATIONS," often identified by the name of the prophet through whom this was accomplished. The prophet whom the Lord chose to head the second dispensation was Enoch, who is remembered most for the tremendous work he did in converting the entire city of ZION so thoroughly that it was taken into heaven because of the people's righteousness. Satan again gained influence over those who remained behind, and a second apostasy followed.

On the surface, there appears to be a discrepancy between the priesthood lineage given in sections 84 and 107. The first traces the priesthood through Abel, and the latter through Seth (D&C 84:6–16; 107:41–52), but this make sense when one recalls that Seth was appointed to take the place of the slain Abel in terms of posterity and priesthood blessings (see Moses 6:2).

The third great prophet was Noah, who preached for 120 years but with little success. The people were so wicked that only Noah's immedi-

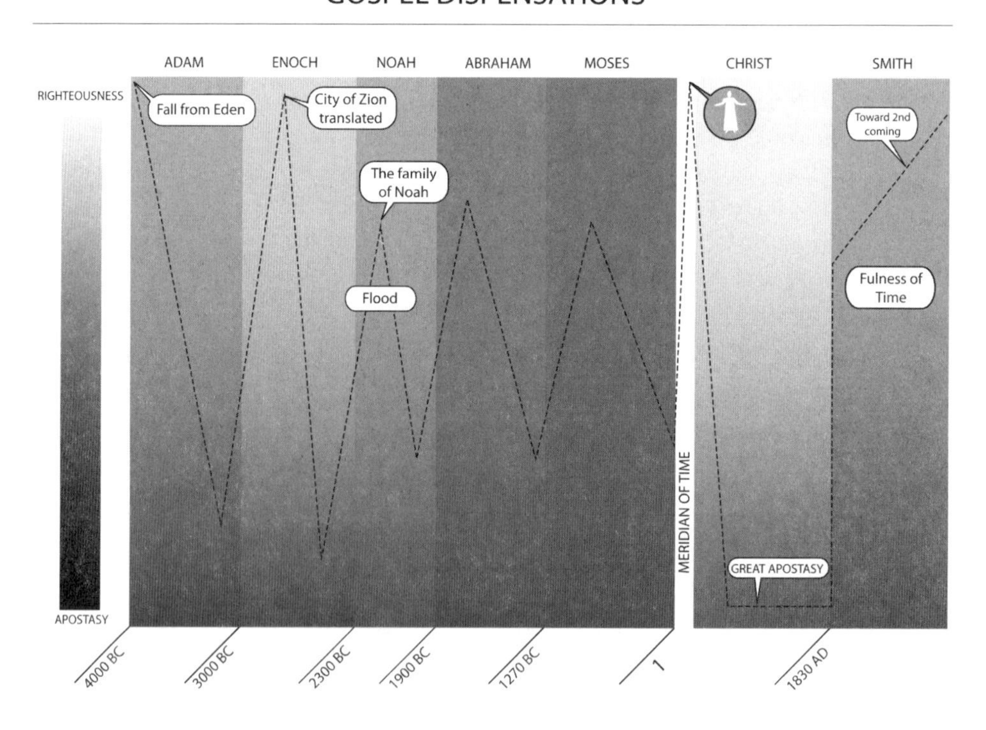

ate family accepted his message. Thus, when the floods came, only eight were saved in the ark (see 1 Pet. 3:18–20.) For a time, Noah's descendants lived in righteousness, but eventually they again fell into apostasy.

The prophet sent to head the fourth dispensation was ABRAHAM, the father of God's covenant people. Like his predecessors, Abraham held the priesthood, having been ordained by Melchizedek, a HIGH PRIEST of God and the king of Salem (see D&C 84:14). At this time, the name of the priesthood was changed to the Melchizedek Priesthood. This was done in order to avoid the too-frequent mention of the name of Deity (D&C 107:2–4). Although it had a new name, this was the same priesthood which Adam, Enoch, and Noah possessed.

Following a period of physical bondage in Egypt and a time of spiritual apostasy, God sent MOSES to head the fifth great dispensation. As a prophet, Moses held the higher priesthood. His older brother AARON was appointed to assist him and was given a lesser priesthood that became known as the Priesthood of Aaron. Section 107 explains the relationship that exists between these two orders of priesthood.

The Aaronic Priesthood may be regarded as "lesser" because it deals with temporal things, because it administers the outward ordinances per-

Restoration of the Melchizedek Priesthood

taining to the "preparatory gospel" (which prepares the individual to receive greater spiritual blessings), and because it is an appendage to the greater priesthood (compare D&C 107:13–14, 20, with D&C 13 and D&C 84:26–27.) The Melchizedek Priesthood, on the other hand, has the right of presidency and administers spiritual things. Through the authority and ordinances of the Melchizedek Priesthood, the power of God is manifested. By this same authority, a person may receive the "mysteries of the kingdom," or the knowledge of God that prepares the individual to have the heavens opened to him and to enjoy communion with the Father and the Son (compare D&C 107:18–19 with D&C 84:19–22.)

Because of the wickedness of the children of Israel, the Melchizedek Priesthood was taken from their midst. Although a few prophets were especially ordained to the higher priesthood, only the Aaronic Priesthood was passed down through the Israelite nation as a whole (D&C 84:25–26).

Because members of the tribe of Levi, or SONS OF LEVI, were assigned to serve in the lesser priesthood, this authority also became known as the Levitical Priesthood. Hence "Aaronic Priesthood" and "Levitical Priesthood" are two names for the same lesser order (see D&C 107:6). All who bore this priesthood were called "priests" in the Old Testament. Nevertheless, the direct descendants of Aaron were called to preside, as do bishops in our dispensation. As the centuries passed, another period of spiritual darkness came over Israel, and even most of the Aaronic priests became corrupted (see D&C 84:23–28).

In the meridian of time, God sent more than a prophet; He sent his Only Begotten Son in the flesh, Jesus Christ. The Savior restored a knowledge of the gospel to mankind and organized a Church in which both the Melchizedek and Aaronic Priesthoods were again found on the earth (see Heb. 7:11). Christ's Apostles were personally ordained by Him (John 15:16); PETER, JAMES, and JOHN received additional KEYS from Moses and ELIAS (ELIJAH) on the Mount of TRANSFIGURATION (Matt. 17:1–3; *TPJS,* 158). Following the death of Christ's Apostles, the Great Apostasy fell over the earth.

In our own day, the Lord opened the dispensation of the fulness of times by following the well-established pattern—sending a prophet through whom He could restore the priesthood and a knowledge of the gospel. The Aaronic Priesthood, together with its keys, was restored May 15, 1829 (D&C 13). The Melchizedek Priesthood was restored soon afterwards by the ancient Apostles Peter, James, and John (D&C 27:12–13;

128:20). Then, in 1836, following the dedication of the KIRTLAND TEMPLE, specialized keys were restored by Moses, Elias, and Elijah (D&C 110:11–16).

Bearers of the priesthood are ordained to specific offices. Aaronic Priesthood offices include deacon, teacher, priest, and bishop; Melchizedek Priesthood offices include ELDER, high priest, PATRIARCH, SEVENTY, and APOSTLE. These titles are meaningful descriptions of what each office does. For example, the title *deacon* comes from the Greek word referring to one who serves. Teachers are called to teach and watch over the Church (D&C 20:53–59). Priests are authorized to perform sacred priesthood ordinances (D&C 20:46–52). *Elder* is an archaic form of the word *older;* those who hold this office are regarded as more mature and are given spiritual responsibilities (D&C 20:38–45). Those holding priesthood offices are organized into QUORUMS.

In one of the "Revelations on Priesthood," the Lord set forth what He called the "oath and covenant" (D&C 84:33–41). For those who are faithful in receiving the Aaronic and Melchizedek Priesthoods and "magnifying their calling," the Lord promised marvelous blessings. They are made pure through the Holy Ghost and their physical bodies are also strengthened. They become the sons of Levi (Moses and Aaron were members of that tribe). They inherit the blessings promised to Abraham and his descendants (see Abr. 2:9–11). They participate in establishing God's Church or kingdom on earth, are the "elect" or those chosen for EXALTATION, and receive all that the Father has.

In his letter to the Saints from Liberty Jail, the Prophet spoke of the spirit in which the priesthood should be exercised (see D&C 121:36–46). It can be used only righteously or "the heavens withdraw themselves" and the effectiveness of the priesthood bearer is brought to an end. Joseph listed various attributes that should characterize faithful priesthood service, and promised marvelous spiritual blessings.

Prophet: One who speaks for God. Also, a title of the PRESIDENT OF THE CHURCH (D&C 21:1). In Old Testament times, prophets were spiritual leaders, and often more than one functioned at the same time. Amos 3:7 reads, "Surely the Lord God will do nothing, but he revealeth his secret unto his servants the prophets." Their writings, together with "the law," constituted the scriptures during the time of Christ (see Matt. 22:40). Today, members of the FIRST PRESIDENCY and QUORUM of the Twelve APOSTLES are sustained as "prophets, SEERS, and revelators" (compare D&C 21:1; 107:92; and 124:125). The Lord declared, "Whatsoever they shall speak when moved upon by the Holy Ghost shall be scripture, shall be the will of the Lord, shall be the mind of the Lord, shall be the word of the Lord, shall be the voice of the Lord, and the power of God unto salvation" (D&C 68:4). JOHN affirmed that "the testimony of Jesus is the spirit of prophecy" (Rev. 19:10).

— Q —

Quorums: A group of men or young men holding a particular PRIESTHOOD office. Quorums are at the heart of Church government. They are organized for those holding each of the priesthood offices, although there are no quorums uniquely for BISHOPS or PATRIARCHS. In 1974, however, the FIRST PRESIDENCY directed that an ELDERS quorum be organized in every ward or independent branch even if the formerly required minimum number is not present (First Presidency circular letter, Apr. 16, 1974; *Church News,* Oct. 19, 1974, 10). Similarly, ward quorums were to be organized for each Aaronic Priesthood office regardless of how few members there might be. Quorums are normally headed by a president and two counselors, although the SEVENTIES quorum has seven presidents with no counselors. The bishop presides over the priests quorum (D&C 107:88), with two quorum members as his assistants.

Priesthood quorums are designed to help their members function better as priesthood bearers (see D&C 124:133–134). Quorums are also important sources of brotherhood. Presidencies are to teach quorum members their duties (see D&C 107:85–89). Elder Henry B. Erying said, "I have learned over the years that the strength in a quorum doesn't come from the number of priesthood holders in it. Nor does it come automatically from the age and maturity of the members. Rather, the strength of a quorum comes in large measure from how completely its members are united in righteousness. That unity in a strong quorum of the priesthood is not like anything I have experienced in an athletic team or club or any other organization in the world. . . . The quorum is a service unit, and the members learn in their service. A quorum can give greater service than the members could give alone. And that power is multiplied by more than their numbers. Every quorum has a leader with authority and responsibility to direct priesthood service. I have seen the power that comes when quorums are called to move out to help in times of disaster. Time and again I have had people outside the Church express surprise and admiration for the effectiveness of the Church in organizing to give help. It seems to them like a miracle. In all priesthood service the miracle of power comes because leaders and members honor the authority of those who direct the service in priesthood quorums across the earth. Miracles of power can come as quorums reach out to serve others. They come as well when the priesthood service is to members within the quorum" (*Ensign,* Nov. 2006, 43–45).

Quorum also refers to the minimum number of priesthood members necessary to vote upon or conduct the business of the Church (D&C 107:28). The Lord specified that the majority of the revealed maximum number may constitute a quorum (D&C 107:28). For example it is necessary to have at least two members of a bishopric or stake presidency, and at least seven members of a high council. This serves as protection for the Church.

— R —

Remission of Sins: FORGIVENESS or pardon achieved specifically through REPENTANCE and BAPTISM.

Remnant: A part that remains, specifically of the house of Israel. In the Doctrine and Covenants, this term refers to the LAMANTIES or Native Americans. In the LATTER DAYS, they will "vex the GENTILES" (D&C 87:5), but they were the subject of a petition included in the dedicatory prayer for the KIRTLAND TEMPLE (D&C 109:64–66).

Remuneration for Church Service: Financial compensation for those required to devote full time to a Church calling. Three months after the Church was organized, the Lord told Joseph Smith to magnify his office by devoting his full time to the Church, that his strength lay in spiritual rather than in temporal things, and that it was the duty of the churches (or BRANCHES) to support him (see D&C 24:3, 7, 9). In February 1831, the Lord directed the Church to build a house for the Prophet (see D&C 41:7). That same month, those who wanted to know the glorious mysteries of the gospel were told to provide other temporal necessities (see D&C 43:12–13). Thus, Latter-day Saints believe that anyone who is called to devote his full time to the Church should receive support from the Church. There are at least two major differences between this practice in the restored Church and the "paid ministry" in the churches of the world:

1. A Latter-day Saint cannot elect to enter the ministry as a vocation to earn his living; one assumes Church assignments only upon a call through those in authority.

2. In contrast to the pattern common in most denominations in which a full-time professional clergy is the rule, among the Latter-day Saints relatively few (such as the GENERAL AUTHORITIES, mission presidents, etc.) are asked to devote their full time to Church work. Instead, most give only part of their time and so are able to support themselves. Thus, many share in the blessings of Church service.

SECTION 42 related the principle of remuneration for full-time service to the LAW OF CONSECRATION (see v. 70–73). For such individuals, their Church assignment was their stewardship, the magnifying of which qualified them to receive support, just as ordinary stewardships provided income. Subsequently, the Lord explained that even though those who administer spiritual things may receive an abundance through the Spirit, they should be equal in temporal things with those whose stewardships were temporal (see D&C 70:12–14).

Repentance: The process through which we must go to obtain a remission for our SINS, and the second principle of the gospel (Article of Faith 4). To be FORGIVEN of sins, one must both confess and forsake the sin. When one truly repents of his sins, he is forgiven, and God promises to forget the sins (D&C 58:42–43; see also D&C 1:32; 18:11–12). President Ezra Taft Benson stated, "Repentance involves not just a change of actions, but a change of heart. Thousands of you have experienced this change. You have forsaken lives of sin, sometimes deep and offensive sin, and through applying the blood of Christ in your lives, have become clean. You have no more disposition to return to your old ways. You are in reality a new person. This is what is meant by a change of heart" (*Ensign,* Oct. 1989, 2). Because of the Lord's ATONEMENT, we can repent and be forgiven for even the most grievous sins, except for the UNPARDONABLE SIN (Isa. 1:18). However, if we repeat a sin that we have already repented for, the previous sin returns and the repentance process becomes more difficult (D&C 82:7). Because we are all imperfect, we must repent and improve ourselves each day so that we may be clean when we stand to be JUDGED and receive EXALTATION.

Resurrection: The reuniting of the body and spirit, which are separated at death. The Lord referred to resurrection as the "redemption of the soul" (D&C 88:16). BOOK OF MORMON prophets testified that the body will be "restored to its perfect frame," and that not even "a hair of the head" shall be lost (Alma 11:43–44; 40:23).

Even though every resurrected body will be physically perfect, not all will be prepared to enjoy the same degree of glory. In his great chapter on the resurrection, Paul spoke of CELESTIAL, terrestrial, and other bodies (see 1 Cor. 15:40–42). Earlier in the same chapter, the APOSTLE spoke of an order or sequence of resurrection (see 1 Cor. 15:20–24).

Sequence of Resurrections*

First Resurrection (Resurrection of the Just)		Second Resurrection (Resurrection of the Unjust)	
Morning	*Evening*		
Celestial	Terrestrial, some Celestial	Telestial	Sons of Perdition
Resurrection of Christ	Second Coming	End of the Millennium	Final Judgement

*1 Cor. 15:20–24, 40–42; D&C 88:22–32, 96–102.

There are two major phases of the resurrection (John 5:28–29; Acts 24:15):

1. The "first resurrection" or "resurrection of the just" began with the Resurrection of Christ and will close with the end of the MILLENNIUM; those inheriting the celestial or terrestrial kingdom will be resurrected during this phase.
2. The "second resurrection" or "resurrection of the unjust" will follow the Millennium and will include those going to the telestial kingdom and those who are sons of perdition (D&C 43:18, 88:100–102).

Only those going to the celestial kingdom are to be resurrected before Christ's SECOND COMING; this period is generally called the "morning of the first resurrection." Many people were resurrected at the time of Christ's Resurrection (see Matt. 27:52–53). Since that time, there have been relatively few, but just before the Second Coming a large number of candidates for the celestial kingdom will be resurrected and "caught up" to descend with Christ in His coming in glory (see D&C 76:63; 88:97–99).

Terrestrial resurrection will begin upon Christ's arrival when He comes to reign over the earth. Those going to this glory will be "Christ's at his coming" (compare D&C 88:99 with D&C 76:72–74). These resurrections will then continue throughout the Millennium. This period may be termed the "evening" of the first resurrection. There will also be some celestial resurrections during this time—those who have lived as mortals during the Millennium on earth and who are worthy of the celestial kingdom, as well as those whose preparations in the spirit world were not yet complete when many of the celestial resurrections occurred at the beginning of the Millennium.

The rest of the dead will also be judged at the beginning of the Millennium but will be found unworthy, so will spend the thousand years in spirit prison. They will be resurrected after the Millennium (compare D&C 88:100–102 with D&C 43:18 and 76:84–85). There is no mention of a "morning" and an "evening" in the second resurrection, but it is probable that the same principle of orderliness will apply in this resurrection as it did in the first.

Joseph B. Wirthlin taught, "We know what the Resurrection is—the reuniting of the spirit and body in its perfect form (see Alma 11:43). President Joseph F. Smith said 'that those from whom we have to part here, we will meet again and see as they are. We will meet the same identical being that we associated with here in the flesh' (*Teachings of Presidents of the Church: Joseph F. Smith* [1998], 910). President Spencer W. Kimball amplified this when he said, 'I am sure that if we can imagine ourselves at our very best, physically, mentally, spiritually, that is the way we will come back' (*The Teachings of Spencer W. Kimball,* ed. Edward L. Kimball [1982], 45). When we are resurrected, "this mortal body is raised to an immortal body. . . . [We] can die no more' (Alma 11:45). Can you imagine that? Life at our prime? Never sick, never in pain, never burdened by the ills that so often beset us in mortality? The Resurrection is at the core of our beliefs as Christians. Without it, our faith is meaningless [1 Cor. 15:14]" (*Ensign,* Nov. 2006, 28–30).

Revelation: Communication from God to man, just as PRAYER is communication from us to Him. Modern revelation is one of the unique claims of The Church of Jesus Christ of Latter-day Saints. The Doctrine and Covenants is a compilation of some of the more significant revelations received by JOSEPH SMITH and others, primarily during the early years of the Church. These have come by various means. Some, including the FIRST VISION, the coming of MORONI (see D&C 2), restoration of the PRIESTHOOD by JOHN THE BAPTIST (D&C 13) and by PETER, JAMES, AND JOHN (D&C 27:12; 128:20), and the restoration of KEYS by MOSES, ELIAS, and ELIJAH (D&C 110:11–16), involved personal visitations. Others came as VISIONS (such as D&C 76). Most came directly from the HOLY GHOST to the PROPHET. This is also the means by which we may—and should—receive divine communication in answer to our prayers. The "spirit of revelation" is when the Holy Ghost speaks to a person in both the mind and the heart (D&C 6:2–3).

Richards, Willard: A member of the QUORUM of the Twelve APOSTLES, an eyewitness to the martyrdom of JOSEPH and HYRUM SMITH, CHURCH HISTORIAN, and second counselor in the FIRST PRESIDENCY. Willard was born June 24, 1804, and at a young age pursued the course of herbal medicine. He was known by the SAINTS as Dr. Richards. Convinced by the message of the Book of Mormon, Willard joined the Saints in KIRTLAND, OHIO, where he was baptized by his cousin, BRIGHAM YOUNG. While serving a mission in Great Britain, Willard was called to the Quorum of the Twelve Apostles. Upon his return, he was appointed as the PROPHET's private secretary. Willard was one of the men held in Carthage Jail and was a witness to the martyrdom of Joseph and Hyrum. Willard's account of the murders is titled "Two Minutes in Jail." During the NAUVOO era, Willard was called as Church historian and recorder, a position he held for the rest of his life. When the First Presidency was reorganized in Kanesville, Iowa, Willard was sustained as second counselor to President BRIGHAM YOUNG. Willard remained a faithful member of the Church and moved to Salt Lake City with the other Saints, where he died on March 11, 1854.

Rigdon, Sidney: A scribe to JOSEPH SMITH while working on the JOSEPH SMITH TRANSLATION of the BIBLE. Sidney also dedicated INDEPENDENCE, MISSOURI, as the land of ZION (D&C 58:50), and was a member of the original FIRST PRESIDENCY. Sidney was born February 19, 1794, in Pennsylvania, and later became a Campbellite preacher. He was BAPTIZED along with most of his Campbellite congregation, on November 14, 1830. In 1832, Sidney was greatly persecuted for his beliefs by being tarred and feathered in Hiram, OHIO. He was severely wounded, and received serious injuries to his head that caused him to suffer delusions from that day forward. Despite his ailments, Sidney became a member of the First Presidency on March 18, 1833 (D&C 90:6–9). After the martyrdom, Sidney claimed to be a guardian to the Church. But his claims were rejected by the Saints, and the QUORUM of the Twelve assumed leadership. Sidney died in Friendship, New York, on July 14, 1876.

— S —

Sabbath Day: A day set apart by the Lord as a time for rest and worship (see D&C 59:10, 77:12). President Spencer W. Kimball suggested the following as appropriate Sunday activities: "Prayer, studying the gospel, preparing lessons, meditating, visiting the ill and distressed, writing to missionaries, taking a nap, reading wholesome material, and attending all the meetings of that day at which [we are] expected" (*Ensign,* Jan. 1978, 4). Prophets have repeatedly counseled the Saints to abstain from shopping and working on the Sabbath Day. President Gordon B. Hinckley lamented, "The Sabbath of the Lord is becoming the play day of the people. It is a day of golf and football on television, of buying and selling in our stores and markets. Are we moving to mainstream America as some observers believe? In this I fear we are. What a telling thing it is to see the parking lots of the markets filled on Sunday in communities that are predominately LDS. Our strength for the future, our resolution to grow the Church across the world, will be weakened if we violate the will of the Lord in this important matter" (*Ensign,* Nov. 1997, 67).

Sabaoth, the Lord of: Sabaoth is the plural form of the Hebrew word *Sabah,* meaning "hosts or armies." Therefore, the phrase "Lord of Sabaoth" emphasizes the power and majesty of the Lord Jesus Christ. Doctrine and Covenants 95:7 also highlights His role as Creator. Other references in the Doctrine and Covenants using this title emphasize the Lord's hearing our prayers (see D&C 87:7; 88:2; 98:1–2). This title is used in two biblical passages referring to Christ's role as Judge (see Rom. 9:29 and James 5:4).

Sacrament Meeting: The key worship service held by Latter-day Saints. Church members are commanded by the Lord to meet to partake of the sacrament often (see D&C 59:9). Elder Dallin H. Oaks said, "The ordinance of the sacrament makes the sacrament meeting the most sacred and important meeting in the Church. It is the only SABBATH meeting the entire family can attend together" (*Ensign,* Nov. 2008). We renew our baptismal COVENANTS each week when we partake of the sacrament (D&C 20:75–79). At the meeting where the Church was organized on April 6, 1830, the sacrament was administered; this was the first sacrament meeting of this dispensation. During Latter-day Saint sacrament meetings, members of the congregation speak on an assigned gospel principle or topic. Sacrament-meeting talks are meant to edify the rest of the congregation and encourage them to use the gospel principles to lead more Christlike lives.

Saint: Literally, one who is holy. The term also refers to a member of the Church. In some languages (including Spanish and German), the words for "saint" and "holy" are the same. Paul addressed some of his epistles to Church members, calling them "Saints" (see, for example, Rom. 1:7; Eph. 1:1; Philip. 1:1; Col. 1:2). He recognized that these members were not perfect, but insisted that the Church had been established "for the perfecting of the Saints" (Eph. 4:12). We should strive for SANCTIFICATION so that we might become Saints in deed rather than in name only.

Sanctification: A state of cleanliness and purity. Following our JUSTIFICATON through obedience to the laws and ORDINANCES of the GOSPEL, we must also be sanctified. Scholars have explained, "Through FAITH in Christ, REPENTANCE, BAPTISM, and receiving the gift of the HOLY GHOST we are first rendered innocent (justified) and then we are made holy (sanctified), and may be called Saints" (*CDC,* 137). The phrase "baptism of fire" refers to how the Holy Ghost symbolically burns all impurities or unholiness from our being. Being "sanctified by the Spirit" is one of the promises made to those who faithfully magnify their callings (D&C 84:33). Sanctification comes from the Latin word *sanctus,* from which the word *saint* is derived. Therefore, sanctification is the process by which we become Saints, not only in name, but in reality. Alma described some who had achieved this state: "Now they, after being sanctified by the Holy Ghost, having their garments made white, being pure and spotless before God, could not look upon sin save it were with abhorrence; and there were many, exceedingly great many, who were made pure and entered into the rest of the Lord their God" (Alma 13:12). Elder Bruce R. McConkie remarked: "Sanctification is a personal reward that follows personal righteousness. The good works of one person cannot be transferred to another" (*MD,* 676). SECTION 20 declares that "sanctification through the grace of our Lord and Savior Jesus Christ is just and true," but can be enjoyed only by "those who love and serve God with all their mights, minds, and strength" (v. 31). Even those who have achieved this exalted condition "may fall from grace," so are cautioned to "take heed and pray always" (v. 32–34). Those who are sanctified are promised that they will be "endowed with power" (D&C 43:16) and receive ETERNAL LIFE in the presence of God forever (see D&C 76:21; 133:62).

Satan: Literally, "the slanderer" (BD, 769). A title of the devil. The Doctrine and Covenants and other scriptures shed light on his status and activities during the PREMORTAL EXISTENCE. He was an "angel in authority" and "Lucifer," meaning light bearer and "a son of the morning," meaning he was one of the prominent members of God's spirit family (D&C

76:25–26). When God announced the Creation of this EARTH as a place where His children could be proved (see Abr. 3:25–28), Satan offered a counter plan which would "redeem all mankind" by destroying man's AGENCY (Moses 4:1–4). When his plan was rejected, Satan rebelled and was cast out, drawing "a third part of the hosts of heaven" with him (D&C 29:36–38; compare Rev. 12:4, 7–9). We learn that Satan's temptations are necessary to give us opposition and to allow us to be agents unto ourselves (D&C 29:39), but we are assured that he cannot tempt us beyond our power to resist (see 1 Cor. 10:13). We actually give Satan power over us as we choose to yield to his temptations (see D&C 29:40). Teachings in the Doctrine and Covenants tell us how to avoid being deceived by Satan and how to resist his enticings (see D&C 10:5; 45:57; 46:8).

School of the Prophets: An educational program for Church leaders that began in 1833. The Lord directed the Saints to seek knowledge and to organize the School of the PROPHETS (see D&C 88:76–80, 118–141). The school was organized on January 22, 1833, less than four weeks after SECTION 88 was given. In accordance with instructions in this revelation, all who participated in the School were admitted by receiving the ordinance of the washing of feet, symbolizing their being clean from the sins of the world (see D&C 88:74, 138–39; *HC,* 1:323).

According to BRIGHAM YOUNG, the School met in a small room, about 10 by 14 feet, situated above JOSEPH SMITH's kitchen at the back of NEWEL K. WHITNEY's store (*JD,* 12:157). The brethren studied such subjects as theology and Hebrew. Sessions would begin about sunrise and continue until about 4:00 p.m. Those attending were instructed to bathe, put on clean linen, and come to school fasting.

Many important events occurred in meetings of the School of the Prophets. This is where SECTION 89, the Word of Wisdom, was revealed by the Lord. Significant spiritual manifestations accompanied the organization of the FIRST PRESIDENCY.

A "school of ELDERS" convened in ZION or MISSOURI during the late summer and autumn of 1833. PARLEY P. PRATT instructed these weekly sessions in a grove of trees (see D&C 97:3–5).

A "school for the Elders" was conducted in Kirtland during the winters of 1834–35 and 1835–36. On December 1, 1834, Joseph Smith recorded the following: "Our school for the Elders was now well attended, and with the lectures on theology, which were regularly delivered, absorbed for the time being everything else of a temporal nature. The classes, being mostly Elders gave the most studious attention to the all-important object of qualifying themselves as messengers of Jesus Christ, to be ready to do His will in carrying glad tidings to all that would open their eyes, ears and hearts" (*HC,* 2:175–76). The "lectures on theology" mentioned here are also known as the "Lectures on Faith" and were published in the Doctrine and Covenants prior to 1921.

When the Prophet opened the School of the Prophets' second season on November 3, 1835, he urged the elders to prepare for "the glorious ENDOWMENT that God has in store for the faithful" (*HC,* 2:301). Theology, history, and grammar were among the subjects studied. By January 18, 1836, the KIRTLAND TEMPLE was sufficiently completed for these schools to move into the small rooms on the third floor. Three days later, Joseph Smith received his vision of the CELESTIAL kingdom (see D&C 137).

These schools were among the earliest adult-education programs in the United States. However, an increase in persecution interrupted their progress for several years. During the second half of the nineteenth century in Utah, groups known as "schools of the prophets" met, but these were more similar to priesthood councils than educational programs.

Scrip: A symbol for material preparation. Literally, a scrip was a satchel or bag used by shepherds or travelers for carrying food. The term *scrip* has also been use to refer to coupons that are used at fairs or carnivals as a substitute for money. A *purse* was a bag used specifically to carry money. Hence, the counsel for early ELDERS preaching the gospel to go without purse or scrip (see D&C 24:18; 84:78, 86) indicates that they should not be preoccupied with material concerns, and that their preparation should primarily be spiritual rather than temporal.

Sealing Keys: The power to bind on EARTH and have it bound in heaven. Jesus promised to give this power to PETER (D&C 124:93; 132:46; Matt. 16:19). One week later, this promise was fulfilled when MOSES and ELIJAH appeared on the mount at the time of the Savior's TRANSFIGURATION and bestowed KEYS (Matt. 17:1–3; *TPJS,* 158). The sealing keys were restored in the present DISPENSATION when Elijah came to the KIRTLAND TEMPLE on April 3, 1836, and bestowed them upon JOSEPH SMITH and OLIVER COWDERY. All priesthood ordinances, including those performed before 1836, are made effective through these keys.

Second Coming: The glorious return of Jesus Christ to the earth, where He will reign personally for a thousand years. Referred to as the "great and dreadful day of the Lord" (D&C 2:1; compare Mal. 4:5), the Second Coming will be the finale of several climaxing events. The LOST TEN TRIBES of ISRAEL will return when the ice melts and "an highway shall be cast up." They will bring treasures and scriptures with them and be "crowned with glory, even in Zion, by the hands of the servants of the Lord, even the children of Ephraim" (D&C 133:26–33; 2 Ne. 29:12–14). The circumstances surrounding their return will be regarded as even more marvelous than MOSES' leading the ancient Israelites across the Red Sea on dry land (see Jer. 16:14–15). Twelve thousand HIGH PRIESTS will be chosen from each of the twelve tribes to help prepare the way for the Savior's return (Rev. 7:1–8; D&C 77:11). A great council will convene at ADAM-ONDI-AHMAN, where those holding KEYS from various DISPENSATIONS will turn them over to the Lord in preparation for His reign. "A great sign will appear in the heavens" (D&C 88:93; Matt. 24:30; JS—M 1:24–26, 36). Orson Pratt explained that its purpose will be to warn the faithful to prepare for the Lord's imminent Coming (*JD,* 8:50). The world will explain it away as an astronomical phenomenon such as a planet or comet (*TPJS,* 287), but the PROPHETS will declare its meaning to the SAINTS.

The "Second Coming" will actually be a series of appearances. The Lord will visit the Saints in the NEW JERSUSALEM to give them instructions regarding the events about to unfold (see 3 Ne. 21:23–29). He will appear to the Jews after two prophets have preached in Jerusalem for three and a half years (Rev. 11:1–13; D&C 77:15). As the Lord sets foot on the Mount of Olives, it will split in two (D&C 45:48–52; Zech. 14:2–5). Then He will appear to the whole world at once, wearing red to symbolize the blood He shed in the ATONEMENT and His having trodden the wine press alone, or having overcome the forces of evil (D&C 133: 46–48). After a half hour of silence, the heavens will be unveiled, and this will be like the unrolling of a scroll (D&C 88:95).

At time of the Savior's coming, certain judgments will occur. The earth will be "renewed" and returned to its "paradisiacal" or terrestrial state (Article of Faith 1:10). Those who are living at that time will be judged; those worthy of at least a terrestrial glory will be "quickened" (D&C 88:96), while those not worthy will be burned as stubble by the intensity of His presence (Mal. 4:1; D&C 133:41). Among the dead, those worthy of CELESTIAL or terrestrial glories will be RESURRECTED, while the rest will have to wait a thousand years for the "Second Resurrection" (D&C 88:98–102; compare 43:18). During the MILLENNIUM, Christ will reign personally and in glory upon the earth. The basic message of the

Doctrine and Covenants is an invitation to prepare to be part of these glorious events (D&C 1:12).

President Gordon B. Hinckley asked, "How do you prepare for the Second Coming? Well, you just do not worry about it. You just live the kind of life that if the Second Coming were to be tomorrow you would be ready. Nobody knows when it is going to happen. . . . Our responsibility is to prepare ourselves, to live worthy of the association of the Savior, to deport ourselves in such a way that we would not be embarrassed if He were to come among us. That is a challenge in this day and age" (*Church News,* Jan. 2, 1999, 2).

Second Death: The fate suffered only by SONS OF PERDITION. When a person sins, he brings a condition of SPIRITUAL DEATH upon himself in that he thereby impairs his ability to communicate with the Lord. Through the ATONEMENT of Christ, spiritual death will be overcome for all people, at least temporarily while they are brought into God's presence to be judged according to their works. Those who have committed the UNPARDONABLE SIN will be cast out of the Lord's presence to be cut off forever from His glory or influence; this is what the scriptures call the second spiritual death (see Hel. 14:15–18; see also D&C 29:41–45; 76:37).

Seer: One who sees spiritually. This is one of the titles given to the PRESIDENT OF THE CHURCH (see D&C 21:1; 107:92; 124:125). In the BOOK OF MORMON, Ammon explains to King Limhi that "a seer is a revelator and a PROPHET also; and a gift which is greater can no man have." He also explains that "a seer can know of things which are past, and also of things which are to come, and by them shall all things be revealed, or, rather, secret things be made manifest, and hidden things shall come to light, and hidden things shall come to light, and things which are not known shall be made known by them" (Mosiah 8:16–17).

Seer Stone: Used by JOSEPH SMITH in receiving REVELATION and translating scriptures (*CHC,* 1:128–133). The seer stone worked according to the PROPHET's righteousness, FAITH and mental exertion. The seer stone is not the same as the URIM AND THUMMIM, although each was used for the same purpose and they functioned in a similar manner.

Seventies: Like the Twelve, the seventies are called to be especial witnesses (D&C 107:25). At the time section 107 was received, the words *special* and *especial* were used interchangeably (compare D&C 107:23;

27:12). Unlike the high priests or elders, the seventies have the major responsibility of being ready to travel when necessary to preach the gospel to the world. Thus, they are called "traveling ministers" or "traveling elders" (D&C 107:34, 97; 124:138–39).

Unlike other PRIESTHOOD quorums, the seventy would be presided over by seven presidents (D&C 107:93). When the initial Quorum of the Seventy was called in 1835, only its seven presidents—known as the First Council of the Seventy—were regarded as General Authorities. By the latter 19th century, the number of seventies quorums multiplied greatly, and they were scattered from Canada to Mexico. By 1975, more help was needed to administer the worldwide Church, so for the first time, additional General Authority Seventies were added to the First Quorum of the Seventy. By the following year, the total, including Assistants to the Twelve (another body of General Authorities with similar responsibilities) exceeded thirty-six, the minimum number required to form a quorum because it is a majority of seventy. Therefore, the First Quorum of Seventy was formally organized. At this time, the title "First Council of Seventy," referring only to the quorum's seven presidents, was discontinued.

The Quorum of the Seventy is "equal in authority" to the Quorum of the Twelve and to the FIRST PRESIDENCY. The seventies were now in a better position to provide the assistance to the Twelve, as called for in D&C 107:38. Note the similarity of the assignments given to these two quorums: both were to be "special witnesses" (D&C 107:23, 25), and both were to "build up the Church and regulate all the affairs of the same in all nations" (D&C 107:33–34).

Boyd K. Packer stated: "Teenagers also sometimes think, 'What's the use? The world will soon be blown all apart and come to an end.' That feeling comes from fear, not from faith. No one knows the hour or the day (D&C 49:7), but the end cannot come until all of the purposes of the Lord are fulfilled. Everything that I have learned from the revelations and from life convinces me that there is time and to spare for you to carefully prepare for a long life" (*Ensign,* May 1989, 53).

Sheaves: "Large bundles in which cereal plants are bound after reaping" (www.merriam-webster.com/dictionary). In the Doctrine and Covenants, sheaves are used to symbolize missionary success. The Lord uses the imagery of a field that is "white already to harvest" to represent those on the EARTH who are prepared and are receiving the GOSPEL message. He promised that the faithful missionaries will be "laden with many sheaves"

(D&C 14:13, 75:5). This means that just as harvesters gather in sheaves of wheat, missionaries will being many souls to the restored Church.

Signs: Miracles on which to build faith, or indicators of that which is to come. The Master condemned those who wanted proof before they would have faith in Him: "A wicked and adulterous generation seeketh after a sign" (Matt. 16:4). Later, He told Thomas, "Blessed are they who have not seen, and *yet* have believed" (John 20:29). In the present DISPENSATION, the Lord warned: "He that seeketh signs shall see signs, but not unto salvation" (D&C 63:7). Korihor, for example, demanded a sign and was struck dumb (see Alma 30). He continued: "Faith cometh not by signs, but signs follow those that believe" (D&C 63:9; compare Mark 16:17). Faith is a gift from God; when a person with faith sees signs, he can discern them by the power of the HOLY GHOST as evidences of God's power. The Lord affirmed that "signs come by faith," yet "not by the will of men . . . but by the will of God" (D&C 63:10–11).

Speaking of signs as indicators of things to come, the Lord declared that the faithful in the LATTER DAYS "shall be looking forth for the great day of the Lord to come, even for the signs of the coming of the Son of Man. And they shall see signs and wonders" (D&C 45:39–40). Later, the Lord assured the SAINTS that "unto you it shall be given to know the signs of the times and the signs of the coming of the Son of Man" (D&C 68:11).

Sin: The breaking of God's law. This word implies that the disobedience is done willingly and with understanding. Notice, for example, the distinction made in the second Article of Faith: "We believe that men will be punished for their own *sins* and not for ADAM's *transgression*" (italics added). Thus the severity with which a sin is viewed depends on our understanding (see D&C 82:3; compare Luke 12:47–48). For example, the UNPARDONABLE SIN can be committed only in the light of sure knowledge through the HOLY GHOST (see D&C 76:31).

Smith, Emma Hale: Wife of JOSEPH SMITH, and the first president of the Relief Society. Emma was born July 10, 1804, in HARMONY, Pennsylvania, and was baptized in June 1830 by OLIVER COWDERY. Emma was the only woman addressed by name in a Doctrine and Covenants REVELATION (SECTION 25). This revelation identified Emma as an elect lady, which the PROPHET declared referred to her calling as the first Relief Society president. During the translation of the BOOK OF MORMON, Emma acted as scribe for a brief time. Although Emma was often outgoing and charitable toward others, she quietly suffered many of her own challenges. Only four of her nine children lived to maturity, and her married life with Joseph was tried by religious persecution. Emma did not go west with the rest of the Saints, and later married Major Lewis Bidamon. She died April 30, 1879, and was buried next to Joseph in NAUVOO.

Smith, Hyrum: Elder brother of the PROPHET Joseph Smith. Hyrum was one of the Eight Witnesses of the BOOK OF MORMON, the PATRIARCH to the Church, and an Assistant President of the Church. He was born in Turnbridge, VERMONT, on February 9, 1800, to Joseph and Lucy Mack Smith. When Hyrum wished to assist with the work of the kingdom, the Lord directed him to "seek not to declare my word but first seek to obtain my word" (D&C 11:21). Joseph entrusted the Book of Mormon manuscript to his brother as he prepared the pages for printing. Hyrum, along with seven others, was shown the gold plates of which he bore testimony the remainder of his life. Hyrum was instrumental in building the temple, participated in ZION'S CAMP, and served an extended mission for the Church in 1831, traveling to Missouri, Michigan, Indiana, and ILLINOIS. While serving as second counselor in the FIRST PRESIDENCY, he was imprisoned in Liberty Jail from November 1838 to April 1839. Hyrum was one of the great and noble ones, chosen in the beginning and "reserved to come forth in the fulness of times to help lay the foundation of the great latter-day work" (D&C 138:53–56). The Lord declared, "Blessed is my servant Hyrum Smith; for I, the Lord, love him because of the integrity of his heart, and because he loveth that which is right before me" (D&C 124:15). He and his brother Joseph died a martyr's death on June 27, 1844. JOHN TAYLOR said, "In life they were not divided, and in death they were not separated. . . . They lived in glory and died in glory" (D&C 135:3, 6).

Smith, Joseph Jr.: PROPHET, SEER, revelator, TRANSLATOR, and first President of The Church of Jesus Christ of Latter-day Saints. The son of JOSEPH SMITH SR. and Lucy Mack, he was born at Sharon, VERMONT, on December 23, 1805. Joseph's birth had been foretold by prophets of past DISPENSATIONS (see 2 Ne. 3). During Joseph's boyhood, the Smith family suffered many difficulties, including crop failures, which required them to move from place to place. On one occasion, Joseph contracted a serious leg infection that prompted the doctor to suggest removing a portion of the bone in his left leg—without anesthetics.

In 1816, following a particularly disastrous growing season, the family moved to PALMYRA, NEW YORK and soon after settled on one hundred acres in the adjoining township of MANCHESTER. It was here in the early spring of 1820 that Joseph experienced the FIRST VISION, which opened the DISPENSATION of the fulness of times. Three years later, in 1823, in answer to Joseph's prayer, he was visited by MORONI, who told him of an ancient record deposited in a hill nearby. Over the next four years, Joseph prepared himself to receive the plates that he would translate into the BOOK OF MORMON by the gift and power of God.

Joseph Smith Jr.

On January 18, 1827, Joseph married EMMA HALE of HARMONY, Pennsylvania. In the midst of the translation, they moved to Harmony. There he was visited by JOHN THE BAPTIST, who restored the AARONIC PRIESTHOOD on May 15, 1829. Shortly thereafter, he was visited by PETER, JAMES, AND JOHN, who restored the MELCHIZEDEK PRIESTHOOD. The Book of Mormon was published in March 1830 and on April 6, the Church of Christ was organized at FAYETTE, New York.

Persecution plagued the young Prophet almost from the beginning and by the end of 1830, Joseph received a REVELATION that he and his growing number of followers should move to "the OHIO" (D&C 37). Arriving at KIRTLAND, he found a number of converts who had accepted the Book of Mormon at the hands of elders serving in the Lamanite Mission. From 1831 to 1838, Kirtland was the headquarters of the Church, during which time the Church's first TEMPLE was dedicated. Also in Kirtland, Church government was put in place, with the creation of the FIRST PRESIDENCY, the QUORUM of the Twelve APOSTLES, and the Quorum of the SEVENTY. Sixty-five revelations now included in the Doctrine and Covenants were received during the Kirtland period, the most fruitful time of revelation during the Prophet's lifetime.

In 1831, a revelation directed Joseph to take a group of ELDERS to Missouri; there they were told that INDEPENDENCE, JACKSON COUNTY, would be the center place of ZION. This became another area of focus in the Church. The dedication of the KIRTLAND TEMPLE on March 27, 1836, followed weeks of marvelous spiritual experiences. One week later, on

April 3, the Savior appeared and accepted the TEMPLE; MOSES, ELIAS, and ELIJAH also appeared and restored KEYS of priesthood authority.

In 1837, opposition mounted again, and early the following year, Joseph and other faithful Saints were forced to leave KIRTLAND. They gathered at FAR WEST, Missouri, with Saints who had already been forced to flee Jackson County. The Saints' sojourn in Far West was brief. In October, Governor Lilburn Boggs ordered that the Latter-day Saints be driven from the state. At the same time, Joseph and other Church leaders were seized and imprisoned and spent many months in Liberty Jail.

In 1839, the Latter-day Saints began settling in ILLINOIS. Under Joseph's leadership, they built up a city called Nauvoo, which became the largest city in the state. The central focus of the city was the NAUVOO TEMPLE, where significant doctrines and practices were unfolded. BAPTISMS for the dead extended blessings to those who had died without the opportunity to accept the gospel. The temple ENDOWMENT taught Saints their true identity as SONS AND DAUGHTERS OF GOD and what they needed to do to return to His presence. MARRIAGE for eternity was introduced, and couples were sealed. In addition, Joseph taught the Saints about their eternal potential.

Persecution continued to follow Joseph and the Saints. On June 27, 1844, he and his brother HYRUM were martyred at the Carthage Jail. Apostle JOHN TAYLOR, who was with Joseph and Hyrum in Carthage Jail, left this testimony concerning the Prophet's contributions: "Joseph Smith the Prophet and Seer of the Lord has done more, save Jesus only, for the salvation of men in this world than any other man that ever lived in it. In the short space of twenty years, he has brought forth the Book of Mormon, which he translated by the gift and power of God and has been the means of publishing it on two continents; has sent the fulness of the everlasting gospel which it contained to the four quarters of the earth; has brought forth the revelations and commandments which compose this, the book of the Doctrine and Covenants" (D&C 135:3).

Smith, Joseph Sr.: The father of the PROPHET Joseph. He was born July 12, 1771, to Asael and Mary Duty Smith in Topsfield, Massachusetts. Joseph married Lucy Mack at age twenty-four in Turnbridge, VERMONT, and they became the parents of eleven children. "Father Smith," as he was affectionately known, readily accepted the words of his fourteen-year-old son as he explained his visitations from God the Father, His Son JESUS CHRIST, and the angel Moroni. Having kept himself aloof from the various churches of the day, to his family's delight he was baptized the day the Church was organized, April 6, 1830, in Seneca Lake. SECTION 4 of the Doctrine and Covenants, directed to Joseph Smith Sr., reviews the qualifications to serve in the kingdom of God. The Prophet's father was ordained the first Patriarch in this dispensation in December 1833, and at age sixty-four Joseph Sr. served a mission with his brother John in the East. Father Smith loved his family dearly, and many people noted the special bond he had with his son Joseph. Father Smith gave each of his family members a final blessing before he died on September 14, 1840. Speaking of Joseph Smith Sr., the Lord declared, "When he shall finish his work I may receive him unto myself. . . and blessed and holy is he, for he is mine" (D&C 124:19).

Smith, Samuel H.: Younger brother of JOSEPH SMITH JR., Samuel served as one of the Eight Witnesses of the BOOK OF MORMON, was one of the six original members of the Church, and is traditionally recognized as the first missionary of the Church. Samuel was born March 13, 1808, in Turnbridge, VERMONT, and was the third member baptized into the Church on May 25, 1829. He served missions with WILLIAM E. MCLELLIN and ORSON HYDE (D&C 75:13). Hearing of his brothers' deaths, Samuel rode to Carthage to retrieve their bodies. As he neared Carthage the mob recognized him and gave chase. While riding low over his horse to avoid the volley of bullets, he injured himself. Soon afterward, on July 30, 1844, he died.

Sons and Daughters of God: The faithful who keep God's commandments. All of us are begotten sons and daughters of God in the spirit. Yet we can become the children of God or of JESUS CHRIST in still another sense. The Lord affirmed to HYRUM SMITH that "as many as receive me, to them will I give power to become the sons of God, even to them that believe on my name" (D&C 11:30). Similarly, He told EMMA SMITH "all those who receive my gospel are sons and daughters in my kingdom" (D&C 25:1). In ancient America, after King Benjamin's people testified that the HOLY GHOST had made a mighty change in them and that they covenanted to obey all of God's commandments, he declared: "Because of the covenant which ye have made ye shall be called the children of Christ, his sons, and his daughters; for behold, this day he hath spiritually begotten you" (Mosiah 5:7). We should live so that our Father can say of us what He said of the Savior: "This is my beloved Son [or daughter], in whom I am well pleased" (Matt. 3:17).

Sons of Levi: Those who will "offer an offering in righteousness" in the LATTER DAYS (D&C 13; 84:31). References to the sons of Levi and their offering can be understood in two senses. Literally, they are the actual members of the tribe of Levi who are assigned to function in the lesser PRIESTHOOD (BD, 724). JOSEPH SMITH taught that the Levites would offer a blood sacrifice, perhaps only on a one time basis, as part of the "restitution of all things" (Acts 3:19–21; *TPJS,* 173). In a more spiritual sense, as part of the "oath and covenant that belongeth to the priesthood," faithful brethren who magnify their callings in the Melchizedek and Aaronic Priesthoods respectively are promised that they will "become the sons of MOSES and of AARON" (D&C 84:33). Moses and Aaron were members of the tribe of Levi, so faithful priesthood bearers become the sons of Levi. Their "offering in righteousness" is their faithful service in the callings they have received.

Sons of Perdition: See, PERDITION, SONS OF; HELL; UNPARDONABLE SIN.

Spirit: See HOLY GHOST.

Spirit World: The realm inhabited by those without physical bodies. During our unembodied PREMORTAL EXISTENCE, we lived in a spirit world with our Heavenly Parents. There we learned of the great plan of salvation and of the creation of this EARTH. Following our experiences in MORTALITY, as disembodied spirits we will once again enter a spirit existence. "Where is the spirit world?" asked Brigham Young. "It is right here" (*JD,* 3:368–69). This post-earthly spirit world will have two divisions, often designated as paradise and spirit prison or HELL. Alma declared that when we leave this life our spirits are JUDGED and assigned to either "paradise, a state of rest, a state of peace" or to "outer darkness," where there is "weeping, wailing, and gnashing of teeth" (Alma 40:11–14). Between Christ's DEATH and RESURRECTION, He visited the spirit world. He did not go to the wicked or unrepentant but rather went to the righteous among whom "he organized his forces and appointed messengers, clothed with power and authority, and commissioned them to go forth and carry the light of the gospel to them that were in darkness, even to all the spirits of men; and thus was the gospel preached to the dead" (D&C 138:28–30). Thus this post-earthly spirit world is a continuation of our probationary second estate. REPENTANCE will not be easier there, because "that same spirit which doth possess your bodies at the time that ye go out of this life, that same spirit will have power to possess your body in that eternal world"

(Alma 34:34). We will remain in the spirit world until the time of our resurrection.

Spiritual Death: Estrangement from God caused by SIN. The Lord declared that He "cannot look upon sin with the least degree of allowance" (D&C 1:31). Therefore, when we first committed sin we brought the condition of spiritual death upon ourselves. Through the ATONEMENT of Christ, we can overcome spiritual death through wholehearted REPENTANCE and BAPTISM for the remission of sins (D&C 1:32; 18:11–12; 58:42–43). Samuel the LAMANITE explained that all will be brought back into the presence of God to be judged. Most will inherit one of the kingdoms of glory, but those who have committed the UNPARDONABLE SIN will be cast out from His presence, thus returning to a condition called the SECOND DEATH, which is a permanent spiritual death (Hel. 14:15–19).

Stake: A geographical Church unit comprising several wards and BRANCHES. The designation *stake* is taken from the writings of Isaiah, who likened latter-day growth to the Lord's people being accommodated in a tent; as numbers grew, the tent would need to be enlarged—cords lengthened, the cloth covering made larger, and the "stakes" or tent posts made stronger. Thus, the stake is a unit with sufficient leadership and faithfulness to *give* strength to the Church, while a mission district is a unit that must *receive* strength from the Church. The first latter-day stake was established at KIRTLAND on February 17, 1834, with the organization of the HIGH COUNCIL there (see D&C 102). The Lord identified stakes of ZION (their full designation) as GATHERING places (D&C 101:20–22) and described them as places of "defense and refuge" from the tribulations prophesied to sweep the EARTH in the LATTER DAYS. They were also to serve as a light or example to the world (D&C 115:5–6). Stakes have continued to be formed. At the end of the year 1900, there were 43 stakes. The 100th stake was organized in Utah in 1928. The 1000th stake was created at NAUVOO in 1979. Today there are well over 2500 stakes, and they are found on every continent.

— T —

Taylor, John: Eyewitness to the martyrdom of JOSEPH and HYRUM SMITH and third President of the Church. John was born November 1, 1808, in Milnthorpe, England, and baptized on May 9, 1836, by PARLEY P. PRATT in Toronto, Canada. At the PROPHET's direction, John moved to Missouri in 1837. On July 8, 1838, John was called to the apostleship by revelation to the Prophet Joseph Smith (D&C 118), and was ordained an Apostle on December of that year by Brigham Young and Heber C. Kimball. John assisted in opening the mission field in Ireland and helped new members migrate to NAUVOO to join the rest of the SAINTS. Taylor was in Carthage Jail when Hyrum and Joseph Smith were murdered, receiving four balls himself. In SECTION 135, he recorded his experience and gave his appraisal of the Prophet's contributions to the kingdom of God and to the world. Though he felt a great loss at the death of the Prophet, John pressed on through the persecution that followed. He later served additional missions to England, France, and Germany, where he assisted in making arrangements for the translation of the BOOK OF MORMON into French and German. In 1857, he joined the Saints in the Salt Lake Valley, where he focused on building the kingdom. John Taylor served as President of the Church from October 10, 1880, until his death on July 25, 1887, in Kaysville, Utah.

Temples: Special houses of the Lord dedicated for sacred purposes. In former DISPENSATIONS, temples had two basic functions: First, they were regarded as places of contact between heaven and EARTH, or places of REVELATION between God and man. When the Lord directed MOSES to build the tabernacle, He promised to reveal Himself there (Ex. 25:8, 22). Second, temples were the place where sacred priesthood ordinances were performed (see D&C 124:38). "Because such ordinances are sacred and not for the world," Elder Joseph Fielding Smith explained, no detailed account of them has been made available. "There are, however, in the Old Testament references to covenants and obligations under which the members of the Church in those days were placed, although the meaning is generally obscure" ("Was Temple Work Done in the Days of the Old Prophets?" *Improvement Era* 52 [November 1955]: 794; see *TDE,* ch. 1).

When the ancient Israelites became established in the promised land, they built a permanent structure. Because Solomon's Temple was to be the house of the Lord, it was made with the finest materials and best workmanship available. This temple was destroyed at the time the Babylonians conquered the Israelites and carried them off captive. When the Israelites were permitted to return, the temple was rebuilt under Zerubabel as best they could. Just before the Savior's ministry, Herod rebuilt the temple on a larger and more lavish scale. Even though Herod's Temple had been defiled, Jesus still regarded it as His Father's house (John 2:13–17). Evidence suggests that the New Testament SAINTS received their temple ordinances in the Galilee area particularly during the forty days between the Lord's RESURRECTION and ascension.

Both major functions of temples needed to be restored in the dispensation of the fulness of times, when there was to be a "restitution of all things" (Acts 3:19–21). The first latter-day temple was dedicated at KIRTLAND in 1836. The two months prior to the KIRTLAND TEMPLE'scompletion were a time of rich spiritual outpouring, culminating with the dedication on March 27 and with the appearance of the Savior, Moses, ELIAS, and ELIJAH one week later (see SECTION 110). Surely this temple filled the first major function—a place of revelation (see D&C 109:5).

Temple service was restored "line upon line." During the early 1840s while the Saints were establishing the city of NAUVOO, temple ordinances were restored, including BAPTISMS for the dead, the ENDOWMENT, and eternal MARRIAGE. Hence the NAUVOO TEMPLE, dedicated in 1846, fulfilled both major functions of temples (see D&C 124:27–30). It contained a baptismal font in the basement and other facilities for ordinances on the attic level.

Following the pioneers' epic journey to the Rocky Mountains, four temples were dedicated in Utah during the second half of the nineteen century. Endowments for the dead were inaugurated with the dedication of the St. George Temple in 1877. The dedication of the great temple at Salt Lake in 1893 represented a significant spiritual achievement for the Saints.

During the twentieth and twenty-first centuries, temples have been built in many lands. In 1900, there were only four temples in service—all of them in Utah. By 1950, the number had doubled to eight and by 1975, it had doubled once again to sixteen. In 1997, President Gordon B. Hinckley announced the concept of much smaller temples to bring the blessings of the house of the Lord closer to the Saints, wherever they might be found. In the year 2000, thirty-four temples were dedicated, exactly one-third of all the temples then in service; the one-hundredth temple went into service that year.

Ordinances for the dead constitute a major part of temple service. JOSEPH SMITH'S VISION of the CELESTIAL kingdom in 1836 revealed that those who died without the opportunity to hear the gospel, who would have received it if they had been permitted to tarry, are heirs of the celestial kingdom (D&C 137:7). The KEYS restored by Elijah on April 3 of that year made all ordinances, including those in the temple, effective on earth and in heaven. Baptisms for the dead were inaugurated at Nauvoo during 1840. The following year, the PROPHET warned, "Those Saints who neglect it [performing ordinances] in behalf of their deceased relatives, do it at the peril of their own salvation" (*HC,* 4:425–26). Endowments for the dead were inaugurated at St. George in 1877. Reflecting on these vicarious service for the dead, President Gordon B. Hinckley asserted that God's plan would be unfair if these gospel ordinances were available only to those who were privileged to hear about them during mortality ("Why These Temples," *Temples of the Church* [Salt Lake City: Intellectual Reserve, 1999], 17).

Throughout the ages, temples have been thought of as sacred places apart from the world. President Gordon B. Hinckley said, "Each of our temples has on its face the statement, 'Holiness to the Lord,' to which I should like to add the injunction 'Keep His House holy!' I submit that every man who holds the Melchizedek Priesthood has an obligation to see that the House of the Lord is kept sacred and free of any defilement. This obligation rests primarily and inescapably upon the shoulders of bishops and stake presidents. They become the judges of worthiness concerning those eligible to enter the temple. Additionally, each of us has an obligation—first, as to his own personal worthiness, and secondly as to the worthiness of those whom he may encourage or assist in going to the House of the Lord. In earlier times, Presidents of the Church felt so strongly about this matter that they required that the President of the Church himself personally sign each recommend. With the growth of the Church, that became impractical" (*Ensign,* May 1990, 49).

President Howard W. Hunter challenged, "I invite the Latter-day Saints to look to the temple of the Lord as the great symbol of your membership. It is the deepest desire of my heart to have every member of the Church worthy to enter the temple. It would please the Lord if every adult member would be worthy of—and carry—a current temple recommend. The things that we must do and not do to be worthy of a temple recommend are the very things that ensure we will be happy as individuals and as families. Let us be a temple-attending people. Attend the temple as frequently as personal circumstances allow. Keep a picture of a temple in your home that your children may see it. Teach them about the purposes of the house of the Lord. Have them plan from their earliest years to go there and to remain worthy of that blessing" (*Ensign,* Nov. 1994, 7).

Joseph Smith taught that "The main object [of gathering] was to build unto the Lord a house whereby He could reveal unto His people the ordinances of His house and the glories of His kingdom, and teach the people the way of salvation; for there are certain ordinances and principles that, when they are taught and practiced, must be done in a place or house built for that purpose" (*HC,* 5:423).

Ten Tribes: See LOST TEN TRIBES.

Tithing: A tenth part of one's increase. Members of the Church are commanded to pay a tithing to the Lord (D&C 119:4). Genesis 14:20 gives the first written account of tithing as ABRAHAM pays tithes to Melchizedek (compare Heb. 7:4–10). SAINTS in the present DISPENSATION are still required to pay tithing and cannot hold a TEMPLE recommend if they do not faithfully observe this commandment. The Lord has promised that when we pay our tithing, we are blessed both temporally and spiritually, and those who neglect to pay their tithes "rob God" (Mal. 3:8–18). At the day of the Lord's coming, those who pay their tithing "shall not be burned" (D&C 64:23). Tithing may be a monetary sacrifice, but it is primarily a matter of FAITH. The Lord has given us every blessing we have and asks for only one-tenth in return. For some, it may seem like a burden to pay tithing, but JOSEPH SMITH counseled us to remember that, "a religion that does not require the sacrifice of all things never has power sufficient to produce the faith necessary unto life and salvation" (*Lectures on Faith,* 69). The Lord does not need our money, but He wants to see if we will give up things that we want and give a portion to Him. Finally, Elder Robert D. Hales stated, "The law of tithing prepares us to live the higher law of consecration—to dedicate and give all our time, talents, and resources to the work of the Lord" (*Ensign,* Nov. 2002, 27).

Times of the Gentiles: See GENTILES.

Transfiguration: A temporary change caused by the power of the HOLY GHOST. It may involve a change in appearance. Normally, Jesus looked like any other person (see Isa. 53:2), but when He was transfigured on the holy mount, "his face did shine as the sun, and his raiment was white as the light" (Matt. 17:2). Similarly, when BRIGHAM YOUNG addressed the SAINTS concerning who should lead the Church after the Martyrdom, some present testified that he seemed to take on the appearance and even the voice of JOSEPH SMITH; this experience is sometimes called "the transfiguration of Brigham Young."

Transfiguration may also refer to the Spirit resting upon a person, giving him special capabilities. For example, MOSES acknowledged that he could not behold the face of God in the flesh unless he was transfigured by the Spirit (Moses 1:11).

Translated Beings: Persons who are physically changed so that they can perform some future service. JOSEPH SMITH taught that "translated bodies are designed for future missions" (*TPJS*, 191). For example, MOSES and ELIJAH were to bestow the KEYS of the PRIESTHOOD to PETER, JAMES, AND JOHN on the Mount of TRANSFIGURATION (see *TPJS*, 158). Because this is done by the laying on of hands, Moses and Elijah would need tangible bodies. Since these keys were to be conferred before Christ inaugurated the RESURRECTION, Moses and Elijah retained their MORTAL bodies much longer than the normal lifespan (they would be resurrected when they restored keys at the KIRTLAND TEMPLE). Similarly, JOHN THE BELOVED (John 21:20–23) and the three Nephite disciples (3 Ne. 28) were "translated" so that they could remain on earth and labor to prepare the world for Christ's SECOND COMING.

Joseph Smith clarified that translated beings are not "taken immediately into the presence of God," but that "their place of habitation is that of the terrestrial order" which frees them from physical suffering (*TPJS*, 170–71). "Translated bodies cannot enter into rest until they have undergone a change equivalent to death" (*TPJS*, 191). The three Nephite disciples have already undergone a change (probably from telestial to terrestrial); at Christ's Second Coming, they would undergo a greater change, from mortality to immortality (see 3 Ne. 28:7–9, 36–40).

Types of Bodies

	Spirit	**Mortal**	**Immortal**
Celestial	Holy Ghost; (Our premortal life)		Father and Son; resurrected in celestial kingdom
Terrestrial		Translated beings: mortals during Millennium	Resurrected in terrestrial kingdom
Telestial		Our present state	Resurrected in telestial kingdom
Sons of Perdition	Those who followed Satan in premortal life		Those who committed unpardonable sin (resurrected)

Translator: One who translates written messages from one language to another. The Prophet Joseph Smith accomplished this role in two distinct ways. References to translating in sections 1 through 17 refer to Joseph Smith translating the Book of Mormon plates by the gift and power of God. Later references to translating point to the prophet's preparing his inspired revision, or the Joseph Smith Translation of the Bible (see D&C 45:60–61; 73:3; 76:15–21; 90:13; 93:53; 94:10; and 124:89). This latter project did not involve translating material from a foreign language, but rather making clarifications, corrections, or restorations of text through the power of inspiration. Joseph's sustaining as a translator (D&C 21:1; 107:92; 124:125) refers to his role in both senses.

United Order: Often used as a synonym for the law of consecration. A group of Church leaders who supervised the law of consecration and directed the work of the bishop were also known as the united order or United Firm. This group was established by revelation (see D&C 78:1–14; 82:11–24; 92:1–2). As persecution intensified, the united orders in Kirtland and Zion were separated (see D&C 104) and eventually dissolved. The title *united order* was also given to some later cooperative ventures in Utah that did not involve consecration.

Unpardonable Sin: The sin against the Holy Ghost, which qualifies one to become a son of Perdition. Those who receive a sure witness of Jesus Christ through the Holy Ghost and knowingly turn away from it—i.e., sin against God—have committed the unpardonable sin. They not only deny Jesus Christ but also defy His power (D&C 76:31). Alma emphasized that to deny the Savior in this manner is a willful and knowing rebellion (Alma 39:6). In a sense, such offenders shed "innocent blood" in that they would assent to the Lord's death (see D&C 132:27).

Concerning those who become sons of perdition, Joseph Smith asked, "What must a man do to commit the unpardonable sin? He must receive the Holy Ghost, have the heavens opened unto him, and know God, and then sin against Him. After a man has sinned against the Holy Ghost, there is no repentance for him. He has got to say that the sun does not shine while he sees it; he has got to deny Jesus Christ when the heavens have been opened unto him, and to deny the plan of salvation with this eyes open to the truth of it; and from that time he begins to be an enemy.

This is the case with many apostates of the Church of Jesus Christ of Latter-day Saints" (*TPJS*, 358).

Alma's counsel to his son Corianton makes it clear that the sin of denying the Holy Ghost is even more serious than committing murder or committing adultery (Alma 39:5). These last two sins are very serious because they involve the giving or taking of life. In the case of murder, a sin that is pardonable but not forgivable, it is impossible to make restitution. Likewise, one who commits adultery or fornication will find it very difficult or impossible to make restitution; however, forgiveness is possible.

Urim and Thummim: A sacred instrument used for receiving REVELATION. The Urim and Thummim is mentioned in the Bible, although no details are provided concerning its appearance or use (Ex. 28:30). JOSEPH SMITH received this instrument along with the plates containing the BOOK OF MORMON (JS–H 1:35). The PROPHET later described them in his letter to John Wentworth, a newspaper editor.

Joseph Smith described the Urim and Thummim as "two transparent stones set in the rim of a bow fastened to a breast plate." He used the Urim and Thummim as he TRANSLATED the Book of Mormon "by the gift and power of God" (*HC* 4:537). Those authorized to use a Urim and Thummim are called SEERS (Mosiah 8: 13). Less known is the Prophet's use of this sacred instrument in receiving revelation. Some of the Doctrine and Covenants revelations received through 1829 were received by this means (see headings to sections 3, 6, 14, 17). After the Prophet received the Melchizedek PRIESTHOOD, no further revelations were identified as coming through this source. Orson Pratt remarked, "The speaker had been present many times when he was translating the New Testament, and wondered why he did not use the Urim and Thummim, as in translating the Book of Mormon. While this thought passed through the speaker's mind, Joseph, as if he read his thoughts, looked up and explained that the Lord gave him the Urim and Thummim when he was inexperienced in the Spirit of inspiration. But now he had advanced so far that he understood the operations of that Spirit, and did not need the assistance of that instrument" ("Two Days' Meeting at Brigham City," *Millennial Star* 36 [11 August 1874]:498–99).

— V —

Vermont: Birthplace and childhood home of JOSEPH SMITH JR. On December 23, 1805, Lucy Mack Smith, the wife of JOSEPH SMITH SR., gave birth to her fourth child at their home in Sharon, Windsor County, Vermont. Joseph Sr. gave his name to his son—Joseph Smith Jr. Vermont was also the birthplace of BRIGHAM YOUNG, HYRUM SMITH, OLIVER COWDERY, Heber C. Kimball, and Erastus Snow.

Visions: One means by which REVELATIONS come from God. They involve seeing something by the power of the HOLY GHOST. SECTION 76, known as "The Vision," is actually a series of visions. Although the appearances of heavenly beings as recorded in SECTION 110 are referred to as "visions" (v. 11, 13), those including the restoration of KEYS must have involved an actual visitation so that PRIESTHOOD authority could be committed by the laying on of hands.

— W —

War: A means of settling differences by force. According to prophecy, the number of wars will continue to increase. When SATAN rebelled against God during our PREMORTAL EXISTENCE, the war in heaven resulted (Rev. 12:7–9). Wars have also existed throughout most of recorded history. The BOOK OF MORMON states that "the Nephites were taught to defend themselves against their enemies, even to the shedding of blood if it were necessary" (Alma 48:14). Specifically, they fought "for their homes and their liberties, their wives and their children, and their all, yea, for their rites of worship and their church" (Alma 43:45). Wars have been prophesied to be widespread during the LATTER DAYS (D&C 45:26; 87:1–4). At the time the SAINTS were being driven by the mobs in Missouri, the Lord counseled them to "renounce war and proclaim peace" (D&C 98:16). If attacked, "they should first lift a standard of peace." Still, He acknowledged that there could be circumstances in which He would justify them in going to war, and promised that He "would fight their battles" (D&C 98:34–37).

During World War II, the FIRST PRESIDENCY affirmed, "When . . . constitutional law . . . calls the manhood of the Church into the armed service of any country to which they owe allegiance, their highest civic duty requires that they meet that call" (CR, Apr. 1942, 94). Decades later, just weeks after the attack on the World Trade Center, President Gordon B. Hinckley counseled, "Now, brothers and sisters, we must do our duty, whatever that duty might be. Peace may be denied for a season. Some of our liberties may be curtailed. We may be inconvenienced. We may even be called on to suffer in one way or another. But God our Eternal Father will watch over this nation and all of the civilized world who look to Him. He has declared, 'Blessed is the nation whose God is the Lord' (Ps. 33:12). Our safety lies in repentance. Our strength comes of obedience to the commandments of God" (*Ensign,* Nov. 2001, 74).

Whitmer, David: One of the Three Witnesses to the Book of Mormon. David was born January 7, 1805, near Harrisburg, Pennsylvania, to Peter Whitmer Sr. and his wife Mary. David became acquainted with the Church through his friend Oliver Cowdery during the New York period. He, along with Oliver and Martin Harris, was shown by an angel the gold plates and other artifacts of the Book of Mormon (D&C 5, 17). Unique to the calling of the Three Witnesses was the assignment to select members of the first Quorum of the Twelve Apostles (D&C 18:37). After a brief stay in Ohio, David took his family to join the Saints in Missouri and in 1834 was appointed president of the High Council in Clay County. In 1837, David united against Joseph Smith's leadership of the Church. He was excommunicated in April 1838, and he and his extended family left the Church and settled in Missouri. His final dying words were his testimony of the truthfulness of the Book of Mormon. David died January 25, 1888, in Richmond, Missouri.

Whitmer, John: One of the Eight Witnesses to the Book of Mormon and the second Church Historian. John was born August 27, 1802, in Fayette, New York, the third son of Peter and Mary Whitmer. Baptized in 1829 by Oliver Cowdery, John was called to act as scribe for Joseph Smith during the translation of the Book of Mormon plates. In section 47, John was called to write a history of the Church, which he faithfully did for a time. John was excommunicated in 1838 as a result of the financial irregularities in his purchase of tracts of land in Caldwell County for the Saints. In 1856, John became the last survivor of the Eight Witnesses and testified of the truthfulness of the Book of Mormon until he died in July 1878.

Whitmer, Peter Sr.: Father of five witnesses of the Book of Mormon and father-in-law of two others. In Peter's home, the restored church was was organized by Joseph Smith on April 6, 1830. He was born on April 14, 1773, in Pennsylvania and baptized in 1830, twelve days after the Church was organized. Peter, along with all his children, left the Church during the Far West period. He moved with his family to Richmond, Missouri, and died on August 12, 1854.

Whitney, Newel K.: Presiding BISHOP of the Church. Newel was born February 5, 1795, in Marlborough, Vermont. Newel became a merchant by trade, establishing businesses in New York and OHIO. His business partner in OHIO was ALGERNON SIDNEY GILBERT. Newel and his wife Elizabeth were PRAYING one night to receive the HOLY GHOST and received a vision in which a cloud overshadowed the house. The voice of the Lord told them to "prepare to receive the word of the Lord, for it is coming." Soon after, men from New York who were called to the LAMANITE MISSION came to their house and taught them the gospel, resulting in their BAPTISM in November 1830 by SIDNEY RIGDON. The Whitneys opened their home to JOSEPH SMITH and his family when they came to OHIO early the following year. Newel was called to be a bishop in the KIRTLAND area (D&C 72:7–8). He was to keep the bishop's storehouse in Kirtland and give out certificates to those who heading for ZION (D&C 72:10, 17). The Whitneys left Kirtland in the fall of 1838, eventually settling at Quincy, ILLINOIS, and then NAUVOO. When the Nauvoo STAKE was organized, Newel was called as Middle Ward bishop. At Winters Quarters, he was sustained as the Presiding Bishop of the Church on April 6, 1847, which position he held until his death in Salt Lake City on September 23, 1850.

Williams, Frederick G.: Second counselor to JOSEPH SMITH in the FIRST PRESIDENCY, and paymaster of ZION'S CAMP. Born in Hartford, Connecticut, on October 28, 1787, he later served his country in the War of 1812 before finding work as a boat navigator on Lake Erie. While practicing medicine and teaching school in OHIO, Frederick was taught the gospel and BAPTIZED by the LAMANITE MISSIONARIES: OLIVER COWDERY, PARLEY P. PRATT, Ziba Peterson, and PETER WHITMER JR. Williams joined the missionaries as they continued their labors to the borders of the Lamanites in Missouri. Once they reached KIRTLAND, he gained the confidence of the Prophet JOSEPH SMITH and was called to be the trustee of the SCHOOL OF THE PROPHETS and paymaster in Zion's Camp. When Jesse Gause proved unworthy to fill his calling as a counselor in the First Presidency, Williams was called in his place (D&C 81:1–3). He was admonished to "be faithful and stand in the office which I have appointed unto you" (D&C 81:4). He also became president of the Kirtland Safety Society; unfortunately, when this bank failed in 1837 he blamed the Prophet and turned against him. Nevertheless, he made the exodus with the members of the Kirtland Camp from Kirtland to Missouri. He was released from the First Presidency at a conference in FAR WEST. The evidence is inconclusive as to whether or not he lost his Church membership, but the records of the Prophet indicate he was rebaptized August 5, 1838. He died in Quincy, ILLINOIS, on October 10, 1842, from the effects of the suffering he endured during the Missouri persecutions and exodus.

Woodruff, Wilford: The fourth PRESIDENT OF THE CHURCH. He wrote the MANIFESTO (Official Declaration 1) and was a prolific journal keeper. Wilford was born at Farmington, Connecticut, on March 1, 1807, and BAPTIZED December 31, 1833, by Zera Pulsipher. In April 1834, Wilford made his way to KIRTLAND, where he joined ZION'S CAMP. In 1837, he served a mission in the East, where he preached the gospel and converted his family. Wilford was ordained an APOSTLE on April 26, 1839, in FAR WEST, MISSOURI. Shortly thereafter, he departed on a mission to the British Isles, where he was instrumental in bringing over 1800 people into the Church. Wilford served two more missions in England before returning to the States to unite with the SAINTS as they began their exodus to the Iowa Territory. In 1877, he gave the dedicatory prayer for the St. George Temple and was appointed its first president. Elder Woodruff was sustained as President of the Church on April 7, 1889, and shortly before General Conference in October 1890, he introduced the Manifesto. President Woodruff died on September 2, 1898, in San Francisco.

— Y —

Young, Brigham: Second PROPHET and PRESIDENT OF THE CHURCH. President Brigham Young was the recipient of two revelations now included in the Doctrine and Covenants, SECTIONS 126 and 136. Born in Vermont on June 1, 1801, Brigham had humble beginnings and was a victim of poverty in his early life. After reading the BOOK OF MORMON, he became fully converted to the gospel. He was ordained a member of the QUORUM of the Twelve APOSTLES shortly after his BAPTISM and remained a dear friend to JOSEPH SMITH throughout the Prophet's lifetime. After Joseph and Hyrum's martyrdom, Brigham returned from Boston to NAUVOO. When he stood to speak to the Saints in Nauvoo, he appeared and sounded like the Prophet Joseph Smith. Brigham was ordained as President of the Church in 1847. Continuing persecution forced the Saints to once again relocate. Brigham Young led the Saints to the Salt Lake Valley and declared that it was the place where they should dwell. Brigham led the Church until his death on August 29, 1877, in Salt Lake City.

Z

Zion: The "pure in heart" (D&C 97:21) and their dwelling place. (This name may refer either to a location or to a condition.) Enoch called his city Zion because "they were of one heart and one mind, and dwelt in righteousness" (Moses 7:18). A hill in the city of Jerusalem was called Mount Zion. It became a symbol for the Jews who wanted to return to their promised land; hence, this movement was called Zionism. The city of the NEW JERSUSALEM in the Western Hemisphere is also called Zion. In 1831, the Lord declared that Missouri was "the place for the city of Zion," and that "Independence is the center place" (D&C 57:1–3). Many revelations in the Doctrine and Covenants use the name Zion in reference to this specific place. While the "center place" of Zion will not be moved, the Lord has established STAKES as additional places of gathering (D&C 101:20–22). The name of every stake ends with the suffix "Stake of Zion." JOSEPH SMITH taught that all of America and even all the world is Zion. At the present time, Church leaders are not directing us to gather to one certain place, but rather they teach the SAINTS to become worthy to establish Zion in preparation for the Lord's SECOND COMING.

Zion's Camp: A military group of men, mostly from OHIO, organized to help restore the SAINTS to their homes in JACKSON COUNTY. The governor of MISSOURI had suggested that the Latter-day Saints raise a force to work with the state militia in restoring the exiled Mormons to their property in Jackson County. Section 103, given in February 1834, directed the Saints to raise such a force from among the strength of the Church. This group, known as Zion's Camp, left KIRTLAND in May 1834 and arrived in Missouri in June 1834. Along the way the Kirtland contingent was supplemented by volunteers from other areas, bringing the total to 205 men. Purposes of Zion's Camp also included taking provisions for the relief of the exiles, who had by that time settled in CLAY COUNTY. After the Camp had reached Missouri, the governor wanted to avoid a violent confrontation, so he withdrew his offer of support. Even though the immediate objective of Zion's Camp was not realized, it sifted those who were willing to respond to the Lord's call from those who were not. The Lord gave a revelation (D&C 105) explaining what needed to be accomplished before ZION could be redeemed.

This experience demonstrated the faith and devotion of several future Church leaders. During the 900-mile march, JOSEPH SMITH associated intimately with and instructed these men. The original Twelve APOSTLES and First Quorum of the Seventy (Section 107) were chosen from among those who marched with Zion's Camp. This lengthy cross-country trek provided valuable experience to Church leaders who later had to direct the forced evacuation, not just of a military force but of men, women, and children, from Nauvoo under much more difficult circumstances.